MEDICAL BREAKTHROUGHS 2005

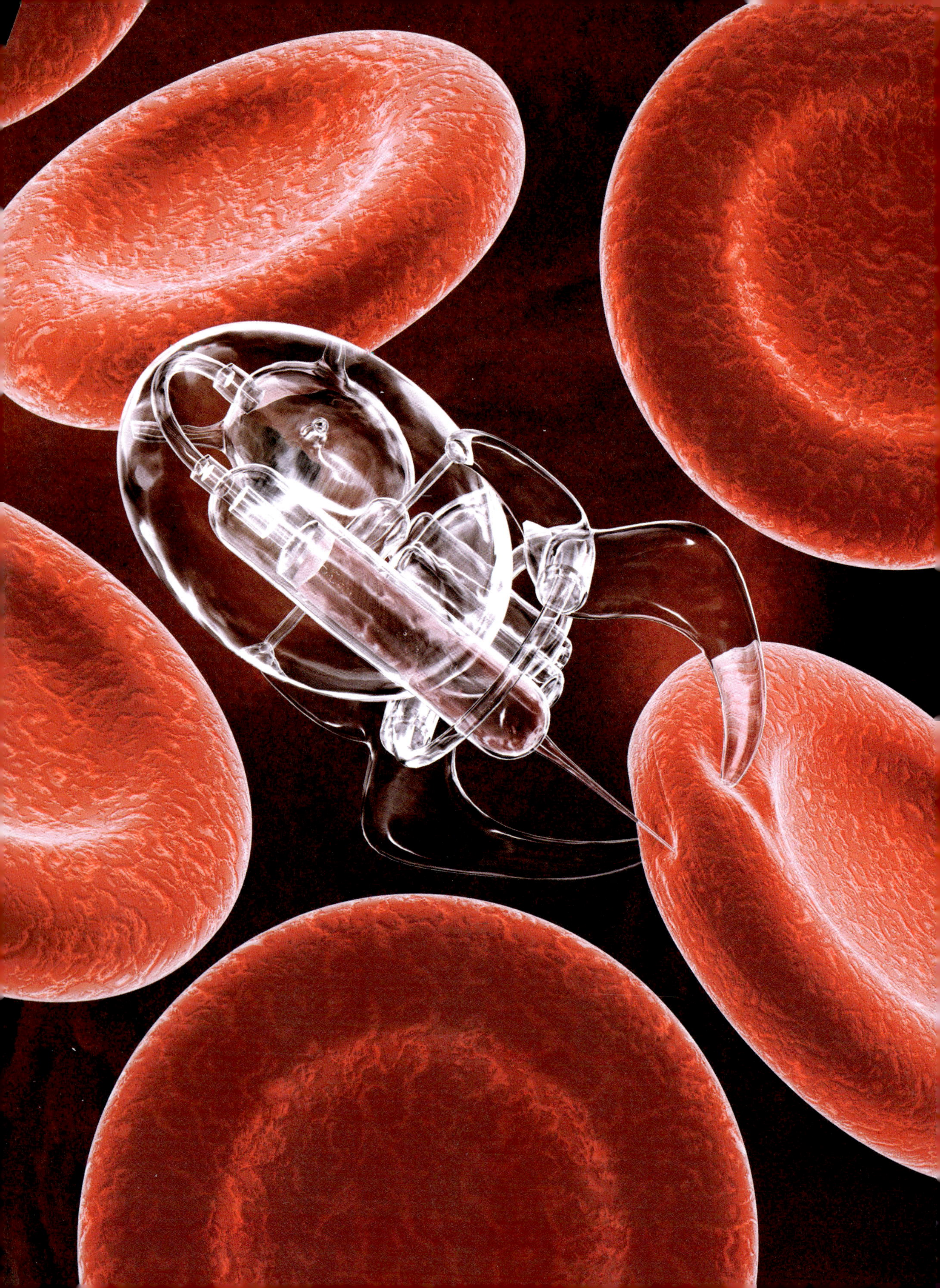

MEDICAL BREAKTHROUGHS 2005

The Year's Most Important Health Developments

The Reader's Digest Association, Inc.
Pleasantville, New York • Montreal

MEDICAL BREAKTHROUGHS 2005

READER'S DIGEST PROJECT STAFF

Senior Editor
Marianne Wait

Senior Design Director
Elizabeth Tunnicliffe

READER'S DIGEST HEALTH BOOKS

Editor in Chief and Publishing Director
Neil Wertheimer

Managing Editor
Suzanne G. Beason

Art Director
Michele Laseau

Production Technology Manager
Douglas A. Croll

Manufacturing Manager
John L. Cassidy

Marketing Director
Dawn Nelson

Vice President and General Manager
Keira Krausz

READER'S DIGEST ASSOCIATION, INC.

President, North America Global Editor-in-Chief
Eric W. Schrier

ISSN 1537-0674

Address any comments about *Medical Breakthroughs 2005* to:
The Reader's Digest Association, Inc.
Editor-in-Chief, Home & Health Books
Reader's Digest Road
Pleasantville, NY 10570-7000

To order copies of *Medical Breakthroughs 2005*, call 1-800-846-2100.

Visit our Web site at rd.com

NOTE TO OUR READERS
The information in this book should not be substituted for, or used to alter, medical therapy without your doctor's advice. For a specific health problem, consult your physician for guidance.

Any references in this book to any products or services do not constitute or imply an endorsement or recommendation.

Printed in the United States of America
1 3 5 7 9 10 8 6 4 2

IE 0088A/IC-US

CONTRIBUTORS

Editor
Jeff Bredenberg, Sheridan Warrick

Writers
Susan Arns, Kelly Garrett, Debra Gordon, Joely Johnson, Eric Metcalf, Ron Sauder, Marc Schogol, Carol Svec, Rob Waters

Contributing Designer
Marian Purcell

Copy Editor
Jane Sherman

Indexer
Ann Cassar

Picture Research
Jeanne Leslie

MEDICAL ADVISORS

Charles Atkins, M.D.
Medical Director, Western Connecticut Mental Health Network; Assistant Professor, Yale University School of Medicine, New Haven, Connecticut

Jacob Bitran, M.D.
Professor of Medicine, Finch University of Health Sciences/The Chicago Medical School; Section Chief, Hematology/Oncology, Lutheran General Hospital, Park Ridge, Illinois

Lawrence C. Brody, Ph.D.
Senior Investigator, Head, Molecular Pathogenesis Section, National Human Genome Research Institute, National Institutes of Health, Bethesda, Maryland (contributions rendered as an individual, not in the name of the U.S. government)

Nicholas A. DiNubile, M.D.
Orthopaedic Consultant, Philadelphia 76ers Basketball and Pennsylvania Ballet; Clinical Assistant Professor, Department of Orthopaedic Surgery, Hospital of the University of Pennsylvania, Philadelphia

Marygrace Elson, M.D.
Associate Clinical Professor of Obstetrics and Gynecology, University of Iowa Hospital and Clinics, Iowa City

Bradley W. Fenton, M.D.
General Internist, Clinical Associate Professor, Thomas Jefferson University Hospital, Philadelphia

Joel A. Kahn, M.D.
President, WorldCare Global Health Plan Ltd., Boston

Barry Make, M.D.
Director, Emphysema Center, National Jewish Medical and Research Center, Denver; Professor of Medicine, University of Colorado School of Medicine, Denver

Randolph P. Martin, M.D.
Director, Emory Non-Invasive Lab, Emory University Hospital, Atlanta; President of the American Society of Echocardiography (for 2003)

Vincent Yang, M.D., Ph.D.
Director, Division of Digestive Diseases, Emory University Hospital, Atlanta

Contents

PART 2 : GENERAL HEALTH

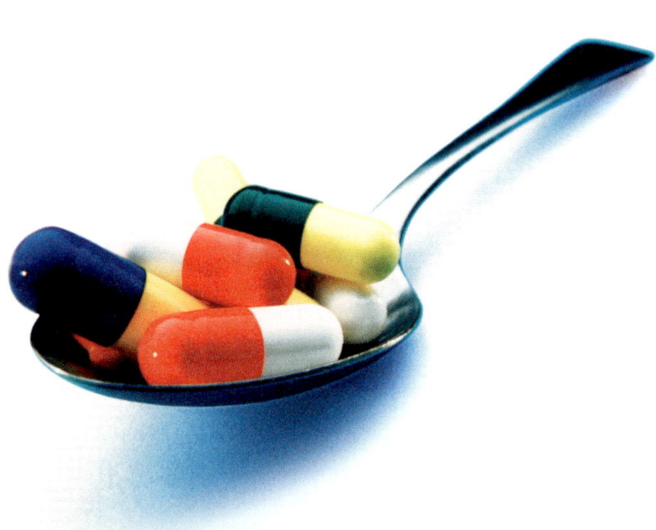

PART 3 : YOUR BODY HEAD TO TOE

BRAIN AND NERVOUS SYSTEM 118-129

CANCER 130-149

DIGESTION AND METABOLISM 150-159

PART 3 : YOUR BODY HEAD TO TOE (continued)

About This Book

These days, you can rely on your daily newspaper to be filled with stories of war, heartache, and woe. *Medical Breakthroughs 2005,* on the other hand, is packed from cover to cover with good news—hope in the form of new lifesaving drugs, faster cures, and discoveries to help all of us stay healthy.

Among our top stories this year: Scientists are experimenting with a drug that appears to reverse heart disease so effectively that they call it "drain opener for arteries." Pills to restore your memory to a more youthful state may start appearing in your drugstore within a few years, and a powerful colon cancer drug kills tumors by cutting off their blood supply. On the lighter side, new cosmetic surgery procedures are giving thousands a lift.

Even the most casual follower of medical news will find this book fun and inspiring to read. In these pages, you'll learn about bat saliva used to dissolve blood clots that cause strokes, deep-sea sponges that yield cancer cures, and newly discovered healing powers of everyday substances such as coffee. You'll also read about the future, a time when microscopic robots will be sent in to repair damage to cells and cure disease, when you'll get your medicine from needles that are too tiny to hurt, and when you'll use biological bandages that speed wound healing and pop a daily pill that could slash your risk of ever developing heart disease.

Medical Breakthroughs 2005 is organized to make the reading easy. Part 1, The Year's Top Stories, is a series of in-depth articles on some of the biggest medical stories in the news. Part 2, General Health, provides updates in chapters on Aging, Children's Health, and Wellness. In Part 3, Your Body Head to Toe, news about specific diseases is organized by body system—Brain and Nervous System, Heart and Circulatory System, Reproduction and Sexuality, and so on.

As you read, keep in mind that many of the breakthroughs unveiled here are experimental, and it could be years before some of these discoveries become available to the general public. If you feel you can't wait, you may be able to enroll in a clinical trial that tests the safety and effectiveness of a new treatment. In that case, a good place to start is the National Institutes of Health Web site at www.clinicaltrials.gov. You should also remember, though, that in many cases, older, time-tested treatments are the best approach. Read the latest news here, talk it over with your doctor, and make an informed decision.

Charles Atkins, M.D., medical director at Western Connecticut Mental Health Network and one of the advisors who helped us ensure the accuracy of this book, puts it nicely: "Increasingly, we need to take more responsibility for our own health and health care choices. Reader's Digest's *Medical Breakthroughs* is a helpful tool that gives us up-to-date information in a way that's both understandable and useful."

PART 1

THE YEAR'S TOP STORIES

SOME OF THE YEAR'S biggest health stories unfolded at the microscopic level: Viruses that pass from animals to humans have scientists scrambling to prepare for the next post-SARS killer outbreak—perhaps of a new strain of bird flu. Researchers cloned the first human embryo and used it to create a new line of stem cells, the controversial cells that could one day be used to cure the major diseases of our time. And scientists have developed unimaginably tiny particles that bring the old sci-fi movie *Fantastic Voyage* a big step closer to reality. In other major stories, researchers accidentally discovered that a certain type of MRI may help cure

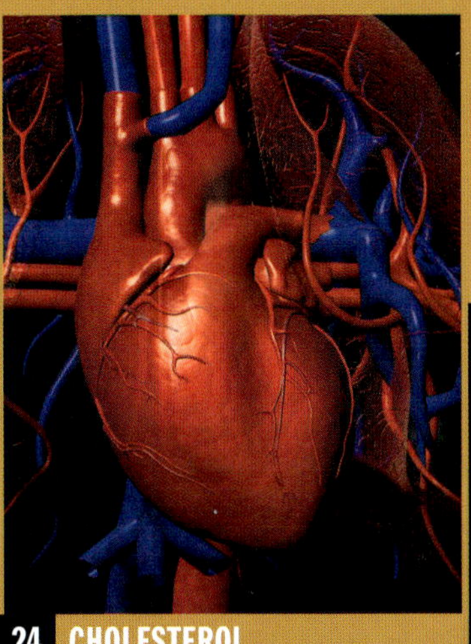

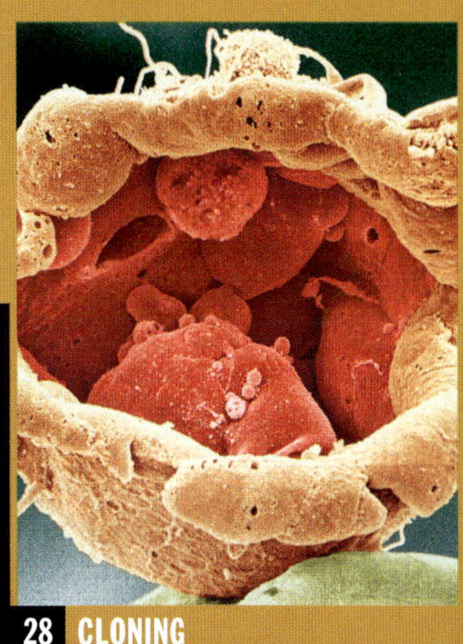

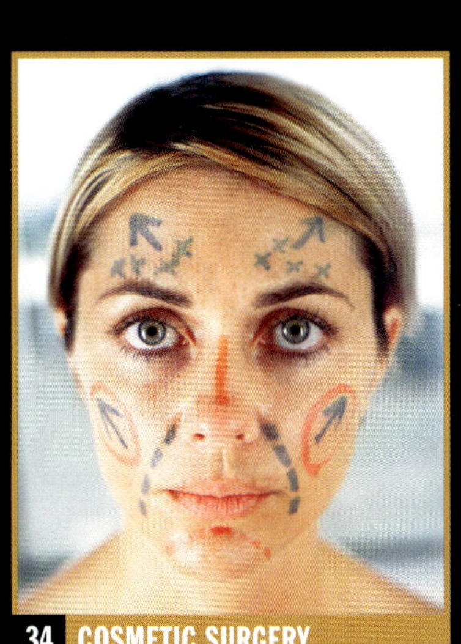

MORTGAGE PAYMENT

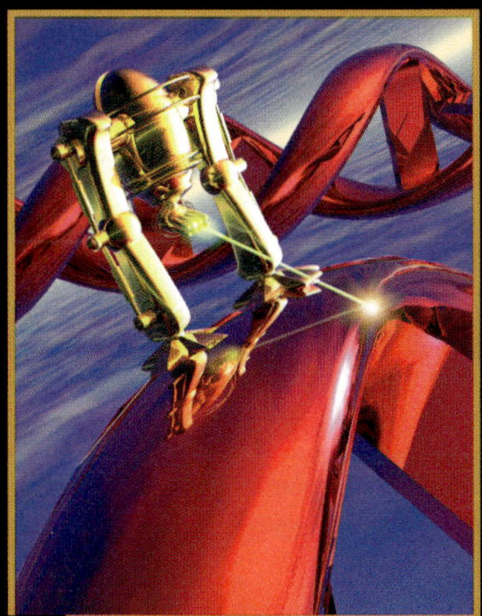

THE NEXT KILLER VIRUS: HEADED YOUR WAY?

Thai soldiers carry off chickens that may be infected with a deadly strain of bird flu. Millions of chickens have been destroyed in Asian countries to protect the public.

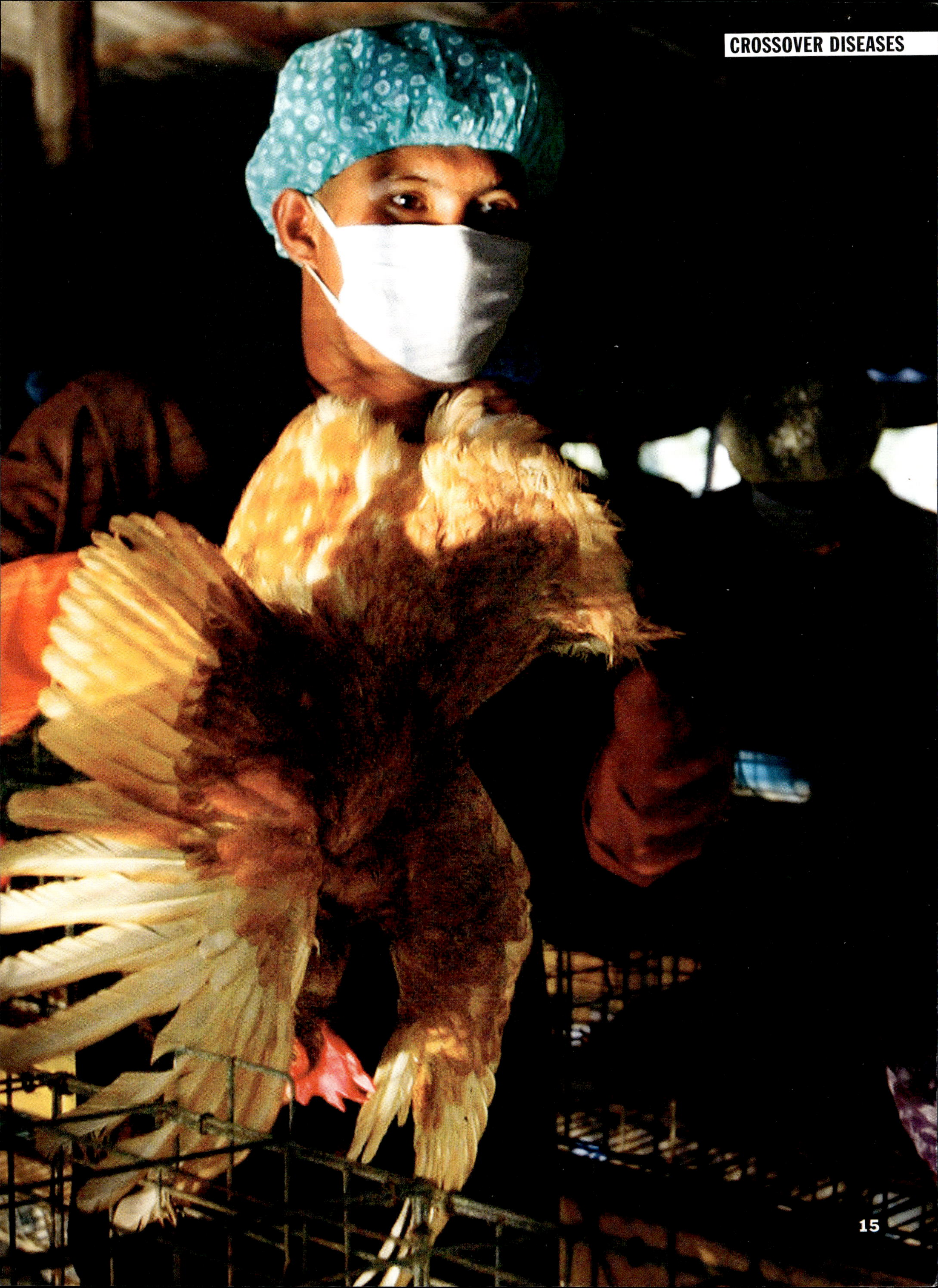

A fever-sensing scanner screens tourists arriving in the Philippines after suspected cases of SARS were reported in China in the spring of 2004.

For his 79th birthday, Ed and his wife, Marie, took a once-in-a-lifetime, three-week trip to China. On the return flight, Marie felt sicker than she remembered ever feeling before. "Some strange bug," she said to her daughter on the telephone the day after they arrived home in San Diego. The conversation was punctuated by Marie's deep, rib-rattling coughs, and she complained of fever, chest pains, and runny nose. "It feels like a cold and the flu rolled into one," Marie said. A couple of days later, Ed also fell ill.

Concerned, the couple's daughter Karen flew from North Carolina to help. Within a week, she was in her doctor's office. "It feels like I'm going to cough out a lung," she said when asked to explain her symptoms. The doctor noted a fever, then held a stethoscope to Karen's back. "I don't think it's the flu," the doctor said. She picked up Karen's chart. "Have you traveled outside the country recently?"

When Karen reported that she had just returned from visiting her parents, who had become sick while touring China, the doctor's eyes widened. With practiced calm, she walked to the sink and washed her hands, then reached into an overhead cabinet for a surgical mask. As she fastened the mask over her mouth and nose, the doctor asked, "What part of China did they visit?" The unspoken question was, could this be SARS (severe acute respiratory syndrome), the virus that in 2003 spread through two dozen countries and infected more than 8,000 people? Or, worse still, could it be the start of the world's next pandemic?

From Animals to Humans

The question was hardly farfetched. Infectious disease experts are growing increasingly alarmed that a deadly new virus could leap national borders and, in a matter of months, reach every corner of the world. SARS is just one of a growing number of threatening diseases that have a particular trait in common: They begin among wild or domestic animals and spread to people.

Animal-borne diseases that cross over to infect humans have existed for eons. In fact, scientists believe that virtually all human viral diseases originated in animals and that every living species of bird, mammal, or reptile is a possible source of new human illness.

"The universe of potential emerging diseases from animals is huge and is, to a great extent, unknown," says David Morens, M.D., a research scientist at the National Institute of Allergy and Infectious Diseases (NIAID), part of the National Institutes of Health (NIH). "Because we don't know how big it is, we don't know what's 'behind the screen.' It's difficult to get a handle on the exact scope of the problem." Not every organism that infects animals has the ability to jump to people, and an organism won't necessarily cause disease if it does. But the potential for a novel bug to cause an epidemic is what keeps virus hunters on their toes.

One of the first recorded epidemics that may have originated among animals began about 430 B.C. during the Peloponnesian War, when an unknown illness killed about one-third of the population of Athens. Recent epidemics that are thought to have begun as animal diseases include Ebola hemorrhagic fever in Africa, which started in an unknown animal and killed 1,261 people between 1976 and 2004, and acquired immune deficiency syndrome (AIDS), which is caused by the human immunodeficiency virus (HIV). Although HIV was first found in humans in the 1950s, it took until 1999 for scientists to trace its source to a particular species of chimpanzee in Africa. The disease jumped to people when hunters came in contact with infected blood.

Even as scientists begin to get a handle on how to prevent or control these viruses, new diseases continue to crop up—some of them deadly.

How Viruses Make the Leap

Most diseases infect only one or a handful of species. That's why your dog or cat doesn't catch a cold each time you get the sniffles. Every now and then, though, an infectious agent, through mutation or adaptation, gains the ability to cross the species boundary. The threat is bigger now than ever before, for several reasons. With more than six billion of us on the planet, we have created a kind of global sprawl—humans as far as the eye can see. All those people need someplace to live. Moving into previously uninhabited land brings us into closer and closer contact with the animal world, where viruses hide. We end up living side by side with exotic diseases that can strike swiftly and lethally.

All those people also need to eat. Feeding billions means that domestic animals—chickens, pigs, and cows—are no longer free to roam on family farms. High production often entails corralling the animals side by side and tail to nose. In high-density pens, the viruses shed by a single sick chicken can potentially infect an entire flock. Of course, the risk to human handlers rises with every infected animal. In this way, previously "safe" animals, such as chickens or pigs, can end up causing human diseases. Depending on the strength and action of the virus, the people who get infected may experience no illness at all or only mild illness, or they may become very sick and possibly die.

Scientists point to the rodent-borne disease called hantavirus pulmonary syndrome (HPS) as a prime example of what happens when people and wild animals compete for living space. Hantavirus is an old virus that was recognized only in 1993 when an outbreak of HPS occurred in the southwestern part of the United States. In 1992, the rodent population in that area increased so much that a large number of mice sought shelter in people's homes. Although mice are common in rural areas, the problem was worse in that unusually wet year. What's more, some of the mice harbored hantavirus.

Of course, where there are mice, there are droppings—and infected mice leave infected droppings. After the rodents left the houses, the droppings dried up and turned to dust. In 1993, as people cleaned out storage areas around their homes, they inhaled the virus-laden dust particles. For 22 people that year, spring cleaning was fatal. The deaths were painful, marked by fever, muscle aches, and so much fluid accumulation in the lungs that it must have seemed like drowning on dry land. Scientists have since learned that about 430 species of mice can carry hantavirus, but only about 10 percent are infected. It was the mouse population explosion that exposed people to this deadly disease.

Evolution of an Epidemic

Although diseases that jump from animals to humans are frightening, they are generally self-contained. That is, only the people who come in contact with infected animals become ill. In order for a virus to spread throughout the world, it must develop the

Viruses spread more easily among domestic animals crowded shoulder to shoulder in modern, high-density pens.

ability to spread from person to person through mutation. Imagine, for example, a farmer who catches influenza—nothing special, just the regular flu bug that goes around among humans every year. If he also contracts a virus from a sick mouse or chicken, he will have two different viruses in his cells at the same time. Viruses in such proximity may swap some genes, thus creating a totally new virus that contains genetic material from both the original viruses. How that virus will act depends on which genes came together. It could end up being harmless, or, in a nightmare situation, it could be as deadly as Ebola and as contagious as the common cold.

In Asia, a deadly strain of bird flu crossed from chickens to humans who handled them.

Meanwhile, just about anyone can leave home and arrive in any city on Earth within 24 hours—even people who are deathly ill. The result? "All diseases are basically one plane flight away," says Lyle Petersen, M.D., director of the division of vector-borne infectious diseases at the Centers for Disease Control and Prevention (CDC). What that means in terms of illness and death depends on the type of bug being spread. If the germ is one of the quick-spreading varieties, scientists estimate that it could take only a few weeks before an outbreak becomes a worldwide threat. In short order, 25 to 40 percent of the world's population could become infected.

The Biggest Threat: Asian Influenza

When the next worldwide outbreak occurs—and scientists agree that it will happen—the most likely source will be an influenza virus.

"Am I worried about this? Yes, I am," says Dr. Morens. "Most people who have spent their careers working in infectious diseases, as I have, will put influenza at the very top of the list or very close to the top of the list of Andromeda strains—really bad things that could, and probably eventually will, come out of the environment and cause a terrible epidemic. We should remember that the 1918 influenza pandemic killed between 50 and 100 million people.

Workers place chickens into bags for burial in Ho Chi Minh City, Vietnam, to control an outbreak of bird flu.

That's more than the Black Death of the 14th century. That's more, so far, than AIDS. There's nothing that we know to assure us that it cannot happen again." Although the exact cause of the 1918 pandemic is not known, genetic evidence found in tissue samples suggests that it started as a bird flu that spent time in another species—possibly pigs or horses—before becoming a threat to people.

The rise of a deadly strain of bird flu in Asia in 2003 was particularly worrisome. The strain was 100 percent lethal in chickens. When it began infecting humans, it became an imminent threat. By the spring of 2004, 34 people in Asia had contracted bird flu through touching, handling, butchering, or being in proximity to infected birds. Of those who became infected, 23 died. That's about a 68 percent mortality rate.

Although the virus hasn't yet adapted to spread from person to person, the steep rise in the number of infections in chickens suggests that it may be only a matter of time until that lethal mutation occurs. In 1997 and 1998, about 1.4 million chickens died of the disease or were destroyed to prevent its spread. In 2001 and 2002, 2.5 million birds were killed. In 2003 and 2004, more than 100 million chickens in eight Asian countries had to be sacrificed to protect the public health.

"It's very clear that this virus poses a much larger risk than many other viruses," says Klaus Stöhr, D.V.M., Ph.D., head of the World Health Organization (WHO) Global Influenza Programme. "The virus is transmitted to humans. It replicates in humans. It causes disease in humans." If a human is infected with both this avian strain and a human strain, he says, it's possible the viruses could swap genetic material and create a more virulent strain. The current concern is that the most extreme efforts can't seem to contain the virus. Despite careful surveillance and immediate action when even a single sick chicken is discovered, outbreaks have continued to erupt, most notably in Thailand.

An Epidemic Arrested: SARS

Another new human disease that originated in Asia, of course, is SARS. It killed 774 people during its first major outbreak in 2003 and is also thought to have jumped from animals. In 2003 and 2004, SARS, which made its first appearance in the Guangdong province of southern China, had medical professionals around the world on red alert. Everything about it was a mystery.

"When SARS emerged, we didn't know what it was, we didn't know where it came from, and we didn't have any drugs or vaccines," says Dr. Morens. "In the early stages, we didn't even have any prevention measures that would allow us to stop it." For a while, it looked as if SARS could be the virus to cause the next worldwide disease outbreak.

In China, a woman on a Shanghai street wears a surgical mask to protect herself from SARS in the spring of 2004.

Although SARS is evidently a crossover disease, no one is sure which animal was the original host. "Traces of the virus were found in civet cats, which are a delicacy in the southeast part of China," says Francois Meslin, D.V.M., coordinator of zoonosis and food-borne diseases in the Communicable Disease Cluster of the WHO. "What we don't know is if SARS really originated from this animal species or if those civet cats were victims as much as humans."

What quickly became clear was that SARS was a coronavirus—one of the family of viruses that can cause the common cold—and that it could be spread from person to person. Once a disease no longer requires animal contact to be transmitted, it becomes a full-fledged human disease. After much investigation, researchers learned that SARS can be spread in the same ways as the flu—by breathing in virus-tainted droplets after an infected person sneezes or coughs or by touching a person or a surface that the virus has contaminated.

That knowledge came too late for the nearly 800 people who died of SARS. Once the outbreak was identified, health authorities in all 29 affected countries acted swiftly to isolate patients and anyone who had come in contact with them. Despite the highly contagious nature of the virus, medical personnel were able to prevent it from spreading throughout the world. The toll could have been much higher.

Public health specialists are wiser for having come through the SARS crisis. The WHO has issued procedures for preventing the spread of a virus within hospitals. These include guidelines on wearing surgical masks, gloves, and eye protection and instructions for the use of negative pressure, venting, and air conditioning in rooms that house SARS patients. "We now know what to do to prevent exposure to contacts of the patient and of the people at the hospital who work with the patient," says Dr. Morens. "It seems like simple knowledge, but it's a big step. I feel that if SARS breaks out again, we have the theoretical knowledge to contain any epidemics." Indeed, when a laboratory worker in China acquired SARS in early 2004, nine people—but no more—became infected before the outbreak was contained. No one knows whether SARS will return soon, but just in case, a vaccine is being prepared. So far it has proved effective in protecting monkeys against the virus, and in May 2004, the first human tests began in China.

The Danger in Your Backyard: West Nile Virus

Although lately it may seem that new strains of human disease emerge from Asia, that's not actually the case. The West Nile virus, discovered in northern Uganda in 1937, has probably been at large for thousands of years. It typically causes very mild, flu-like symptoms with no long-term effects. But in the 1990s, there were reports of outbreaks of West Nile in the Mediterranean region, Russia, and Romania—only this time, hundreds of people developed severe neurological disease in addition to the aches, pains, and fatigue caused by the older strain. A genetic mutation, according to one theory, changed a relatively weak virus into one capable of causing meningitis (inflammation of the lining of the brain or spinal cord), encephalitis (inflammation of the brain), paralysis, and death. That strain was the one that made its way to New York in 1999.

This virus is capable of infecting numerous species, including birds, horses, and dogs, but it is spread by mosquitoes, not by direct contact with the infected animal. When an infected animal is bitten, the mosquito sucks up the virus circulating in the animal's blood. The next time that mosquito bites, a small amount of the blood-borne virus is injected before fresh blood is removed. In this way, the tiny mosquito carries disease from animal to animal—or from animal to human. Although not all mosquitoes carry West Nile, enough do to make even wary scientists sick. "I got West Nile last summer," says Dr. Peterson. "I just went out to my mailbox, thinking I would be out there for a minute. Then I ran into one of my neighbors, we started talking, and we both got bitten by a bunch of mosquitoes. Three days later, both of us got West Nile." Gone are the carefree summer nights when the only risk of lingering outdoors was a few itchy bites. Now, every mosquito is suspect.

No one knows exactly how the virus got to the United States, says Dr. Petersen. "It probably arrived by an infected animal that was imported, or an infected person came, or possibly an infected mosquito hitchhiked on an airplane, which is actually fairly common." Since it hit U.S. shores, West Nile virus has marched relentlessly

A policeman in central China guards a civet cat captured by a farmer. The cats are one possible source of the country's outbreak of SARS.

Call in the swat team: The *Aedes albopictus* mosquito can pass the West Nile virus from one animal to another—or to humans.

across the nation, each year moving a little farther west. In 2003, 9,858 cases of West Nile were reported in the United States. Of those, 2,863 people had severe forms of the disease that affected their brains and nerves, and 262 died. In 2004, the disease expanded its reach into New Mexico, Arizona, and California. By 2005, West Nile virus will have reached just about every corner of the country.

After that, no one can predict exactly what will happen. "Once the disease enters an area, it tends to stick around," says Dr. Petersen. "West Nile virus will be a significant public health problem for the foreseeable future. Fortunately, there's no indication that the virus is mutating to become even more severe than it already is." Nonetheless, a vaccine is in the works. Initial testing has begun, but it will be several years before it becomes widely available.

Preparing for the Next Global Outbreak

Public health specialists are scrambling to keep up with the latest virus threats. Surveillance is the first line of defense. Once a disease reaches a country with a sophisticated medical communication and reporting system, it cannot hide. For example, if an influenza epidemic hits in the United States, the CDC will know within a week through its nationwide influenza monitoring program.

The best weapons against influenza are vaccines, which can prevent or at least lessen the effects of the virus, but vaccines take a minimum of six months to manufacture and distribute. Also, because we never know the exact strain of virus until it hits, a vaccine prepared in advance and stockpiled may not work against the strain that subsequently appears. As Dr. Stöhr puts it, it's like owning a gun for protection but having to wait until your enemy is shooting at you to make the ammunition. The virus will spread more quickly than we are able to make the vaccine.

Antiviral medications are also effective, and they should work during a global influenza outbreak, but

FAST FACTS

ASIAN INFLUENZA

- It started as a disease of wild waterfowl, such as ducks, but is now commonly found in domestic chickens in many parts of Asia.
- Scientists believe the virus is spread through the blood, feces, and mucus secretions of infected birds. This means that people who butcher live birds, or those who work without face masks in an area populated by infected birds, are most likely to catch the disease.
- People do not become sick by eating infected chickens. Normal cooking temperatures kill the virus.
- It is not yet transmissible from person to person.

SARS

- No one knows which animal first spread the disease to humans.
- No one knows exactly how the disease travels from person to person, although it appears to be spread in the same ways as the common cold.
- Vaccine development began in 2004, but years of testing are required before vaccines can become available to the public.
- It is not yet transmissible from person to person.

WEST NILE VIRUS

- About 99 percent of all cases are transmitted by mosquitoes, which pass the virus from birds, horses, and other mammals to humans.
- People in the western part of the United States may be at greatest risk because the most efficient carrier—the culex species of mosquito—is prevalent in that part of the country.
- The disease can also be spread through blood transfusions. Blood is now routinely screened for the virus, however, so the risk is minuscule.
- The best preventive is to use an insect repellent containing DEET (N,N-diethyl-3-methylbenzamide). When used as directed on the product label, this compound is considered safe for people of all ages. Insect repellents containing permethrin can be applied to clothing—never to skin—for extra protection.

MAD COW DISEASE: **BURGERS THAT BITE BACK**

The world's most mysterious animal-borne disease reared its head again in 2004, when the agents that cause mad cow disease were discovered in sheep muscles—the parts commonly cut into portions such as chops or leg of lamb. Scientists used to think that these tiny infectious agents, bits of misshapen protein called prions (pronounced PREE-ons), were found only in brain, nerve, and lymph system tissues.

Finding prions in muscle means the risk of mad cow disease may be greater than previously suspected. Scientists believe people get the human form of the illness, called variant Creutzfeldt-Jakob disease (vCJD), by eating meat from animals that had the disease. Until 2004, they believed that careful butchering could separate the untainted meat, but the new study, published by researchers in France in June 2004, raised fresh worries. Although prions are fewer in muscle than in brain, no one knows how many are needed to cause disease.

A case of mad cow was found on this Washington State ranch.

"We know very little about prions," says David Morens, M.D., a scientist at the National Institutes of Health. Unlike bacteria and viruses, prions do not seem to contain DNA or RNA. They can withstand heat, disinfectant chemicals, immune attack, and even ultraviolet radiation.

In people and animals, prions act like toxic seeds that start a cascade of destruction. Scientists believe they proliferate by encouraging normal proteins in the body to mutate in imitation of the prions. When enough prions accumulate in the brain, cells die, leaving so many holes that the organ ends up looking like a sponge. People and animals lose their ability to think and control their bodies. Eventually, they become delirious, then fall into comas before dying. Millions of infected cattle have been destroyed, and more than 100 people have died of vCJD.

Many health experts believe it is within our power to eradicate mad cow and vCJD. This will require vigilance in detecting sick animals, strict regulations to protect herds, and compliance by those who tend the cattle. The surveillance and testing have already begun, and statistics suggest the mad cow epidemic is fading. That's not certain, however. A study published in May 2004 raised the chilling possibility that there may be thousands of people in Great Britain who are carrying vCJD prions. The concern is that even while seemingly healthy, they may be able to transmit the disease to others through blood transfusions, organ donations, or tainted surgical or dental instruments.

they are very expensive, and the world's drug companies aren't currently set up make the large amounts that could be needed. This means that if a pandemic begins, antiviral drugs will become a hot commodity. "They're completely out of reach for every developing country. They cannot afford it," says Dr. Stöhr. "And developed countries may even start fighting for the very little which is available. There is no one who can produce enough."

Once a pandemic is recognized, the goal will be to control it and minimize the number of infections and deaths. Success will depend in part on how quickly we are able to produce vaccines and antiviral medications. "Currently, we are not very well off in this part," says Dr. Stöhr. "The disease and the public will not forgive complacency." He warns that the next pandemic will catch everyone unprepared unless governments, health agencies, and pharmaceutical companies come up with innovative ways to make these therapies available. Some researchers are striving to shorten the vaccine production time by using genetically engineered viruses instead of growing actual viruses in eggs (the current procedure). Because these techniques are new, though, extensive testing will be needed before they can be approved and licensed.

Ideally, we would prevent emerging diseases instead of merely reacting to them once they strike. To do so, however, would require international cooperation on an unprecedented scale—as well as some economic sacrifices. The virus hunters' "wish list" includes keeping rainforests, wetlands, and other

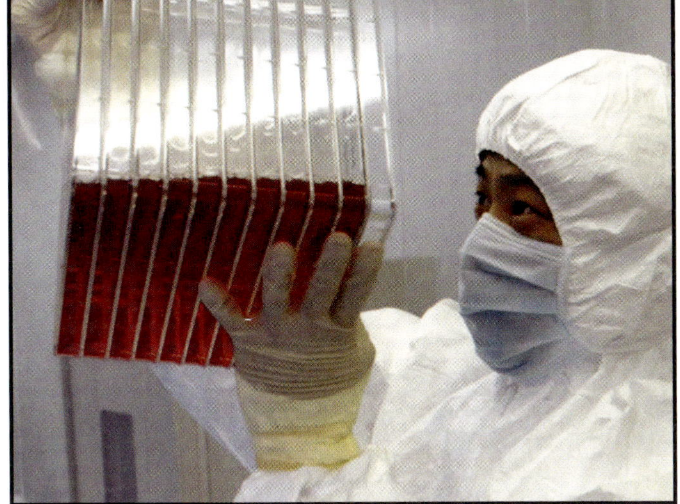
A Chinese scientist examines a SARS vaccine being developed for human use.

undeveloped environments safe from human intrusion; developing rules for importing and exporting wildlife; and changing farm practices so animals are kept in more spacious conditions.

"We need to consider the continuum from animals to humans with respect to the infectious diseases," says Dr. Meslin, "not divide this [issue] into small sectors, saying wildlife diseases are not our problem because our problem is domestic animals, or our problem is public health. We have to look at all beings as one—including the infectious diseases—and realize that whatever is done in one sector affects all the other sectors." Agriculture, industry, housing, wildland, and pollution policies are all part of the same tangled public health issue.

Crisis Averted for Now

Such matters were far from the thoughts of Marie, Ed, and their daughter Karen as they suffered through the flu-like symptoms of the "strange bug" picked up in China. It turned out that they didn't have SARS, but rather an infection that was never identified and never spread beyond the household.

Had it been SARS, everyone on Marie and Ed's plane from China would have been exposed, as well as everyone they met or talked to in the airport or during the week after they arrived home. Similarly, everyone on Karen's plane back to North Carolina would have been at risk, plus everyone in the doctor's office and in the supermarket and drugstore she visited on the way. And all of the people those people came in contact with might also have had the potential to catch the disease. A once-in-a-lifetime vacation could have turned into a regional or national disaster. When the laboratory worker in China was exposed to SARS in 2004, about 1,000 people were quarantined to keep the disease from spreading. But next time? No one is sure. Maybe a more virulent strain of virus will sweep the globe faster than physicians can react—or maybe the experience of dealing with SARS taught us enough.

"We have learned a lot," says Dr. Stöhr. "One lesson is that however creative nature is going to be in producing new pathogens, I believe that we will be even more creative to stem those outbreaks, to control them." ■

How to Make Bird Flu Vaccine

A technique called reverse genetics allows scientists to mix and match genes from different viruses. This should allow them to create a harmless flu virus that triggers immunity to a pandemic strain.

Harmless human flu virus

RNA

Plasmid

The flu genome consists of 10 genes encoded on eight strands of RNA.

Two of the strands contain genes for surface proteins. Each strand can be put on a different plasmid (a loop of DNA) and transferred into a cultured monkey cell.

Bird flu virus

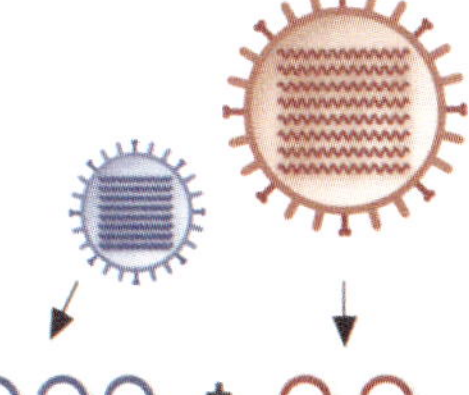

To make a vaccine, you need to mix the two surface protein genes from bird flu with the other eight genes from a harmless human strain.

Monkey cell

The eight plasmids are inserted into monkey cells grown in culture.

The monkey cells start producing a virus that is harmless but has surface proteins from bird flu. When killed and used as a vaccine, this will prime the immune system to recognize the bird flu virus and create antibodies to it.

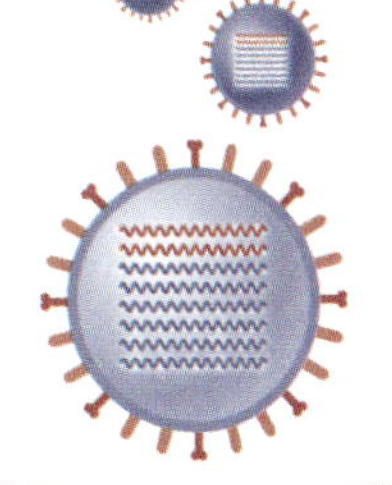

The traditional vaccine manufacturing process is to inject the virus into eggs. After a few weeks, large quantities of virus can be harvested for vaccines.

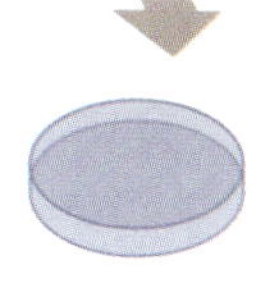

If a bird flu pandemic takes off, manufacturers may also be able to grow the virus in cell cultures. This will increase manufacturing capacity, but so far no such plants are licensed.

NEW DRUG ACTS LIKE DRAIN OPENER FOR ARTERIES

A scientific mystery that dates back a quarter century to a small group of people in an Italian lake resort may have produced a powerful and unexpected new weapon that could revolutionize the fight against heart disease, America's number one killer.

Infusions of a special, bio-engineered version of "good" cholesterol can shrink plaque in the arteries in a matter of weeks, putting heart disease in reverse.

Back in the 1970s, doctors began scratching their heads when they came across a curious family in Limone sul Garda, a picturesque Italian village. Blood tests showed that three people, a father and two of his children, had very low levels of HDL (high-density lipoprotein, or "good" cholesterol, the kind that protects against heart disease) and very high levels of dangerous blood fats called triglycerides. The combination was a recipe for heart attacks, yet their arteries appeared to be perfectly healthy, and they all lived long lives remarkably free of heart disease. What could account for the paradox?

Research revealed that they had a "mutant" form of HDL that made it extremely effective at cleaning up LDL (low-density lipoprotein), the "bad" cholesterol that gums up arteries. About 40 people in the town were eventually

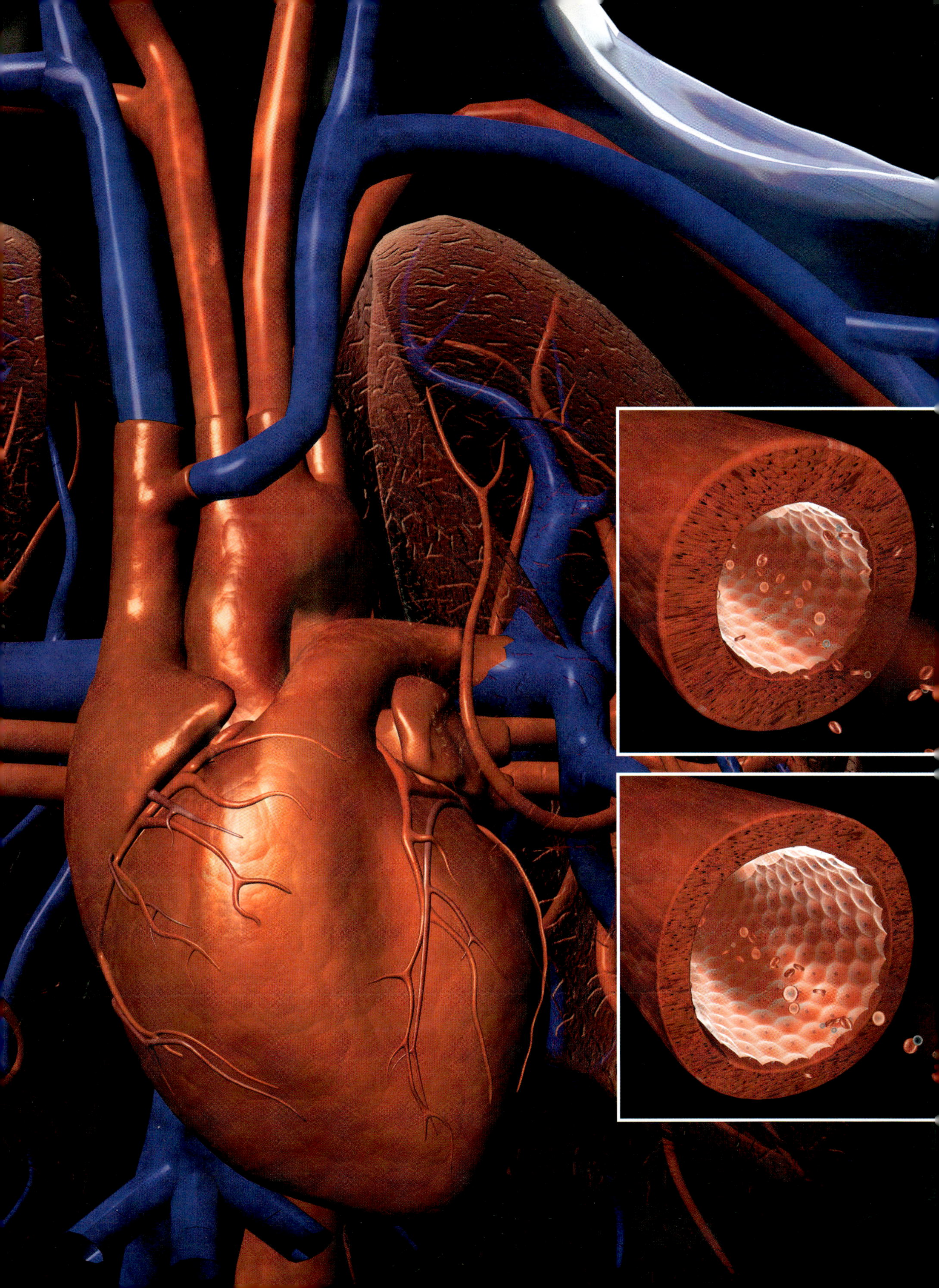

found to have this unique type of HDL, and all had lower-than-expected rates of heart disease. The altered HDL responsible for their heart health was eventually named ApoA-I Milano, after the region where it was found.

Eventually, a bioengineered version of ApoA-I Milano was created, and when scientists fed it to rabbits and other lab animals over a period of 10 years, the results were remarkable: The plaque buildup inside the animals' arteries stopped, and the existing plaque shrank.

Scientists know that what works in animals does not always work in humans, so when doctors at the Cleveland Clinic in Ohio and nine other sites gave ApoA-I Milano intravenously to 47 patients with coronary artery disease, they were astounded at the outcome. Both the speed and the scale of improvement were stunning. After five weekly infusions, intravascular ultrasound scans showed that the plaque in the patients' arteries had shrunk by an average of about 4 percent. By comparison, in patients treated with an LDL-lowering statin drug and niacin over a three-year period, the reduction in plaque was less than 1/2 of 1 percent.

A SUPER HDL SUCCESS STORY

Since taking part in an ApoA-I Milano study two years ago, Bob Garrison, a retired postal services manager in his seventies from Oklahoma City, has been largely free of heart disease symptoms, including chest pain. Garrison, who currently takes atorvastatin (Lipitor), one of the cholesterol-lowering statin drugs, was 59 and about to embark on a fishing trip when he had his first heart attack. Over the next decade, he had a second heart attack and multiple angioplasties. But now his story has changed. "I haven't had any problems. I haven't had to have any more angioplasties. I used to have pain in my chest every once in a while, but I have had hardly any pain. I haven't had anything go wrong with me since I took that."

Garrison is very aware, however, that the super HDL needs to be tested for several years before it can be approved for use by the general public. "The only thing I dislike about it," he says, "is that at my age, it may take so long to get out on the market that I may never get to use it."

"Good" Cholesterol Can Clear Plaque

Infusions of a synthetic component of "good" cholesterol, or HDL, reduced artery disease in just five weeks in a small study that could have bigger implications for treating the nation's leading killer.

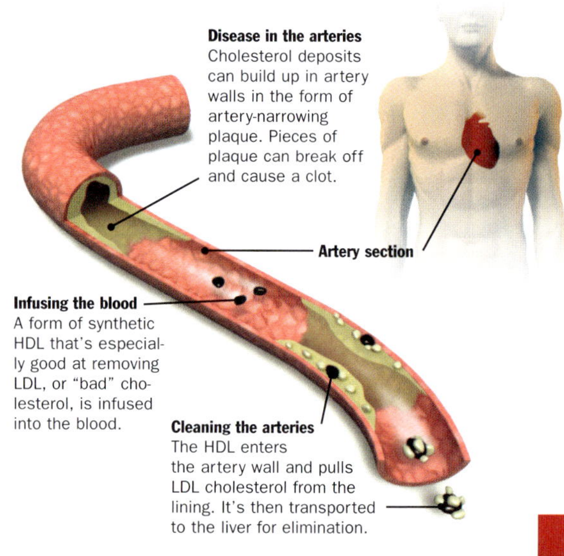

The implication is huge: Someday in the foreseeable future, heart disease could be treated not with invasive bypass surgery or angioplasty (an artery-opening procedure) but with a drug that would actually reverse the disease.

The Role of "Good" Cholesterol

The regular old HDL in most people's blood helps protect them from heart disease, which is why high levels—more than 40 mg/dL—of this type of cholesterol are good. (Losing weight and getting more exercise are two ways to boost your HDL numbers.)

"I tell my students that HDL is like a maid," says David Harrison, M.D., director of cardiology at Emory University in Atlanta. "HDL cleans the house. HDL comes into a messy artery and sees all the junk lying around—the LDL—and picks it up and throws it away. If you happen to have a low LDL count, you're a neat freak. You don't need as much attention from a maid. If you have a high LDL count, it's like you're a slob. Your arteries are messy, and you need regular housekeeping service. So it is important for you to have a high HDL count." Regular HDL also has other beneficial functions, including possible roles in fighting inflammation (now considered a major contributor to heart disease) and offsetting the tendency of blood to clot.

The Italians in the Milano region had HDL that was only slightly different from what most of us have. In one of the main proteins making up their HDL, apolipoprotein A-I, the amino acid cysteine was substituted for the amino acid arginine. The chemical switch appears to make the protein unusually good at its job of latching onto LDL molecules, lifting them out of artery walls, and carrying them to the liver for disposal.

Scientists also discovered that the "super" HDL appears to have especially strong antioxidant properties, meaning that it helps prevent damaging molecules called free radicals from oxidizing LDL particles and making them more likely to stick to artery walls. (Similar to the process of rusting, oxidation occurs when cells are attacked by free radicals, which are byproducts of body processes that involve oxygen.)

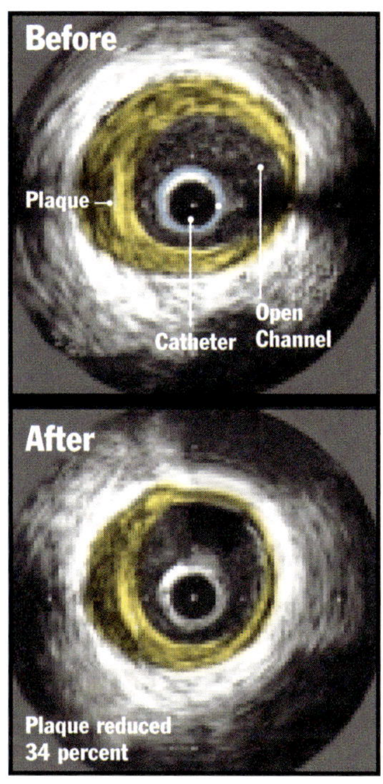

"Super HDL" shrank dangerous plaque, visible in this cross-section of an artery before and after treatment.

Liquid Drano for the Arteries

The biggest potential benefit of ApoA-I Milano may be its ability to act on the whole circulatory system at once, cleaning out the arteries like a liquid drain opener. In heart disease, the arteries are narrowed due to the accumulation of plaque. If a plaque is unstable, it can burst, spewing its contents into the artery. The body sends chemicals that trigger a clotting response, and if the resulting clot blocks the artery, it can cause a heart attack.

Most people with heart disease have plaque in more than one place, says researcher Muhammad Yasin, M.D., of Integris Southwest Medical Center in Oklahoma City, who was involved in the study. "You look at the arteries with ultrasound—they are studded with plaques," he says. Angioplasty—the catheter-based procedure commonly used to open blocked arteries—opens only one area of an artery at a time. ApoA-I Milano, on the other hand, unclogs the whole plumbing system.

In the future, when someone is diagnosed with unstable angina (chest pain caused by narrowed arteries) and is clearly at risk of having a heart attack, a drug such as ApoA-I Milano might be used to stabilize the patient long enough to let other treatments, such as an LDL-lowering statin drug, get him out of danger.

Esperion Therapeutics, the small company that made ApoA-I Milano, was purchased for $1.3 billion by the giant drug company Pfizer in December 2003. Pfizer will need to invest in several more years of drug trials to prove the effectiveness and safety of ApoA-I Milano before it can be approved for use. Among the lingering issues: As an editorial in the *Journal of the American Medical Association* noted, ApoA-I Milano has yet to be tested head to head against regular HDL to prove that it's better at fighting heart disease.

Nevertheless, the study results are "very promising," says lead researcher Steven E. Nissen, M.D., of the Cleveland Clinic. "It produced a lot of excitement. How far can we go with this? What happens if we give it for 12 weeks? There are many things we don't know. All we know is that it was a big surprise—a large effect, occurring rapidly—and we hope that it will be proven to be very beneficial in larger studies." ■

what does it mean to you?

Rome wasn't built in a day, and similarly, ApoA-I Milano must undergo several years of further testing before it can earn FDA approval for use in combating heart disease. Nonetheless, if the results of future studies support the prior findings, the "super HDL" may be part of a trend in new drugs and therapies aimed at controlling coronary artery disease chemically rather than surgically. The potential advantages:

- Super HDL may buy time for patients clearly at risk of having heart attacks, giving them the chance to let treatments, such as LDL-lowering statin drugs, get them out of the woods.
- Unlike angioplasty and stents, which open just one or two blocked arteries at a time, super HDL acts on all plaques simultaneously, providing a more efficient, clean-sweep approach to reducing artery-clogging plaque.

HUMAN EMBRYOS CLONED, DEBATE IGNITED

"Cloned human." The two words side by side last year in a research paper published in the journal *Science* would have captured almost anyone's attention. Indeed, the report unleashed a slew of ethical, legal, social, moral, and religious conundrums that nearly eclipsed the scientific achievement.

South Korean scientists, using human eggs and human DNA, had created human embryos through cloning, but they had no plans to make babies who would grow up into walking, talking duplicates of the women who had produced the eggs. Instead, the scientists extracted stem cells from the microscopic balls of dividing cells. Embryonic stem cells can become virtually any type of human tissue, potentially offering powerful treatments—even cures—for damaged or diseased organs, spinal injuries, diabetes, Parkinson's disease, multiple sclerosis, and more.

With this experiment, the scientists took a critical step toward therapeutic cloning—that is, cloning for the purpose of obtaining stem cells for treating disease. Their announcement, though, renewed calls for a worldwide ban on all forms of human cloning—both therapeutic and reproductive—and left American scientists feeling like kids who had arrived too late for the party.

Dr. Woo Suk Hwang *(top right)* and Dr. Shin-Yong Moon *(top left)* of Seoul National University in Korea were the first in the world to clone a human embryo. Above, the cloning process.

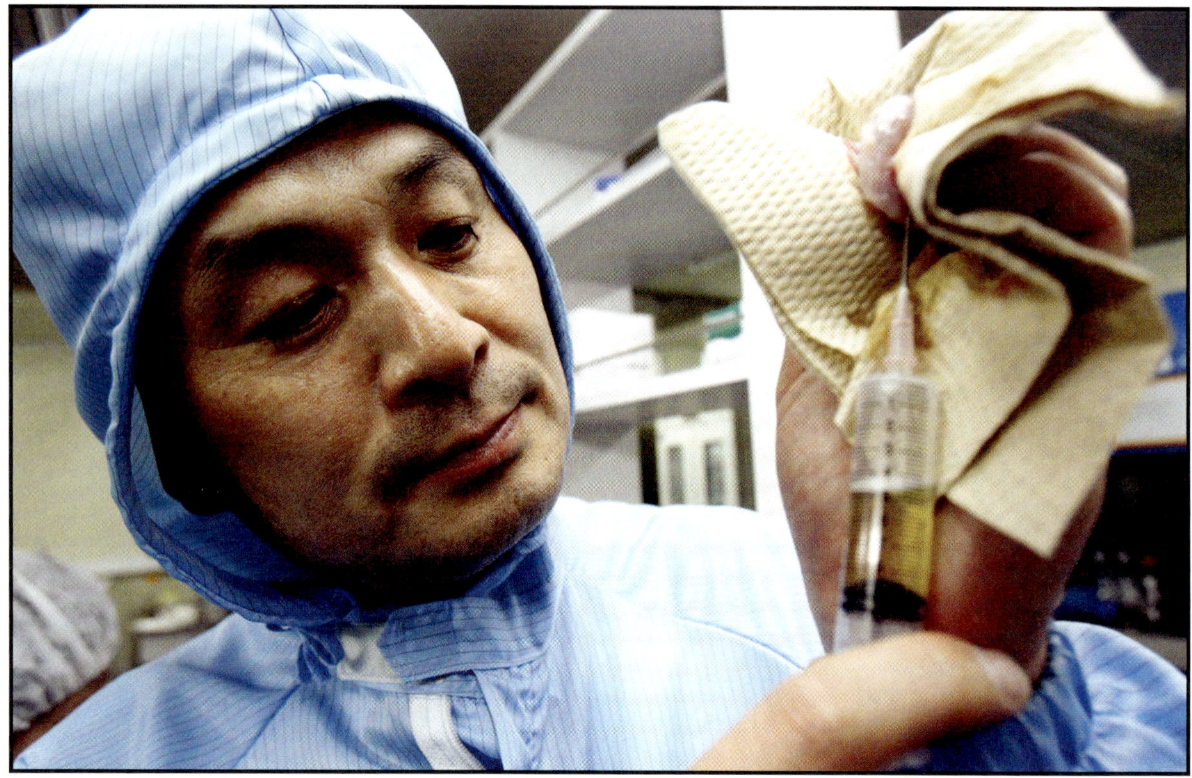

Cloning pioneer Dr. Woo Suk Hwang, shown in his Seoul laboratory, is working to make therapeutic cloning a reality. A veterinary medical researcher, he has also cloned cows and pigs.

Cracking the Egg

Of course, someone, somewhere was bound to attempt human cloning, an event the world has been simultaneously anticipating and dreading. So why did it take eight years from the birth of Dolly the sheep, the first cloned mammal, to clone human cells? Blame the egg. That's the view of Gerald Schatten, Ph.D., professor and vice chair of the department of obstetrics, gynecology, and reproductive sciences at the University of Pittsburgh School of Medicine and a leader in the world of cloning and stem cell research. In fact, in a paper published in *Science* in April 2003, he predicted that human cloning might never be possible.

Dr. Schatten and his team attempted to use the same method that worked with Dolly and other mammals in their own efforts to clone rhesus macaque monkeys. But more than 700 times, they failed. The problem, Dr. Schatten says, has to do with the way monkey and human eggs divide. Removing the DNA from one of these eggs—a critical first step in cloning—effectively "paralyzes" the egg, rendering it unable to divide into the multiple cells that form an embryo.

The South Korean researchers eventually solved the division problem. They first "harvested" eggs from 16 volunteers, using classic in vitro fertilization (IVF) techniques (the women were given drugs to stimulate their ovaries to produce multiple eggs, which were then harvested through an outpatient surgical procedure). Then the scientists replaced the nuclei in the eggs from each woman with nuclei from cells in the woman's body, thereby exchanging the eggs' incomplete DNA for the woman's complete DNA. Ordinarily, an embryo has two DNA sources, a woman's egg and a man's sperm, and it's the fusion of the two that triggers cell division, notes lead researcher Woo Suk Hwang, D.V.M., Ph.D., of Seoul National University in South Korea. In this case, the researchers gave the eggs a chemical bath to kick-start their division.

The new cloning attempt might well have failed right then, just as the monkey cloning attempts had, if the South Koreans hadn't done something different: use eggs at an earlier stage of development. Researchers have long known that egg cells possess special "motor" proteins, which, as the cells divide, neatly pull apart tight packets of DNA, or chromosomes. Removing the DNA at the start of the cloning process also removes the motor proteins, stopping cell division and bringing the process of therapeutic cloning to a screeching halt. The eggs used by the South Korean researchers, however, were young enough that motor proteins hadn't yet gathered around the DNA (think of them as hanging out at the edges of the cell instead), so they remained in the egg after the DNA was removed.

The scientists had another advantage: They had harvested an amazing 242 eggs from the 16 volunteers. Having so many eggs to work with meant they could take more risks, experimenting with different techniques until they found the one that worked. They wound up with 30 embryos that reached the blastocyst stage. A blastocyst is a ball of about 100 cells, and deep in the center of the ball are the all-important stem cells. The South Koreans managed to extract 20 of these inner cell masses, one of which grew into a batch, or "line," of stem cells. The rest were destroyed, as were the embryos.

Their procedure managed to dodge one major ethical issue involving embryonic stem cell

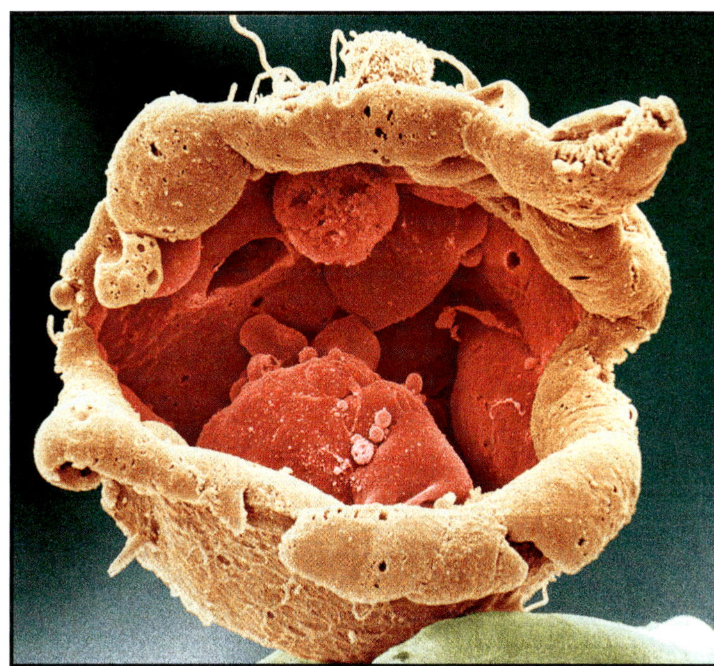

This human embryo, at the blastocyst stage, has been opened to reveal the inner cell mass, where stem cells can be harvested. Stem cells can be coaxed into becoming virtually any kind of tissue, making powerful new treatments possible.

A New Path to Stem Cells

South Korean researchers have created cloned embryos and grown them for about six days, until they formed spheres of about 100 cells. At that stage, stem cells, perhaps useful for treating disease, can be extracted.

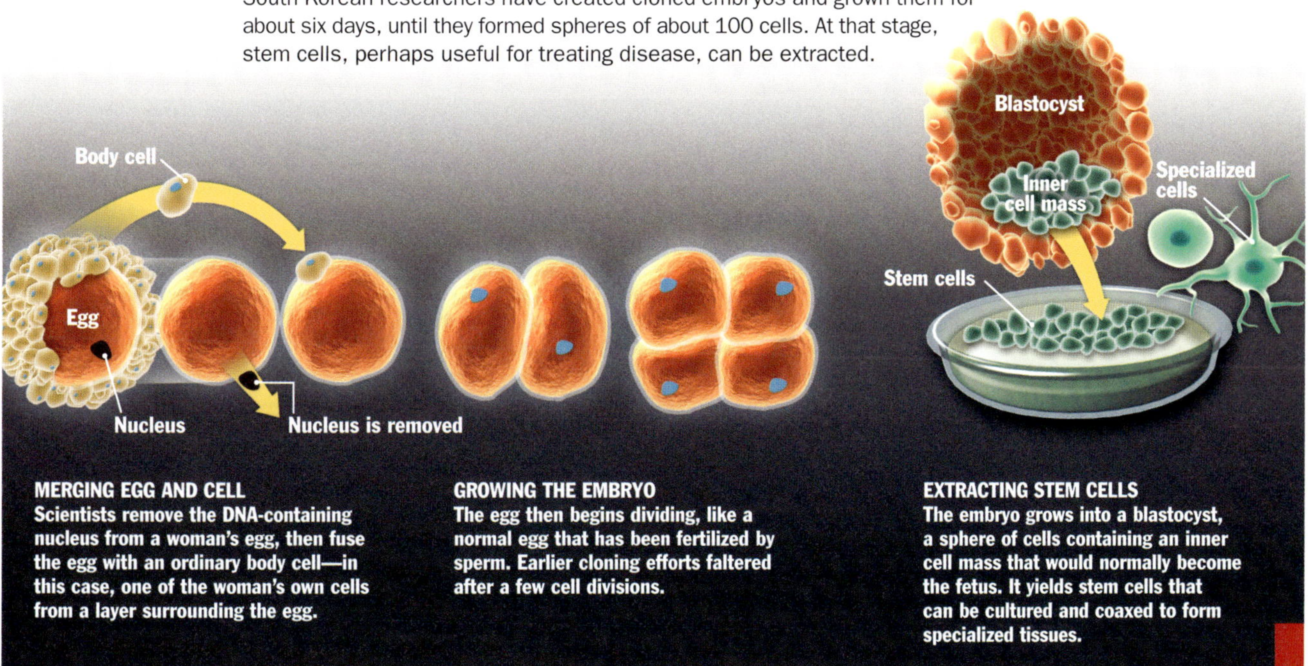

MERGING EGG AND CELL
Scientists remove the DNA-containing nucleus from a woman's egg, then fuse the egg with an ordinary body cell—in this case, one of the woman's own cells from a layer surrounding the egg.

GROWING THE EMBRYO
The egg then begins dividing, like a normal egg that has been fertilized by sperm. Earlier cloning efforts faltered after a few cell divisions.

EXTRACTING STEM CELLS
The embryo grows into a blastocyst, a sphere of cells containing an inner cell mass that would normally become the fetus. It yields stem cells that can be cultured and coaxed to form specialized tissues.

research: They didn't have to use embryos left over from attempts at IVF. The eggs they harvested were identical to ones the women would ordinarily have lost during their monthly menstrual cycles. What's more, the eggs were never fertilized, so there was no conception, biologically speaking. That means the cells the scientists made were identical to those of each egg donor. That's important when it comes to creating stem cells for therapeutic use, says Dr. Hwang. A doctor attempting to treat a spinal injury can transplant cloned stem cells into the egg donor, and her body will welcome them as its own. Cells derived from another person could be rejected.

Former First Lady Nancy Reagan has become an outspoken advocate of stem cell research.

his work in the lab had the potential to enable the young man to walk again.

The nation of South Korea also plays a role. Although it bans reproductive cloning, it allows therapeutic cloning in certain circumstances. At the same time, like most Asian countries, it does not allow organ transplants. Cloning to create stem cells that can develop into hearts, lungs, and other organs is the only hope for people in these nations who need transplants. Additionally, Dr. Hwang's religious beliefs—he is a Buddhist—support his actions. "Buddhist faith is that all living things are given new life after they die," he says. "Cloning also means new life."

A Workaholic at the Cloning Academy

"This couldn't have been done anywhere else in the world except in South Korea, for a number of reasons," says Dr. Schatten. First, there is the technological prowess of South Korean scientists. "They are among the best cloners on Earth," he says. He notes that they have already cloned cattle resistant to mad cow disease and pigs that could be used for human organ transplants.

What's more, notes Dr. Schatten, Dr. Hwang is exceptionally focused, even by the standards of academic science. He is at his lab—dubbed the cloning academy—by 6:30 A.M. 7 days a week, 365 days a year. It took him just a couple of years to succeed in his therapeutic cloning efforts.

Dr. Hwang's drive is fueled by his own vision of what successful stem cell research would mean. In fact, he and his partners have structured the patents for their work so the doctors receive no financial rewards. "I would like to find the way to treat patients with degenerative disease," he says. "I would like to bring therapeutic cloning into real life."

When his research flagged at one point, and he became frustrated, he visited a young couple just back from their honeymoon, during which the man had fallen and been paralyzed. Dr. Hwang realized

The Debate Catches Fire

Nevertheless, Dr. Hwang's work set off a firestorm of protest, largely because therapeutic cloning involves the destruction of embryos, which some people view as human life. The United States

In New Brunswick, New Jersey, protesters gather outside a forum on the state's stem cell research initiative.

government now restricts federal funding for stem cell research to batches of embryonic stem cells that already existed in 2001, when the policy was announced. Those stem cell lines, of which about 18 remain, are not very good, says James A. Grifo, M.D., Ph.D., professor in the department of obstetrics and gynecology at New York University and a member of the NYU Program for IVF Reproductive Surgery and Infertility. "They were created when the techniques were not well established, and they offer very limited potential for furthering this field," he says.

Scientists who are using cloning to obtain embryonic stem cells are the ones calling most loudly for a worldwide ban on cloning for the purpose of creating babies.

Federal policy aside, human cloning of any kind is banned in several states, including Pennsylvania, where Dr. Schatten has his lab, which is why he works with only primates and other animals.

The U.S. stalemate leaves many scientists frustrated. This situation, Dr. Grifo says, would be akin to closing Alexander Fleming's lab in the early 20th century to halt the development of penicillin. "The current policies and politics are taking an incredibly promising technology and basically preventing it from happening," he says.

The result, he and others say, is that the world's best and most well funded scientists are going to find themselves on the sidelines as countries such as South Korea and China take the lead. "The bottom line is that there are people and patients who are going to suffer because we're so short-sighted," Dr. Grifo explains.

Ironically, the scientists who are using cloning to obtain embryonic stem cells are the ones calling most loudly for a worldwide ban on cloning for the purpose of creating babies. They're urging world governments to officially support therapeutic cloning, the kind of work done in South Korea. "We have to drive the last nail in the coffin of reproductive cloning," says Dr. Schatten. "It's unsafe, ineffective, and thoroughly immoral and unethical."

New Hurdles Ahead

The South Korean achievements are just the first step into therapeutic cloning. Next up: Figuring out whether the newly created stem cells will be useful in medicine. Research reported in 2004 found that human embryonic stem cell lines grown in the lab over several months may have genetic abnormalities. Additionally, no one yet knows whether embryonic stem cells can really generate the many types of cells the scientists want, from heart muscle to motor neurons.

In South Korea, Dr. Hwang and his team are exploring whether the stem cells they retrieved will in fact produce specific cell types, such as nerve cells and pancreatic cells. They're also working to develop artificial eggs that could be used for cloning in nations where politics slams the door on embryo research. They have voluntarily halted any new cloning of human eggs while the world debates the issues. ■

what does it mean to you?

By cloning human embryos and extracting stem cells from them, the South Korean scientists moved the research into stem cell therapy further along. Here's what their achievement means.

■ Scientists can now create their own batches, or lines, of stem cells. They no longer have to use human embryos left over from in vitro fertilization attempts in order to get embryonic stem cells.

■ Cloning allows scientists to create embryos that genetically match the person who needs the therapy. Most likely, this will improve the chances that the treatment will work.

■ Researchers hope one day to use stem cell therapy to treat conditions such as Alzheimer's, Parkinson's disease, diabetes, multiple sclerosis, heart disease, and spinal injuries, among others.

■ Experts estimate it will be at least a decade before anyone applies to the FDA for permission to conduct studies of stem cell treatments in humans. That's because so much remains unknown about how embryonic stem cells act in the body. Until researchers convince the FDA that human experiments are safe, they won't gain permission to conduct them. Once they do get the go-ahead, experts say, it will be many years before the technology could be used to treat any of the conditions for which it looks so promising.

THE NEW FACE OF PLASTIC SURGERY

While watching television one night, Doris Newton decided she was tired of not liking the way she looked. "It always looked like I had a wrinkled turtleneck sweater on," she says—and it was time to do something about it.

Blueprint for a younger face: This patient, marked up for surgery, is among millions swarming to cosmetic surgeons' offices since TV shows such as *Extreme Makeover* erased the stigma.

Newton wasn't watching a sitcom with gorgeous babes and hunks who make the rest of us feel like Plain Janes and Johns. The show was one of the new wave of "reality" makeover programs, which follow people as they get everything from plastic and reconstructive surgery to injections of the latest "line fillers" that plump out wrinkles.

Although Newton's no kid (she wouldn't give her age but acknowledged having three grandchildren), she decided there was no reason to look any older than necessary. So, brushing aside the old moral judgment—that plastic surgery strictly for appearance's sake is sinfully vain—Newton, who lives near Philadelphia, had a face-lift and a few other cosmetic procedures. It was not quite an extreme makeover, but it was definitely a change. Looking in the mirror afterward, she says, "I feel better about myself.

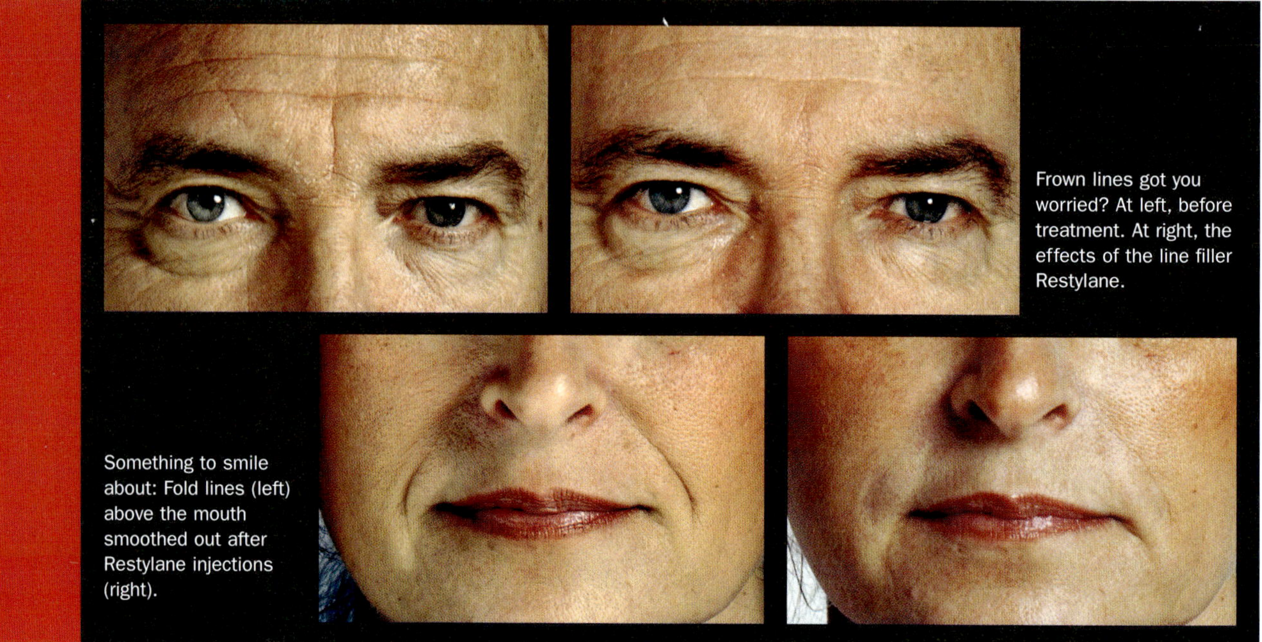

Frown lines got you worried? At left, before treatment. At right, the effects of the line filler Restylane.

Something to smile about: Fold lines (left) above the mouth smoothed out after Restylane injections (right).

I do look younger, but I don't look artificial. My face isn't looking tight. I look just like a regular woman."

Newton is just one among millions of people in the past year who watched Cinderella-like, top-to-bottom transformations on programs such as *Extreme Makeover*, *The Swan*, and *I Want a Famous Face* and then rushed out to get makeovers of their own. While some doctors fear such programs create an unrealistic picture of plastic surgery, people nevertheless are voting with their feet—and their faces, breasts, and bellies.

"I have a waiting list as long as your arm," says Lori Saltz, M.D., a plastic surgeon in La Jolla, California. By the middle of 2004, she says, her business was already up a whopping 60 percent from 2003. Before, "it was as if people were saying, 'You go first.' 'No, you go first,' " she says. Then the reality shows appeared. "It was like—boom!—and the dam breaks."

It's not just a big-city and bicoastal trend, either. "At least 40 percent of the people in my practice mention having seen these reality shows," says plastic surgeon Clark Taylor, M.D., D.D.S., of Missoula, Montana.

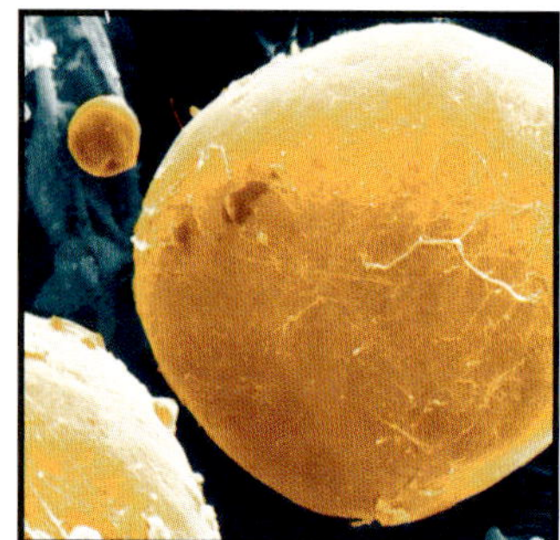

Microscopic view of collagen, part of the connective tissue in skin.

Injections of Restylane last longer than collagen injections.

In all, more than 8.7 million cosmetic plastic surgery procedures were performed in 2003—a 32 percent increase from about 6.6 million procedures the year before, according to statistics compiled by the American Society of Plastic Surgeons. The patients are still overwhelmingly women, but a growing number of men are also going under the knife or needle.

The New Wrinkle Erasers

The TV shows are only a piece of what's driving the trend. Cosmetic surgery is in fact getting easier. The new era began with Botox, a toxin that's injected to paralyze the tiny muscles that give us crow's-feet and laugh lines. Botox has become a household word since it was approved in 2002 because of all of the celebrities who've reportedly used it. Then, in 2003, the movement got a fresh boost when the FDA approved two new line fillers.

"One of the things we've begun to realize is that the face doesn't just age by sagging," says Brent Moelleken, M.D., a plastic surgeon who has been featured on *Extreme Makeover*. Instead, he says, "We are now realizing that a tremendous component of aging is loss of volume—the face is actually shrinking and facial fat is atrophying."

The basic component of the new line fillers, Restylane and Hylaform, is hyaluronic acid, a body component that pads tissue by attracting and binding water molecules to the skin. When natural levels of hyaluronic acid fall as the years go by, skin becomes less resilient and looks older. Injections of Restylane and Hylaform can counter this decline more safely and quickly and last longer than other fillers now available.

The older generation of fillers included a person's own fat cells plus collagen, a fibrous protein that's a constituent of the connective tissue in skin and tendons, but the life span of fat injections was unpredictable, Dr. Moelleken says.

Before Restylane and Hylaform, there were hyaluronic acid–based facial fillers called Synvisc and Hyalgan. They are made from animal products (such as cow cartilage or rooster combs) that may cause allergic reactions in people sensitive to foods such as beef, eggs, and chicken.

What's more, classic collagen—derived from cows—may also cause allergic reactions, requiring time-consuming preinjection testing, says David E. Bank, M.D., of Mount Kisco, New York, who is on the teaching faculty of the department of dermatology at Columbia Presbyterian Medical Center in New York City. New laboratory-grown strains of human collagen give better results, he says.

The new fillers are ready to go when you are. "People can walk in and say, 'I'm going to my reunion this weekend, and I really want this corrected,' and we can do it on the spot," says Dr. Bank.

These treatments aren't permanent. The body eventually absorbs the added material, and then new injections are required. Collagen injections generally

A HUGE APPETITE FOR **SKIN-TRIMMING SURGERY**

Severely overweight people who are desperate to trim down have been lining up to get stomach-shrinking surgery to quell their appetites. Such procedures are so popular and successful that they're resulting in a boom in another kind of surgery—procedures that reshape the folds of skin left behind after massive weight loss.

Plastic surgeons are doing more and more "body-contouring" procedures after stomach-shrinking surgery to give a lift to the figure fore and aft and to trim sail-like expanses of skin. They report a surge in the number of buttock lifts, upper-arm lifts, thigh and lower-body lifts, tummy tucks, and face jobs. And they expect to be doing even more in the future: The number of people in the United States having gastric bypass surgery—the most common stomach-shrinking procedure—rose from 67,000 in 2002 to 103,000 in 2003 and was projected to hit 144,000 in 2004. In 2003, plastic surgeons did 52,000 body-contouring procedures on patients who had lost large amounts of weight, and that figure was expected to increase by 36 percent in 2004.

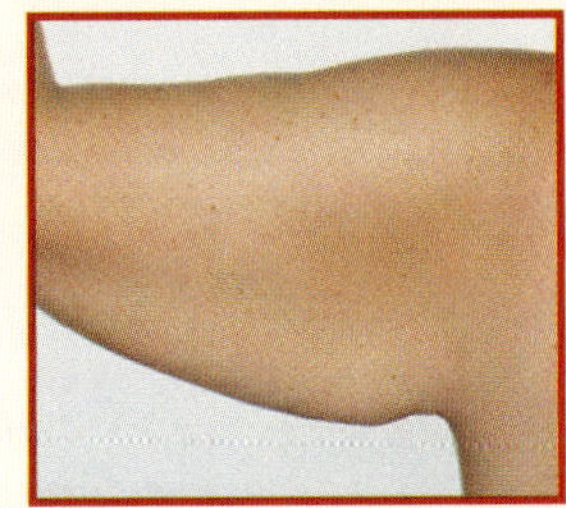

Losing large amounts of weight can leave sagging skin under the arms and elsewhere.

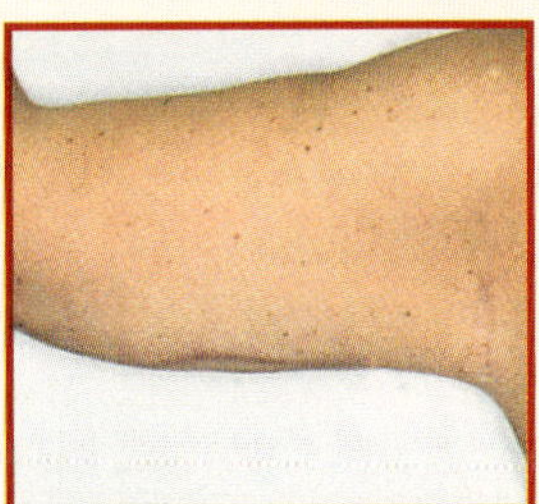

Getting your "wings" clipped: Arm lift surgery removes excess skin.

Such skin-tightening surgeries are not only getting more frequent, they're getting better as well. For example, one procedure commonly done after gastric bypass corrects an excess of skin that looks like a bat's wing between the elbow and the chest wall, says Berish Strauch, M.D., author of a study on new arm-contouring techniques.

Previous techniques to restore normal shape to this area often left unsightly scars that didn't heal well because those methods didn't take into account how skin is pulled when an arm is flexed and extended, the study found.

Dr. Strauch—a general, plastic, and hand surgeon and microsurgeon at the Albert Einstein College of Medicine in New York City—recommends some improvements in the procedures. For instance, he says the scar can be made less visible by making the incision on the underside of the arm. Using an S-shaped incision allows the scar to expand and contract with the arm's natural movements and thus heal better. New, improved procedures also allow the skin to settle back into the armpit as naturally as it did before.

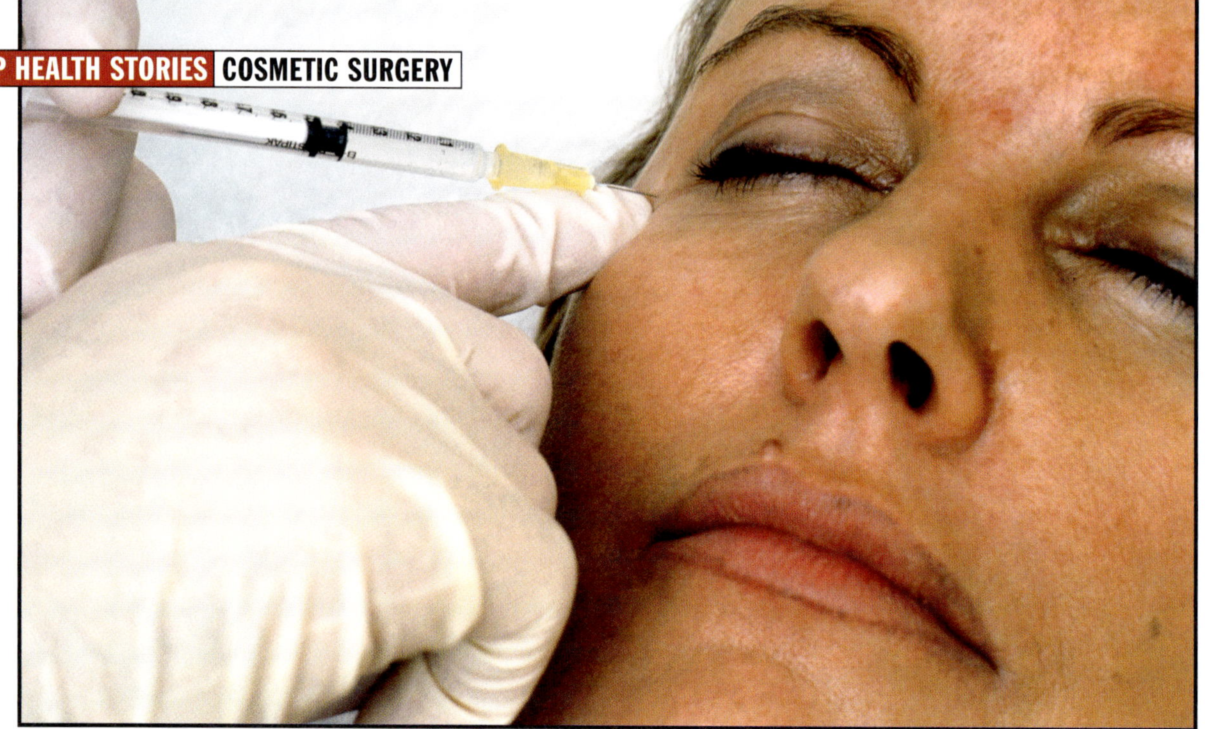

Better than Botox? While Botox injections (above) paralyze facial muscles that cause wrinkles, the newer line fillers actually plump out the skin, padding tissue by attracting and binding water molecules to the skin.

are good for about four to six months, Hylaform for six to nine months, and Restylane for up to a year. But the treatments are quick and relatively cheap. Botox, Hylaform, and Restylane shots cost between $500 and $1,000, whereas the average face-lift runs about $5,000.

It's no wonder that in 2003, medical trend watchers saw a 41 percent increase in these so-called minimally invasive procedures over the previous year. Collagen treatments rose by 30 percent, and Botox injections shot up by 157 percent. (Studies are now being conducted on a new, improved botulism toxin called Dysport, already in use in Europe, Dr. Bank says.)

Plastic Surgery "Lite"

With new techniques on the rise, face-lifts were down 24 percent in 2003. There are still many people, however, who want the kinds of makeovers they're seeing on TV—face-lifts, nose reshaping, liposuction, breast augmentation, eyelid surgery, breast and butt lifts, tummy tucks, lip augmentation, and all the other types of totally new-look looks.

To keep up with demand and the times, plastic surgeons increasingly are "minimalizing" many of those procedures, too. They are using smaller incisions and sutures for face-lifts (which people increasingly want done on only certain parts of the face). For a traditional face-lift, surgeons make a big cut, lift the skin and tissue beneath it, and use multiple stitches like bridge cables to pull it all up. Recovery takes weeks.

Cosmetic Surgery Trends

More and more people—including younger women—are opting for cosmetic surgery. Botox injections were the most popular noninvasive treatment in 2003. Since then, line fillers have surged in popularity.

COSMETIC SURGERY BY AGE

	% OF ALL OPERATIONS, 2003
Ages 51–64	24%
Ages 35–50	40%
Ages 19–34	26%
Other ages	10%

NONINVASIVE TREATMENTS

MOST POPULAR	2003 TOTAL
Botox injections	2,891,390
Chemical peel	995,238
Microdermabrasion	935,984
Laser hair removal	623,297
Collagen injections	576,255

GROWTH IN PROCEDURES

	% CHANGE 2002-03
Lip augmentation	+21%
Tummy tuck	+18%
Breast lift	+17%
Liposuction	+13%
Face-lift	+9%
Eyelid surgery	+7%

SURGERIES

TOP FIVE	2003 TOTAL
Nose reshaping	356,554
Liposuction	320,022
Breast augmentation	254,140
Eyelid surgery	246,633
Face-lift	128,667

With a new method, sometimes called a feather lift, surgeons can thread barbed sutures through a small incision to lift and anchor underlying slack tissue. Recovery takes days instead of weeks, which means it's a procedure people can practically have done to get ready for a heavy date.

Also revolutionizing face-lifts is endoscopic surgery, in which tiny instruments and cameras are inserted through small incisions. "Instead of doing long incisions ear-to-ear, we make three small incisions at the hairline," says Rod Rohrich, M.D., president of the American Society of Plastic Surgeons. Small incisions heal faster and get patients back in action sooner, he says. For breast augmentation, Dr. Rohrich says, incisions below the breast are being replaced by small endoscopic incisions under the armpit, through which the implants are inserted and then filled.

Like fillers, surgery doesn't necessarily last forever, but the less invasive procedures last just as long as the original treatments. The life span of a face-lift is still 7 to 10 years.

Some Surgeons' Frown Lines Are Deepening

Although business is booming, plastic surgeons have mixed feelings about the TV-fueled trend. Cosmetic surgery is clearly called for in the case of people who have suffered body damage—accident victims, for instance, as well as cancer and AIDS patients. And plastic surgery proponents argue that extremely unsightly features, such as a large or misshapen nose, can seriously damage a person's professional and personal life and cause such self-loathing that life doesn't seem worth living. Anecdotal evidence suggests that plastic surgery can turn many such lives around.

Like any surgery, though, plastic surgery isn't risk-free. There are complications and, in rare cases, fatalities. For instance, on January 16, 2004, Olivia Goldsmith, author of *The First Wives Club*, died of complications from surgery to remove loose skin from her chin.

Seeking to toss a big bucket of water on what they see as an overheated trend, the British Association of Aesthetic Plastic Surgeons criticized the new TV makeover craze. Plastic surgeons' organizations in the United States also sound cautionary notes. "The new wave of plastic surgery reality television is a serious cause for concern," says Dr. Rohrich. "Some patients on those shows have unrealistic and, frankly, unhealthy expectations about what plastic surgery can do for them."

Urging that people go to board-certified plastic surgeons for advice and treatment, Dr. Rohrich says, "I have witnessed plastic surgery disasters where someone tried to look like someone else. Patients need to be careful of any physicians claiming they can make you look like someone else."

Emily Pollard, M.D., the Philadelphia-area plastic surgeon who eliminated Doris Newton's "turtleneck," cautions, "We're not going to fix everything—we don't have a life coach here."

And plastic surgeon Terry Dubrow, M.D., who appeared on *The Swan*, emphasizes that reality shows are for entertainment, not education. "Does *Survivor* give you an idea of what camping is about? Does *The Bachelor* give you an idea of what dating is about? We're not saying this is what plastic surgery's about." ■

what does it mean to you?

Inspired by "reality" makeover television shows and less invasive treatments, people who want to erase wrinkles and shore up sagging flesh are swarming to cosmetic surgeons. Here are some things to consider if you're thinking about having surgery:

- With cosmetic procedures being "legitimized" on popular television shows, expect less tongue-clucking and disapproval by others regarding your plastic surgery.
- New noninvasive and minimally invasive procedures cause less trauma and require less recovery time. Wrinkle-erasing filler treatments typically cost $500 to $1,000 and last for several months.
- If you're considering having plastic surgery, find a surgeon who is certified by the American Board of Plastic Surgery. Ask whether your surgeon has hospital privileges to perform your surgery and whether the facility where your surgery will be done is accredited. Ask how many of these procedures your surgeon has done.
- Make sure your surgeon discusses the risks involved, which may include serious or even life-threatening infection.
- Be realistic about what cosmetic surgery can do for you. The results may not be exactly what you expected. Cosmetic surgery may boost your self-esteem, but it can't fix your career, love life, or emotional problems.

MAGNETS ERASE DEPRESSION

The young woman at McLean Hospital near Boston had bipolar disorder and was so depressed she could barely speak. She responded to questions with one-word answers. She made no eye contact. Then she lay on a platform and disappeared into the tunnel of a magnetic resonance imager, or MRI. Forty-five minutes later, she emerged, seemingly a new person.

"I think therapy for depression is really going to be effective when behavioral treatments are combined with electrical ones."

Eric Wassermann, M.D.

"Something had changed," says Aimee Parow, who was then a research assistant for a study of bipolar patients and is now a medical student. "She was talking, she was sociable." After the scan, Parow and the patient walked together to another part of the hospital, with the patient chattering away.

Parow thought the woman's mood shift must have been a fluke and dismissed it. Then she scanned another patient, a middle-aged woman whose depression took a different form. "She was cranky, irritable, and

A wire coil that generates brief magnetic pulses is used to stimulate the brain's frontal lobes. For some people, this transcranial magnetic stimulation relieves depression.

really didn't want to talk to me," Parow says—but she came out of the machine smiling and cracking jokes.

Parow was baffled—and excited. The MRI scans, using a special imaging method known as spectroscopy, were designed to measure patients' responses to antidepressant medications, but it seemed the scans themselves might be having an effect. Parow lay in bed that night, unable to sleep. In the morning, she told her boss what had happened, and the study was quickly redesigned to measure patients' moods before and after their scans.

Over the next year, 30 patients with bipolar depression got the same type of scan, a series of magnetic pulses delivered much more rapidly than in standard imaging MRIs. When it was all over, 23 of them said their moods had brightened. Meanwhile, among 10 patients who received sham scans, only 3 felt relief.

The study, published in the *American Journal of Psychiatry* in 2004, provided tantalizing support for an idea that could have come from an old Buck Rogers movie: that an electric coil poised over the skull could zap a person's brain with magnetic energy and improve the way it functioned. In fact, scientists have been exploring magnetism's power over the brain for many years. While an MRI had never been known to have this effect before the McLean study, a therapy called transcranial magnetic stimulation (TMS) has been tested widely—and with some success—on people with depression, as well as on patients with Parkinson's disease, obsessive-compulsive disorder, and even chronic pain. Now, with this and other findings, momentum is building, and these treatments may well make the jump from science fiction to everyday therapy for people with psychiatric and neurological disorders.

A Magnetic Idea Takes Off

The first uses of magnetic energy to trigger activity in the brain date back to the 19th century, but the early devices produced magnetic fields just strong enough to make volunteers see flashes of light. It wasn't until 1985 that Anthony Barker, Ph.D., a medical physicist at the University of Sheffield in England, built the first effective TMS device, a single, doughnut-shaped coil of wire. When powered with electricity, it created a short-lived magnetic

Brain Mapping

Scientists were able to map out functions of the brain by aiming magnetic pulses at different sections.

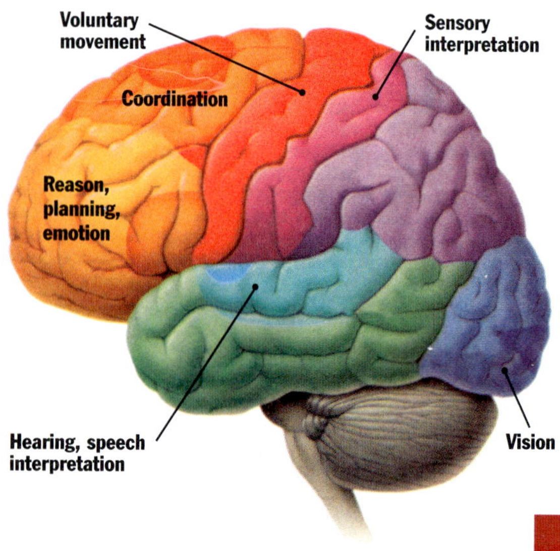

After the treatment, two of the patients showed what the reseachers called "robust" improvement, and another had complete freedom from symptoms for the first time in three years.

field. Dr. Barker's gizmo delivered just a single pulse of magnetic energy, and the magnetic field it created was weak and diffuse.

Within a few years, however, designs of the devices improved: Figure-8-shaped coils created a more targeted magnetic field, and scientists were able to deliver a flurry of very brief pulses—up to 50 a second. At that point, TMS was being used as a diagnostic tool: Much as a doctor might tap a knee with a mallet to test a person's reflexes, researchers used magnetic pulses to stimulate areas of the brain's motor cortex, causing patients' legs to kick and their arms to jerk.

As the technology improved, and researchers began aiming magnetic pulses at brain structures beyond the motor cortex, they found they could briefly block or inhibit certain brain functions. For example, by stimulating areas of the cortex known to control speech or vision, they could prevent people from speaking or perceiving some images.

From Research Tool to Treatment

Before long, some researchers began to envision TMS as a tool not just for mapping the brain but also for healing it. In 1994, Eric Wassermann, M.D., a neurologist and neurophysicist at the National Institute of Neurological Diseases and Stroke, was using TMS for brain mapping. He was approached by Mark George, M.D., a psychiatrist and neurologist at the National Institute of Mental Health. Dr. George had made an interesting observation: He'd noticed that the PET scans of some depressed patients showed that their frontal lobes were inactive, and he wondered if this might be a cause of their depression.

"He asked us, 'Can we take your stimulator and aim it at the frontal lobes and make their depression better?'" Dr. Wassermann recalls. Although skeptical, Dr. Wassermann thought it was worth a try.

"The prefrontal cortex is the part of the brain that's uniquely human," says Dr. George, who now directs the Brain Stimulation Laboratory at the Medical University of South Carolina in Charleston.

CREATIVITY ON TAP?

Imagine sitting under a machine that looks a little like a hair dryer, flipping a switch, and suddenly possessing the extraordinary abilities of an autistic savant—hearing a piano sonata just once and then being able to play it perfectly, for instance, or recalling an entire page of phone numbers.

That possibility is not so far-fetched. Allan Snyder, Ph.D., a physicist turned neurobiologist who directs the Center for the Mind in Sydney, Australia, believes a device that delivers magnetic pulses to the brain can literally fling open the doors of perception.

Dr. Snyder has persuaded dozens of people to undergo transcranial magnetic stimulation, or TMS, aimed at the left-front temporal lobe, the gray matter just under the left temple. The goal: To temporarily shut off higher brain functions and give free rein to the detail-obsessed "perceptual" brain, mimicking the brain damage in autistic savants and people with left-brain injuries, who sometimes develop savant-like skills. The perceptual brain takes in raw information with astounding accuracy, but most of us lose track of the details when they're processed and simplified by the conceptual mind.

Allan Snyder, Ph.D., uses magnetic pulses to simulate brain damage in a volunteer to see if savant-like skills emerge.

While TMS had no effect in seven of the volunteers in Dr. Snyder's most recent experiment, it created a change in four others. They drew more realistic pictures of animals after looking briefly at photographs or were more likely to notice a subtle mistake when asked to proofread a sentence. For Dr. Snyder, these seemingly small differences amount to a sharper—more perceptive—view of the world. And one day, he says, we may be able to focus such heightened powers of observation and recall on challenging creative tasks, such as writing memoirs or painting landscapes.

"This could be the ultimate creativity-enhancing machine," he says. "That's profound, isn't it?"

"It does nothing in particular but a lot of things in general—it helps us plan and hope and dream. And we also think that it helps regulate some of the deeper emotional parts of the brain." His idea was that magnetic pulses aimed at the lobes of "the prefrontal cortex—the area just above the eyes—could create changes in the cortex or in its relationship with deeper brain structures. The goal, he explains, was "to reset mood regulation and treat depression."

The two scientists used TMS on six depressed patients who had not improved with numerous trials of antidepressants. After the treatment, two of the patients showed what the researchers called "robust" improvement, and another had complete freedom from symptoms for the first time in three years. These results generated a lot of excitement among neurologists and psychiatrists and led to dozens more studies, although most have been quite small. With no drug company paying the bills, most of the studies have been government funded, and the largest one to date included only 70 people.

The results have been encouraging but not stellar. Overall, a minority of patients found their moods greatly improved, but most experienced relatively little change. Still, taken together, Dr. Wassermann says, the studies suggest that TMS does help many people with depression.

Altering Brain Chemistry without Drugs

The big question, of course, is why would TMS improve mood? Studies with other high-tech machines show that magnetic stimulation affects blood flow and sugar use in parts of the brain. But most researchers think that TMS may work for some of the same reasons as another poorly understood treatment: electroconvulsive therapy (ECT), better known as shock therapy. With ECT, doctors jolt the brains of anesthetized patients with electricity, inducing seizures. Many ECT patients show significant improvement, although these gains often come at a price: cognitive problems, including a sometimes profound loss of memory, that scientists believe are caused by the zapping of the hippocampus, a key center of memory formation. In the early days of TMS research, the powerful magnetic fields also induced seizures in some patients. That hasn't happened in many years, Dr. Wassermann says, because researchers follow protocols governing the place, length, strength, and timing of treatments.

Dr. George says TMS amounts to electrical stimulation without the electrodes. "We're electrically stimulating the cortex, but we're using the magnetic field as the trick to get past the skull," he says. As the magnetic pulses penetrate past hair, skin, and bone and reach brain cells in the cortex, on the surface of the brain, they cause the nerve cells to electrically discharge and send a signal in the form of electrons flowing from cell to cell. As this signal spreads through the brain, it triggers changes in neurotransmitters, brain chemicals that are the target of antidepressant medications.

Dr. George believes depressed people have problems in the mood-regulating circuitry of their brains, centered in the prefrontal cortex. He thinks ECT, perhaps by inducing a seizure, interrupts the normal flow of electrons and "resets" the regulatory circuit. "My idea with TMS is that instead of inducing a generalized seizure, we could reset that circuit with daily, gentle nudges," he says.

But Dr. George's theory doesn't explain the improvements Aimee Parow saw in the MRI patients at McLean Hospital. That's because the low-frequency magnetic fields emitted during the MRI scans were too weak to make neurons fire and send a signal, says Michael Rohan, the physicist who led the study.

He speculates that the unique sequence of magnetic pulses in his spectroscopic MRIs somehow altered the chemistry of the brain cells without causing them to fire. "We think we've hit some kind of a magic spot in the timing" so the pulses are synchronizing up with processes taking place in the cells and correcting some kind of chemical imbalance. "It's a mystery to us, but the effect was rather profound," Rohan says.

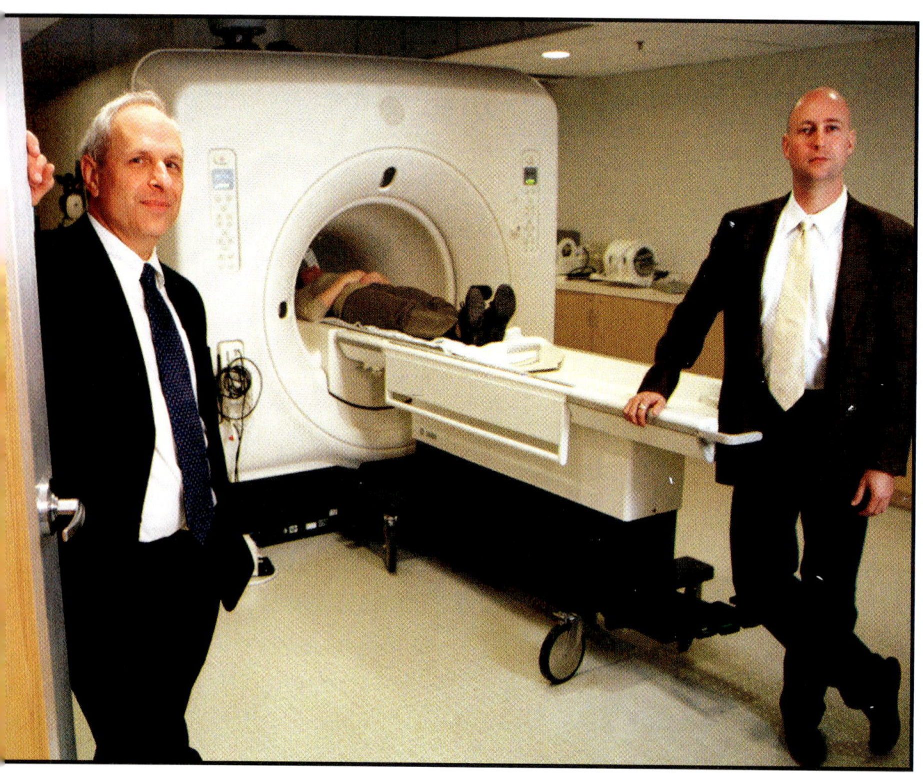

Bruce Cohen (left) and Michael Rohan explored the antidepressant effects of a special MRI at McLean Hospital near Boston.

The Pulse of the Future

Rohan and his colleagues have designed a tabletop device that emits the same kind of pulses as their specialized MRI. They hope to replicate the results of their first study.

Meanwhile, other scientists are exploring the effects of TMS on a range of other psychiatric and neurological disorders. Working with schizophrenic patients who hear voices, Ralph Hoffman, M.D., a Yale researcher, has applied low-frequency TMS to the auditory cortex—the part of the brain that processes and

Transcranial Magnetic Stimulation

When a transcranial magnetic stimulation (TMS) coil is turned on near a patient's scalp, a powerful and rapidly changing magnetic field passes safely and painlessly through skin and bone. The shallow, precisely focused magnetic pulses stimulate brain cells to start signaling.

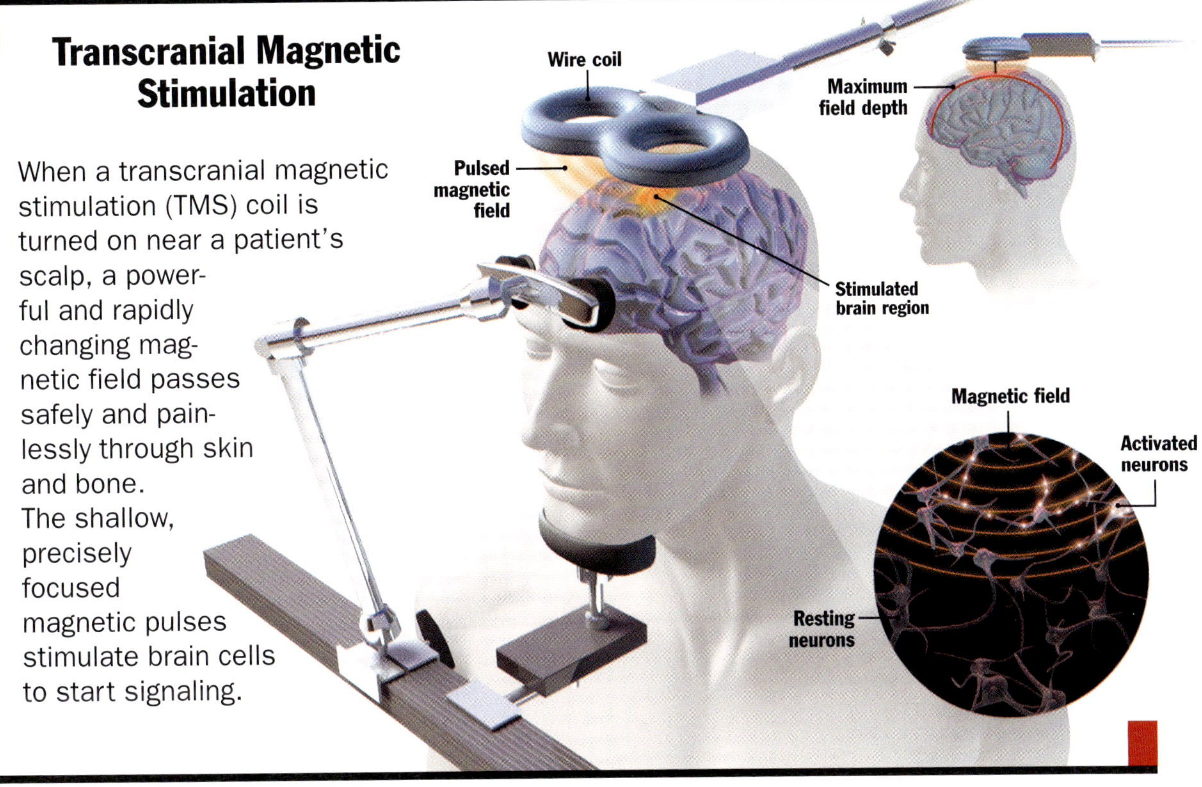

interprets sound—and found that the patients' auditory hallucinations declined markedly. What's more, French researchers have reported that stimulating the motor cortex seems to give relief to people with chronic pain. However, results have been mixed in studies using TMS to relieve the palsied movements of Parkinson's disease and seizures caused by epilepsy.

"Most pathological and neurological disorders are related to deeper structures in the brain," says Abraham Zangen, Ph.D. While working at the National Institutes of Health (NIH), he developed a coil that may be able to penetrate farther into the brain than standard TMS devices. Dr. Zangen, who now consults for an Israeli-American company that bought the coil's patent from the NIH, hopes its deeper reach may make it an effective treatment for autism, Parkinson's disease, addiction, obesity, and depression. He is organizing a study of several dozen depressed patients.

Thus, depression remains the hot spot in studies of magnetic stimulation. "Now that we know it works," says Dr. George, "how do we begin to optimize it? What's the best way to make it work? We have a lot more work to do." ■

what does it mean to you?

Using magnetic energy to treat brain disorders is not as far out as it may seem. The technique called transcranial magnetic stimulation (TMS) has the full attention of brain researchers and psychiatrists, who see it as a noninvasive way to treat a number of different problems.

■ Treatment of depression holds the most promise. Overall, numerous studies suggest that TMS can help relieve the symptoms of many depressed patients.

■ Experts believe that TMS may act in ways quite similar to electroconvulsive (shock) therapy, but without causing seizures or impairing patients' memories.

■ Scientists also believe that TMS may help relieve the shaking experienced by people with Parkinson's disease, reduce the scary voices sometimes caused by schizophrenia, and bring some relief to people with chronic pain.

■ The technique is still being tested. If all goes well, a TMS device could be available for use in medical clinics by 2006.

SHARPER MEMORY FROM A PILL?

Can a pill sharpen memory dulled by age or even disease? Several promising drugs are currently being tested in humans.

Most people accept reading glasses as a bothersome but bearable price to pay for maturity. When they keep forgetting where they left the blasted things, though—well, that's when they start to worry. Three-quarters of people over 50 complain of memory lapses—the name that won't come to you, the bafflement as to why you're in a room you just entered, and, of course, the 15-minute search for those specs that were perched on top of your head the whole time. While a degree of memory loss is a natural consequence of aging, don't tell that to these middle-aged and older people; they're not amused by what some like to call "senior moments." A big part of what it means to be alive is being taken away, and there really ought to be a pill to stop it.

In fact, dozens of memory-enhancement drugs are now being tested, and this year, several of them showed enough promise to advance into new phases of human trials. The first memory pills may be available in just a few years. Even better ones will follow.

The drugs are arriving in the nick of time. The entire U.S. baby boom generation will be 50 or older by 2014. That's more than 75 million potential memory problems right there, without even counting the boomers' aging parents.

"Hanging onto memory is important for maintaining quality of life," says Axel Unterbeck, Ph.D., chief scientific officer of Memory Pharmaceuticals in Montvale, New Jersey, which is developing several drugs. Memory impairment makes daily tasks harder. It impedes communication, which can contribute to depression. And as you lose the ability to form memories, you lose part of what makes you, you.

The promised pills aren't mere refinements of the modestly effective medications prescribed since the early 1990s to slow the memory decline of Alzheimer's disease. They spring from far-reaching studies of exactly how the brain takes in sights, sounds, and scents and stores them as memories.

"These new drugs work on entirely different mechanisms in the brain than anything that's come before," says Tim Tully, Ph.D., a pioneer in the memory-enhancement field who's overseeing the development of some of the drugs at his Helicon Therapeutics biotech lab in Farmingdale, New York. "They directly upgrade the biochemical process of memory storage."

As it turns out, notes Gary Lynch, Ph.D., who pioneered memory-enhancing drugs called ampakines and is scientific advisor for Cortex Pharmaceuticals in Irvine, California, the act of storing a new memory causes real chemical and physical changes among the brain's billions of nerve cells—changes that scientists are at last learning to manipulate. In fact, experiments in enhancing memory have been stunningly successful in animals. Dr. Tully, for example, created memory-enhanced fruit flies that performed 10 times better than normal fruit flies in tests such as learning to remember—and avoid—sources of electric shocks.

How Memories Are Made

To understand what the drugs can eventually do for you, it helps to understand a little bit about how memory works.

"Memory is a process, not a thing," says Dr. Tully, "and it's not one process but many." First comes alertness. If you're not paying attention to what's coming in through your eyes or ears or other senses, the memory-forming interplay of chemical reactions in the brain never gets started. Can't remember the name of a person you just met? Maybe you never actually listened in the first place.

Forming a memory and calling it up (retrieval) are also distinct processes. Improving retrieval is a low priority in memory research for the simple reason that calling up existing memories is much less of a problem for older people than forming new ones. An 80-year-old American, for example, can probably tell you what she was doing when she heard about the attack on Pearl Harbor more than 60 years ago.

Likewise, separate processes control the two main types of memories. Short-term memories are the many temporary, workaday impressions—such as

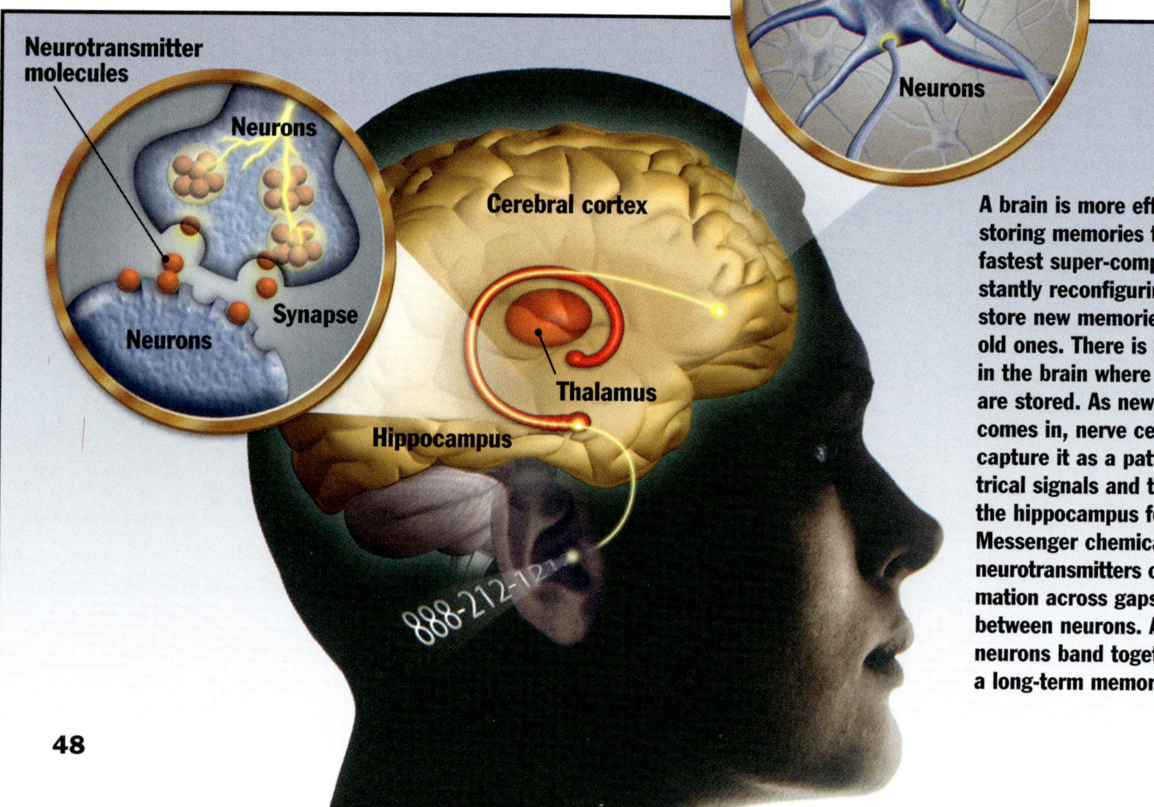

A brain is more efficient at storing memories than the fastest super-computer, con stantly reconfiguring cells to store new memories and purge old ones. There is no one place in the brain where memories are stored. As new information comes in, nerve cells (neurons) capture it as a pattern of elec trical signals and transmit it to the hippocampus for processing. Messenger chemicals called neurotransmitters carry the information across gaps (synapses) between neurons. A group of neurons band together to store a long-term memory.

the location of your reading glasses—that help you get things done but are soon discarded. Long-term memories consist of information you can recall days, months, or decades down the line.

Sensations entering the brain create short-term memory by triggering an intricate multichemical cascade that causes changes in the junctions (synapses) between brain cells (neurons). New or altered connections give memory a physical structure. Since any two of your billions of neurons may have thousands of synapses, there's no shortage of storage space.

These changes are temporary unless another chemical sequence is initiated. To convert an experience from a passing event into a long-term memory, the identical cascade must run many times, forming a permanent point of contact between neurons where nerve impulses can pass. That's why today you remember what 9 times 5 equals: not because you once read it somewhere but because you were forced to repeat the times tables over and over again.

"I would characterize it as very promising that the drugs in the pipeline will help people improve their long-term memory function."

Axel Unterbeck, Ph.D.

The new drugs don't promise you more memory per se but instead help new memories lock themselves in. When you take one of these pills, memorizing poetry is no longer a lost ability from your youth but a doable proposition.

So is remembering that new acquaintance's name. While sharpening long-term memory is the primary effect of most memory pills being developed, short-term memory is also improved. That's because the processes, though distinct, "speak to each other," as Dr. Tully puts it. "Conversion to long-term memory depends on short-term memory, or otherwise there would be nothing to convert," he says. "Anybody with short-term memory deficits will benefit from the drug as a secondary effect."

Squaring Off against Alzheimer's

Creating smarter humans has a certain futuristic appeal, but it isn't what's driving the new research into memory drugs. The idea is to make sick people better—to help those whose memory has been impaired by clinical conditions. The most serious of those conditions, of course, is Alzheimer's disease, which is where Helicon, Memory, Cortex, and most other memory drug developers are focusing their efforts.

No memory drug will "cure" Alzheimer's, a brain-degenerating disease of which memory loss is just one of many grim consequences. But helping patients maintain some ability to form long-term memories will surely make their remaining years more meaningful. "And if a drug to halt Alzheimer's is found, you'll still have to rehabilitate the brain and give them back some of what they've lost," Dr. Tully says. "That's where our drugs will be effective."

Alzheimer's may be especially debilitating, but it accounts for just a small percentage of people whose memory isn't what it used to be. About 50 percent of people over 65 clearly suffer from some degree of impairment, while another 25 to 30 percent may or may not (researchers haven't been able to say). Most have either mild cognitive impairment (MCI) or age-associated memory impairment (AAMI).

The symptoms of both conditions run the gamut from episodes of forgetfulness to a noticeably reduced capacity to form short- and long-term memories. However, MCI is a far more serious diagnosis than the more common AAMI because about 80 percent of those who have it develop Alzheimer's within seven years.

That makes MCI a top target of the memory drug developers, not just to spare its victims from memory problems now but perhaps to get a head start on treatment for Alzheimer's-related memory loss. "If we can help MCI sufferers postpone their progression to Alzheimer's disease by even a year, it would have a hugely beneficial impact on their health and the economy," Dr. Unterbeck says.

Meanwhile, there's also good news for the memory-challenged masses. Even though they are lower on the priority list, people with AAMI are most likely to benefit from memory drugs. "These drugs are potentially extremely effective in restoring memory with age-related impairment," says Dr. Unterbeck.

The New Drugs Take the Test

Drug developers are focusing on three main types of memory pills, all of which are being tested now.

Ampakines. These manmade molecules boost the electrical signals that trigger the memory-forming chemical exchanges that take place between neurons. Since those signals weaken with age, memory impairment is in part a problem of power supply. An ampakine turns up the power by attaching itself to a protein on the brain cell surface, called an AMPA receptor, and helping it respond to the hormone glutamate—a response that generates most of the electrical signals running through brain cells. "It's surprisingly simple," says Dr. Lynch. "All ampakines do is help the AMPA receptor's function to increase the current. It's like turning up the dimmer on a light switch."

Ampakines were the first memory drugs out of the gate in the 1990s and were predicted to be the first across the finish line. But the drug developers were forced to abandon testing of an ampakine that was chosen for its safety but proved too weak to consistently deliver the desired effects in humans (although some study subjects still showed marked improvement). "The concern with any of these drugs is to make sure they don't cause brain damage," Dr. Lynch says, "so we were very cautious."

A more powerful ampakine with the working name CX717 has also proved safe in humans. In 2004, it entered Phase II studies, in which the drug's effectiveness is tested by comparing memory improvement in volunteers taking it daily with that in other volunteers taking a placebo. The next step, Phase III, repeats the testing but in a much larger pool of volunteers, usually hundreds. Success in that phase could lead to approval of the drug.

CREB enhancers. These drugs are perhaps the most eagerly awaited because they deliver to humans essentially the same benefits that gave Dr. Tully's fruit flies their super-powered memory. The drugs boost the amount of a brain protein called CREB (cAMP response element binding protein), which plays a huge role in memory formation.

Like a shop foreman, CREB organizes the other chemical workers involved in memory formation. When its levels are raised, the process kicks into high gear. CREB enhancers achieve that effect by blocking the action of another protein that normally keeps CREB levels in check.

Higher CREB levels make the brain much more efficient at creating permanent connections between synapses—and the faster those connections form, the fewer times you have to repeat the words of a song or poem to store them for good. Take a daily CREB enhancer, and you may find that you can able to talk about the details of that novel you read last month instead of struggling just to recall the title.

New Help for Fading Memory

Dozen of drug developers are testing different approaches to memory enhancement. Here are three of the most promising types of memory drugs and when they might come to market.

DRUG	EXAMPLE	ACTION	OPTIMISTIC ARRIVAL DATE
Ampakines	CX717 (Cortex Pharmaceuticals)	Speed and strengthen the formation of new memories by boosting the electrical signals between brain cells.	2007
CREB enhancers	HT712 (Helicon Therapeutics), MEM 1414 (Memory Pharmaceuticals)	Bolster cell-to-cell connections in the brain by raising levels of the protein CREB, a key organizer in memory formation.	2009
Calcium channel modulators	MEM 1003 (Memory Pharmaceuticals)	Optimize levels of calcium inside and outside of each brain cell, which counteracts memory decline by making cells more responsive to incoming signals.	2008

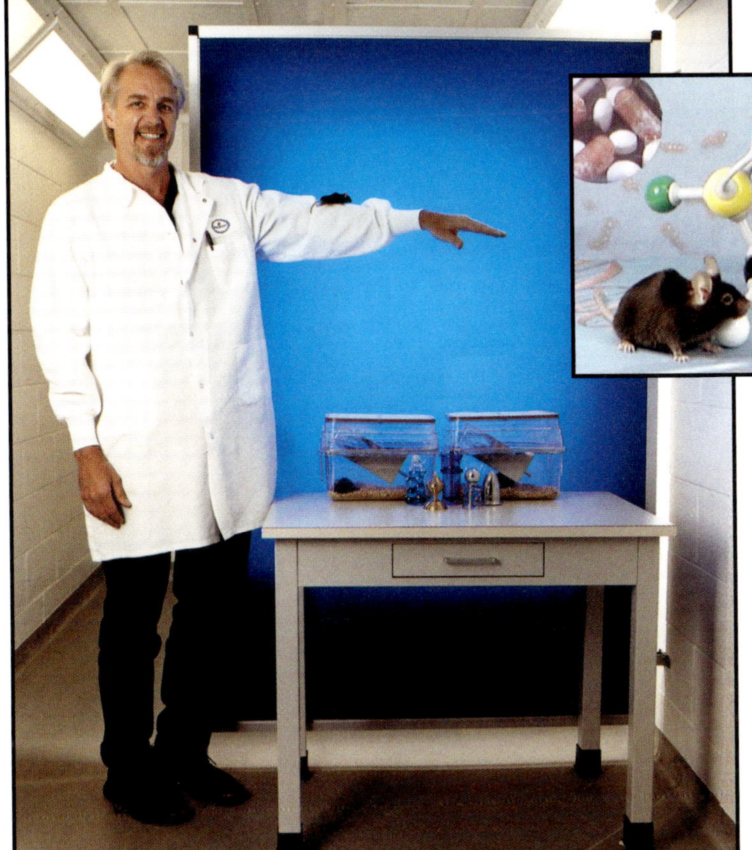

At his Helicon Therapeutics lab, Tim Tully, Ph.D., oversees development of drugs that will improve memory storage.

Say "cheese": Dr. Tim Tully's memory-impaired lab mice got relief with new drugs under development.

Both Dr. Tully's Helicon Therapeutics and Dr. Unterbeck's Memory Pharmaceuticals are working on CREB enhancers. Helicon's main drug, HT712, was slated to begin Phase I testing (mainly to establish human safety) by the end of 2004. Phase II, to test effectiveness, could begin in 2005. "So maybe by the summer of 2006, we'll know if HT712 does what we think it will do for memory," Dr. Tully says. Phase III trials would follow, "so we're talking at least five years from 2004 if all goes well."

Memory Pharmaceuticals' version is called MEM 1414. (Don't worry; the drug names will get more memorable down the road.) It's a bit further along in testing, with Phase I safety trials nearly complete.

Calcium channel modulators. At Memory, another drug, dubbed MEM 1003, is at a similar stage of testing. It's a calcium channel modulator that improves memory in patients with Alzheimer's and MCI (but not those with AAMI) by restoring the balance of calcium inside and outside the neurons.

The Race to Market

Best-case scenarios put memory drugs in consumers' hands in 5 to 10 years, although ampakines may well arrive sooner. "There's no guarantee that all will go well," Dr. Tully says. Nevertheless, many people have their fingers crossed. Remember, some major memory drugs, such as ampakines, have already sharpened human memories in small pilot studies. And perhaps because researchers have proceeded cautiously, the drugs furthest along in development have not caused any side effects. Still, advances are slow. "There's no way to predict exactly how long it will take before these drugs are available," Dr. Tully says, "but it's a question of when, not if." ■

what does it mean to you?

Insights into the way the brain forms memories have opened a new era of memory-enhancement drugs. When the pills become available, just about everybody over 50 will benefit.

■ Alzheimer's patients will be able to slow or even reverse memory decline with drugs that are much more effective than the ones currently available.

■ Although memory drugs themselves will never cure Alzheimer's (which involves much more than memory loss), they will play a big role once a drug that stops the disease is found. Recovering Alzheimer's patients will take the pills during "brain rehabilitation" to restore memory capacity that the disease took away.

■ People with mild cognitive impairment—a memory disorder that often leads to Alzheimer's—will be able to repair memory loss and slow or perhaps prevent the progression to Alzheimer's.

■ By taking once-a-day memory pills, people over 50 who are bothered by increasing memory lapses and declining ability to form new long-term memories—a condition known as age-associated memory impairment—will restore their recall to near-peak levels.

NANOTECHNOLOGY
HUGE HOPES FOR TINY MEDICINE

A mere flaw in your DNA is no match for an astoundingly tiny, laser-armed repair robot in this artist's conception of the future.

Last year, while a dogged little spacecraft dodging the rings of Saturn sent back photos to awestruck outer-space scientists, inner-space scientists received astounding images as well. They used manmade particles a million times smaller than a pencil dot to do what most people never dreamed was possible: Take live-action movies of genes at work inside living cells.

The researchers were actually able to watch the same cellular events that are targeted by some anticancer drugs. Being able to observe these processes may someday allow experts to create new and more finely tuned cancer treatments. Meanwhile, scientists working with similarly minuscule particles devised new ways to track—and curtail—the spread of breast cancer and even kill tumors.

OLOGY

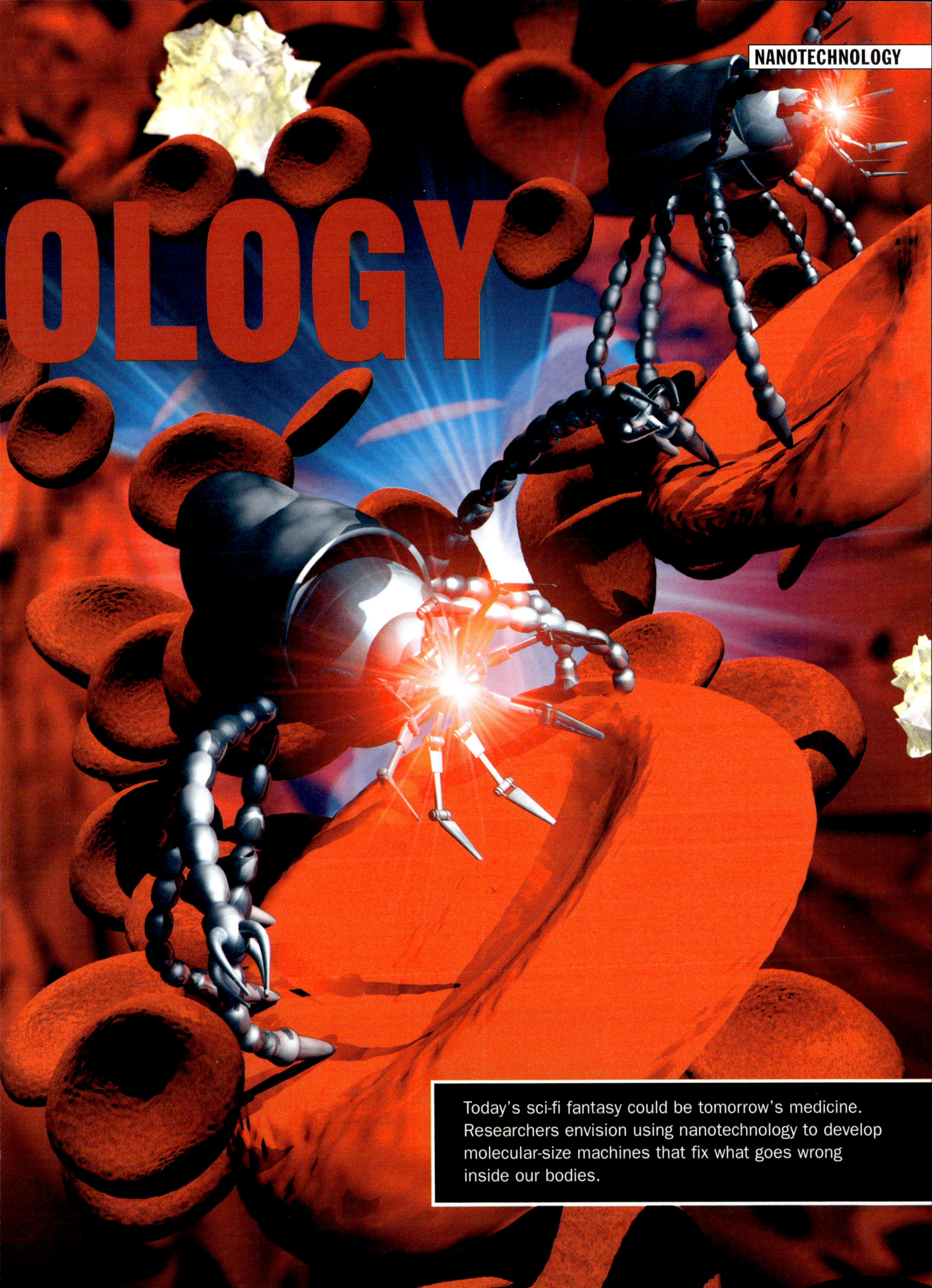

Today's sci-fi fantasy could be tomorrow's medicine. Researchers envision using nanotechnology to develop molecular-size machines that fix what goes wrong inside our bodies.

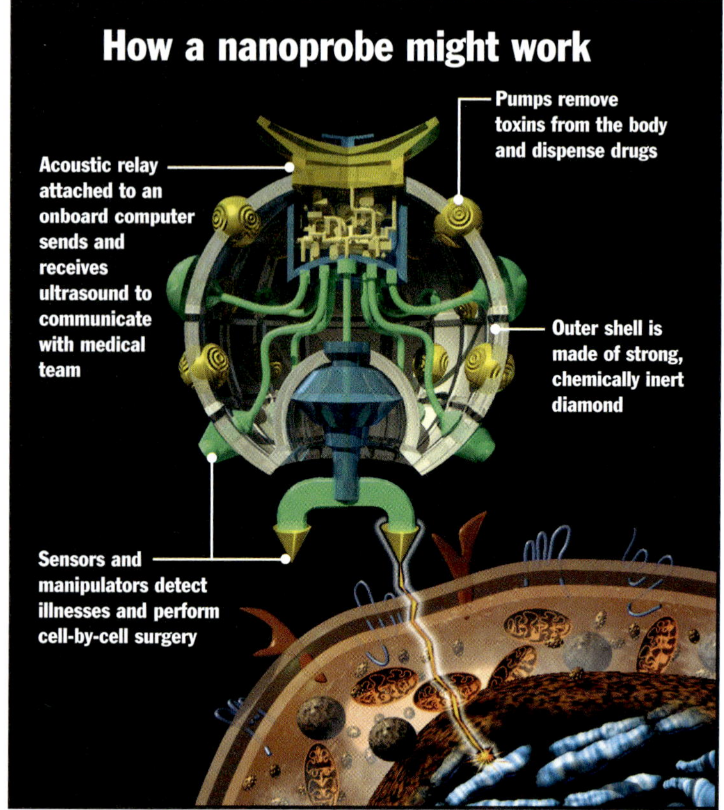

Welcome to the new world of nanotechnology, a science that puts the arcane and bizarre discoveries of particle physics to work on real-life problems. Nanotech researchers are especially excited by the many opportunities in the world of medicine: Sure fire tumor detection. Crystal-clear imagery of blood vessels and tissues hidden deep within the body. Medical tests that provide instant results. Revolutionary methods for defeating cancer, AIDS, and other major diseases.

What's making these developments possible is the outlandishly small size of the tools used in nanotechnology (*nano-* is from the Greek word for dwarf). To get a sense of the scale at which nanoscientists work, first envision a meter—39.37 inches, a bit more than a yard. Narrow down to a centimeter—about a third of an inch. Descend to a millimeter—one-thousandth of a meter, or about four-hundredths of an inch. That's about the size of a mosquito egg. Ever seen one?

We're still not even close to our destination, though: a nanometer, or a billionth of a meter, about the width of 10 hydrogen atoms lined up in a row. In comparison, a red blood cell is a veritable gorilla, measuring 8,000 nanometers, and the period at the end of this sentence is Godzilla—1 million nanometers.

That is the scope of nanotechnology. Using a variety of techniques—such as vaporizing carbon and letting it condense in an inert gas to produce crystals—scientists are able to produce unimaginably tiny tubes, spheres, shells, snowflakes, and other complex "nanoparticles." Several much-heralded nanotech advances in 2004 may help drug companies more quickly develop new cancer drugs and therapies.

Tiny Weapons against Cancer

In one study, researchers at Germany's Max Planck Institute used fluorescent nanoparticles called quantum dots to make the first-ever movies of the signaling mechanisms and chemical processes that control genes, according to a report in the journal *Nature Biotechnology*.

Quantum dots, dubbed Qdots, glow in various colors when "excited" by a light source, such as a laser. They can be customized to link up with, or tag, specific proteins that perform key chores inside cells. Unlike existing imaging tools—such as fluorescent dyes, which fade away in seconds—Qdots can provide extended, real-time images of healthy and diseased cells at work.

According to the Quantum Dot Corporation in California, which created and manufactures Qdots, such live images will provide a better understanding of how cell processes work and may allow researchers to watch close up as cells react to medications and treatments, including some used against cancer.

In a related experiment, scientists at Carnegie Mellon University in Pittsburgh gave quantum dots a special coating that enabled them to enter lab animals' tissues and send back trackable signals for many months. Without the new coating, the Qdots are too fragile to function in the body for more than hours or days. Eventually, these particles could be treated with substances that seek out specific tumors and then be

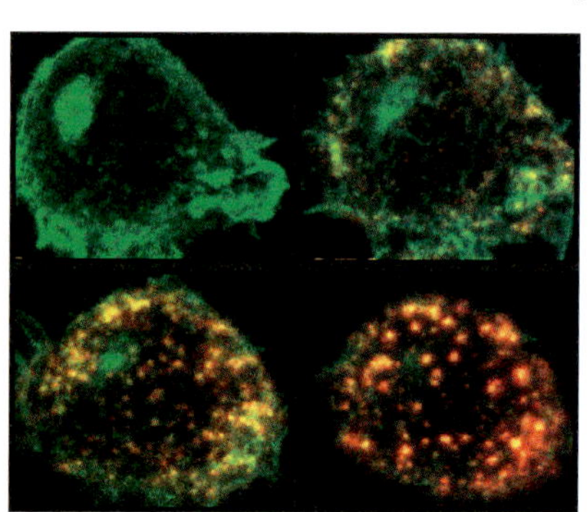
Scientists used minuscule "quantum dots" to make the first movies of signaling within cells.

injected into the body, tracked by laser technology and tiny microscopes called nanoscopes, and used to pinpoint and illuminate tumors so doctors can remove them with greater accuracy and with greater likelihood of getting all of the cancer. They could even be used to deliver antibodies or drugs.

Such possibilities no longer seem fanciful. In 2004, researchers at Rice University in Houston reported that in preliminary tests, "nanoshells" had proven effective at eradicating tumors in laboratory animals. Twenty times smaller than a red blood cell, a nanoshell consists of a silica core covered by a thin layer of pure gold. Because of their small size, nanoshells are able to pass through the poorly formed blood vessels of a tumor and collect inside it. When near-infrared light is aimed at the tumor, it passes harmlessly through soft tissue and strikes the nanoshells' gold coating, raising its temperature the same way sunlight heats a car's metal roof. The concentrated heat destroys the tumor.

"The results of these first animal studies are very promising," says Naomi Halas, Ph.D., professor of electrical engineering and chemistry at Rice. "While we don't yet have a target date for our first human trial, our team is working hard to make this treatment available to cancer patients as soon as possible."

Women may be among such technologies' earliest beneficiaries. At Carnegie Mellon, Byron Ballou, Ph.D., a research scientist at the Molecular Biosensor and Imaging Center at the Mellon College of Science, believes that the first medical use of nanotech tools

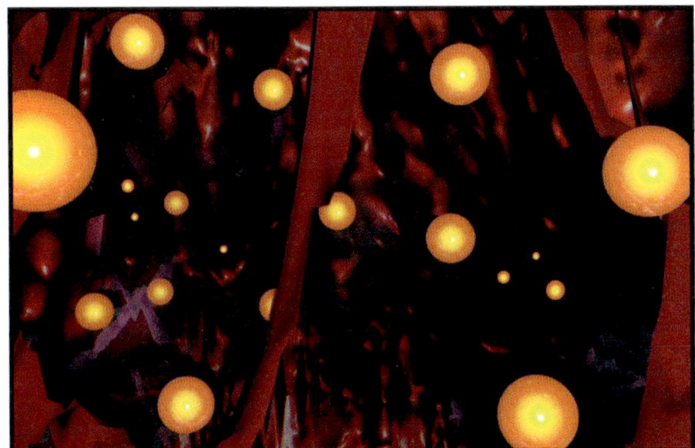

In this artist's conception, gold-covered microscopic particles called nanoshells cluster inside a tumor. When near-infrared light strikes the shells they heat up, destroying the cancer.

will be against breast cancer. That disease spreads through the lymph nodes, which must be removed along with the tumor if they've been affected by the cancer. When surgeons perform breast cancer surgery, Dr. Ballou says, the vital question is, "When should you stop taking nodes? The trick is to find out what nodes you should be taking."

A technician at the New Jersey Nanotechnology Laboratory holds a disk printed with an etched pattern used to make nanotechnology devices.

Currently, he says, surgeons inject radioactive dyes to try to locate "sentinel nodes"—those closest to the tumor that show signs of the cancer's spread. Such detection methods can be slow and inexact, but injecting Qdots instead of radioactive dyes would give surgeons a quicker, more precise picture of where the diseased nodes begin and end. Armed with that knowledge, Dr. Ballou says, they could operate with greater success.

New Arsenal of Disease Fighters

Cancer is just one of many health conditions that nanotechnologists are targeting. In 2004, researchers at Philadelphia's Drexel University reported progress in developing a device the size of a cell phone that would permit people on blood-thinning (anticoagulant) medication to take their own blood-clotting readings at home. The researchers say the device, which is able to analyze submicroscopic particles, would take readings by targeting proteins involved in the clotting process. Determining the right anticoagulant dose has always been a process of trial and error, but the new method would more exactly calculate the required dose.

Nanotechnology is also improving genetic testing and gene therapy. For instance, researchers are exploring ways to test embryos for inherited cystic fibrosis (CF) prior to in vitro fertilization, using nanoparticles that glow when they encounter compounds produced by the CF gene. Other scientists are testing the feasibility of compressing healthy DNA strands from about 200 nanometers to less than 25 nanometers in order to slip healthy genes through the cell membranes of people who have CF and other genetic disorders. The healthy genes would force the cells to perform normally.

Still other researchers, hoping to build better artificial joints and implants, are trying their luck with rolled-up sheets of carbon atoms called nanotubes. Studies have found that among other things, bone cells called osteoblasts bond to titanium coated with nanotubes better than to regular titanium. Among the potential benefits: less chance that the ball and socket of a surgically implanted artificial hip joint will work loose.

Even the war on AIDS may get a boost from nanotechnology. In late 2003, the FDA approved early, small-scale human trials to determine the safety of an anti-HIV vaginal gel developed by the Australian nanotechnology firm Starpharma. The company says the gel, which is inserted prior to sex, contains a protein that prevents the virus from infecting healthy cells. The nanotech components of the gel are dendrimers—super-tiny, snowflake-like molecules to which all sorts of medical substances can be attached for special delivery. Dedrimers, too, are being tested as cancer fighters.

Nanotechnology has even reached the shelves where everyday health and beauty aids are sold. Among the new products are heavy-duty sunscreens made with zinc oxide particles so tiny that they go on clear instead of chalky white, as traditional zinc

Artery Cleaner

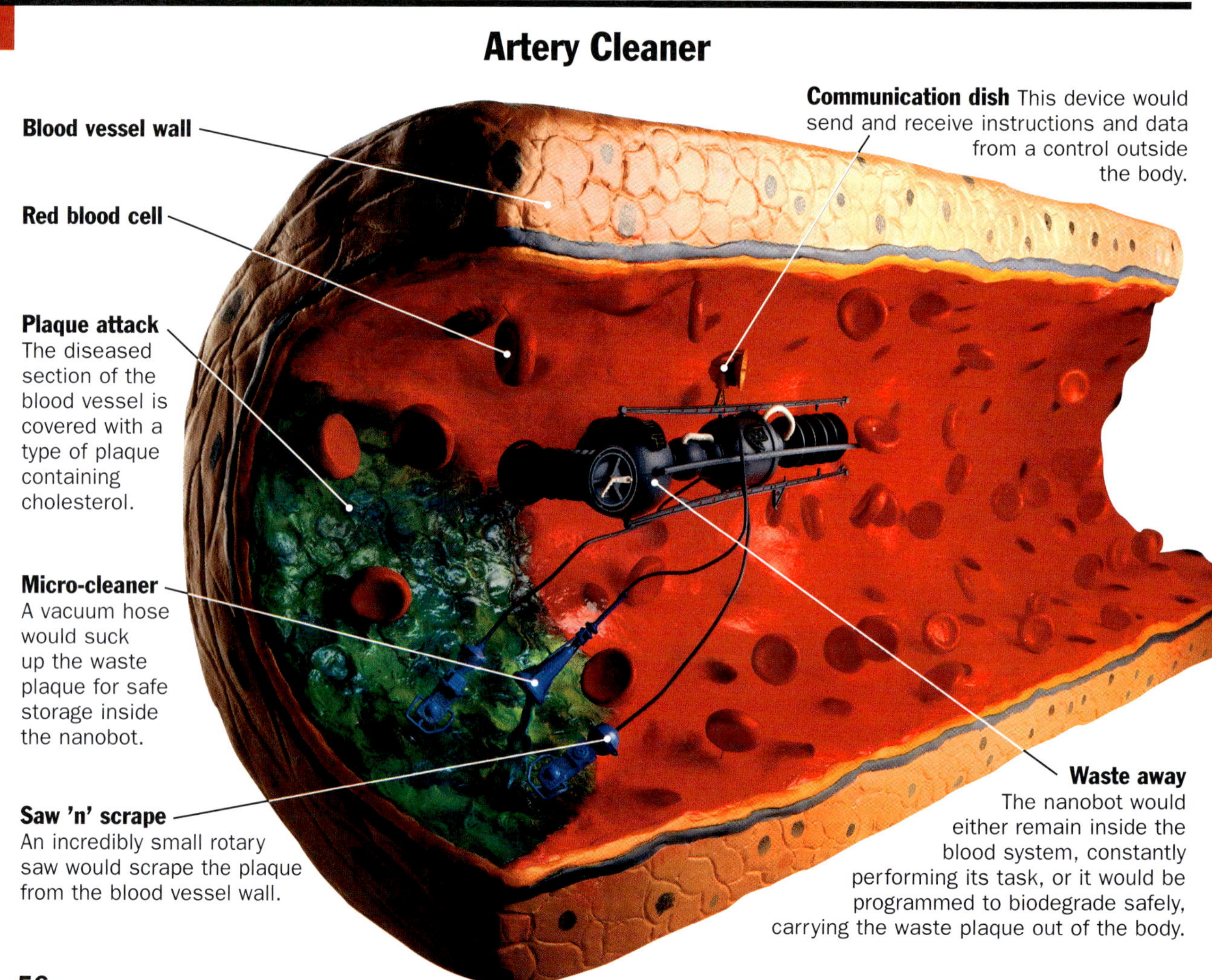

oxide creams do. According to experts, zinc oxide offers superior protection from the sun because unlike other commonly used sunscreens, it provides protection from both ultraviolet A and ultraviolet B rays.

The Truly Fantastic Voyage

What's the ultimate potential of nanotech therapies? It's limitless, say some scientists, who envision nano-size molecular "machines," with gears and propellers and built-in power tools. Other scientists caution, however, that only time will tell whether these dreams will come true.

"Getting molecular-scale control is extremely relevant to medicine," says Christine Peterson, executive director of the Foresight Institute in Palo Alto, California, which promotes nanotechnology. Disease begins with molecular-level damage. If we can send in nano repair kits for such breakdowns, including cancer, "the medical benefits are immense," she says.

The focus is not only on disease but also on the ordinary ravages of time. "We don't know a lot about aging," says James R. Von Ehr II, head of a Texas nanotechnology company called Zyvex, "but it looks like the process is caused by cellular degradation—the little nanomachines inside our cells start to break down. If we had other nanoscale machines that could go in and repair some of those breakdowns, in principle, we could repair them. And if we can repair the cell to the state it was in when it was young and healthy, we might be able to repair the organism."

Dr. Ballou agrees—up to a point. "The future hope is to be able to go in and replace or fix biochemical machinery," he says, "but I don't know exactly how this will come about."

There are also questions about possible harmful effects of nanotech particles and matter. Qdots, for example, are made from the heavy metal cadmium, and researchers from the University of California, San Diego, reported in early 2004 that under certain conditions, the Qdots proved to be acutely toxic. Other researchers say this danger can be countered by coating the dots with protective substances.

Whatever the concerns, they haven't scared off investors. The U.S. government allotted $847 million in 2004 for what's called the National Nanotechnology Initiative. The government of Japan, which for decades has been at the forefront of the miniaturization movement, is also heavily funding nanotechnology research.

When such investments may pay off, no one can say. "You can go for a long time and nothing moves forward, then the next day, everything moves forward," says James Castracane, Ph.D., head of the school of nanosciences at the State University of New York at Albany.

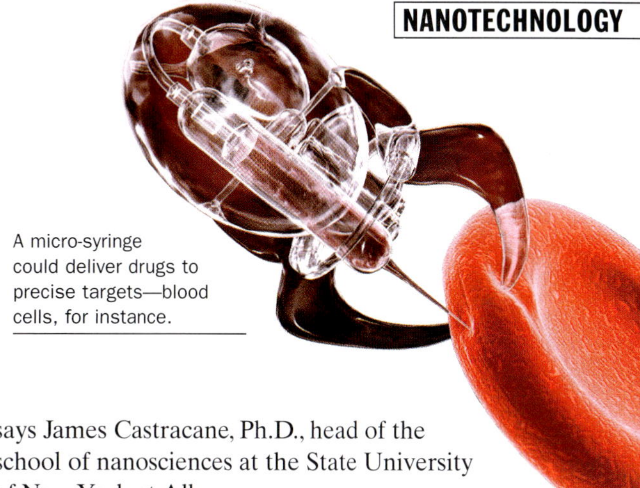

A micro-syringe could deliver drugs to precise targets—blood cells, for instance.

A breakthrough could be just a few years off, says Rick McCullough, Ph.D., dean of the Mellon College of Science and a colleague of Dr. Ballou. "There are multiple startup companies trying to bring this kind of stuff to market," he says. "You have to believe some of them are going to hit."

In 1965, the movie *Fantastic Voyage* told of a microscopic submarine full of medical experts shrunk to cellular size. Their mission: to navigate the body of a dying scientist and save his life. It was science fiction then, but no longer, says Dr. Castracane. "That fantastic voyage is actually happening." ■

what does it mean to you?

In late 2003, the director of the National Institutes of Health issued a list of initiatives called the NIH Roadmap for Research. The goal: To speed research discoveries from the lab to the public. Among the top five priorities was nanomedicine. If nanotechnology lives up to its promise, doctors will be able to:

- Detect diseases such as cancer in their earliest stages and devise treatments to stop them in their tracks. Nanoparticles such as Qdots and dendrimers would reveal tumors that could be either destroyed by the nanoparticles or removed by precise surgery.
- Locate signs of genetic susceptibility to health problems and fight bad genes with good. Researchers are exploring ways to detect a predisposition to cystic fibrosis—or the disease itself—in embryos and eliminate the problem with genetic treatments.
- Make giant strides toward understanding and countering the aging process where it begins—inside the body's cells.

COMING SOON: ANTI-AGING DRUGS

Inside a San Francisco laboratory, some very special worms recently celebrated their 120th day of life. It was no ordinary birthday. For one thing, 120 days is about six times longer than any of these millimeter-long creatures would normally live. Even so, they looked and acted like budding youths.

There's more. The researchers who genetically altered the worms, making their astonishingly long lives possible, had an extra reason to celebrate. They had just recently unlocked the secret of the worms' ultralongevity, revealing the details of the life-expanding process that the gene manipulation had triggered—and they think they can duplicate that process in humans. In fact, they're working right now on an anti-aging drug to do just that.

This isn't wishful thinking. Many people reading this article have a much better chance of happily observing a healthy 100th birthday than they did just two years ago. The "Methuselah worms" are part of the reason, but so is another breakthrough that occurred in 2003 and 2004, when researchers identified two human gene variations that are partially responsible for the

In the not-too-distant future, centenarians will be commonplace, but they won't hold a candle to the folks who are pushing 150 with nary a health problem.

Worm experiments by Cynthia Kenyon, Ph.D., turned scientific thinking on its ear. No longer considered inevitable, aging may be more like a disease that can be cured.

long lives of centenarians. The discovery of these "longevity genes" could lead to a drug that duplicates the genes' life-extending effects.

The science of longevity has moved ahead so rapidly in recent years that many experts now consider it a matter of decades before sprightly, mentally sharp 100-year-olds will be too common to cause a raised eyebrow. The really interesting folks of the not-so-distant future won't be mere centenarians but rather people who are pushing 150 without a health problem worth complaining about.

Aging: Now Just Another Disease

Intrigued? So is Cynthia Kenyon, Ph.D., the University of California, San Francisco, biologist who was one of the first to liberate anti-aging medicine from the milieu of questionable "miracle" products and bring it into the sober world of science. Much of today's optimism about the potential for longer, healthier human lives can be traced back to Dr. Kenyon's work in 1993, when she coaxed some of the current worms' ancestors into living twice as long as normal. That alone was head-turning, but how she did it was revolutionary.

"Basically, we got worms to live much longer and stay very healthy by changing just one gene," Dr. Kenyon says. "That's quite remarkable."

It was so remarkable, in fact, that it helped overturn a concept of aging that had held sway for thousands of years. "People always thought that we just wore out like an old car, and there was nothing to be done about it," Dr. Kenyon says. "But now we think aging may be more like a disease with a cure."

That cure, many researchers are convinced, is hidden in our genes. Some, like Dr. Kenyon, believe that a single gene may hold the key. By 2004, manipulating that one gene had extended not only worm life but also the lives of fruit flies and mice. In 2003, researchers associated with Dr. Kenyon revealed exactly how this gene can, under the right conditions, prolong life and health—knowledge that's necessary to develop a longevity pill for humans.

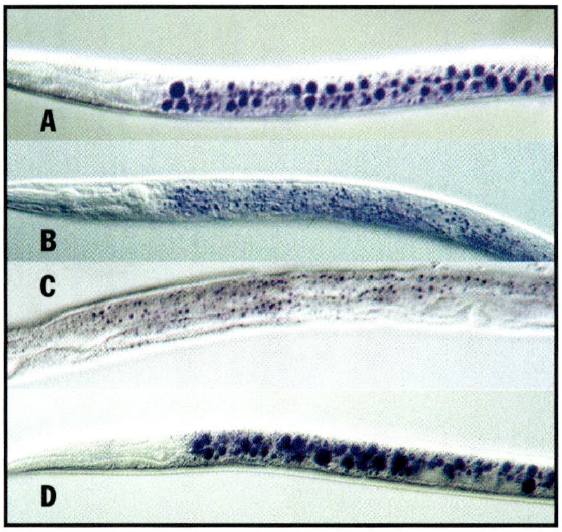

Earlier worm research showed the roles of the DAF-2 and DAF-16 genes in the suppression of fat storage. (Fat storage is suppressed in worms b and c.) It may be possible to make drugs that have a similar effect in humans.

The gene is called DAF-2. Its usual role is to give instructions for producing a hormone receptor—that is, a protein that sits on cells and grabs insulin, the sugar-delivery hormone, as it passes by. Under certain conditions, DAF-2 initiates a series of chemical events that allow the organism to live longer. It does this by causing another gene, called DAF-16, to order up a special protein that activates scores of other genes with widely varying roles. None of these secondary, or "downstream," genes are life extending by themselves, but together, they can potentially keep an organism up and running for as long as the genes are switched on.

Some of those genes make antioxidant proteins that protect cells from destructive oxygen molecules called free radicals and from the age-related diseases those free radicals hasten, such as heart disease. Other genes hold blueprints for antimicrobial proteins that guard against infection. Still others control fat storage, cholesterol transport, insulin output, and other metabolic tasks.

Using a favorite metaphor of gene researchers, Dr. Kenyon describes the group of genes as an orchestra. "The hormone-receptor gene DAF-2 is the master regulator—the conductor," she says, while the longevity gene DAF-16 is the concertmaster, or top assistant in the orchestra. "The antioxidant genes would be the violins, the metabolic genes would be the cellos, the antibacterial genes the French horns, and so on. Each contributes in its own way, and together, [they] produce a very big effect on life span."

"We may not have to find too many more genes to get people to live to 100."

Nir Barzilai, M.D.

Harnessing the Body's Own Powers

Dr. Kenyon and others have shown they can toy with genes and proteins to force the conductor to play the "Longevity Symphony" on demand. Of course, their success so far has been limited to rather humble members of the animal kingdom. Is there a DAF-2 equivalent in humans? Dr. Kenyon thinks so. Before you believe her, though, you may want the answer to an obvious question: If animals really do have a gene that can help them stay younger longer, why isn't it active all the time?

The explanation begins with evolution's preferred strategy for keeping species from going extinct. Our biological imperative is reproduction, not longevity. Once we've had time to procreate, our genes don't bother much with keeping us alive.

Put another way, death is the price we pay for sex. A cruel tradeoff? Perhaps. If you're a parent, though, ask yourself if you'd have given up having children if that meant you could live forever. In that light, evolution's choice seems more acceptable, doesn't it?

But here's the kicker: We may be able to have it both ways—kids and longer lives. How? By exploiting an exception clause in the death-for-sex contract.

Gerontologists have long known that when animals eat just enough to survive, they extend their life spans. As a longevity strategy, such calorie deprivation isn't likely to be a big hit, because who wants to buy extra years by leading a life of near starvation? Even so, the longevity effect of calorie deprivation confirms that deep in our genes, there is an emergency backup mechanism geared toward keeping us alive rather than producing more mouths to feed. It may be, the theory goes, that the DAF-2 chain of events is one such mechanism that's just sitting there, waiting for us to trick it into action.

"It makes perfect sense from an evolutionary point of view for organisms to retain a system for slower aging at the expense of fertility during times of famine, when fertility's not such a good idea anyway," says Aubrey de Grey, Ph.D., a British longevity researcher. "And of course, anything that's evolved has some genetic structure to it that can be manipulated."

A Real Longevity Pill?

Still, Dr. de Grey doubts that DAF-2 or any similar genetic master conductor exists at the human level, at least not in any way that can extend life. Many agree with him, including Nir Barzilai, M.D., a researcher at Albert Einstein College of Medicine in New York City and discoverer of one of the two recently announced human longevity genes. "The idea that a single gene mutation can increase life span is an important research model," Dr. Barzilai says, "but to get results in worms and apply them to humans takes a big leap of faith."

Dr. Kenyon and others have enough faith to see a chance that with the help of drugs, humans are genetically capable of unleashing a DAF-2–style response that will keep us alive and healthy into our hundreds. "We think the human equivalents of the DAF-2 and DAF-16 genes are the genes that encode the insulin receptor and another protein called insulin-like growth factor, or IGF-1," Dr. Kenyon says. "So maybe we can tweak the insulin/IGF-1 systems in humans like we did with the worms."

A researcher extracts DNA from the blood of centenarians at Elixir Pharmaceuticals, which is working to develop an anti-aging drug.

She and like-minded colleagues recently set up a lab called Elixir Pharmaceuticals in Cambridge, Massachusetts, to develop a human anti-aging drug. In 2004, testing was well under way in mice, a necessary step before trying the drug on humans. The researchers won't reveal much until the study is done, perhaps in 2005, but Dr. Kenyon does say, "The early results are very promising."

How would this longevity drug work? Rest assured that the researchers at Elixir are not trying to mutate a human gene to induce the DAF-2 longevity effect, as in worms and flies. Instead, their target is the proteins for which the genes carry instructions. "What we're doing is creating a molecule that will bind to a protein and change it so it acts as if we had changed the gene's instructions," Dr. Kenyon says. "That will lead to turning downstream genes on and off the way DAF-16 does."

If all goes well, and the drug turns out to work safely in humans, pills to add 20 healthy years to the typical life span may be available within a decade. "Whether it's in the next 10 years or 100 years, we really are going to be able to live longer, healthier lives," Dr. Kenyon says.

Why Centenarians Thrive

Even researchers who are skeptical of Dr. Kenyon's single-gene approach agree that drugs to produce longer, healthier lives are on the way. For them, the recent identification of two human longevity genes validates the intensive genetic studies of centenarians that began in earnest at the turn of the new century. Simply put, we can now be sure that people who live to be 100 are more likely to have certain variations of certain genes that predispose them to long life.

While we've long known that having the right parents improves your odds of making it long into your eighties, a healthy lifestyle and a generous dose of good luck are equally important factors. But for ultra-longevity—that is, living to 100 or more—nothing matters except the right gene profile.

"I'm telling you, I studied 300 centenarians, and I didn't have a single yogurt eater, not a single vegetarian, not even anybody who exercises," Dr. Barzilai says. "On the other hand, 30 percent of them were overweight or obese, and one 104-year-old woman was celebrating her 95th year of cigarette smoking. These people have a unique genetic component that makes lifestyle insignificant for longevity."

The two longevity genes are mutations of normal genes. Neither gene variation on its own accounts for more than perhaps 18 percent of centenarians' longevity potential, but Dr. Barzilai thinks it's just a matter of time before the rest of the genetic puzzle is filled in. "And we may not have to find too many more genes to get people to live to 100," he says. "Just a few more might do it."

We can now be sure that people who live to be 100 are more likely to have certain variations of certain genes that predispose them to a long life.

The next step would be for researchers to create drugs that duplicate the biological processes unleashed by each of these genes. One of the genes turns out to be the exact equivalent of one of Dr. Kenyon's worms' "downstream" genes. It has the same name (metasomal transfer protein, or MTP) and the same function of regulating lipids, or blood fats.

The other gene, discovered by Dr. Barzilai and called CTP, also controls lipids. Specifically, the version of the gene found in centenarians creates higher levels of the beneficial cholesterol known as

HDL. More important, it ensures that the molecules that carry cholesterol through the bloodstream, called lipoproteins, are larger than usual. Small lipoprotein particles are more susceptible to damage from free radicals and are more likely to embed themselves in artery walls.

"Everyone who has diabetes, heart disease, or hypertension has the smaller lipoprotein particle size," Dr. Barzilai says. "I've also found evidence that I haven't published yet that the large lipoprotein particle size is associated with much better cognitive function, so CTP may also be protecting centenarians' brains, which is extremely important for longevity."

When will scientists come up with drugs to mimic these genetic benefits? The development process requires identifying molecules that will get the job done, testing them in animals for toxicity and effectiveness, and seeing how they work in humans via a series of rigidly controlled studies. Assuming that pharmaceutical companies immediately jump on the opportunities offered by the recent discoveries, we're looking at a 5- to 10-year process before the first modest longevity drugs are available.

Nevertheless, thanks to some medical serendipity, we may have a drug that will provide at least some of CTP's benefits much sooner. For reasons unrelated to Dr. Barzilai's research, a pharmaceutical company is developing a drug that will simultaneously raise HDL levels and increase lipoprotein particle size. "It does just what the CTP gene mutation in centenarians does," Dr. Barzilai says.

The drug is already in the advanced stages of human testing, so it could be available in 2005 or 2006. It's not meant as a longevity drug per se but rather as a way to reduce the risk of age-related diseases that are in part a consequence of cholesterol imbalance, such as heart disease. The question is: What's the difference?

From one perspective, not much. Except for possible master genes such as DAF-2, DAF-16, and a few others being explored, all of the human and animal longevity-associated genes discovered so far have to do with protecting against disease—through larger lipoprotein particles, special antioxidant proteins, infection-fighting agents, and so on. The logic is obvious: If you delay the age-related diseases that can kill you, you'll probably live longer.

"There's a really powerful medical potential in that," Dr. Kenyon says. "We may be learning how to combat a lot of different diseases at once."

The Next Milestone: 150

The anti-aging drugs of the future should be able to do more than promise better ways to treat age-related diseases such as diabetes, cancer, heart disease, and Alzheimer's. Longevity researchers hope they will alter the behavior of certain genes so such diseases are out of the question for people 100 and older, just as they are for most 25-year-olds.

"We're approaching things from a whole different direction," Dr. Barzilai says. "Many scientists have been studying people with specific age-related diseases and looking for the genes that cause them, but we're studying people who don't get these diseases and finding the genes that cause such long, healthy lives."

Can there also be hidden in our genes a mechanism that doesn't just keep us disease-free but is also able to retard the aging process? Many longevity researchers think so. Dr. Kenyon sees such a possibility in the DAF-2 effect, or something like it. Others point out that women who give birth in their forties are four times likelier to live to 100,

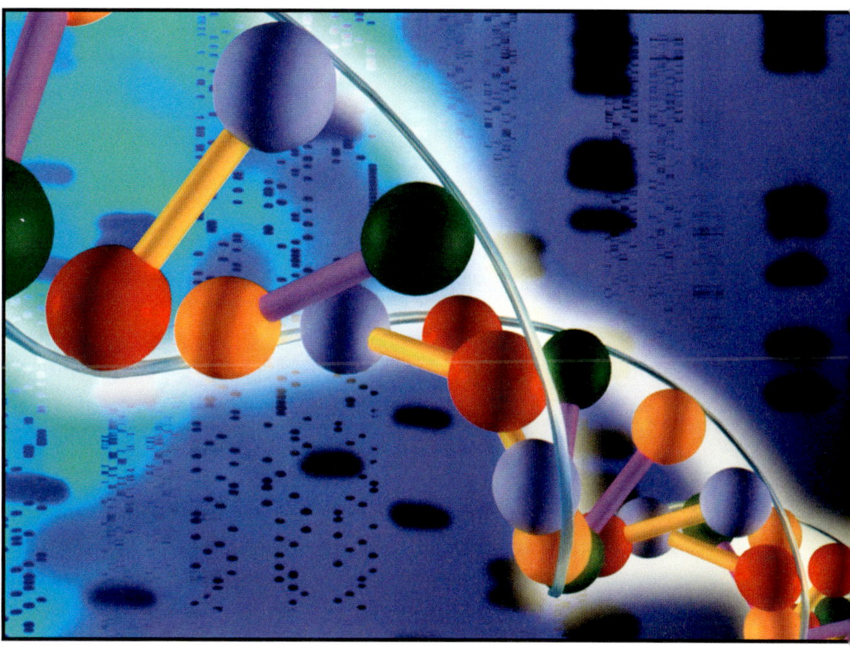

If the secret to long life is in the genes, then drugs that mimic the effects of those genes—such as creating more beneficial HDL cholesterol—could extend our lifespans.

CAN A THOUSAND CANDLES FIT ON A BIRTHDAY CAKE?

Live to 120? Child's play, says Aubrey de Grey, Ph.D. The British gerontologist from Cambridge University is convinced that medical know-how will soon keep human beings alive for hundreds, if not thousands, of years. "Our ultimate goal," he says, "is the availability to the entire human race of technology that will restore them to whatever degree of youth they desire and keep them there for as long as they want."

The way to do that, Dr. de Grey says, is not by duplicating the action of selected longevity genes, as many leading anti-aging researchers advocate. "Tricking the body into doing what it already knows how to do will get you maybe 20 more years," he says. "My approach is to do much better than what evolution has given us."

How? Basically, by getting under the hood and fixing whatever can possibly go wrong. Dr. de Grey, who's also an engineer, has narrowed down the "components of aging" to just seven. He's also identified the "fixes" for all of them, many of which are already found in laboratories. Here are Dr. de Grey's keys to ultralongevity. Whether all seven will be available in 20 years (possibly) or 100 (quite probably), he can't say.

1. Restock the cell supply.
The killer: Aging brings an ultimately fatal net loss of cells in heart, brain, and muscle tissue because more cells die than are replaced by new ones.
The solution: Coax all-purpose stem cells to convert in the lab to the cell type you want, then deliver them to multiply wherever they're needed in the body for a never-ending supply of new tissue. Such "stem cell therapy" has already worked experimentally.

2. Really cure cancer.
The killer: Malignant cells break free from the usual limits on their proliferation, so there's nothing to stop the tissue damage they cause.
The solution: Use periodic gene therapy to reprogram all of the body's cells so that the natural cell death mechanism can't be overridden. It's an ambitious (some would say audacious) but feasible plan to control cancer that has already been partially successful in mice.

3. Move easily mutating genes to a safer home.
The killer: Mitochondria are power-producing units in a cell that induce aging because the 13 genes they contain—the only genes found outside the nucleus—are not well protected from the consequences of mutation. Their unchecked mutations eventually create damaging toxicity.
The solution: Use existing gene therapy techniques to duplicate the codes of the mitochondria's genes and relocate them permanently to the nucleus, where safeguards against runaway mutations are already located.

4. Clear out junk inside the cells.
The killer: White blood cells that don't divide regularly accumulate a variety of unwanted molecules that can't be broken down and eliminated. Over time, the piled-up trash prevents the cells from working properly.
The solution: Genetically reprogram adult stem cells in the blood to include instructions for making a special enzyme that will break down material, then deliver these housekeeping cells via a bone marrow transplant.

5. Clear out junk outside the cells.
The killer: With age, protein deposits called amyloids accumulate between brain cells, destroying brain function—not just in Alzheimer's patients, but eventually in everybody.
The solution: A vaccine to stimulate the body's immune system to get rid of these deposits has already been tested. Dangerous side effects halted progress, but safer versions are being explored.

6. Get rid of unwanted cells.
The killer: Too many fat cells in the abdominal cavity create life-shortening metabolic problems, including diabetes. Also, aging and useless (senescent) cells accumulate in the joints' cartilage tissue, where they become toxic.
The solution: Inject drugs that will either seek out and kill only the unwanted cells or induce the immune system to do the selective killing.

7. Loosen up the arteries.
The killer: Arteries become stiff with age because unneeded proteins and sugars surrounding the cells of the vessel walls eventually bond to each other in a process called crosslinking. The result is high blood pressure, heart disease, or stroke.
The solution: The first drug to break down such crosslinks is in the advanced stages of testing in humans. More drugs need to be found, though, because there are many types of crosslinks.

an indication that some people have genetic structures that allow life events, including getting old, to unfold more slowly.

Dr. Barzilai found more hope for such an age-slowing mechanism as he looked at the characteristics of the centenarians in his study. While tumors were rare in the group, people with the CTP variation were just as likely to have them as those who didn't have the variation—but they developed their tumors an average of 10 years later. "That implies that CTP may combine with other genes to actually slow aging," he says.

Is Super-Longevity Worth It?

What can we really expect from these latest strides? Nobody knows for sure, of course, but the consensus among those doing longevity research is that within a decade, there will be drugs that middle-aged people can take to boost their chances of staying healthy to age 100. Improved versions will soon follow that could make centenarians common. We may also see a gradual increase in the maximum life span, from about 12 decades to 13 or 14.

Some people have qualms about these developments, the most common being that delaying death cheapens life. Dr. de Grey, who envisions life spans measured in centuries, is convinced that people will drop their concerns once longer lives become a reality. "They just don't want to be disappointed," he says.

Dr. Kenyon sees life extension as advancing well-established medical goals. "We've always put a lot of effort and money into treating diseases to keep people alive," she says. "That's wonderful, but all that's been offered them is not being dead. What we're talking about now is prolonged health, the opportunity to enjoy the benefits of youth longer."

If it all comes true, society will have to adjust to the skewed demographics brought on by so many centenarians. Population control will be even more urgent than it is now, and having full retirement and health benefits kick in at 65 may no longer be economically feasible.

For longevity researchers, these and other challenges pale in comparison to the priceless gift of life. As Dr. Barzilai points out, the lucky few who have passed their 100th birthdays have lived some 2 1/2 times longer than their life expectancy at birth, which was about 40 at the time. Maybe it's time for the rest of us to share their good fortune. ■

Ding Yushen of Rugao, China, made it past 100. You may, too—the first longevity drugs should arrive within the next decade.

what does it mean to you?

Advances in genetic research on animals, along with the discovery of human gene variations responsible for centenarians' long lives, have prompted researchers to test anti-aging pills. These drugs could one day give everyone a shot at the extra years that centenarians now enjoy.

■ Drugs that mimic the results of a certain gene that increases worms' life spans by sixfold are currently being tested in mice. Such drugs could lengthen human lives by 20 years, and the first of them could be available within 10 years.

■ Pharmaceutical companies are expected to start working soon on drugs to mimic the disease-delaying benefits of two gene variations recently found in centenarians. These genes give special cholesterol-managing instructions that protect against heart disease, diabetes, and brain deterioration.

■ If enough new longevity genes are discovered in centenarians in the next several years, drug developers could have the insights they need to protect humans from all the major diseases of aging, including cancer.

The New Low-Carb Foods: Welcome but Worrisome

Food options for America's estimated 10 million low-carb dieters exploded in 2004 as low-carb products gobbled up more and more supermarket shelf space.

Shoppers can now fill their grocery carts with low-carb beer, ketchup, barbecue sauce, salad dressing, cookies, and snack chips. Even items that are hard to envision as diet foods have been added to the pack: In late 2003, Hershey's unveiled a line of low-carb chocolate bars, and Breyer's rolled out several types of low-carb ice cream and other frozen desserts. According to the editor of a low-carb industry newsletter, sales of these foods were expected to be $30 billion in 2004—double the sales of the previous year.

A Hunger for New Options

"Consumers are looking at ways to control their carb intake," says Stephanie Childs, a spokeswoman for the Grocery Manufacturers of America, "and it's the consumer demand that has sparked the introduction of the low-carb products."

Food companies cut the carbs in these new foods mainly by replacing wheat flour with soy flour and sugar with sugar alcohols. Measure for measure, soy flour has half the carbohydrates of wheat flour and several times the protein. Sugar alcohols, including erythritol, maltitol, mannitol, sorbitol, and xylitol, are lower in calories and can be used spoonful for spoonful to replace sugar in baked goods, ice cream, and other foods. The virtue of these sweeteners is that they don't cause sharp increases in blood sugar, as regular sugar, white bread, white flour, and other foods like potatoes do. A sharp rise in blood sugar causes a rush of the sugar-handling hormone insulin, which in turn can send blood sugar plummeting and make you hungry again.

People following the Atkins Diet and other low-carb diets are encouraged to tally—and avoid—those carbs known to quickly boost blood sugar. At the same time, they're allowed to turn a blind eye to carbs from sugar alcohols and fiber, the indigestible roughage in whole grains, fruits, and vegetables. Food companies have seized on the idea of "bad" carbs and "good" carbs and have begun offering products that contain only a few grams of blood–sugar–raising "net impact carbs," or "net carbs."

Consumer advocates warn, however, that these terms haven't been officially defined, and the label claims are unregulated. What's more, the claims fail to recognize that some of the supposedly "Atkins-friendly" sugar alcohols do contain calories and may cause gas, diarrhea, or other digestive problems. Meanwhile, when you toss one of these foods into your cart, be aware that it may not be much lower in carbs than its everyday counterpart—and it may be as high or even higher in calories.

Compare, for example, Doritos, the popular snack chips, with Doritos Edge, a low-carb version. A serving of regular Doritos contains 18 grams of carbs and 140 calories, while a serving of Doritos Edge contains half the carbs but the same 140 calories. Or consider spaghetti sauces. A serving of a standard sauce by Ragu has 10 grams of carbs and 130 calories, while a serving of Carb Options Hearty Italian Style with Sausage contains 7 grams of carbs and 160 calories—30 calories more.

What Really Counts

That's the concern about these low-carb products, says dietitian David Grotto, R.D., L.D., a spokesperson for the American Dietetic Association and director of nutrition education at the Block Center in Evanston, Illinois. "Low-carb doesn't necessarily

Salvaged or still sinful? Low-carb cookies like these beckon to dieters looking for an easy fix.

A shopper wheels through the Castus Low Carb Superstore in Fremont, California. Owner Rick Schott started the small chain in 1999 after losing 100 pounds on a low-carb diet.

mean good nutrition or low-calorie," he says. In other words, shoppers who focus too closely on carbs can sabotage their weight-loss efforts.

On the flip side, despite many warnings about shortcomings of the low-carb approach—the weight loss is due to your body shedding water, and the diet is typically high in animal fats, which are known to increase the risk of heart disease—low-carb diets have lately earned some respect from the medical establishment. Studies published in top medical journals in 2003 showed that people could lose at least as much weight on low-carb diets as on other types and at the same time improve their levels of "good" HDL cholesterol. Another study, reported in the May 2004 issue of *Annals of Internal Medicine,* found similar results—plus, fewer of the study volunteers dropped out of a low-carb diet after six months than did those on a low-fat diet.

Low-carb diets may be winning hearts and stomachs across America for now, but, Grotto says, there's no getting around one fact: "The bulk of research holds that calories really are what matter most." He remembers wondering why a client he was counseling in the 1990s kept gaining weight—until he learned that the man was eating a box of low-fat cookies every day. A decade later, he says, he sees the same thing going on—except, of course, the cookies are now low-carb. ■

Antidepressants Prompt Suicide Warnings

Teens taking antidepressants may feel just well enough at the beginning of treatment to take action in the form of a suicide attempt.

Medical authorities in the United States and Great Britain grappled with a most difficult question in late 2003 and 2004: Do certain antidepressant drugs increase the risk of suicide, or would depressed people who attempt suicide do it anyway?

In October 2003, the FDA suggested the drugs may be to blame for some suicides in children. It issued a public health advisory to alert doctors to reports of suicidal thinking and suicide attempts among children with severe depression during clinical studies of eight selective serotonin reuptake inhibitors (SSRIs). These drugs include such commonly prescribed medications as fluoxetine (Prozac) and paroxetine (Paxil). The October advisory followed a similar FDA recommendation in June that doctors not use Paxil to treat children or adolescents with depression.

British regulators went a step further. In December 2003, they warned that Prozac was the only SSRI that should be prescribed to children. For people under age 18, other drugs in the same drug class—including Paxil, sertraline (Zoloft), escitalopram (Lexapro), fluvoxamine (Luvox), and citalopram (Celexa)—carried risks that outweighed their benefits, the regulators said. Prozac wasn't on the list because it's the only SSRI approved for use in treating children with depression in the United States or Great Britain. (The FDA has since concluded that an increased risk of suicidal behavior exists with Prozac, too.) The others are used "off-label," that is, at the doctor's discretion. One other SSRI, Zoloft, is approved for treating obsessive-compulsive disorder in children in the United States, while Luvox is approved for that use in Great Britain.

Adults Warned, Too

The concerns over a possible link between antidepressants and suicide didn't stop with children. After holding committee hearings on the matter in February 2004, the FDA issued another advisory warning doctors, patients, and families to closely monitor children *and* adults with depression—especially at the beginning of treatment or when doses change—for suicidal thoughts.

The warning came even before the publication in a July 2004 issue of the *Journal of the American Medical Association* (JAMA) of a study that found the greatest risk of suicidal behavior came in the first month after starting antidepressants, especially in the first one to nine days. That study, though, found no greater risk of suicide with SSRIs than with two other popular antidepressants, amitriptyline (Elavil, Endep) and dothiepin (Prothiaden, Dolsulepin), older medications that belong to the tricyclic class of antidepressants.

All of this leaves parents of depressed children—and adults struggling with depression—

scratching their heads. Just what is going on with this popular and effective class of drugs?

No one, even experts at the FDA, is quite sure. "It's very hard to tell what is a suicide attempt and what isn't" in clinical studies, says Scott Gottlieb, M.D., senior advisor for medical technology at the FDA. It's also difficult to tell whether a drug is directly spurring suicide attempts.

That's because of the very nature of depression, explains Brian McConnville, M.D., a child and adolescent psychiatrist at Cincinnati Children's Hospital Medical Center. Depression and an inclination toward suicide are clearly linked, he says, but there's a vast spectrum of people with suicidal thoughts. "On any Friday night in any emergency room, you'll see teenagers coming in saying they have suicidal intent," he says. "Distinguishing between those who have a full plan and those who are just mad at the time is difficult."

Also, when they're first diagnosed and begin treatment, many people with the kind of severe depression that warrants medication are often too numb and lethargic to do anything, much less commit suicide. As the treatment kicks in, they begin to regain some energy—just enough, in some cases, to try to kill themselves. The authors of the JAMA study suggest that one reason for the slightly higher risk of suicide early on is that patients are still very depressed. It generally takes about two weeks or more before people taking antidepressants start to feel better. This is the point of the FDA advisory, says Dr. Gottlieb. "Doctors should be more vigilant during this initial treatment time."

Hidden Clinical Trials

The issue of antidepressants and suicide took a legal turn in June 2004, when New York State Attorney General Eliot Spitzer sued GlaxoSmithKline, maker of Paxil, charging that the giant drug maker concealed clinical evidence that the drug could lead to suicidal thinking in children and adolescents and that it didn't work any better than a placebo (dummy pill).

The controversy opened the public's eyes to what the *Wall Street Journal* called the "black hole" in medical research, in which as many as half of all studies, particularly those with negative results, are never published or publicly presented.

Timeline: SSRIs under Scrutiny

- **June 2003:** FDA recommends that Paxil not be used to treat children or adolescents with depression because it may increase the likelihood of suicide.
- **October 2003:** FDA issues a public health advisory alerting physicians to reports of suicidal thinking and suicide attempts in clinical studies of various antidepressant drugs used on children with severe depression.
- **December 2003:** British drug regulators warn that SSRIs other than Prozac should not be prescribed to children.
- **January 2004:** American College of Neuropsychopharmacology issues a report stating that Zoloft and similar SSRIs do not increase children's suicide risk.
- **March 2004:** FDA issues another advisory, about the need to "closely monitor both adults and children with depression, especially at the beginning of treatment or when the doses are changed." It also asks for stronger cautions on the labels of 10 drugs.
- **April 2004:** Researchers publish the results of their analysis of six trials of antidepressants in children, finding that the trials consistently exaggerated the benefits of the drugs and downplayed the side effects. Their conclusion was that antidepressants could not be confidently recommended as a treatment for childhood depression.
- **June 2004:** New York State Attorney General Eliot Spitzer files a lawsuit accusing GlaxoSmithKline of "repeated and persistent" fraud for concealing data showing problems concerning the effectiveness and safety of its drug Paxil when used by children and adolescents.
- **July 2004:** A study of 159,810 people who were taking antidepressants for the first time found a slightly increased risk of suicide in the first month of drug treatment, particularly the first one to nine days after starting medication, but noted that the risk is no greater with SSRIs than with drugs in the tricyclic class of antidepressants.
- **September 2004:** An FDA advisory committee recommends that the agency require a black box warning on antidepressants, the strongest warning label issued for drugs.

As of summer 2004, the FDA was reviewing all reports of suicides or suicide attempts linked to antidepressants. It also asked manufacturers to change the labels of 10 drugs—Celexa, Prozac, Paxil, Zoloft, Lexapro, Luvox, bupropion (Wellbutrin), mirtazapine (Remeron), nefazodone (Serzone), and venlafaxine (Effexor)—to include stronger cautions and warnings about the need to monitor patients for worsening depression and the emergence of suicidal thoughts, regardless of the cause. ■

Growth Hormones for Short Kids Raise a Controversy

How does your kid measure up? The FDA recently approved growth hormone for kids who just happen to be very short.

"What's the problem with being short?" Libby Kershner demanded. She was 9 years old and didn't understand why her parents wanted her to take injections of human growth hormone. They tried to explain that without the hormone, she would never grow taller than 4'8". But Kershner wasn't thinking about her adult height. She was thinking about the shots she would have to take every night.

Her parents prevailed, though, and for five years in the 1990s, she had the injections. Today, a college senior who stands 5'2", she's glad she did. "I'm taller than some of my friends," she says proudly. "I had low self-esteem. Growth hormone helped me grow in two ways—mentally as well as physically."

Since 1985, synthetic growth hormones have been helping abnormally short children, and there are thousands of families worldwide who are delighted with the results. But in the summer of 2003, the practice suddenly became the focus of controversy. That's because the FDA changed the rules for who could receive Humatrope, a genetically engineered version of the body's own growth hormone.

In the past, Humatrope shots had been available only to short children whose stature was the result of a medical problem, such as a growth hormone deficiency. In 2003, the regulators said that exceptionally short children with no apparent medical problem could receive it, too. The kids defined as "exceptionally short" are the shortest 1.2 percent of children—girls who, without treatment, would never grow taller than 4'11", and boys who would never shoot past 5'3".

The FDA move raised eyebrows among some people, who questioned the need to "treat" short stature. Others cheered the new rules.

"Don't trivialize what it means to be short," declares David Rothman, coauthor of *The Pursuit of Perfection: The Promise and Perils of Medical Enhancement*. He points out that exceptionally short children often have low self-esteem. They're picked on in school and passed over for sports teams. As teens, they have more trouble getting dates. Studies show that short men even get paid less than taller ones. But even Rothman concedes that parents need to weigh the pros and cons before seeking growth-hormone treatment for their children. There are serious issues to consider.

Small gains. In its decision on Humatrope, the FDA relied on the results of one major trial. After 4 1/2 years of treatment, participants in that trial gained an average of 1 1/2 inches. That may be enough to boost a very short child into the bottom of the normal range, but it's not going to turn a natural jockey into a linebacker. In other studies, higher doses of hormone yielded greater gains. But is an inch or two—or even four—worth the cost of treatment, the aggravation of nightly shots, and the risk of side effects? "How much is an inch worth?" asks Ora Hirsch Pescovitz, M.D., chief of pediatric endocrinology at Indiana University School of Medicine in Indianapolis.

Growing pains: Some parents and children have decided that regular growth hormone shots are worth the discomfort and inconvenience. At right, a "pen" for injecting Humatrope, man-made human growth hormone.

Big costs. That's not an idle question. Treatment currently averages $10,000 to $20,000 a year—and it's not unusual to be treated for four years. The FDA's go-ahead to use the drugs for healthy short kids raises the possibility that insurance may one day cover the costs, but since insurers may consider the hormone treatments "cosmetic," like plastic surgery, it's equally likely that parents will continue to pick up the tab.

The ouch factor. Parents may worry about painful bills, but kids fret about the nightly shots. (Because most growth occurs at night, children take the shots before bed.) The injections can be given with very fine needles that cause less pain than regular needles—but who wants to take shots for a condition that isn't a medical problem? The treatment often continues until late puberty, when the plates in the bones fuse, making further growth impossible. That's a lot of shots.

Safety concerns. All drugs, without exception, can have side effects. Even though growth hormone appears to be very safe, children sometimes develop complications, including swelling of the hands and occasionally of the brain. The swelling disappears when treatment is stopped, but what about long-term consequences? Doctors worry that the treatment could increase the risk of cancer years later. Tall girls with a condition called acromegaly have excessive levels of growth hormone as youngsters—and higher rates of colon cancer as adults. "But their levels of growth hormone are 10 times those that we're giving these children," says Pinchas Cohen, M.D., professor of pediatrics at the Univer-sity of California, Los Angeles, School of Medicine. He maintains that "growth hormone is one of the safest drugs we have."

And for the moment, at least, it ranks as one of the most controversial. ■

Innovative Wound Care Tested in Battle

Stanching the flow: Derived from the "glue" that holds shrimp shells together, this bandage encourages blood clotting and stops severe bleeding.

High-tech wound treatments made military headlines in 2004, as U.S. forces and their coalition partners in Iraq tackled one of the most vexing challenges of battlefield medicine: out-of-control bleeding. The military launched an all-out attack on the problem (the leading cause of death from wartime injuries) after a horrific military death in Somalia, which was immortalized in the 2001 movie *Black Hawk Down*. The film depicted the real-life tragedy of a soldier who died from blood loss before he and his buddies could be rescued.

"That soldier engendered a lot of people to say, 'What can we put in a medic's hands, or in a soldier's hands to help his buddy?' " notes U.S. Army Col. David Burris, M.D., interim chair of the department of surgery at the Uniformed Services University of the Health Sciences in Bethesda, Maryland.

The answers to that question range from a $1,000, still-experimental bandage composed of the clotting factors found in human blood to a kitty-litter-type product that costs just pocket change and is available from Internet sources without a prescription.

The least high-tech but potentially most useful new item is a tourniquet that can be applied with one hand, enabling soldiers with arm wounds to stem bleeding on their own. The tourniquet is especially valuable because the body armor worn by today's soldiers means that most injuries occur in their arms or legs, through which major arteries and veins run, says Dr. Burris. Eventually, he says, all military personnel in the field will carry these tourniquets in their battle packs.

Then there's QuikClot. "It literally looks like kitty litter," says Dr. Burris. In fact, it's even chemically related to the sandy stuff. Made of aluminum silicate, a type of volcanic rock, the powder is poured into a bleeding wound to encourage clotting; the wound is then covered with a bandage until the patient can get to a hospital for more help. "We think it's saved at least a dozen marines and soldiers," says Dr. Burris. At about $20 for a 3 1/2-ounce bag, it will probably be used routinely by homeland emergency workers in the near future. Currently, all marines carry it in their individual first-aid kits, and Dr. Burris says that some army soldiers took it to Iraq on their own, ordering it directly from the manufacturer, Z-Medica, or its distributors. It was approved by the FDA in September 2003.

Researchers also found a high-tech clotting agent in the lowly shrimp. Made from the biological glue that holds shrimp shells together, the chitosan bandage is 1/2 inch thick and about the size of a beverage coaster, with the consistency of a communion wafer. When pressed against a wound, it sticks to the injury and absorbs liquid, thus hastening clotting.

Such technology isn't limited to the battlefield. Because the FDA must first approve any medical product developed for the military, the products become available to civilians at the same time. QuikClot's manufacturer has already begun marketing a trauma pack containing its product to emergency workers, outdoor sports enthusiasts, and motorists around the nation. ■

Switching One Sweet Drink for Another

Which would you rather have your kids drink at school, a beverage with 103 calories and 16 grams of sugar or one with 110 calories and 27 grams of sugar?

If you said the former, you're out of luck. The first is a regular cola, and schools around the United States are kicking sodas out of school vending machines in favor of juice and sports drinks—which, believe it or not, have more sugar and calories than the ubiquitous Coke.

The backlash against soda comes as studies find that 56 to 85 percent of children in school consume at least one soft drink daily (adolescent boys quaff four or more a day). In 2000, 76.3 percent of all U.S. schools offered soft drinks in vending machines. Their proliferation is blamed, in part, for the growing epidemic of overweight kids in the United States, particularly since studies show that calories consumed from sweetened drinks don't fill you up, they just add to your overall daily calorie intake.

Prompted by information like this, thousands of schools across the country have ended exclusive vending machine contracts with soft drink giants—forgoing millions of dollars in income—to bring in healthier alternatives. Los Angeles banned all soft drinks from school campuses beginning in 2004, and New York City replaced all carbonated drinks with either water or 100 percent juice versions of Snapple.

But if it's kids' health they're looking out for, they're looking in the wrong place, says Barry M. Popkin, Ph.D., professor of nutrition at the University of North Carolina in Chapel Hill and an expert on children's nutrition. "There's no difference if the schools get rid of Coke and add a fruit drink," he says. "It's helping no one healthwise."

What few realize is that so-called healthy beverages can have just as much and sometimes more sugar than a can of Coke or Sprite. For instance, 8 ounces of Snapple Mango Madness has 110 calories and 27 grams of sugar. Vendors are stocking machines with sweetened milk products that are so packed with sugar they might as well be marketed as liquid candy.

Overall, says Dr. Popkin, kids get nearly 13 percent of their calories from sweetened drinks, with almost 3 percent from fruit juice alone. "Clearly, I think that in this country, in this context, calories are what count," he says. "There are very few children, except for adolescent girls moving toward anorexia, who aren't consuming too many calories."

Small wonder, then, that in January 2004, the American Academy of Pediatrics urged its members to work toward eliminating all sweet beverages—both carbonated drinks and fruit drinks—from school vending machines and replacing them with healthier alternatives.

They may get some help from parents. A Robert Wood Johnson Foundation national poll released in December 2003 found that 92 percent of teachers and 91 percent of parents favor converting the selections in vending machines to healthy foods and beverages. Just what are healthy beverages? Dr. Popkin doesn't hesitate: "Water and skim milk." ■

If you think fruit drinks are the healthy answer to sodas, think again. Nutritionists say water and milk are the winners.

PART 2

GENERAL HEALTH

DIGGING IN against the ravages of aging? In the Aging chapter, read about two common vitamins that can dramatically cut your risk of Alzheimer's disease and why taking a B-complex vitamin may be the best thing you can do to stay mentally sharp. Also discover which antibiotics appear to significantly slow the devastating effects of Alzheimer's.

In the Children's Health chapter, learn why old standbys—including breastfeeding, exercise, and watching less television—are looking better and better for improving your child's well-being. Parents will also want to read the shocking news about children's diets, learn about a software program that benefits kids with ADHD, and find out why antibiotics may not be the answer to ear infections. In the Wellness chapter, there are compelling new reasons to take vitamin D, cut back on salt, and buy wild—or canned—salmon instead of the farmed variety.

76 AGING

EALTH

102 WELLNESS

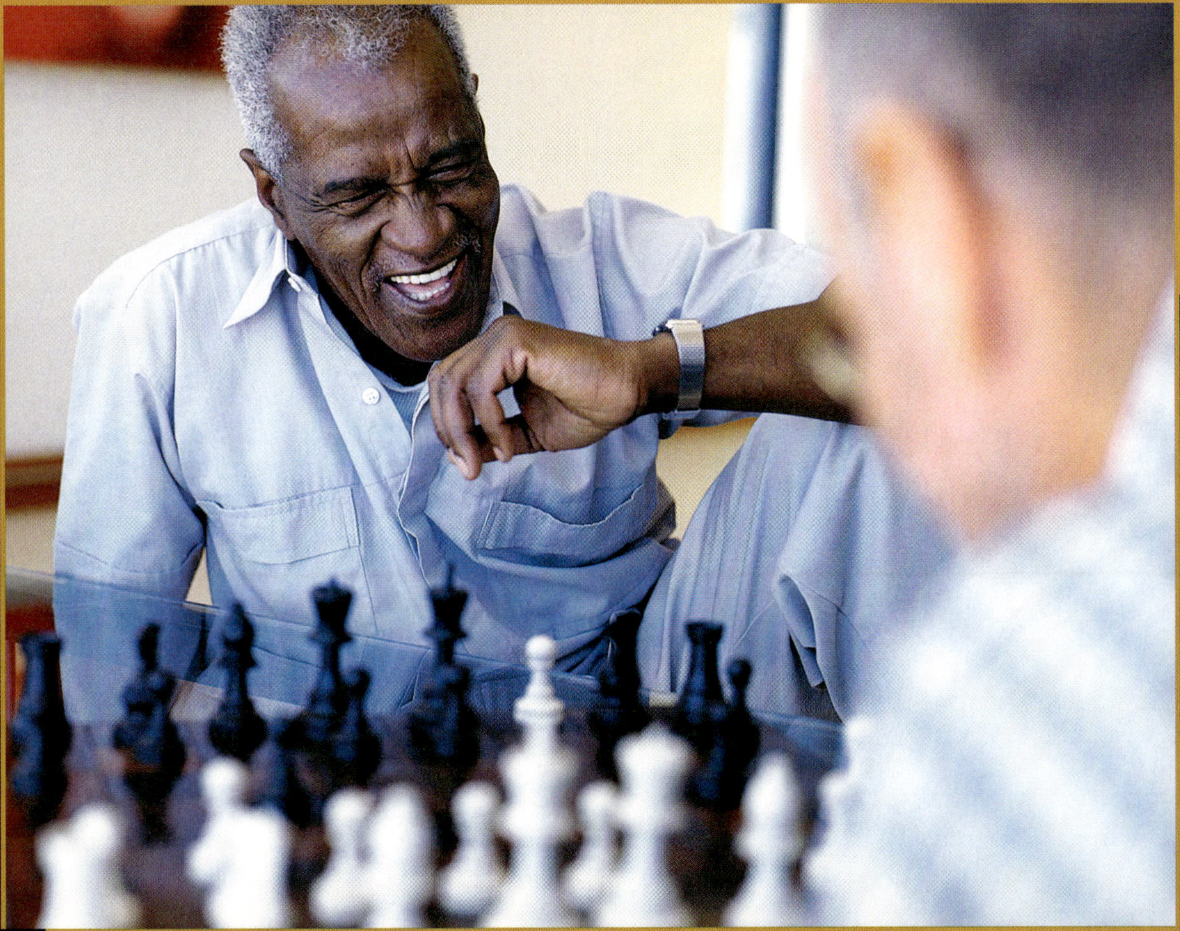

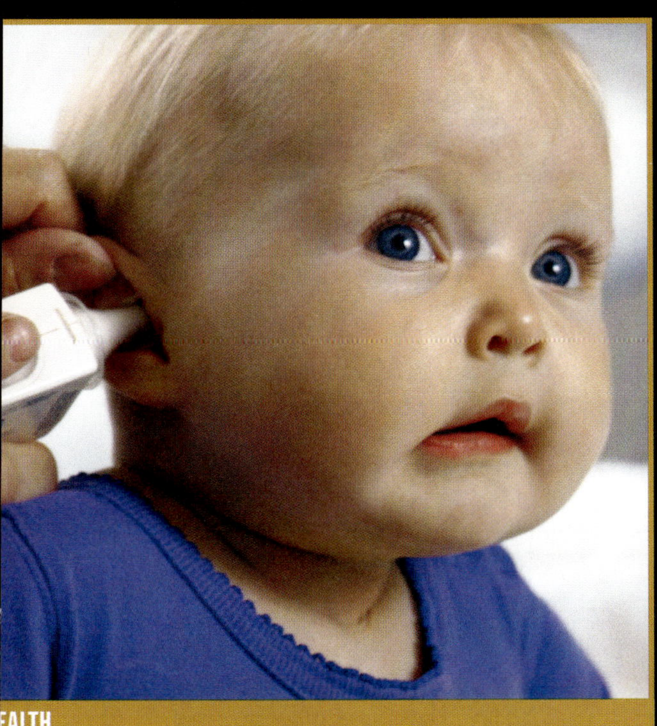

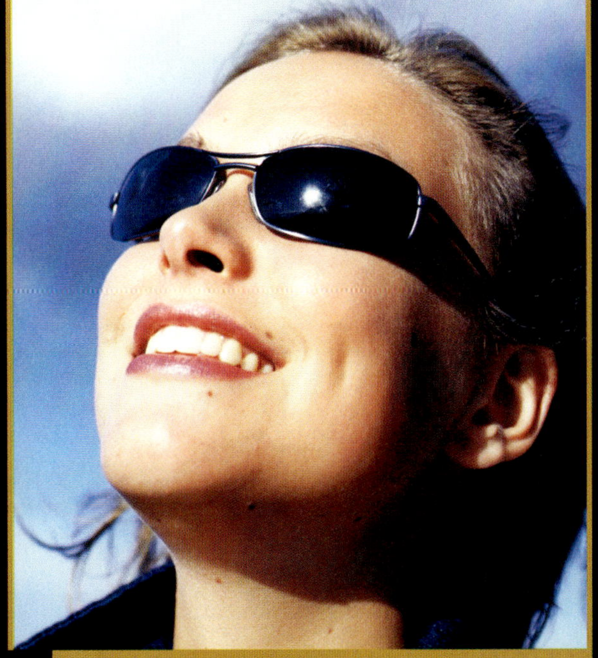

AGING

IN THIS SECTION

MEDICAL ADVANCEMENTS OFFER MORE THAN A LONGER LIFE—THEY PROMISE A BETTER LIFE WELL INTO OLD AGE.

On the high-tech front, vibrating insoles for your shoes may soon help you keep your balance and avoid falls by subtly tickling nerve endings in your feet. And scientists have begun testing a system that uses artificial intelligence to help people with memory problems get through the day with a minimum of difficulty and a maximum of independence.

Alzheimer's disease, of course, is the cruelest memory robber, but a new way to peer into the brain promises a warning of the disease—a warning that would allow doctors to start treatment sooner. That treatment may include antibiotics, as new discoveries have shed light on the role of bacteria in Alzheimer's as well as the ability of antibiotics to slow the disease's progress.

If you're hoping to avoid Alzheimer's, it turns out that a combination of two common vitamins should help you do it. And there are more good reasons to take your vitamins, especially a B-complex supplement: sharpening your memory and protecting your bones.

Alzheimer's Disease

Coming Soon: A Snapshot of Early Alzheimer's

It's your 65th birthday—time for your first Alzheimer's scan. A quick injection near your inner elbow is followed by a painless PET (positron emission tomography) scan. If your brain tests "clean," you look forward to many happy years without serious memory loss. If the doctors see warning signs of Alzheimer's, they put you on a drug regimen to keep you from developing the full-blown, memory-robbing disease. You go back in a year for another scan to make sure the drugs are doing their job.

No part of that scenario is possible today. Doctors have no tool that allows them to peer into a living brain in a way that reveals the markers of Alzheimer's—clumps of protein deposits called amyloid plaques. Although there are drugs in the pipeline designed to reduce the accumulation of these plaques, there's been no way to see if the drugs accomplish that. And without being able to follow the plaques' progression visually, researchers can't even be sure that a reduction in these clumps will result in a reduction of symptoms.

That's about to change, thanks to a landmark discovery that will finally give researchers a window on plaques in the brain. Researchers at the University of Pittsburgh School of Medicine and their counterparts at Sweden's Uppsala University announced in a January 2004 issue of the journal *Annals of Neurology* that a newly invented imaging agent has been shown to make plaques visible during PET scans.

The dye, dubbed Pittsburgh Compound B, ushers in a new era of Alzheimer's research that will probably speed up the development of plaque-reducing drugs or other treatments. It also provides a diagnostic tool that for the first time will allow Alzheimer's to be spotted and treated well before mental decline sets in. Millions of baby boomers about to enter their sixties may be able to fend off the disease with drugs that reduce amyloids—the proteins that make up plaques—just as they fend off heart disease with cholesterol-lowering drugs.

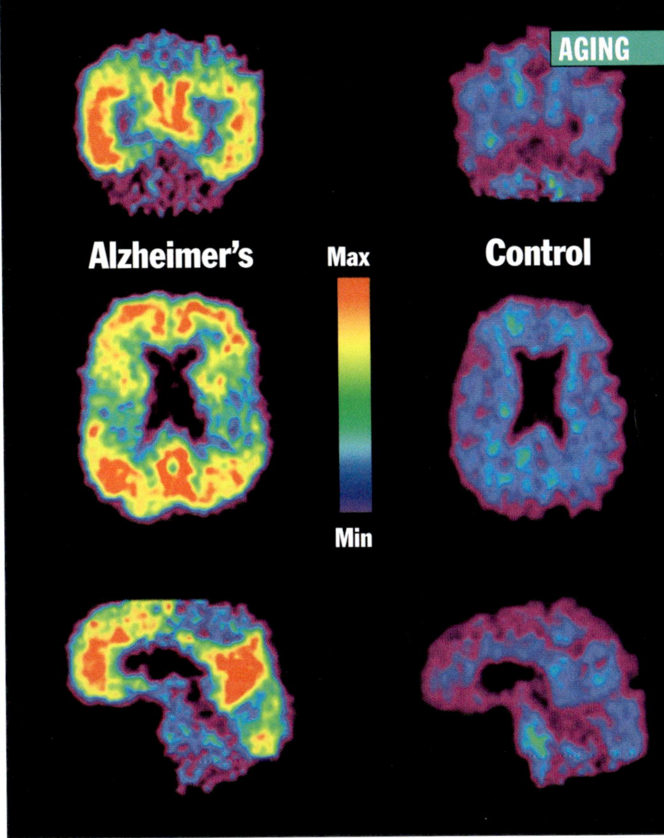

The column of three scans on the left shows amyloid plaque buildup (red and orange) in a brain with Alzheimer's disease. On the right, a healthy brain. A new dye makes detection of the plaque possible.

How it works. The Pittsburgh compound is an injectable radioactive dye, a variation on the dye used to detect plaques in autopsied tissue. The difference is that the new dye can safely enter the brains of living human beings through the bloodstream; prior to its invention, plaques could be imaged only after death. Once in the living brain, the new dye sticks only to amyloid deposits, making them easily detectable with a PET scan. Within 2 hours, the dye is gone from the body.

Availability. The dye's inventors are working with the British firm Amersham Health, which specializes in diagnostic tools, to fine-tune the new imaging agent for affordable, practical use in diagnosing Alzheimer's. That will require more lab work and then more tests on human volunteers. Thus, even though the Pittsburgh researchers and others can move ahead with studies that use the new dye to find out more about the cause and treatment of the disease, the rest of us will probably have to wait several years before we can walk into a local clinic for an Alzheimer's test.

Alzheimer's Disease

A New Alzheimer's Treatment from Old Drugs

In the twentieth century, infection-fighting antibiotics tamed many afflictions. Now, two of these widely used drugs have been shown to slow the mental decline of Alzheimer's disease.

It's not just a token improvement that antibiotics are offering. Results of a carefully controlled study at five clinics across Canada revealed that the 43 Alzheimer's patients who took the antibiotics for six months experienced significantly less mental decline than the 39 who were given placebos (dummy pills). The study authors, who presented their work to the Infectious Diseases Society of America in October 2003, rated the antibiotics' performance at least as effective as that of any of the three most common current drugs for Alzheimer's treatment—donepezil (Aricept),

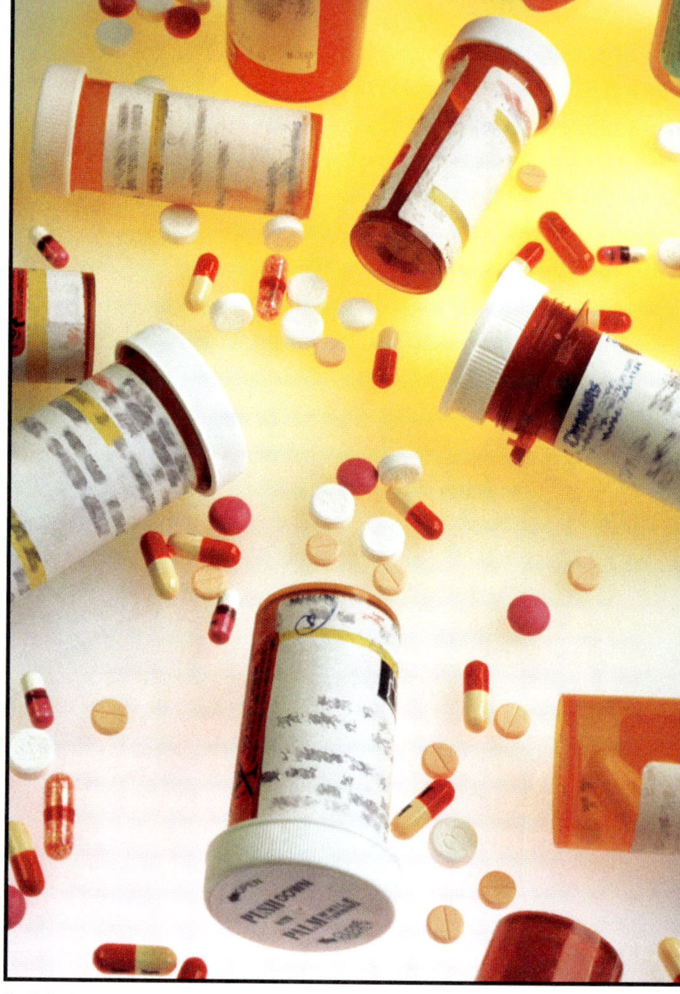

Antibiotics could hold back the mental deterioration of people with Alzheimer's disease, potentially giving them more good years.

IS THERE AN INFECTION CONNECTION?

If antibiotics work as a treatment for Alzheimer's, could the disease be caused by infection? Neurologists have known for some time that bacteria called *Chlamydia pneumoniae*—the ones responsible for a number of respiratory ailments—are found in the brains of most Alzheimer's patients. But just what those bugs are doing in those brains has been hard to pin down. Even the researchers who discovered the antibiotic treatment for Alzheimer's don't think the drugs work by killing bacteria.

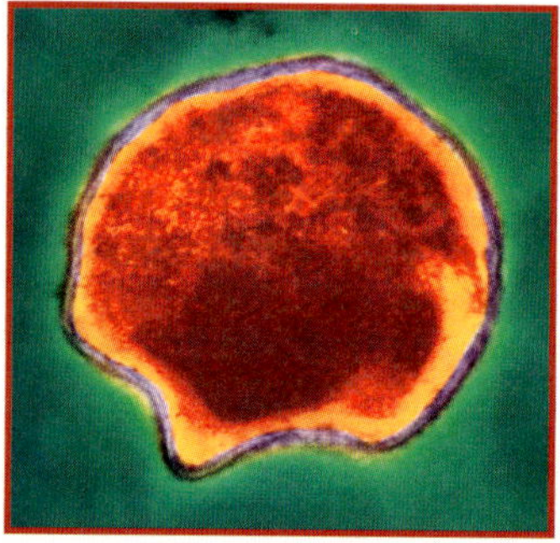

C. pneumoniae *bacteria are a culprit in respiratory infections. In Alzheimer's, too?*

Nevertheless, there's new evidence that *C. pneumoniae* does contribute to Alzheimer's. According to researchers from the Philadelphia College of Osteopathic Medicine, healthy mice who had the bacteria sprayed into their noses soon developed amyloid plaques, the protein deposits in the brain that are the hallmark of Alzheimer's. That doesn't prove that the bacteria cause Alzheimer's, but the researchers think the bugs might act as a trigger for other causes.

Blood tests can confirm the presence of *C. pneumoniae* by testing for antibodies mobilized to fight the bacteria, but such testing is neither common nor recommended at this point as an Alzheimer's indicator. More research is needed before the blood tests can be advised.

rivastigmine (Exelon), and galantamine (Reminyl)—all of which belong to the class of drugs known as cholinesterase inhibitors.

How they work. The two antibiotics found to fight Alzheimer's, doxycycline (Adoxa, Periostat) and rifampin (Rifadin, Rimactane), are best known for their activity against *Chlamydia pneumoniae*, a bacterium that causes a number of respiratory illnesses, from sore throat to pneumonia. Although there's been some suspicion in the past that the chlamydia germ may be associated with Alzheimer's, the researchers don't think the antibiotics' effectiveness has anything to do with fighting infection. Doxycycline and rifampin may instead slow the disease's progress by reducing inflammation in the brain, or perhaps by discouraging accumulation of the protein clumps known as amyloid plaques that are a central feature of the disease.

Availability. Doxycycline and rifampin are established antibiotics with good safety records, and doctors can prescribe them for Alzheimer's treatment right now. Most physicians, however, will probably be reluctant to do so until a new, larger study duplicates the positive results of this one. Long-term treatment with any antibiotic increases the risk of germs developing resistance to that drug. Still, the Canadian study authors say it makes sense for people who've had no success with other Alzheimer's treatments to discuss the possibility of an antibiotic regimen with their doctors. ■

RESEARCH ROUNDUP

How Long Will Mom or Dad Live?

Doctors now have a way to answer the one question that families of Alzheimer's patients find hard to ask: How long is our loved one expected to live? By following the long-term progress of 521 newly diagnosed Alzheimer's patients, Seattle-area researchers have made available to doctors a formula for a fairly reliable estimate of an Alzheimer's patient's prospects. That means families and caregivers can better plan for the care of their loved ones. The formula will also help physicians choose the appropriate treatment strategies.

When Blood Pressure Is Too Low

Middle-aged folks are usually advised to keep their blood pressure down to protect against heart disease and stroke. However, elderly people who are concerned about Alzheimer's would be well advised to make sure it doesn't go too low. Low blood pressure, according to a new study of more than 400 senior citizens age 75 and over, significantly raises the risk of Alzheimer's-related dementia, or mental decline.

After 21 years of monitoring the health of the study subjects (all of whom were dementia-free at the start), researchers at Albert Einstein College of Medicine in New York City found that those who had consistently low blood pressure in the early years of the study were twice as likely to develop dementia later on. In the study, any reading of 70 or lower for diastolic blood pressure (the second number in a blood pressure reading) was regarded as low.

The study authors, writing in the December 2003 issue of the journal *Neurology*, suspect that the connection between low blood pressure and dementia is related to an inadequate supply of blood to the brain. They also believe that the connection is age dependent—that is, the increased risk of dementia from low blood pressure applies only to people over 75. Nevertheless, since high blood pressure has also been linked to increased Alzheimer's risk, all adults now have even more reason to ask their doctors about how to keep their blood pressure where it should be.

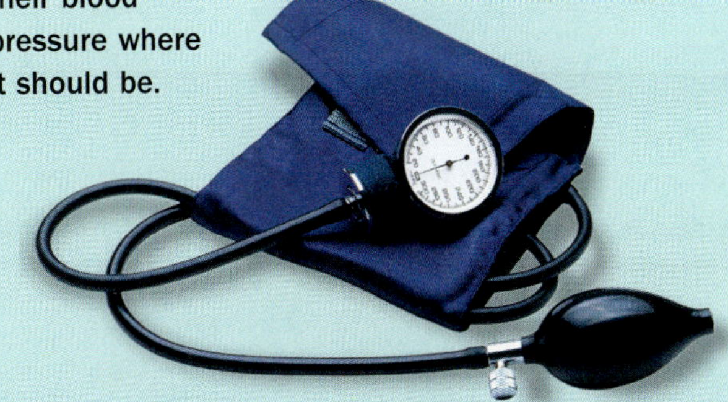

C Plus E Equals Less Risk of AD

Want to avoid Alzheimer's disease as you get older? Take your vitamin C—and your vitamin E. Both vitamins act as powerful antioxidants with a host of health benefits, including protecting the brain from free radicals, the unstable molecules that inflict damage on cells.

Together, the vitamins form a mighty duo that can drastically cut your risk of Alzheimer's disease. In fact, a study of 4,740 Utah residents age 65 and over found that the prevalence of Alzheimer's among those who took both vitamins E and C daily for three years was a whopping 78 percent lower than among those who didn't.

Just one of the vitamins alone won't get the job done. According to results reported in the January 2004 issue of the journal *Archives of Neurology*, the Utah residents who reported taking either vitamin C or vitamin E alone showed no decline in Alzheimer's risk. Taking multivitamins had no effect either, probably because the dosage wasn't high enough. The doses found to offer Alzheimer's protection were 500 milligrams of vitamin C and 400 IU of vitamin E—far more than the amounts found in multivitamins.

Alzheimer's Disease

Low Testosterone Linked with Alzheimer's

All men have less of the male sex hormone testosterone circulating in their bloodstreams as they get older. Now it appears that the less you have, the higher your risk of Alzheimer's disease.

Researchers who followed 574 men, ages 32 to 87, over two decades found that those who eventually developed Alzheimer's had, on average, half the amount of "free" or unbound testosterone in their blood as those who stayed Alzheimer's-free. And here's the big news: The low free testosterone levels were detected as much as a decade before Alzheimer's could be diagnosed. That's a strong indication that low testosterone is a precursor, and perhaps even a cause, of Alzheimer's in men.

Only a small amount of a man's total testosterone circulates unbound in the blood. This "free testosterone" enters the brain, and in so doing, appears to have a beneficial effect on the nerve cells there. Previous studies have connected healthy free testosterone levels with a better ability to remember things that were heard and seen. Now, the new study, published in a January 2004 issue of the journal *Neurology*, seems to show that the sex hormone also protects the brain against Alzheimer's.

Since a simple blood test can reveal a man's free testosterone level, this new finding suggests that testosterone supplementation may make sense in men whose levels are low. However, that's something the researchers aren't yet ready to recommend—not until more research confirms the link between testosterone levels and Alzheimer's and until safety concerns about testosterone replacement therapy are addressed. Testosterone supplementation is suspected of raising men's risk of prostate cancer and stroke.

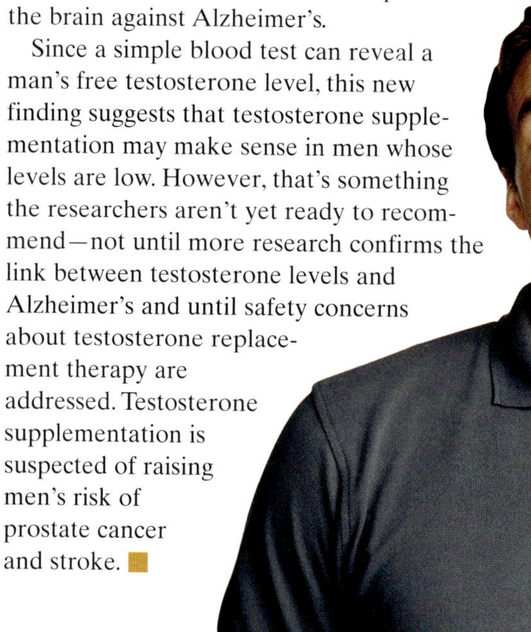

Balance

Shaky Footing Provides Better Balance

By the end of 2005, a lot of older adults may be walking around in shoes that shake. New research shows that continuous vibrations on the soles of the feet dramatically improve balance control in elderly people while limiting sway in their standing posture. Most important, the steadying effect of these vibrations should cut down on serious falls, the number one cause of death due to injury in elderly people.

The breakthrough was announced in October 2003 in the British medical journal *Lancet* after an unusual series of tests was conducted on adults both young and old. The volunteers were asked to stand on special gel-based vibrating insoles for about 30 seconds at a time. Since the vibration intensity was set at just below the lowest level that a human can feel, the participants had no idea when the vibrating mechanism was on or off. Special cameras aimed at reflector points on the volunteers' bodies clearly showed less side-to-side swaying in each body when the insoles were vibrating, especially among the elderly people.

How it works. Humans can stand and walk on two feet without tipping over only because nerve endings in the skin of our soles are constantly reading pressure changes at the point where our feet meet the ground. The nerves fire off signals to the brain, which in turn instructs the muscles to adjust accordingly—so in reality, we're never "standing still." Tiny muscle contractions are constantly taking place to balance us.

The problem for elderly people is that the nerve endings lose sensitivity over the years and fail to pick up many of the pressure changes. The vibrating insoles solve that problem because continuous exposure to uneven vibrations "tickles" the nerve cells into heightened sensitivity. The nerve-brain-muscle performance thus improves, and better balance results.

Availability. The Boston University researchers who ran the study have been working with a medical device manufacturer to design an affordable, battery-powered insole that can be inserted into shoes. The prototype will have to be tested to gain FDA approval. Since the device is noninvasive, the researchers expect the process to move quickly and predict that the vibrating insoles could be available, with a prescription, before the end of 2005.

Fancy Footwork

Video cameras aimed at reflector points on volunteers monitored their balance. When researchers activated subtly vibrating insoles, balance improved.

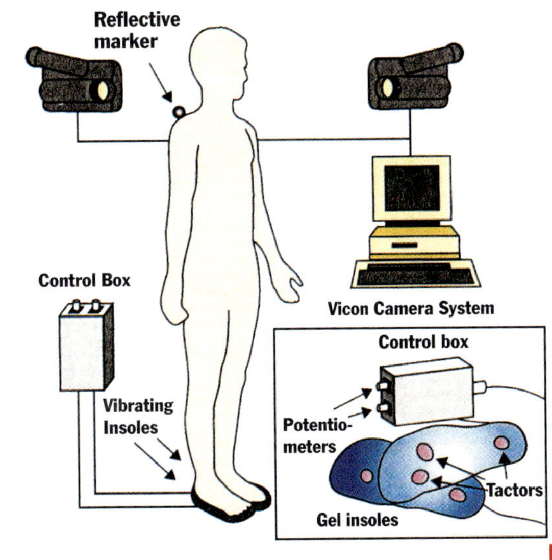

Earthshaking discovery: Vibrating insoles may better the balance of older people who have lost some of the sensitivity in their feet.

Falls

Vitamin D Keeps Older Adults on Their Feet

Preventing falls is easier than you might think. Just by making sure to get enough vitamin D every day, an older adult can cut his risk of falling in half. That means a simple multivitamin may be all that's needed to avoid the debilitating and often life-threatening consequences of fracturing a hip or other bone.

Swiss researchers gave a vitamin D supplement to half of 378 elderly residents of a retirement community. After about nine months, those who took their daily dose of D were a whopping 55 percent less likely to fall than those who didn't, according to the study results, published in the February 2004 issue of the *Journal of the American Geriatrics Society*.

That's because vitamin D does more than team up with calcium to build bone strength. It helps older muscles maintain strength by regulating the release of parathyroid hormone (PTH). Too much PTH weakens muscles needed for balance. It also weakens bones, increasing the likelihood of a fracture resulting from a fall.

Vitamin D deficiency is surprisingly common in developed countries. That's especially true among the elderly people, who tend to stay indoors, depriving their bodies of the sunlight needed to manufacture vitamin D. Older people also tend not to get enough vitamin D from foods. That's why the researchers recommend supplements.

How much D do you need? Many multivitamins contain 10 micrograms (400 IU), which is adequate for most of us. However, if you're over 65, ask your doctor about taking a heftier dose. Many studies indicate that 20 micrograms (800 IU) is the most effective dose for preventing falls. Also make sure you're getting enough calcium: The Swiss study showed that the vitamin D is wasted if you're not. Most people need 1,000 to 1,200 milligrams of calcium per day. ■

General Health

The B Team Makes the Anti-Aging A-List

B vitamins are shaping up to be among the most valuable anti-aging supplements on the market. A bevy of recent studies has shown that certain B vitamins protect older folks against two of the most debilitating age-related maladies: failing memory and weakened bones. Add the well-known heart benefits of B vitamins, and you've got a virtual wonder drug sitting right there on the drugstore shelf.

In fact, some researchers say, supplementing with a B-complex vitamin—or simply taking a daily multivitamin—could be the most important simple step you can take toward ensuring a sharp-minded, fracture-free old age.

Folate for bones. The family of B vitamins, especially one called folate or folic acid, helps to keep older bones strong by reducing levels of homocysteine, an amino acid. Experts already knew that an elevated level of homocysteine increases heart attack risk, but now research also links it to the brittle-bone disease osteoporosis. In Dutch and American studies published in a May 2004 issue of the *New England Journal of Medicine*, the 25 percent of people with the most homocysteine in their blood had at least double the risk of an osteoporosis-related bone fracture compared with the rest.

Clearly, having too much homocysteine making the rounds in your system is something to avoid. But the study authors aren't recommending routine homocysteine tests (which cost $100 to $200). Rather, they say, typical daily multivitamins that include folic acid and the other B vitamins are usually enough to keep your homocysteine levels in the healthy range.

B_{12} for memory. The other anti-aging superstar in the B family is vitamin B_{12}. New research from Sweden confirms that getting enough B_{12} makes you less likely to develop age-related memory loss. After taking blood samples and giving memory tests to 167 people with an average age of 83, Swedish and British researchers found that people with sufficient levels of vitamin B_{12} in their bloodstreams scored much better on the memory tests than those with B_{12} deficiencies. The vitamin made the biggest difference for those people who carried a gene variant known as APOE4—the so-called Alzheimer's gene—but people without the APOE4 gene also benefited. Vitamin B_{12} has also been shown to combat bone loss (see page 196).

The study authors recommend that people over age 50 get their vitamin B_{12} from supplements, since some older adults have trouble absorbing B vitamins from foods. Many nutritionists recommend that older adults take 100 to 400 micrograms per day, the amount found in many B-complex supplements. ■

Hard Facts about Who Lives Longest

Where and to whom you were born has a lot to do with when you'll die, sociologists have discovered. Scientists delved into the life stories of more than 5,000 men born between 1906 and 1921. Their main conclusions: Men born into blue-collar homes risk earlier death than those from white-collar families. Those born in urban areas die earlier than their rural counterparts. If they grew up with one or more step-parents, their risk of dying early is higher. And if one or both of their parents were immigrants, they're more likely to live longer than offspring of native-born parents. The results were published in March 2004.

The researchers emphasize that it's not the birth situation itself that makes the difference but rather the habits it tends to foster. For example, men who grow up on farms are less likely to be obese, and children of immigrants are less likely to smoke.

Want to improve your chess game? Take a vitamin B-complex supplement. Older people who get enough vitamin B_{12}, found in the supplements, have sharper memories.

Memory Loss

A Nicotine Fix for Your Memory

Patching up your memory: Small doses of nicotine may give your brain a boost, making "senior moments" less frequent.

Why would a nonsmoker wear a nicotine patch? Because she's trying to quit—that is, quit forgetting things. Researchers have discovered that small, steady doses of nicotine reduce the mild but annoying memory loss that accompanies aging even in healthy people. This means that memory-boosting patches may one day become common.

By putting a group of seniors "on the patch" for a month and then testing their memories, a research team at Duke University in Durham, North Carolina, redeemed some of nicotine's dismal reputation. Nicotine, it was found, can alleviate symptoms of age-related memory loss—by reducing the number of those forgetful "senior moments," for instance. It may even prevent, or at least slow down, the decline of memory function in the first place.

How it works. Most people think of nicotine only as the addictive ingredient in tobacco. But, as many a chain-smoking college student cramming for exams can testify, it can also enhance mental function. That's because nicotine duplicates the action of a natural brain chemical called acetylcholine, which is released at nerve endings to help with learning and memory. When nicotine is introduced into the brain, it's like boosting the workforce at a construction site. Beams are lifted and walls erected more easily.

Earlier research had suggested that nicotine's ability to mimic acetylcholine can help people with major brain disorders such as Alzheimer's disease. The new study, reported in October 2003 in the journal *Psychopharmacology*, unveiled nicotine's beneficial effects on a much less serious malady known as age-associated memory impairment. This is the unwelcome "I can't find my keys" and "where'd I put my glasses?" syndrome that's common in older adults. Subjects who wore the nicotine patches noticed a marked improvement in their memories. Those who (without knowing it) had fake patches noticed no change at all.

Availability. The study volunteers wore the same patches that are used for quitting smoking, which feed small, metered doses of nicotine into the bloodstream through the skin to help smokers get through the withdrawal stage of smoking cessation. However, the researchers warn against using these patches for memory enhancement. For one thing, the study was very small, involving only 11 subjects. Its findings, as impressive as they are, need to be duplicated in larger studies. More important, nicotine is a powerfully addictive drug, and using nicotine skin patches for the long term can be dangerous. The most likely next step will be the development of a nicotine-like drug that delivers nicotine's memory-enhancing benefits without its negative side effects. ■

RESEARCH ROUNDUP

Don't Forget: It's Never Too Late to Quit

It's true that some researchers are exploring the possibility that nicotine may one day be manipulated and used in a patch or drug to slow age-related memory loss. But don't turn to cigarettes for a mental boost in the meantime. The detrimental effect of smoking on mental function in old age is well established, and now there's more proof. Researchers from several European countries examined data on more than 9,000 elderly people and found that aging smokers experience mental decline at five times the rate of aging nonsmokers. The more they smoke, the faster their memories slip away.

No one is sure why smoking has such a disastrous effect on mental sharpness over time, but the reason may be related to blood flow. Smoking narrows arteries, reducing oxygen delivery to the brain. Decreased blood flow may also contribute to "mini-strokes" that kill off brain cells. Think that quitting later in life is pointless? Think again. In the study, former smokers scored much better than current smokers on memory tests.

Memory Loss

A High-Tech Friend Lends a Helping Hand

Older folks with fraying memories can look forward to having a 24-hour friend around the house in the coming years. This particular friend will be made of computer circuits and motion sensors instead of flesh and blood, but it will still offer much of what's needed from a true companion: a helping hand, understanding, and respect for your independence.

Autominder is a computerized creation of University of Michigan scientists that will help memory-impaired seniors manage their daily tasks—everything from using the bathroom and taking medication to finding their way around and even remembering to call their loved ones. It doesn't dole out reminders like an alarm clock. Instead, it uses artificial intelligence to interact with the user.

How it works. All the information about the person's daily routine—eating meals, taking medication, watching favorite TV programs—is programmed into a laptop computer that's set up in a safe place in the house or apartment. The computer communicates with a unit that the user keeps with her (either a handheld device or something that can be attached to her clothes or body). From this unit, she receives reminders, either vocally or displayed in large type on a screen.

And that's just the bare bones of the operation. With strategically placed motion and contact sensors keeping track of the user's whereabouts and activities, the Autominder can use its intelligence to adjust its reminders to suit the situation. For example, if it knows that the user has just spent several minutes in the bathroom, it may delay a programmed bathroom reminder. If it senses that mealtime overlaps with a favorite weekly television program, it may suggest an adjustment to avoid the conflict. It will even learn the best time to gently prod, "Have you called your daughter lately?"

Availability. Much fine-tuning and testing needs to be done before the Autominder (or similar technology under development at other research sites in the United States) will be ready to market. An early version, mounted on a small mobile robot, was recently field tested in a Pennsylvania retirement community. It was a hit with the users. "They actually felt a sense of autonomy that they don't feel with a human caretaker," says Martha E. Pollack, Ph.D., lead researcher on the project. (Autominder's developers are currently focusing less on the robot and more on the handheld or clothes-mounted device paired with motion sensors, which should prove more practical for home use and much cheaper than a mobile robot.) Dr. Pollack expects Autominder to be available to the public around 2010—just as the first wave of baby boomers approaches age 65. ■

Paws to Remember

Guide dogs for the blind are a time-tested blessing. Why not guide dogs for the memory impaired? The idea makes sense, because Alzheimer's patients often lose their way outside their homes, wandering aimlessly until they get some help. Now, an Israeli dog trainer and a social worker have successfully trained and tested the first "Alzheimer's aid dog," which may prompt further research aimed at widespread use of such dogs.

The key to the project was finding the right dog, which turned out to be a female collie from Finland named Polly, who has the crucial ability to stay calm when her master (a 62-year-old volunteer with mild Alzheimer's) becomes confused and frustrated. Polly is her master's constant companion. She knows his habits and routine, as well as the neighborhood around his home. When her master gets lost, he simply tells Polly "Home!" and she leads him there. Perhaps just as important, Polly's playful and attentive manner relieves much of the anxiety and loneliness that sometimes afflict people with Alzheimer's.

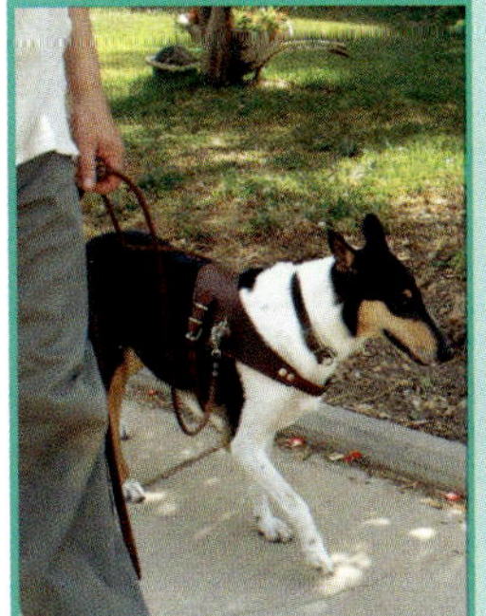

CHILDREN'S HEALTH

IN THIS SECTION

POLITICIANS AND PUNDITS CONTINUED TO SOUND THE ALARM OVER THE CHILDHOOD OBESITY EPIDEMIC.

Meanwhile, one study showed that toddlers' diets are shockingly deficient in fruits and vegetables and laden with far too much fat. In the "good news" column, children of mothers who breastfeed are less likely to be overweight. Breastfeeding even appears to improve kids' cholesterol levels later in life.

Another way to safeguard your children's future health: Get them to exercise. In addition to keeping kids slim, the right type of physical activity strengthens their bones, helping to prevent osteoporosis decades later. Vigorous exercise can even help youngsters catch fewer colds.

In the "why didn't we know this sooner" category, a major study found that the number of hours of TV a toddler watches corresponds with how good—or bad—his attention span is at age 7. For kids already diagnosed with ADHD, research from Sweden shows that "exercising" the brain with a specially designed software program can help improve working memory.

Finally, find out why the use of antibiotics for ear infections and strep throat is losing favor.

RoboMemo to the rescue: When children performed memory exercises regularly on this special computer program, their ADHD symptoms improved.

ADHD

Byte by Byte, ADHD Symptoms Improve

As the number of children with attention deficit hyperactivity disorder (ADHD) continues to rise in the United States and other countries, researchers, doctors, and parents are scrambling to find treatments that don't involve medication. Now, new research from Swedish researchers suggests that "exercising" a certain part of the brain in kids with ADHD can significantly improve their performance on cognitive tasks while reducing symptoms of inattention and hyperactivity.

The problem. Researchers have known for some time that particular regions of the brain that control a type of memory called working memory are impaired in children with ADHD. Working memory involves tasks such as taking notes during a classroom lecture or trying to remember a phone number someone has just given you while you continue to listen to that person talk. If you have problems with working memory, you have trouble remembering plans or instructions and solving problems.

Children and adults with attention deficit have difficulty with working memory because it's dependent on the prefrontal cortex of the brain—a region that's smaller in people with ADHD—and the neurotransmitter dopamine, which isn't used very effectively in those with the condition.

The solution. To strengthen working memory in a group of children with ADHD, researcher Torkel

TOP Trends

CANADA BANS BABY WALKERS

Leading the vanguard of the growing movement against baby walkers, Canada took a gold medal in child safety in April 2004, becoming the first in the world to ban sale of the devices.

Baby walkers, those plastic seats with wheels and oversize trays that babies use to propel themselves around a room or house, are known dangers. In 1999, nearly 9,000 infants age 15 months and younger were injured in the United States alone as a result of them. Such statistics led the American Academy of Pediatrics to call for a ban in 2001—to no avail.

But Health Canada, the Canadian health ministry, decided the facts were too frightening to ignore. "Health Canada has determined that these children do not have the necessary skills, reflexes, or cognitive abilities to safely make use of these products," the ministry said in a prepared statement. It advised parents who have walkers to get rid of them.

SPENDING ON BEHAVIOR DRUGS SOARS

It's no secret that the number of kids diagnosed with behavioral disorders, such as attention deficit hyperactivity disorder (ADHD), has been rising in recent years. And new data released in mid-2004 shows that parents now spend more money on prescription drugs to treat children with conditions such as ADHD, depression, autism, and conduct disorders than on antibiotics.

The number of children taking behavioral drugs jumped by more than 20 percent between 2000 and 2003, outpaced only by the increase in children on drugs to treat stomach disorders, which swelled by nearly 28 percent. Spending on drugs used to treat ADHD soared by 183 percent for children overall and by 369 percent for children under 5. About 5 percent of kids in the survey took one or more behavioral drugs.

Brain researcher Torkel Klingberg, M.D., Ph.D., uses software to strengthen the working memory of kids with ADHD.

Klingberg, M.D., Ph.D., and his colleagues at the Karolinska Institute in Stockholm installed a software program on the children's home computers that was designed to strengthen working memory. For 30 minutes a day, five days a week, the children (ages 7 to 12) completed various exercises on the computer, such as remembering the position of objects and recalling letters or digits. For one group of kids, the exercises got progressively harder over the five-week study; for a second group, the level of difficulty remained low. The results were then uploaded to a mainframe computer, and an expert analyzed them.

When the children were tested immediately after the experiment, those in the first group showed significant improvements in their working memory in comparison to those in the second group. Ninety percent of the improvements remained three months after the program ended, and parents and teachers also reported significant improvements in tasks requiring working memory, as well as less inattention.

Dr. Klingberg and his colleagues presented their findings at the American Association for Child and Adolescent Psychiatry meeting in October 2003.

Availability. The program used in the study, called RoboMemo, is manufactured and distributed by the Swedish company Cogmed Cognitive Medical Systems. The company began distributing its product in Sweden in late 2003 and hoped to begin worldwide distribution in late 2004.

TOP Trends

PAINTBALL EYE INJURIES ON THE RISE

If your kids are into the trendy war game of paintball, which involves shooting paint at the opposing team, you'd better make sure they wear goggles as well as old clothing when they play. A report in the January 2004 issue of *Pediatrics* found that eye injuries from paintball have been increasing among U.S. children in recent years.

Researchers analyzed previously unpublished data from the U.S. Consumer Product Safety Commission and found that the number of paintball eye injuries treated in emergency departments had skyrocketed from an estimated 545 in 1998 to more than 1,200 in 2000, an increase of more than 45 percent. At least 40 percent of those injuries occurred in children under 15, mostly boys.

RESEARCH ROUNDUP

A Clear Picture of ADHD

For more than a decade, researchers have known that attention deficit hyperactivity disorder (ADHD) is a physical disorder of the brain. Now we've gotten our best-ever look at that disorder. In November 2003, scientists from the University of California, Los Angeles, published images from MRI scans of the brains of children with ADHD. While earlier studies had suggested that the brains of kids with ADHD differ from those of other children, the images were never clear enough to show exactly where the differences lay. The new images, published in the British medical journal *Lancet*, clearly showed that the areas of the brain associated with attention and impulse control are smaller in children with the disorder. The pictures' clarity was due to sophisticated computer processing of raw MRI data, and it should be valuable in helping researchers develop more targeted medications and behavioral treatments for ADHD.

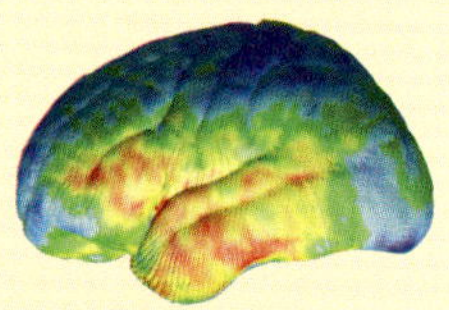

The red, yellow, and, to a lesser extent, green areas of the brain are smaller in kids with ADHD.

Tube and consequences: The torrent of quickly changing images and sounds provided by television may train young brains to expect the same stimulation in real life, thus shortening toddlers' attention spans.

ADHD

TV to Blame for ADHD Epidemic?

Many a parent has wondered how previous generations managed to raise children without television for entertainment. But for all its ability to keep kids quiet and, yes, sometimes educate them, television is also gaining a reputation that's nearly as bad as that of cigarette smoking, with research finding that it contributes to weight problems and aggression. Now, a groundbreaking study suggests that plopping your toddler in front of the tube may predispose him to attention deficit in the future.

What the study found. Researchers from the University of Washington in Seattle compared the amount of TV that 1- and 3-year-olds watched with their rate of attention problems at age 7. They discovered that every hour of television the toddlers watched daily increased their risk of later attention problems by 10 percent. (Attention problems were assessed using a standard questionnaire that probes whether a child has difficulty concentrating, is easily confused, is impulsive, has trouble with obsessions, and/or is restless.) The findings lend additional weight to the American Academy of Pediatrics' recommendation that children under 2 not watch television at all.

On average, the toddlers in the study watched 2.2 hours a day at age 1 and 3.6 hours at age 3. Only a third of the 1-year-olds watched no TV, and just

RESEARCH ROUNDUP

Melatonin Summons the Sandman

Kids with ADHD often have trouble falling asleep, either because of the disorder or as a side effect of the medication they take to manage it. Now, Canadian research suggests that megadoses of the supplement melatonin—a synthetic version of the hormone that guides human sleep patterns—can help.

Researchers gave nine school-age children 6 milligrams of melatonin for one week and a placebo (dummy pill) for one week. Neither the parents nor the kids knew which pills the children were taking. Sleep logs kept by the parents revealed that when the kids got melatonin, they fell asleep in an average of 51 minutes, versus 88 minutes when they got the placebos.

For adults, a usual dose of melatonin is tiny, with some studies finding that just 0.3 milligram is all that's needed. But study researchers say there's no harm in children taking larger doses. "Melatonin is well tolerated, and there are no specific contraindications," says the principal researcher, Margaret Weiss, M.D., Ph.D., director of the ADHD clinic at Children's and Women's Health Centre in Vancouver, British Columbia. "It is a much safer alternative than tranquilizers, hypnotics, neuroleptics, antihistamines, and drugs like clonidine," she says. Those drugs are often prescribed to help kids with ADHD fall asleep.

Children don't seem to build up a tolerance to melatonin, she says, so it doesn't lose its effectiveness over time. The researchers are now conducting a larger trial to confirm their results.

7 percent of the 3-year-olds went without daily tube time.

"I was shocked to incredulity by the amount of television these very young children are watching," says study author Dimitri Christakis, M.D. Since children that young are awake only about 12 hours a day, the data means that they're spending 20 to 30 percent of their waking hours watching TV, he notes.

Reshaping the brain. Dr. Christakis and his colleagues suspect that early and intense TV watching molds children's brains in a way that later affects their ability to pay attention. Studies in newborn rats have shown that high levels of visual stimulation change the architecture of their brains.

Television, with its rapid scene changes, quickly passing images, and stimulating sounds and colors, may condition the brain to expect that high level of stimulation later in life. Obviously, real life moves at a much slower pace.

While researchers didn't have information on whether the children in their study were diagnosed with ADHD, the diagnosis isn't what's important, says Dr. Christakis. What matters is a child's attention span. "We know that children who pay attention better do better in school. And those who do well early in school are more likely to do better later in school, and that's an important predictor of success in life."

Since publishing his study, Dr. Christakis (who has young children of his own) has heard from numerous parents who say they rely on television to entertain their toddlers so they can get things done, such as cooking dinner. Dr. Christakis has a ready answer: "TV has only been around about 50 years, but dinner has been around forever. Obviously, there are other ways to get dinner on the table when you have young children." Although he agrees that plopping your kid in front of the tube is convenient, "not everything that is convenient is necessarily good." ■

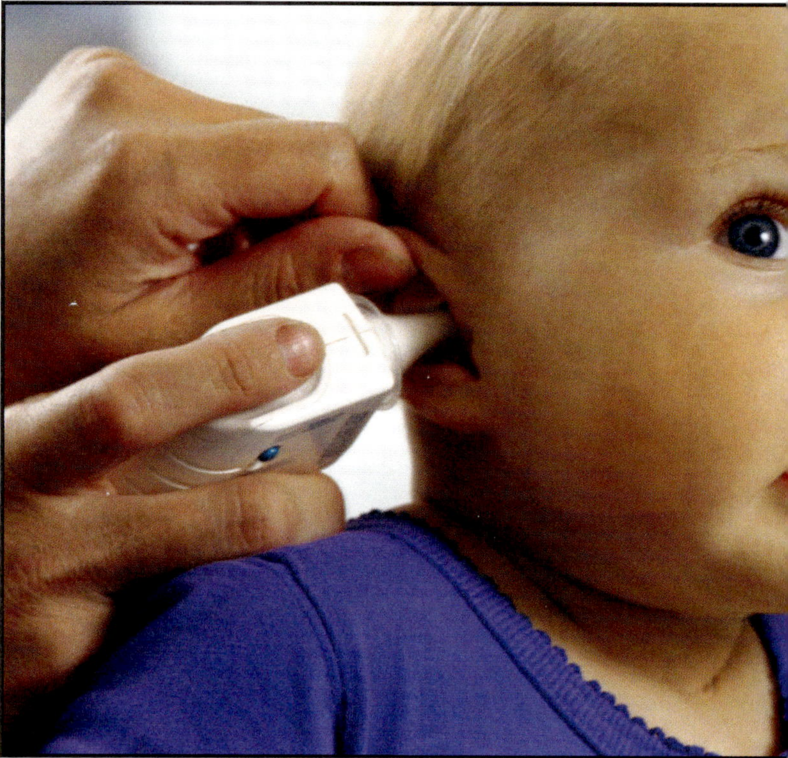

Allergies and Asthma

An Upside to Fevers

The next time your baby spikes a fever, don't panic. It could mean she'll be less likely to develop allergies when she's older. That's what researchers at the Henry Ford Health System in Detroit found when they studied the medical records of 835 children from birth through age 1, then followed the children until they turned 7.

Earlier research had suggested that kids who had illnesses such as measles, tuberculosis, and hepatitis A were less likely to develop allergies. In this study, researchers looked at more common infections, such as upper respiratory tract infections. "And, lo and behold, it appeared that having a fever in the first year was protective," says researcher L. Keoki Williams, M.D., a clinical epidemiologist at Henry Ford.

The fever itself seemed to be the deciding factor, with fever-inducing infections involving the eyes, ears, nose, or throat associated with a lower risk of allergies than similar infections that didn't result in fever, says Dr. Williams. It didn't matter how high the fever was: The effect was the same for temperatures between 100.4° and 101°F, the cutoff used in the study.

The number of fevers did matter, however. Among children who were fever-free during their first year, half

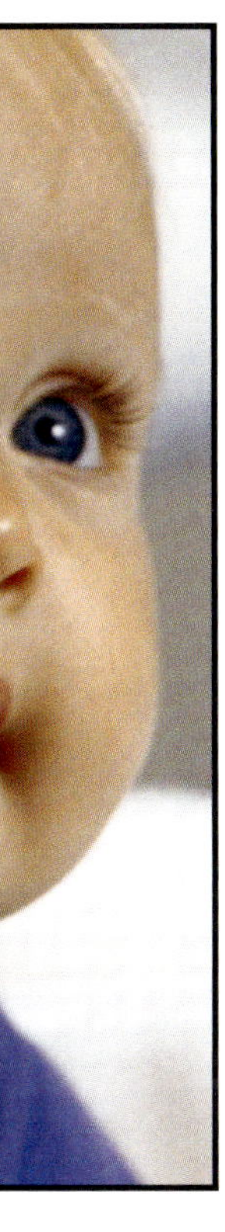

Friendly fire: In the first year of life, fevers caused by infection in the eyes, ears, nose, or throat may train the immune system to tell the difference between germs and harmless intruders such as dust and pollen.

were allergic to one or more irritants by age 7. Among those who had one fever, 46.7 percent were allergy-prone, but only one-third of the youngsters who had two or more fevers in infancy showed allergic sensitivity by age 7.

Stimulating the immune system. The findings lend additional credibility to the so-called hygiene hypothesis. This popular theory suggests that because people in Western industrialized countries are exposed to fewer germs than nature intended, their immune systems become overly sensitive—to the point where they react to harmless "invaders" such as dust and pollen.

"We think there are important decisions going on in the first year of life at the level of the T cell," says Dr. Williams. T cells act as ringleaders for the immune system, telling other immune cells how and when to react to a threat. "If you don't have exposure to early infections, it may be more likely that T cells decide to respond to certain environmental challenges in an allergic way," he explains. Infections significant enough to cause fevers probably stimulate the immune system enough to affect T cell development, he says.

The study's findings may eventually help researchers find a way to immunize children against allergies by manipulating their immune systems early on, says Dr. Williams. In the meantime, he cautions, "I don't suggest you go out and expose your baby to other sick children." ■

RESEARCH ROUNDUP

Are You Smearing Your Baby with Allergens?

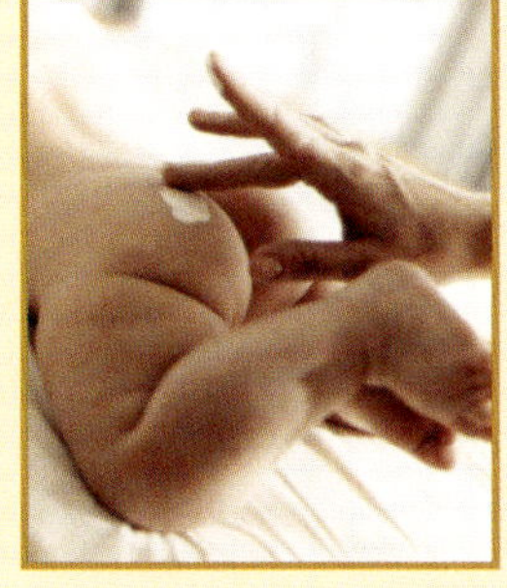

Before you rub baby lotion on your infant, read this. A study presented at the 2004 annual conference of the American Academy of Allergy, Asthma, and Immunology found that pediatric skin care products often contain traces of common allergenic foods.

Researchers at Children's Hospital in Chicago examined 293 pediatric skin care products and found that 26 percent contained such common allergenic foods as cow's milk, soy, wheat, hydrolyzed soy, and tree nuts, and 46 percent contained other foods. Lotions, creams, and baby oils were most likely to contain the foods. The researchers didn't show that these products cause allergies or allergic reactions, but earlier research linked peanut oil found in baby lotions to peanut allergies.

Let Johnny Play

Asthma is no excuse to let your kid turn into a couch potato. Yet researchers at Johns Hopkins Children's Center in Baltimore found that one in five children with asthma don't get enough exercise, even though running and swimming, among other activities, can actually help control the disease.

Researchers interviewed the parents of 137 children ages 6 to 12 with asthma about their children's activity levels and compared them with those of 106 children without asthma. Not surprisingly, they found that the healthy kids were more active overall, spending an average of 146 minutes a day in physical activity, compared with 116 minutes for the children with asthma.

Lack of somewhere to exercise wasn't part of the problem—most families lived within walking distance of a park, playground, or recreation center—but some of the parents were. One-fourth of the parents were afraid their youngsters would get sick if they exercised. The researchers noted that warmup exercises and, if necessary, a change in medication should take care of any exercise-related asthma.

A Little Pressure Prevents Ear Infections

Your child has yet another ear infection. You've been through several rounds of antibiotics, and now your pediatrician is suggesting surgery to insert ear tubes. You're reluctant, but what else can you do?

There may be benefit in an alternative therapy called osteopathic manipulative treatment (OMT), which involves gentle stretching and pressure to move the muscles and joints. During a six-month study of 57 children with frequent ear infections, the ones who received OMT in addition to routine care had fewer ear infections and surgical procedures. Researchers at Oklahoma State University in Tulsa, who published their results in September 2003, say OMT helps partly by relieving compression of the bones surrounding the ear's Eustachian tube, allowing it to drain more freely.

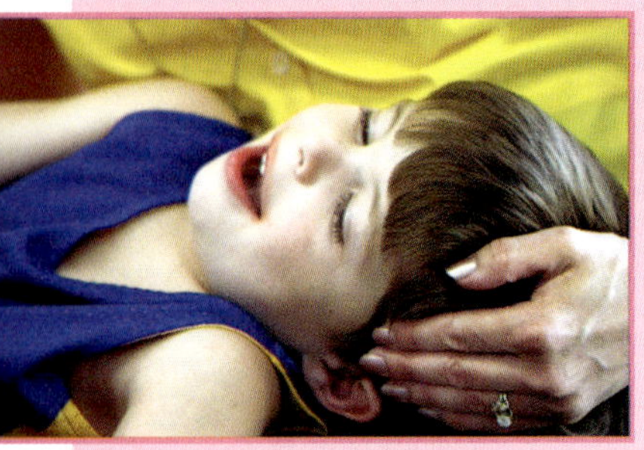

Ear Infections

New Guidelines: Keep the Lid on the Pink Stuff

Your 2-year-old wakes in the night crying, rubbing his ear, and running a fever. The next day, you tote him to the pediatrician, along with your own diagnosis of an ear infection, anticipating the usual prescription for an antibiotic.

Hold on. New guidelines issued in March 2004 by the American Academy of Pediatrics (AAP) and the American Academy of Family Physicians set new standards for just which kids should get antibiotics—and the results may surprise you.

Cutting down on antibiotics. "These are wonderful, wonderful guidelines because they increase the options for parents and doctors," says Ted Ganiats, M.D., professor of family and preventive medicine at the University of California, San Diego, who co-chaired the guideline committee. The recommendations are built on European studies showing that antibiotics benefit only about one in eight kids with ear infections—"nowhere near as many as parents think," Dr, Ganiats says.

The goal is to cut down on antibiotic prescriptions in the United States, thereby slowing the rising rate of antibiotic-resistant bacteria, particularly those that cause ear infections. Currently, more than 5 million cases of acute otitis media (AOM) occur each year in U.S. children, resulting in more than 10 million antibiotic prescriptions annually. In fact, half of all antibiotics prescribed for preschoolers in the United

States are prescribed for ear infections. Following the new guidelines, notes the AAP, could cut the annual number of prescriptions by 3 million.

What the guidelines say. The recommendations direct doctors to focus on relieving pain from ear infections (something even antibiotics don't do), with acetaminophen or ibuprofen in the first 24 hours, then giving parents of most children the option of fighting the infection without drugs for two or three days. Antibiotics would be prescribed only if the child didn't improve in that time. The guidelines also remind doctors to differentiate between traditional ear infections and something called otitis media with effusion, a fancy way of describing fluid in the middle ear. Antibiotics are useless when it comes to this kind of otitis media, and the condition usually improves on its own.

The academies recommend antibiotics for babies 6 months and younger with certain or suspected AOM, children 6 months to 2 years with certain or suspected AOM and severe symptoms, and kids who have underlying health conditions that could make AOM worse, such as cleft palate, Down's syndrome, immune system disorders, cochlear implants, and others. ■

RESEARCH ROUNDUP

Drop the Drops for Ear Infections

If your doctor hands you a prescription for antibiotic eardrops when your baby has an ear infection, you may want to think twice before filling it. A study presented at a meeting of ear, nose, and throat doctors in January 2004 found that the commonly used antibiotic drops ofloxacin (Floxin) and ciprofloxacin (Cipro) can lead to an increase in drug-resistant bacteria and fungi in the ear.

Two doctors at Temple University School of Medicine in Philadelphia found a link between eardrops and fungus in children who had undergone ear tube surgery, prompting them to examine samples from children's ears taken before and after they received eardrops. They found a significant increase in drug-resistant bacteria and fungi in children who used the drops. (Antibiotics kill off all bacteria—even beneficial ones—leaving a disrupted chemical environment that allows fungi to grow.) Their advice: In young children and for minor infections, avoid antibiotic eardrops. In older children, use the drops with care, along with ear suctioning to remove excess fluid.

General Health

New Reasons to Breastfeed

The idea that breastfeeding is best is not new, but the evidence continues to accumulate. Now it appears that infants who are nursed instead of bottle-fed are less likely to be overweight later in life. They may even be less apt to develop heart disease or diabetes.

A heart-smart approach. In a groundbreaking study published in the British medical journal *Lancet* in May 2004, researchers from the Institute of Child Health in London looked at more than 200 teenagers whom they had studied as babies. The babies had been randomly assigned to receive either breast milk or formula.

Compared with teens who were bottle-fed as babies, those who were breastfed had significantly lower levels of LDL, or "bad" cholesterol, as well as lower levels of C-reactive protein, a marker of inflammation in the body that's now thought to play a major role in heart disease and other serious illnesses, including diabetes and cancer. The differences were so great that they translated into a 25 percent reduction in the risk of heart disease.

Researchers suspect the reason for the differences is that the bottle-fed children grew faster than the breastfed babies, spurred on by the nutrient-rich formula. This in turn resulted in the permanent metabolic changes the researchers noticed in the teens, including increased insulin resistance and changes in the cells lining their blood vessels, both of which are risk factors for early cardiovascular disease.

Breastfed babies are skinnier. These findings fit like a puzzle piece with another recent study that found that the longer women breastfed, the less likely they were to have overweight children. That study, published in the February 2004 issue of *Pediatrics,* is one of the largest ever conducted on the link between breastfeeding and weight later in life.

Researchers found that 4-year-old children who were never breastfed or were breastfed for less than a month were much more likely to be overweight than those who were nursed longer. The protective effect of nursing seems to kick in at 3 months and increase from there. The longer the children were breastfed, the less likely they were to be overweight.

Researchers think that breastfeeding reduces the risk of weight problems because breastfed babies learn to self-regulate the amount they eat. For example, they fall asleep or turn their heads when they're finished, as opposed to bottle-fed babies, who continue to have nipples stuck in their mouths. Most major medical societies recommend that women breastfeed their babies for at least a year.

Kids Gotta Go When Kids Gotta Go

If your 6-year-old suddenly starts wetting his pants in first grade, don't blame it on stress or changes in routine. Instead, ask his teacher about her bathroom policy. A University of Iowa survey of 1,000 elementary school teachers found that 80 percent set specific times for bathroom breaks, a policy that contributes to incontinence and can lead to bladder and kidney infections.

Between 5 and 15 percent of school-age children have daytime incontinence, says the study's lead author, Christopher S. Cooper, M.D., associate professor of urology at the university. According to Dr. Cooper, kids in kindergarten and first and second grade are simply not old enough to hold their urine or bowel movements until a set time.

Resisting the urge can result in accidents (which children in one study named as the third most stressful thing that could happen to them, after the death of a parent or going blind) or urinary problems. Kids who learn to "hold it in" continually tighten the muscles that prevent leakage of urine or feces. "They can become very good at this," says Dr. Cooper, "but then they have trouble learning to relax the muscles when they can go to the bathroom." This in turn leads to incomplete emptying of the bladder, which can contribute to infections.

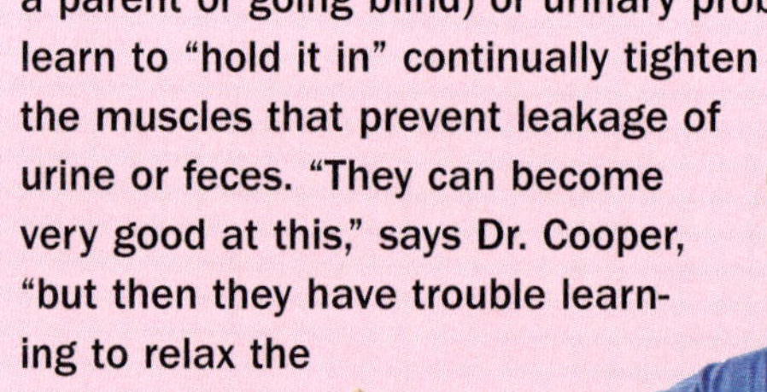

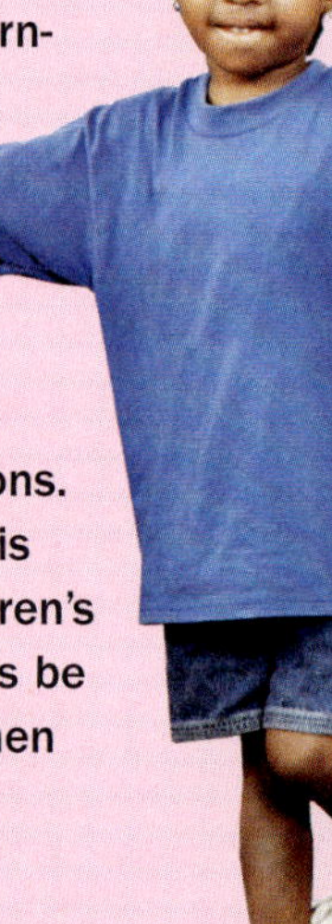

The answer, says Dr. Cooper, is for parents to talk to their children's teachers and ask that their kids be allowed to go the bathroom when they need to.

General Health

Sports Keep the Doctor Away

The more they dribble, the less they sniffle. Kids who participate in active sports apparently have stronger immune systems and are less likely to come down with colds or flu.

There's yet another reason to make sure your kids get some exercise instead of sitting in front of the tube: Not only does exercise keep off excess pounds and strengthen muscles and bones, it also fends off colds and flu. At least that's what Canadian researchers found when they looked at the correlation between playing sports and staying healthy.

In the study, the more kids participated in high-energy activities such as soccer and basketball—anything that significantly increased their heart rates—the less likely they were to get sick enough to miss school.

The researchers, from Brock University in Ontario, knew from earlier studies on adults that moderate exercise could strengthen the immune system, says lead researcher Panagiota Klentrou, Ph.D., associate professor in the department of physical education and kinesiology. But no one had ever examined the effects of exercise on children's immunity. "They are the ones most likely to suffer from viral infections throughout the year, so it was logical to pursue this question," says Dr. Klentrou.

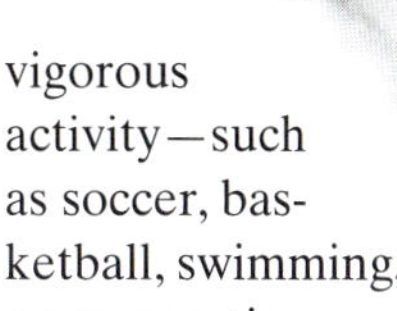

It turned out that 8 hours or more a week of vigorous activity—such as soccer, basketball, swimming, or gymnastics—reduced sick days among the children. The researchers also discovered that kids who had more than 25 percent body fat had far more sick days than thinner children. ■

RESEARCH ROUNDUP

Stopping Nosebleeds Faster

Have you ever tried to stem bleeding from a 7-year-old's nose and wondered how such a tiny appendage could possibly spout all that blood? The next time it happens, you'll have a solution at your disposal that doctors in emergency rooms have been using for more than 40 years.

The secret weapon? Nasal plugs impregnated with micro-dispersed oxidized cellulose, or m-doc, derived from cotton. The tiny fibers (each nine times thinner than a human hair) act as a "scaffold" upon which the blood can clot. The plugs also form a protective gel-like covering over the wound, but they won't stick to the wall of the nose or cause further bleeding when removed. Over-the-counter plugs containing m-doc are now available under the brand name Seal-On, which received FDA approval in 2002 and hit American store shelves in the spring of 2004. (Seal-On has been available in Europe since 2003.) The product is also available in a spray and an adhesive bandage.

Fast Food Nation

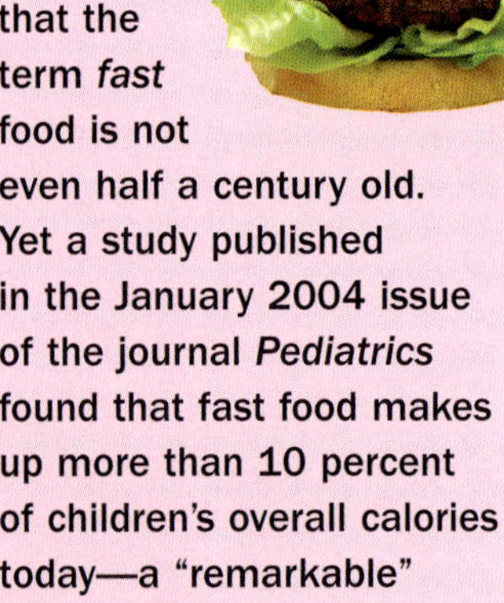

It's hard to believe that the term *fast* food is not even half a century old. Yet a study published in the January 2004 issue of the journal *Pediatrics* found that fast food makes up more than 10 percent of children's overall calories today—a "remarkable" fivefold increase since the late 1970s, according to the study.

Researchers studied the dietary patterns of 6,212 American children and adolescents, ages 4 to 19, and found that on any given day, one-third of the kids ate food from a fast-food restaurant. Their recommendations? Get fast food out of schools, restrict its marketing on TV shows aimed at kids, and nix the free toys and games that are a part of "kids' meals." Those recommendations have some pretty heavy backing, since the American Academy of Pediatrics is already on record as saying that directly advertising anything—including fast food—to young children is inherently unethical.

Obesity

Early Dieting Doomed to Fail

If your kindergarten-age daughter is looking a little pudgy, and you're thinking about putting her on a diet, think again. A study published in the Journal of the American Dietetic Association found that girls who are at risk of being overweight at age 5 and begin dieting often end up putting on extra weight by the time they're 9.

Diets don't work. University of Pennsylvania researchers followed 153 five-year-old girls for four years, evaluating their weight, attitudes about their weight, eating patterns, and satisfaction with their bodies.

The researchers identified 32 girls who had begun to become overweight at age 5. By age 7, those girls were eating significantly more than girls who weighed less, munching snacks even when they weren't hungry. They were also more dissatisfied with their bodies, more concerned about their weight, and more likely to diet. These patterns continued through age 9.

So why the weight gain? The researchers theorize that the girls' dieting backfired in much the same way it does for adults—namely, depriving yourself of the food you want results in binge eating and encourages you to eat whenever food is available, whether you're hungry or not.

The study's message is clear, says Matt Longjohn, M.D., executive director of the Consortium to Lower Obesity in Chicago Children. "Diet is a four-letter word. You have to make lifestyle changes," he says. "If a child is overweight, I'm not saying look the other way, but focus more on creating positive opportunities in her daily life for physical activity rather than focusing on diet and weight."

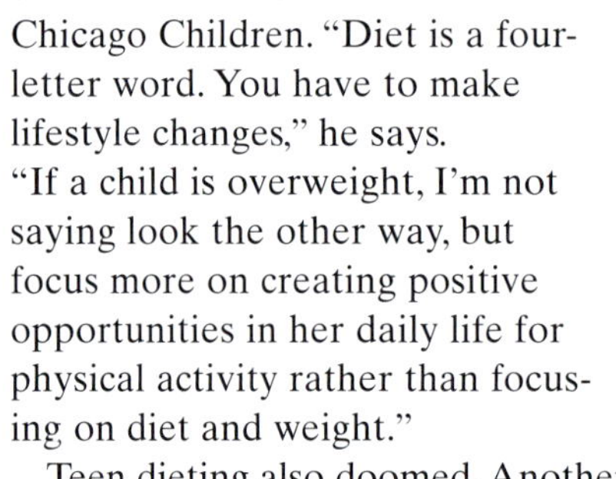

Teen dieting also doomed. Another recent study, this one from Harvard Medical School, found that dieting doesn't work for teenagers, either. After following more than 15,000 boys and girls between the ages of 9 and 14 for three years, the researchers found that the kids who dieted gained more weight on average—about 2 pounds more a year—than those who weren't dieting, possibly because the dieting teens were more likely to binge. ■

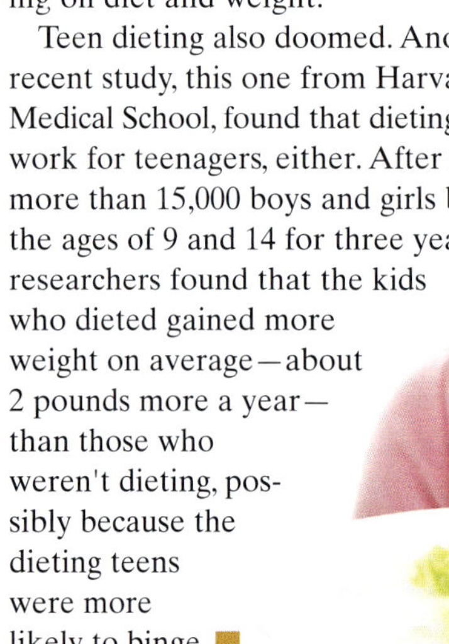

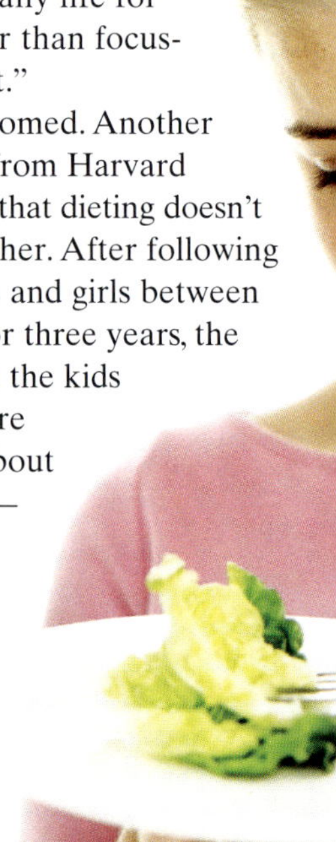

Obesity

Weight-Loss Drug Approved for Teens

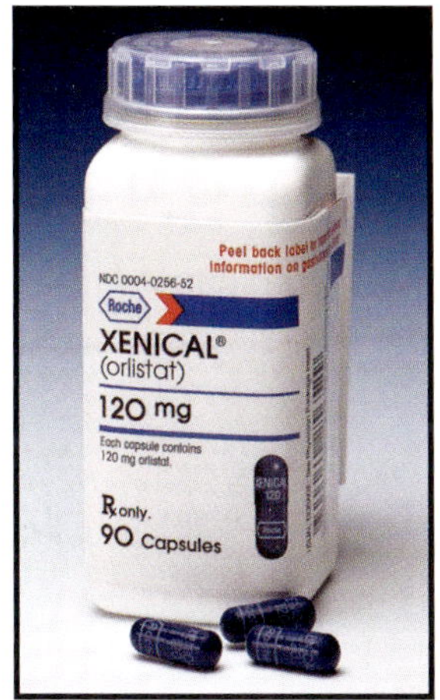

Xenical prevents some of the fat in food from being absorbed into the body.

Like their adult counterparts, seriously overweight teenagers can now turn to a weight-loss drug to help them shed health-threatening pounds. In December 2003, the FDA approved orlistat (Xenical) for kids between ages 12 and 16.

The approval comes amid a growing obesity epidemic among U.S. children. The problem is particularly worrisome for adolescents because studies show that overweight teens are more likely to become overweight adults. Between 1994 and 2000, the percentage of overweight adolescents in the United States increased from 5 percent to 11 percent. Today, about 30 percent of U.S. teenagers are overweight, and 15 percent of those teens are obese.

How it works. Xenical works by blocking the enzyme lipase, which breaks down the fat we eat so the body can absorb it. When this enzyme is blocked, about 30 percent of the fat in food is never absorbed and exits the body via feces.

Xenical doesn't give teens carte blanche to pig out on pizza and Häagen-Dazs, however. People taking the drug still have to follow a low-fat diet and exercise regularly, says Marc S. Jacobson, M.D., director of the Center for Atherosclerosis Prevention at Schneider Children's Hospital of North Shore–Long Island Jewish Health System in New York. Dr. Jacobson directed one of the clinical trials on the drug in adolescents.

"It's not a magic pill, and it doesn't replace healthy habits," he says. Teens taking the drug should also take a daily multivitamin supplement, since Xenical can reduce absorption of fat-soluble vitamins such as vitamins E and A.

Who should take it. Xenical is not for the slightly overweight teenager who wants to lose a few pounds before the prom. It's for the teen whose weight problem is so serious that it affects her health. Specifically, that means someone with a body mass index (a measurement that takes into account height and weight) of more than 30, or more than 27 if the teenager also has type 2 diabetes, high blood pressure, or abnormal cholesterol levels.

Xenical has potential side effects, including increased bowel movements and cramps, but none of the 16 teenagers who used it in Dr. Jacobson's study dropped out because of side effects, and all lost weight. "Some of the kids who really lost significant amounts of weight had dramatic changes in their social life and their ability to play sports and go out with other kids," he says. "It was a great effect."

Availability. Xenical is available in the United States with a doctor's prescription, but as of summer 2004, it had not yet been approved for use in adolescents in Europe. ■

They don't call them small fry for nothing. Young children are eating fatty foods at an alarming rate, to the exclusion of fruits and vegetables.

Obesity

Babies' Diets "Shocking"

When you think of finger foods for toddlers, you might picture Cheerios, cut-up apples and bananas, and little bits of meat. Actually, an image of French fries, pizza, hot dogs, and other unhealthy fare would be more accurate, according to a new national survey. The survey evaluated the eating habits of 3,000 randomly selected children between the ages of 4 months and 2 years and found that little kids are eating the same kinds of bad-for-you food as their parents.

The study, published in the January 2004 issue of the *Journal of the American Dietetic Association*, found that a third of children younger than 2 ate no fruits or vegetables on any given day. Of those who did eat a vegetable, those 15 months and older were most likely to eat French fries.

Overall, the researchers found, the toddlers were also eating far more calories than they needed at their age, setting them up for weight problems later on. The results were "shocking but not surprising," says Kathleen Reidy, Dr.P.H. (doctor of public health), director of nutrition sciences for baby food maker Gerber, which sponsored the study.

"The not-surprising part is that American babies are transitioning onto the American diet, but the shocking part is that we are seeing problematic eating habits we associated with older children—few fruits and vegetables, too many sweetened drinks, too much fat—in children as young as 9 months."

Most worrisome is the fact that the foundation of a child's diet is set in the first two years, says Dr. Reidy. Studies show that what a child likes and eats at age 2 is what he will like and eat at age 8. "The issue we saw screaming out at us was that we're not developing these healthy eating habits early," she says.

Behavior Problems Predict Weight Problems

A University of Michigan study found that children who are antisocial, anxious, dependent, depressed, headstrong, hyperactive, or withdrawn have a much greater likelihood of becoming obese. The study, published in the November 2003 issue of the journal *Pediatrics*, evaluated questionnaires completed by parents of 755 children ages 8 to 11. The researchers theorize that children with such problems are less likely to play outside or on teams, getting less exercise and spending more time in sedentary activities, such as watching television. These children may also use food to make themselves feel better.

Obesity

The Wrong Breakfast May Make Junior Fat

If your child's typical breakfast is a bowl of sugar masquerading as cereal or a couple of pieces of toasted white bread smeared with jelly, it may be contributing to overeating later in the day and, potentially, to weight gain. That's the conclusion of a British study published in the November 2003 issue of the journal *Pediatrics*.

What do white bread and most sugary cereals have in common? They have a high glycemic index (GI), a measurement of how much a food increases blood sugar within 2 to 3 hours after eating it. High-GI foods include refined grains, such as cornflakes, rice puffs, and white bread, and simple sugars, such as sugary jams. Because they are digested and absorbed into the bloodstream quickly, these foods send blood sugar skyrocketing. In response, the body mass-produces the hormone insulin, which escorts blood sugar out of the bloodstream and into cells. The result is extreme: Blood sugar levels plummet, leaving you hungry again in no time—or so the thinking goes.

The popular theory holds that, on the other hand, eating low-GI foods (such as whole grain breads and cereals) helps keep appetite in check, facilitating weight loss. Several studies in recent years have supported this notion, but few of them involved kids. This study, conducted at Oxford Brookes University in Great Britain, was designed to test the effect of high- and low-GI foods in children.

"Test" breakfasts and lunch observations. In the study, a group of 37 children (some overweight, some not) was given one of three breakfasts for three consecutive days: a low-GI breakfast, a low-GI breakfast with added sugar, and a high-GI breakfast. All of the breakfasts included fruit juice, cereal, and milk, with or without bread and margarine, and all contained exactly the same number of calories. All of the kids reported feeling full after eating the meals.

At lunchtime, researchers unobtrusively recorded how much food the kids consumed (lunch was buffet-style). Their conclusions? The breakfast a child ate had a "statistically significant" effect on how much she ate at lunch. Kids who ate high-GI breakfasts were more likely to eat more at lunchtime than children who ate either of the low-GI breakfasts.

"This is the first study to observe such an effect in a group of normal and overweight children, and it adds to the growing body of evidence that low-GI foods may have an important role in weight control and obesity management," wrote the study authors.

Kids who start the day with a low-fiber cereal eat more later in the day than those who dine on whole-grain cereal.

Osteoporosis

Getting a Jump on Osteoporosis

Who would have thought that jumping up and down for just a few minutes a day, interspersed with some skipping, could make a major difference to a kid's bones later in life? Yet that's exactly what researchers in British Columbia found after studying the effects of a two-year exercise program on prepubescent boys and girls.

Starting 9-year-old kids thinking about osteoporosis may seem like overkill, but it's important, says study author Kerry J. MacKelvie, Ph.D., a postdoctoral fellow in endocrinology at British Columbia Children's Hospital and the University of British Columbia in Vancouver. Today, one of every two women and one in eight men over 50 in the United States will have an osteoporosis-related fracture in his or her lifetime. Prevention has to start in childhood, when most bone mass and strength are laid down.

"In the last few years, people who work with kids and think about health started to realize that the lack of physical activity in children was behind a lot of the problems we see emerging in teens and adults," Dr. MacKelvie says.

The exercise program. The study involved 383 children at 14 schools. For the kids at half of the schools, it was business as usual. At the other schools, the children participated in 12-minute circuit training programs three times a week during two seven-month sessions (with summer break in between).The program included nine stations at which the kids did simple activities such as jumping up and down off a step or jumping over hoops set into the ground. The action of jumping puts weight on the femur (the large thighbone) and the hip, both common sites of future fractures.

The key was providing diversity of movement, says Dr. MacKelvie, since research shows that doing activities you're not already used to (such as running or walking) have a greater effect on bone.

The results. After two years, Dr. MacKelvie and her colleagues found that the children who completed the program gained about 4 percent more bone mass in the hip and lower spine than children who didn't follow the program. The boys had no significant change in the lower spine, possibly due in part to the different ways in which boys and girls jump and land, but their bone strength increased 7.5 percent more than that of the boys who didn't participate in the exercises.

"We consider these changes to be substantial," says Dr. MacKelvie. "If you looked up the drug studies for older women, you'd see that bisphosphonates and other therapies for osteoporosis can hope to raise bone mass by only about 1 to 2 percent per

RESEARCH ROUNDUP

Too Many Breaks? Get a Scan

If your child sees an orthopedist almost as often as he sees a pediatrician, you may want to ask for a bone scan. Researchers at the American Academy of Pediatrics national conference in November 2003 reported that when they scanned the bones of 16 children who had had two or more fractures from minor accidents, 11, or 67 percent, were found to have osteoporosis. The researchers recommended that children ages 6 to 13 who have two or more fractures due to "minimal trauma"—such as breaking a wrist while snowboarding—should have a DEXA bone scan, an x-ray that measures bone mineral density.

year. There's greater potential for exercise to prevent osteoporotic-related fractures."

The issue of bone strength is important, she says, since it's the combination of strength *and* bone mass that provides the ultimate protection from fracture. The results were published in the December 2003 issue of the journal *Pediatrics* and the April 2004 issue of the journal *Bone*.

What it means. The study is valuable primarily because it showed that short bursts of activity can make a significant difference in bone mass and strength, according to Dr. MacKelvie. Best of all, "You don't have to take children out of the classroom to do these activities," she says. ■

IN Brief

Ipecac Syrup Gets the Heave-Ho

Ipecac syrup, long used by parents to induce vomiting when a child swallowed something toxic, can actually do more harm than good. A growing body of evidence finds that not only is ipecac often ineffective at making kids vomit, it could also interfere with other poison-control remedies. The American Academy of Pediatrics has called on doctors to urge parents to toss the ipecac. Instead, if you have a poison emergency, call the national poison center at (800) 222-1222.

Fish Oil Linked to Allergy Prevention

An Australian study found that fish-oil supplements taken during pregnancy may help prevent allergies in children who have a high risk of developing them. Fish oil contains omega-3 fatty acids, which reduce inflammation. Researchers speculate that they may affect some part of the fetus's developing immune system, lowering the risk of future allergies.

Be Positive about Potty Training

If you're in the midst of potty-training misery with your toddler, think positive. That's the word from researchers at the University of Pennsylvania in Philadelphia, who found that parents who were told to praise their children and avoid negative terms (for example, "stinky diaper") during potty training had children who became toilet trained sooner than parents who received only basic instructions.

Antibiotics No Salve for Sore Throat

Instead of running to the pediatrician for antibiotics every time your child has a sore throat, try remedies such as hot drinks, soup, and throat lozenges. Chances are, antibiotics won't make much difference. A Dutch study found that even in children with strep throat, penicillin had no more effect on symptoms, school attendance, and recurrence of sore throat than a sugar pill.

IN THIS SECTION

IMAGINE DROPPING BY YOUR DOCTOR'S OFFICE AND PUFFING INTO A TUBE TO FIND OUT WHETHER YOU HAVE A SERIOUS ILLNESS, SUCH AS CANCER.

Or consider never having to have painful injections again, instead receiving medications through needles so small you can't feel them. Both of these developments were in the works in the past year and could become a reality in the near future.

Among the here-and-now developments: Experts are urging people to consume less salt and more potassium. The popular weight-loss supplement ephedra was banned because of the risks it posed, spurring manufacturers to promote new alternatives. And one researcher who tested 2 metric tons of salmon found the farm-raised variety to be loaded with enough contaminants to pose a real health risk.

Want to avoid a cold? Don't put too much faith in antibacterial soaps. Already have a cold? There's something more effective you can do than ask your doctor for antibiotics. Finally, forget the old drink-eight-glasses-of-water-a-day advice. It turns out that when it comes to staying properly hydrated, there's no need to hit a magic number; just use common sense.

Anxiety

Do-it-yourself Acupuncture for Anxiety

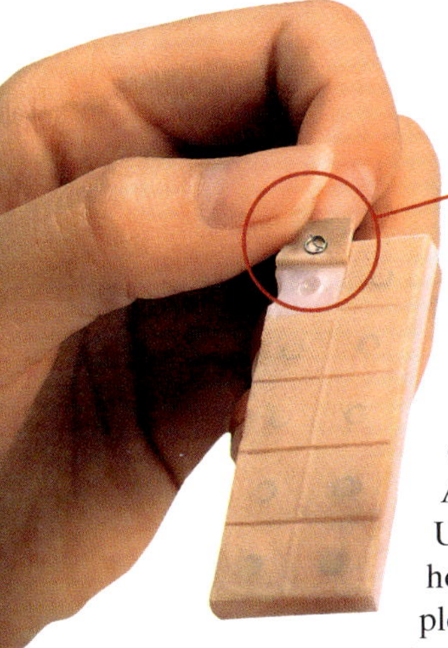

Watching as your child is wheeled into an operating room ranks near the top of life's stressful moments. An anesthesiologist at Yale University School of Medicine, however, has found that a simple acupuncture device can reduce parents' anxiety at such times.

Shu-Ming Wang, M.D., divided the mothers of children who were going to have surgery into two groups. In one group, she inserted tiny acupuncture needles called press needles into each mother's ear at a specific point that's known to produce relaxing effects. (A press needle is a short, fine needle attached to a wire loop covered with an adhesive bandage, which makes it look similar to a thumbtack.) In the other group, Dr. Wang inserted needles into spots that aren't known to produce a calming effect.

The mothers then spent 30 minutes with their children before the kids were anesthetized for surgery. When the women were surveyed about their anxiety levels, those who received the "real" acupuncture treatment were found to be significantly less upset than the moms in the other group. The children of the less anxious moms were also significantly less anxious as they went into the operating room.

According to Dr. Wang, who has taught this acupuncture technique to other doctors at seminars, most hospital clinicians who are familiar with acupuncture should be able to offer this type of anxiety-reducing treatment. And a press needle designed for self-care home use, called Pyonex, will be available in 2005. ■

TOP Trends

OBESITY A TAXING PROBLEM

The obesity epidemic is hitting us where it hurts: in our wallets. According to a report published in the January 2004 issue of the journal *Obesity Research*, if a special tax were created to pay for all the obesity-related illnesses covered by Medicare and Medicaid in the United States, it would cost each adult $175.

Medicare and Medicaid are the federally funded programs intended to provide health coverage for seniors and low-income residents, respectively. The obesity-related costs paid by Medicare each year range from $15 million in Wyoming to $1.7 billion in California. Annual costs to Medicaid range from $23 million in Wyoming to $3.5 billion in New York.

SMALL NEWS FROM THE GOLDEN ARCHES

After 2004, a word commonly associated with fast food will be heard less often at McDonald's. The chain announced it would phase out its "supersized" French fries and drinks, jumbo items that cost just a few cents more. Supersized drinks will remain only as promotional items.

The move came on the heels of a film called *Super Size Me*, which won an award at the 2004 Sundance Film Festival. The documentary, which takes a critical view of the fast-food chain, follows a young filmmaker as he consumes nothing but McDonald's food and drinks for 30 days, making sure to eat everything on the menu and regularly choosing supersized items. He documents his expanding waistline during the month, with a total gain of 25 pounds. In media reports, a spokesman for McDonald's denied that the changes at the restaurant had anything to do with the film. McDonald's also began marketing "Go Active" meals that include a salad, bottled water, and a pedometer.

EGGS-TREME MEASURES

Which came first: the chicken, or the egg? In the case of the new "designer" eggs now occupying grocery store shelves, the answer is definitely the chicken. Some of the eggs contain heart-healthy omega-3 fatty acids, typically found in fish oil and flaxseed. (The hens that lay these eggs are fed a diet rich in these ingredients). Some contain extra lutein, the yellow eye-protecting nutrient in egg yolks. (These hens feast on lutein-rich marigold extract.) And animal rights enthusiasts can buy "cage free" eggs, from chickens that were never kept in cages.

Diagnostic Tests

New Breath Test Will Diagnose Disease

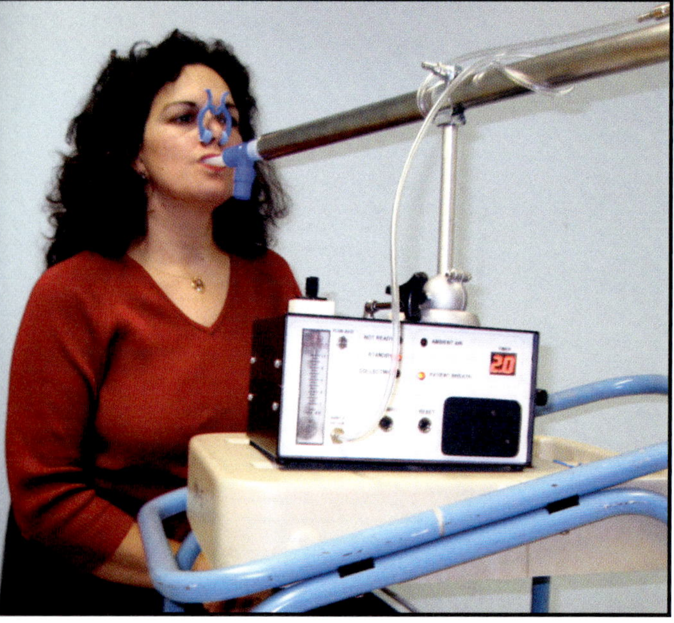

An ill wind? Patients exhale into a breath collection apparatus for 2 minutes in order to capture compounds that provide a "fingerprint" of diseases.

Finding out if you have cancer or another serious condition may soon be as easy as whistling or blowing out a candle.

Each breath you exhale carries chemical hints about processes going on in your body, and a new device can store your breath so it can be analyzed for subtle signs of disease. The device—the breath-collecting apparatus (BCA)—features a tube into which a person exhales for several minutes and a special trap that collects chemicals from the exhaled breath, says Michael Phillips, M.D., professor of clinical medicine at New York Medical College in Valhalla, who developed the BCA.

Analyzing breath to help track down a diagnosis isn't new. Doctors can currently test for lactose intolerance—a problem that keeps some people from properly digesting dairy foods—by measuring hydrogen in a person's breath. Police officers routinely "diagnose" excessive alcohol consumption with breath tests. But the new technology analyzes much tinier amounts of breath components than any other test has been able to do.

A new clue to disease. In the early 1970s, Dr. Phillips says, Nobel Prize winner Linus Pauling froze exhaled breath in a tube and discovered that the air contained traces of volatile organic compounds (VOCs), carbon-based chemicals evaporated in the air. Dr. Phillips has since measured many Americans' and Europeans' breath with his device and discovered that healthy people generally exhale the same 200 or so VOCs, in tiny concentrations. When people have diseases, however, they exhale some *different* VOCs. By comparing the breath of healthy people with that of people who are ill, he's been able to create three-dimensional "fingerprints" of various diseases.

Testing for cancer and diabetes. In early 2004, the FDA approved the device to test for organ rejection in people with recent heart transplants. Additional studies were evaluating its usefulness for detecting diabetes, breast cancer, and lung cancer.

Breath testing may also eliminate a pain that many people with diabetes face daily: needle sticks. Some people with diabetes need to prick themselves several times a day to get blood samples from which to check their blood sugar levels. Researcher Pietro Galessetti, M.D., Ph.D., and his colleagues at the University of California, Irvine, recently conducted tests on 10 people to see if they could use VOCs in the volunteers' breath to measure their blood sugar levels. The painless method appeared to work, and the researchers plan to test it on a larger number of people.

Before this method becomes useful on a large scale, patients will need access to breath-analyzing equipment that's small and cheap. Currently, Dr. Phillips's apparatus is relatively simple, but the technology used to examine the trapped breath is both expensive and cumbersome, so researchers must send breath samples to a central laboratory for analysis. Dr. Phillips's envisions a future when doctors will have their own equipment loaded with different disease fingerprints, providing a rapid diagnosis in the office. Patients will no longer have to endure blood draws or invasive diagnostic procedures to know what's going on in their bodies. "All they'll have to do is sit down and breathe for a couple of minutes," he says. ■

Farm-raised salmon tend to bring more to the table—in the form of contaminants such as dioxins, PCBs, and DDT.

Food Safety

Is Your Salmon Swimming in Contaminants?

"Eat plenty of fish" has been the edict from doctors and nutritionists for years, especially for people who want to stave off heart problems. However, the advice applies only if the fish isn't contaminated, says David Carpenter, M.D., director of the Institute for Health and the Environment at the University at Albany in New York. In an analysis of more than 2 metric tons of salmon, Dr. Carpenter and fellow researchers discovered that a lot of the fish—particularly the farm-raised variety—were loaded with enough contaminants to pose a health hazard.

Farm-raised vs. wild. The researchers purchased whole salmon and fillets from vendors in Europe and North America for testing and also analyzed samples of feed given to farm-raised salmon in Europe, North America, and South America. As reported in a January 2004 issue of the journal *Science*, the researchers found that levels of dioxins and PCBs in farm-raised salmon were more than 10 times higher than in wild salmon. Dioxins are formed by burning oil and coal, and they can persist in the environment for many years. PCBs are industrial chemicals. Concentrations of the pesticide DDT, long banned in the United States, were also higher in farm-raised salmon.

The differing levels of contaminants are probably due to the different diets of the fish. The researchers found contaminants in the food given to farmed salmon, which is rich in fish oil and fish meal. The food samples from Europe were more contaminated than those from North or South America. Accordingly, levels of contaminants were higher in European-farmed salmon than in farmed fish raised in North or South America.

SKIMP ON FISH, MOMMY

Pickles and ice cream started sounding even better to expectant mothers in December of 2003. That's when the FDA and the Environmental Protection Agency jointly issued an advisory urging pregnant and nursing women, as well as women considering becoming pregnant, to severely limit their fish intake.

Some types of seafood contain unacceptably high levels of mercury, which can damage a fetus or infant. The advisory warned that these women should avoid shark, swordfish, king mackerel, and tilefish. It's safe to consume up to 12 ounces a week of other types of store-bought fish–including canned tuna–although you should eat a variety of types. Canned light tuna tends to have less mercury than tuna steaks or canned albacore.

If you fish for your own dinner, consult your local health department about whether locally caught fish is safe to eat. If they can't offer any guidance, you can eat as much as 6 ounces a week, but avoid eating any other fish that week.

What's the risk? The contaminants detected are fat soluble, meaning that they're stored in the fat of the fish that are processed into food for farmed salmon. In turn, they are stored in the fat of salmon that eat the food and then in the fat of people who eat the fish.

That's a problem, Dr. Carpenter says. Some of these contaminants are known to cause cancer, and some can lower the IQs of babies born to mothers who have the toxins in their bodies. DDT can cause liver cancer and damage humans' nervous and reproductive systems. The chemical was banned in the United States in 1972, but it takes more than a decade to break down in the environment, and it's still used in other parts of the world.

In light of his findings, Dr. Carpenter suggests that only people who stand to gain from salmon should eat the farm-raised fish. Middle-aged people with heart disease who are at risk for arrhythmia (irregular heart rate) can benefit from the omega-3 fatty acids in the fish, which are shown to help reduce the risk of this problem.

On the other hand, says Dr. Carpenter, the risks of eating farm-raised fish outweigh the benefits for children and young adults, who are less likely to have heart problems and have more decades of life in which to develop cancer from the accumulated contaminants.

Shopping savvy. To find wild salmon, look for fish labeled "wild Alaskan salmon" or "wild Pacific salmon." Expect to pay about three times more for wild salmon fillets than for fillets of farm-raised salmon. Canned salmon, however, is almost entirely derived from wild fish, and it's inexpensive. You can also get omega-3 fatty acids from other sources, including walnuts, canola oil, and flaxseed oil.

The term "fresh Atlantic salmon" means it's farmed. If you want to eat farm-raised salmon, look for fish from Chile or the state of Washington. The research showed fish from these areas to be less contaminated.

Poultry Consumers Can Breathe Easier

The chicken you purchase at the supermarket may soon be safer. A product containing a mouthwash ingredient has won FDA approval as a method of reducing harmful germs on chickens during processing. When it's used in a mouthwash, the chemical—cetylpyridinium chloride—kills germs that cause bad breath and helps prevents plaque on teeth. Research shows that it also reduces campylobacter, salmonella, and E. coli bacteria when it's sprayed on poultry.

Most campylobacter infections occur after people touch raw poultry or eat raw or undercooked poultry meat. The bacterium causes diarrhea and abdominal pain but is generally not fatal. Salmonella and E. coli infections are also commonly linked to raw or undercooked meat, and both can be deadly.

According to the maker of the new chicken-cleansing product, called Cecure, more than half the poultry producers in the United States were in the process of adding it to their production facilities in early 2004. The company says the product that remains on the poultry is harmless to humans. People would have to eat more than 90,000 pounds of treated poultry each year to swallow the same amount of cetylpyridinium chloride that they would ingest by gargling with mouthwash every day for a year.

Heart Health

Ulcer Bug Is Also a Cholesterol Suspect

Helicobacter pylori, a bacterium that lives in the stomach, is best known for causing ulcers, but the sneaky germ may also play a role in unhealthy cholesterol levels, researchers from Austria and Germany have discovered. On the positive side, getting rid of the bug may be a quick and easy way to improve your cholesterol profile.

In a study published in a January 2004 issue of the *American Journal of Cardiology*, researchers looked at 87 people with ulcers who tested positive for *H. pylori* and took drugs, including two antibiotics, to eradicate the bacteria. The patients' cholesterol levels were tested before they began taking the drugs and again a year later.

Once the bacteria were eliminated, the participants' total cholesterol increased significantly—but the increase was mostly in their HDL, or "good" cholesterol, the kind that gobbles up "bad" cholesterol and helps prevent the formation of artery-clogging plaque. Their HDL levels increased by almost 25 percent.

It's unclear why *H. pylori* would affect cholesterol, says lead researcher Hubert Scharnagl, Ph.D., of the University of Graz Clinical Institute of Medical and Chemical Laboratory Diagnostics in Austria. One theory is that the bacteria trigger inflammation in the body that affects cholesterol balance. When the bacteria are eradicated, the inflammation subsides, and the ratio of good to bad cholesterol improves.

Although more studies are needed to establish the connection between *H. pylori* and cholesterol, people whose cholesterol tests show they have low HDL should consider being tested for the bacteria, Dr. Scharnagl says. ■

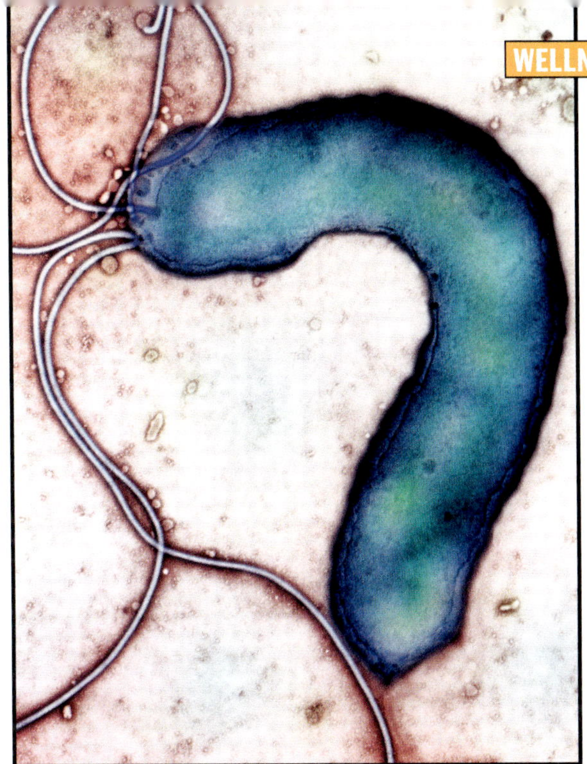

The curved (or sometimes spiral) *Helicobacter pylori* bacteri is involved in ulcer formation. It may throw your cholesterol levels a curve, too.

RESEARCH ROUNDUP

Hard Water May Be Soft on Your Heart

Hard water is a hassle when it leaves stains on your sink and tub, but the benefits it may offer to your heart could be a consolation.

A Finnish study found that increased water hardness—the concentration of minerals such as calcium and magnesium—was linked to reduced risk of heart attack. Rates of heart attack vary widely in Finland, which has relatively soft water. Researchers looked at data on nearly 19,000 men ranging in age from 35 to 74 and compared it with data on water hardness throughout the country. They found that for each increased unit of water hardness, risk of heart attack fell by 1 percent.

The magnesium in hard water may be responsible for the beneficial effect. Earlier research linked higher magnesium intake or higher blood levels of the mineral with reduced risk of high blood pressure and heart disease.

Heart Health

Chest Pain? Make the Right Call

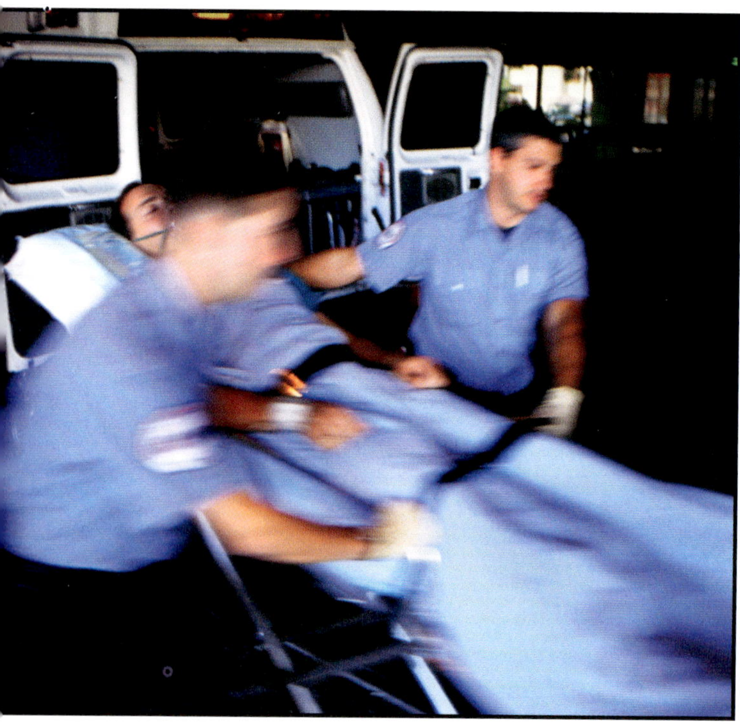

Think fast: You're having chest pain. Should you jump in the car or call 911? Heading to the hospital by car will probably get you through the emergency room door sooner, but you're likely to get faster medical treatment if you go by ambulance.

That's the finding of a study published in a January 2004 issue of the *American Heart Journal*, which examined data on patients with chest pain from 20 cities around the United States. People who went to the emergency room by private vehicle arrived an average of 4 minutes faster. Those who went by ambulance, though, received crucial medications to dissolve the blood clots causing their heart attacks 17 minutes sooner once they reached the hospital.

The authors say the faster treatment may be due to the ambulance crew's ability to relay information about the patient's condition to the hospital en route, so doctors can more quickly diagnose the problem and begin treatment.

RESEARCH ROUNDUP

Is Your Grandkid a Heartbreaker?

Being around your grandchildren gladdens your heart, right? Well, if you're a grandma who's caring for your grandchildren, even part-time, you could be putting your heart at risk.

A team of researchers from Harvard studied data on more than 54,000 middle-aged and senior women from the Nurses' Health Study, an ongoing study of female nurses that began in 1976. They found that grandmothers who cared for healthy grandchildren for as few as 9 hours a week had a 55 percent greater chance of developing heart disease than those who weren't caregivers. The study was published in the November 2003 issue of the *American Journal of Public Health.*

Although the researchers didn't explore exactly why caregivers would have a higher risk of heart disease, it's possible that more stress or less time to focus on maintaining their health could play a role in the results.

Living Happily–And Longer–Ever After

Men tend to derive more health benefits from being married than women do; that much researchers already knew. Now, a new study shows that women, too, are healthier when they're married—but only when they're happy in the relationship.

The 13-year study assessed the marital status and cardiovascular disease risk of 493 women. Researchers measured the women's physical risk factors, including blood pressure and glucose and cholesterol levels; their lifestyle risk factors, such as smoking and exercise; and their psychological risk factors, such as stress, depression, and anxiety.

Women who were highly satisfied with their relationships showed healthier measurements—for instance, lower cholesterol, less weight gain, and less depression—than women who were unhappy in their relationships or were single, widowed, or divorced, says Linda Gallo, Ph.D., the lead researcher at the University of California, San Diego.

Nutrition

Vitamin D Takes Center Stage

Chances are you know that you should be taking plenty of calcium for your bones. Many calcium supplements also contain vitamin D because the two work as a team to protect your skeleton, but now it turns out that vitamin D may be important in its own right in more ways than we knew.

Recent research shows that the "sunshine vitamin" may play a key role in preventing certain cancers as well as multiple sclerosis (MS). It also showed up in one study as an effective treatment for widespread musculoskeletal pain. Unfortunately, some researchers fear that too many of us have woefully low levels of the nutrient.

The body makes vitamin D when the skin is exposed to sunlight. People who live far from the equator, though, and those who rarely venture outdoors or always wear sunblock, are at risk for deficiencies. Most of us could use more vitamin D in the winter, and older people may need supplements because with age, the skin becomes less able to convert sunlight into vitamin D.

Protection from colon polyps. For four years, researchers coordinated through Dartmouth Medical School in New Hampshire followed people who'd had precancerous colon polyps removed. Half were given calcium supplements, and the other half got placebos (dummy pills). The vitamin D levels of 803 subjects were also assessed twice with blood tests.

The people who took calcium supplements were less likely to develop more polyps—provided they also had higher-than-average vitamin D levels. Vitamin D was also associated with a reduced risk of recurrent polyps, but only in the people who received the calcium supplements. The combination of calcium and vitamin D is also thought to help protect against cancers of the breast and prostate.

Multiple sclerosis prevention. Researchers have long known that people who live near the equator have lower rates of multiple sclerosis than those who live farther away. Vitamin D may be the reason, says Kassandra Munger, M.Sc., a Harvard researcher who led the first prospective study exploring the relationship between vitamin D and MS. This kind of study follows a group people without a disease to see who develops it and how they differ from people who don't.

The study evaluated data from nearly 200,000 women. Those who took at least 400 IU of supplemental vitamin D daily had 40 percent less chance of developing MS than those who didn't take it. The researchers' next step is to examine samples of blood from millions of individuals, which are stored in a military repository, to see if people with low levels of vitamin D in their blood are more likely to develop MS. In MS, the immune system attacks the protective insulating sheath around nerves, and vitamin D may protect against the disease by preventing that kind of assault.

The pain connection. A study published in the December 2003 issue of the journal *Mayo Clinic Proceedings* uncovered a surprising link between persistent pain and low levels of vitamin D. Greg Plotnikoff, M.D., noticed that many patients he saw at a University of Minnesota community health clinic suffered from unexplained pain despite having otherwise normal checkups. He remembered reading European studies that connected pain with vitamin D deficiency and decided it was worth testing for the deficiency in his patients.

Nearly all of the 150 patients whom Dr. Plotnikoff studied turned out to be low in vitamin D—including all of those under age 30. The people who were severely deficient required prescription-strength doses of the vitamin to restore normal levels.

Vitamin D deficiency is believed to lead to changes in the inner bone that cause it to become rubbery and press outward on the outer layer of bone, probably causing the aches and pains. If you have unexplained pain, ask your doctor for a blood test that measures vitamin D, Dr. Plotnikoff suggests.

How much is enough? The current Recommended Dietary Allowance (RDA) for vitamin D is 200 IU for adults under age 50, 400 IU for people ages 51 to 70, and 600 IU for people 70 and older. Some experts now believe that these recommended levels—set back in 1997—are too low. Meanwhile, most people don't even get the RDA.

Nutrition

Vitamin E: Better from a Box than from a Bottle

If you want your daily supplement of vitamin E to do the most good, taking it *in* your breakfast may work better than taking it *with* your breakfast. That's the finding of a small study that compared the vitamin's "bioavailability"—how well the body can use it—when it's consumed in pill form versus in a cereal with added vitamin E.

Three women and two men participated in the trial, conducted at the Linus Pauling Institute at Oregon State University in Corvallis. They first took vitamin E in a 400 IU capsule—typical for a vitamin E supplement—with a glass of fat-free milk. Later, they ate cereal containing 30 IU of the vitamin (the Daily Value) with fat-free milk. Next, they ate cereal containing 400 IU of the vitamin with fat-free milk. Finally, they consumed a 400 IU vitamin E capsule with cereal that had no vitamin E, along with fat-free milk. The vitamin E in the capsules and cereal was specially tagged with deuterium—an isotope of hydrogen—so the researchers could measure it in the subjects' bloodstreams. The cereal company General Mills sponsored the research.

The subjects' bodies were able to absorb the 400 IU in the cereal far more readily than the same amount in capsule form. Even eating the 30 IU cereal got more of the vitamin into the participants' bodies than taking the 400 IU capsule. The results were published in the January 2004 issue of the *American Journal of Clinical Nutrition.*

What it means. Vitamin E is an antioxidant that may help reduce the risk of heart disease. Previous studies have found fewer protective results from supplements than from vitamin-rich diets. Unfortunately, says Maret Traber, Ph.D., a researcher for the study, it's hard to get much vitamin E from foods, since those that contain it tend to be unusual (wheat-germ oil), be high in fat (almonds and olive and canola oils), or provide only small amounts (spinach and kale). Thus, eating a low-fat, vitamin-fortified cereal is a reasonable way to consume the vitamin, she says. ■

RESEARCH ROUNDUP

Snap, Crackle, and Drop Your Insulin

If you have insulin resistance—a condition that makes you more likely to develop diabetes—pouring a bowl of high-fiber cereals may be a smart way to start your day. A Canadian study compared the effects of high-fiber and regular cereals on the blood sugar and insulin levels of 77 men, 42 of whom had insulin resistance. In all of the men, the high-fiber cereal caused a smaller rise in blood sugar than the regular cereal, which wasn't surprising. But in the men who had insulin resistance, the high-fiber cereal caused less of a rise in insulin than the regular cereal—and this was not the case in the healthy men. This means that a high-fiber cereal might help people with insulin resistance manage their condition.

Nutrition

New Guidelines: Shake That Salt Habit

New nutritional guidelines suggest that most Americans should put the saltshaker under lock and key and go peel themselves a banana.

The Institute of Medicine, a private organization that advises the U.S. government on nutritional guidelines and other scientific matters, issued its report on salt and potassium in 2004. It recommended that young adults get no more than 1,500 milligrams of sodium each day. Adults between the ages of 50 and 70 should take in 1,300 milligrams daily, and people older than 70 need only 1,200 milligrams per day.

Although it's considering revising its advice, the government currently recommends that Americans consume no more than 2,400 milligrams of sodium a day, but most people get far more. According to studies, the average person consumes more than 4,000 milligrams daily. Much of it comes from restaurant meals and processed foods, such as frozen dinners, canned soups, and prepackaged meals. In some people, consuming excessive sodium can contribute to high blood pressure, which plays a role in heart and kidney disease and strokes.

The American Heart Association suggests that people who want to lower their sodium intake should limit:

- Ham, bacon, lunchmeats, and sardines
- Canned foods and juices
- Cheese and buttermilk
- Ketchup, sauces, and salad dressings
- Monosodium glutamate (MSG), baking soda, and baking powder

Other ways to reduce sodium consumption include rinsing canned vegetables and beans before eating, using low-sodium peanut butter, and flavoring foods with herbs and spices instead of salt.

While you're cutting back on salt, you may want to beef up your intake of another mineral—potassium—according to the same report. People need 4,700 milligrams daily, which is roughly twice the amount that young adults generally consume. Potassium helps maintain proper fluid levels in your body and may help prevent high blood pressure. Sources include bananas, spinach, citrus fruits, tomatoes, and potatoes.

FUTURE BREAKTHROUGHS

MICRONEEDLES: Too Tiny to Hurt

By 2010, doctors may be able to put medications into your body with new devices that combine the efficiency of a hypodermic needle with the painlessness of a patch.

The devices are microneedles, which are so small that they're invisible to the naked eye. In fact, they're measured in millionths of a meter in length—too short to cause pain when they poke into your skin. They may be hollow or solid and made of silicon, metal, glass, or polymer.

Microneedles could be affixed to a medicinal patch that's applied to the skin, allowing the medication to seep into your body through the tiny holes made by the needles, says Mark Prausnitz, Ph.D., associate professor of chemical and biomedical engineering at the *Georgia Institute of Technology in Atlanta.*

The tiny needles offer an option for delivering drugs that can't be taken by mouth or supplied via conventional patches. Dr. Prausnitz is particularly interested in using microneedles to administer vaccines, saving infants and children from the pain of getting multiple injections. The BioValve company has licensed Georgia Tech's microneedles and is developing drug-delivery methods that use them.

Nutrition

Super Foods Pack Powerful Antioxidant Punch

Your body is constantly under assault by tiny troublemakers called free radicals, but two studies published in the summer of 2004 show which foods offer you the best protection against their vandalism.

Free radicals are unstable oxygen molecules that can damage your cells' DNA. Your body naturally generates some free radicals when you breathe or eat, and you take in more when you're exposed to cigarette smoke and pollution. Damage from free radicals — a process called oxidation — is thought to play a role in many ailments, including heart disease, cancer, and Alzheimer's disease, as well as the general wear and tear of aging.

The "antidote" to oxidation is antioxidants, compounds that neutralize free radicals. Fruits and vegetables are rich in antioxidants, which include vitamins E and C as well hundreds of other such compounds.

The strongest antioxidant foods. The new studies, conducted by the USDA, tested the antioxidant capacity of various foods. Among the fruits studied, the highest in antioxidants per serving are blueberries, cranberries, blackberries, and prunes. Taking top honors among vegetables are red beans, red kidney beans, and pinto beans, followed by artichokes. Some nuts pack a wallop, with pecans having more antioxidant capacity than many fruits and vegetables. Also on the list are potatoes, currently maligned by advocates of low-carbohydrate diets.

Among spices that the researchers tested, ground cloves, ground cinnamon, dried oregano, and turmeric top the list of those with antioxidant power. And there's one powerful antioxidant food that will appeal to chocoholics: baking chocolate.

Eat your vegetables. The bottom line of this research is that "individuals should eat more fruits and vegetables.... I am coming to the conclusion that there needs to be at least one food with high antioxidant capacity included in each meal," says Ronald Prior, Ph.D., a research chemist with the USDA and one of the study authors.

TOP 20 ANTIOXIDANT FOODS

The following foods are ranked according to their antioxidant power per serving (strongest first), using portion sizes set by the USDA. Some spices and baking chocolate are also high in antioxidants but weren't measured per serving and aren't included in the list.

SMALL RED BEANS
LOWBUSH BLUEBERRIES
RED KIDNEY BEANS
PINTO BEANS
CULTIVATED BLUEBERRIES
CRANBERRIES
ARTICHOKES
BLACKBERRIES
PRUNES
RASPBERRIES
STRAWBERRIES
RED DELICIOUS APPLES
GRANNY SMITH APPLES
PECANS
CHERRIES
BLACK PLUMS
RUSSET POTATOES (COOKED)
PLUMS
GALA APPLES
WALNUTS

Nutrition

Fructose's Reputation Sours

You may want to think twice before you pop open your next soft drink, particularly if you're concerned about your weight. The soda may quench your thirst, but the type of sugar it contains may also trigger your hunger.

A study reported in the June 2004 issue of the *Journal of Clinical Endocrinology & Metabolism* investigated the different ways that common types of sugar affect the hormones in the body that tell us when we're full or hungry. What it found inflicted more injury on the already-damaged reputation of fructose.

Sodas are sweetened with high-fructose corn syrup, a thick liquid made from cornstarch. The sweetener gets its name from the fructose—a type of sugar—it contains, although it also contains glucose, another form of sugar. Food and beverage manufacturers increasingly use high-fructose corn syrup instead of regular sugar (sucrose) because it's cheaper, and the liquid is easier to mix into sodas.

What the study showed. The researchers looked at 12 healthy, normal-weight young women who ate three meals in a lab, each accompanied by a specially prepared beverage sweetened with either fructose or glucose. After a month, the experiment was repeated, but this time, the volunteers drank the beverage they hadn't had the first time. In each instance, blood was drawn frequently for testing.

The researchers found that when the women drank the fructose drinks—which contained as much fructose as two cans of soda—their bodies produced less of a hormone called leptin, which makes you feel full, thus encouraging you to stop eating. The volunteers also had higher levels of a hormone called ghrelin after eating the meals accompanied by fructose. Ghrelin stimulates the appetite, making you want to eat more.

According to the study, Americans are consuming at least 26 percent more fructose than they were three decades ago, primarily because they're drinking more soda. This increase in fructose consumption may be playing a role in the national increase in obesity, the authors state—possibly by making people eat more because of their altered hormone levels. Many fruit drinks are also high in high-fructose corn syrup.

Not solely to blame. "Sodas contain a lot of calories with no nutrients. They result in a metabolic pattern that may promote hunger," says Karen Teff, Ph.D., lead author of the study and adjunct associate professor at the University of Pennsylvania School of Medicine in Philadelphia. "If you want to lose weight, cutting out soda is a good idea. However, many factors play a role in obesity, and this is just one variable."

Lowering your total sugar consumption is also a wise move, since in the body, table sugar breaks down into both glucose and fructose. And of course, burning more calories through exercise is a sure way to lose weight or keep it off. ■

Nutrition

Old Hydration Advice Doesn't Hold Water

Forget the traditional advice that says you must drink eight 8-ounce glasses of water a day. New guidelines say it's fine to just drink—try not to find this too startling—*when you're thirsty*.

The Institute of Medicine (IOM), a private group that sets guidelines for nutrients that Americans need, released its recommendations for water intake in the spring of 2004. Its report stated that for the average sedentary man, taking in 3.7 liters of water each day—which is more than eight 8-ounce glasses—is adequate. For women, a daily intake of 2.7 liters, or a little less than 3 quarts, is adequate. But those amounts include the fluids found in foods. Also, according to the IOM, healthy people can often get by with less than that amount; there's no magic number. Drinking when you're thirsty will keep you properly hydrated. Of course, if you're out in the heat or engaged in exercise, you should drink more.

The amount of fluid in foods can be significant. For instance, whole wheat bread is 38 percent water by weight, roast turkey is 62 percent water, and a whopping 90 percent of cantaloupe is water.

The institute also shot down another common myth: that caffeinated drinks count against your daily fluid intake because they cause you to urinate more. Actually, the report says, caffeine doesn't appear to have much effect, so you can include coffee, tea, and caffeinated soda in your daily fluid intake.

Another report in 2004 shot more holes in common assumptions about water. Researchers from the University of Queensland in Australia reported in a February issue of the *British Medical Journal* that the age-old advice to drink more fluids during illness may actually be harmful in some cases. A hormone produced when people have pneumonia or bronchitis causes them to store water rather than passing it in urine. Although drinking water can help thin mucus, drinking too much could theoretically cause excessively low sodium in people with these conditions. This is because water can dilute sodium in the body too much—a condition called hyponatremia—leading to confusion, lethargy, and possibly even coma. ■

Supplements

Herbal Heavyweight Takes a Beating

As 2004 dawned, fans of the herb ephedra descended on health food stores in the United States, emptying shelves of the popular weight-loss supplement. The spree came on the heels of word that the FDA would soon ban sales of the herb because it posed "unreasonable risk of illness or injury." In February 2004, the FDA followed through, prohibiting the sale of any supplement containing ephedrine alkaloids, which are components found in ephedra.

Widely touted as a way to help people lose weight and enjoy better athletic performance, ephedra was found in a variety of products with pumped-up names like Ripped Fuel, Thermonex, and Speed Stack. The stimulants purportedly stoked users' metabolisms, helping them burn calories faster. The side effects, however, included higher blood pressure, irregular heart rate, and jitters.

A risky herb. The ban followed years of contemplation by the FDA as reports of harm linked to the herb accumulated. A February 2003 study commissioned by the National Institutes of Health looked at 16,000 "adverse events" reported after ephedra use, which included several heart attacks, strokes, and deaths that may have been attributable to the supplement. The study found some evidence that ephedra could be useful for short-term weight loss, but there was little to support its use for improved athletic performance.

Ephedra gained even more negative attention on a hot Florida day the same month, when Baltimore Orioles pitcher Steve Bechler, just 23, died of organ fail-

[THE NEXT EPHEDRA?]

For a year or two before the FDA ban on ephedra, a number of companies producing ephedra supplements started marketing other products for weight loss. You're likely to see more of the following in the near future, according to Annette Dickinson, Ph.D., president of the Council for Responsible Nutrition, and Michael McGuffin, president of the American Herbal Products Association. But that's not to say that *these* will be devoid of controversies of their own.

- **Bitter orange.** Also known as citrus aurantium, this supplement contains synephrine, a mild stimulant. Some research has shown that it helps promote weight loss, but it's chemically similar to ephedrine and can raise blood pressure. The same week that the ephedra ban was announced, a U.S. senator urged the FDA to ban bitter orange, too, and the agency is reportedly monitoring the supplement closely.
- **Garcinia cambogia.** This supplement, extracted from an Asian fruit, contains a chemical called hydroxycitric acid. It's said to facilitate weight loss, but a study published in the *Journal of the American Medical Association* in 1998 found that dieters who took it lost no more weight than dieters who took placebos.
- **Green tea extract.** The Internet is filled with claims for this supplement, but evidence supporting those claims is scant. A small Swiss study back in 1999 did find that people who took green tea extract burned more energy—and thus calories—over a 24-hour period than those who took a placebo. The researchers claimed that the results weren't attributable simply to the caffeine in the tea.

ure after succumbing to the heat during spring training. A supplement containing ephedra was found to be a contributing factor in his death.

The legal status of ephedra varies from country to country. Canada allows ephedra or ephedrine use only for short periods in limited doses in certain drugs, such as nasal decongestants. It's illegal when combined with caffeine and used for weight loss or body building. In the United Kingdom, ephedra remains legal, although it's restricted to set doses and must be obtained from a pharmacist, registered medical herbalist, or doctor.

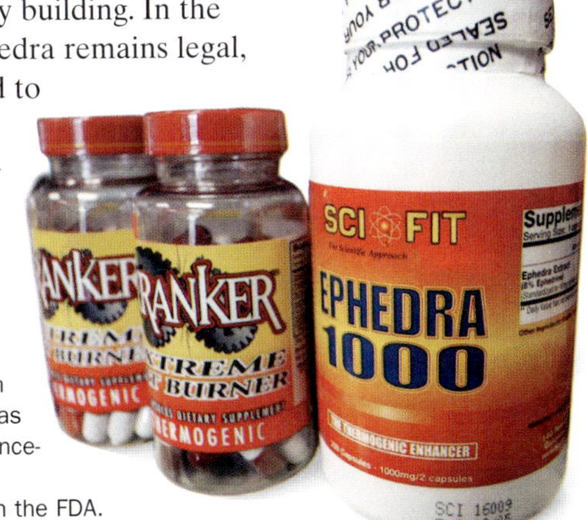

Bottles of ephedra were pulled from store shelves in the United States. Popular as a weight-loss and performance-enhancing supplement, the stimulant scored poorly with the FDA.

IN Brief

You Can't Always Judge a Hospital by Its Workload

If you're deciding where to have a specific type of surgery, you might think the hospital that performs the largest number of those surgeries is the best place to have your operation. You could be wrong, though.

A study published in the *Journal of the American Medical Association* examined the outcomes of more than 260,000 coronary artery bypass surgeries. It found that hospitals that performed a high number of such surgeries had only "modestly" lower death rates for the procedure.

These findings won't necessarily hold true for all surgeries, says lead author Eric Peterson, M.D., of the Duke Clinical Research Institute in Durham, North Carolina. A patient undergoing a complex operation, such as brain surgery, will probably have a better outcome at a hospital that does such procedures frequently. On the other hand, Dr. Peterson says, hospital volume doesn't matter as much for someone having a more routine operation, such as an appendectomy.

If you're planning elective surgery and want help in judging a hospital's success rate, ask if the hospital collects figures on the outcomes of its surgeries and, if so, how its success rates compare with those of other hospitals, he suggests.

Slam That Door—You'll Live Longer

According to a study of hot-tempered nuns and priests, showing your anger when you're upset may help you enjoy more years of life. The study followed 851 Catholic clergy members in their seventies for about five years. During the study, those who were most likely to be depressed and direct their anger inward were almost twice as likely to die as those who most often expressed their anger openly with actions such as slamming doors.

YOUR BODY HEAD TO TOE

RESEARCHERS are leaving no stone unturned in search of medical breakthroughs. Their discoveries include anticancer compounds from the deep sea, a miraculous clot buster for stroke patients modeled after the saliva of vampire bats, and a hormone derived from the saliva of Gila monsters that could be the next major weapon against type 2 diabetes. Old thinking is being turned on its ear as scientists put forth revolutionary theories about the origins of cancer and osteoarthritis—theories that could lead to new and better treatments. And doctors are pulling out the big guns—actually, tiny new instruments—to grab artery-blocking clots and remove them before they cause permanent damage.

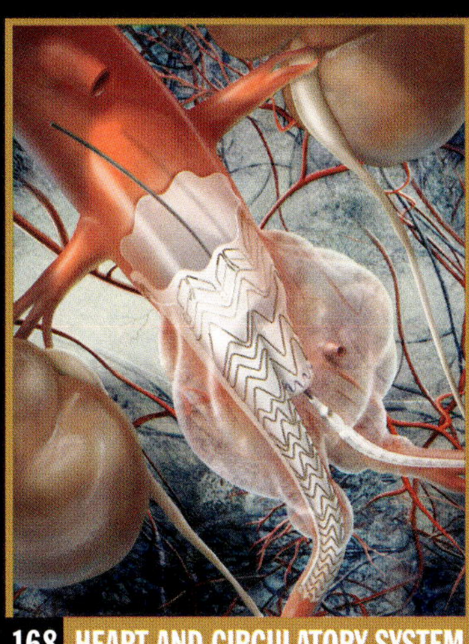

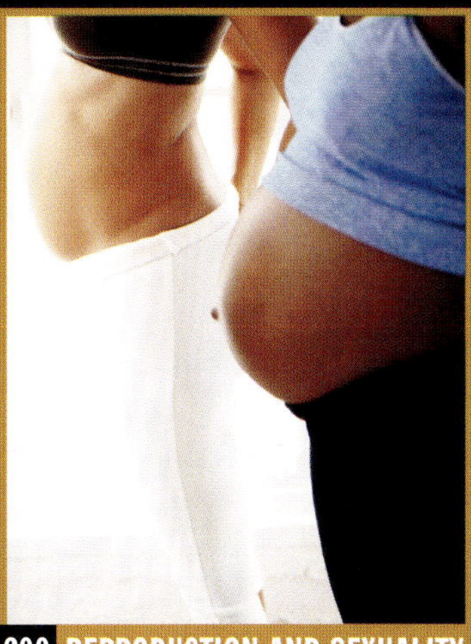

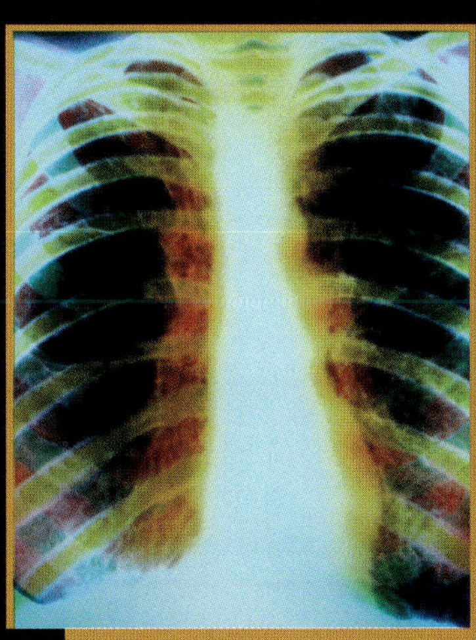

BRAIN

AND NERVOUS SYSTEM

IN THIS SECTION

SOME OF THE LATEST APPROACHES TO TREATING STROKE SOUND LIKE THE WORK OF MAD SCIENTISTS.

But the scientists are sane, and their methods are sound. To save lives and reduce disability, they're experimenting with a clot-dissolving drug derived from the saliva of vampire bats and a tiny, corkscrew-shaped device that doctors can use to reach into the brain and retrieve a clot before it can cause further harm. In some stroke patients, the device has actually reversed paralysis and speech loss.

How's your mood? If you're depressed and you're a woman over 50, research shows you have an increased risk of dying of a heart attack or stroke. On a lighter note, one researcher went looking for the "funny bone" and found out why humor makes us feel good.

Laughing so hard your head hurts is one thing, but chronic headaches are another. People who have them may soon benefit from drugs used to treat epilepsy. Acupuncture is also proving effective for headaches, including migraines. And there's a new reason to get migraines under control: Research shows they can actually damage the brain.

Cerebral Palsy

Helping Kids with Cerebral Palsy Reach for Independence

Children with cerebral palsy, a disease that impairs areas of the brain that control movement and muscle tone, often have weak or stiff muscles in their limbs and poor control over them. When one side of the body is more affected than the other, the kids tend to favor the stronger side, sometimes to the point of ignoring the weaker side altogether. So what can we do to help these children use both sides of their bodies and learn to do everyday tasks, such as dressing and feeding themselves, that add up to independence?

Traditional physical therapy sometimes helps a little, but not much. A better way may be a technique called constraint-induced (CI) movement therapy. CI therapy has been around for a while, helping adults recover function after strokes or brain injuries. Now, researchers at the University of Alabama at Birmingham are using the technique for children with cerebral palsy, bringing new hope to parents who had given up on having their children ever show improvement.

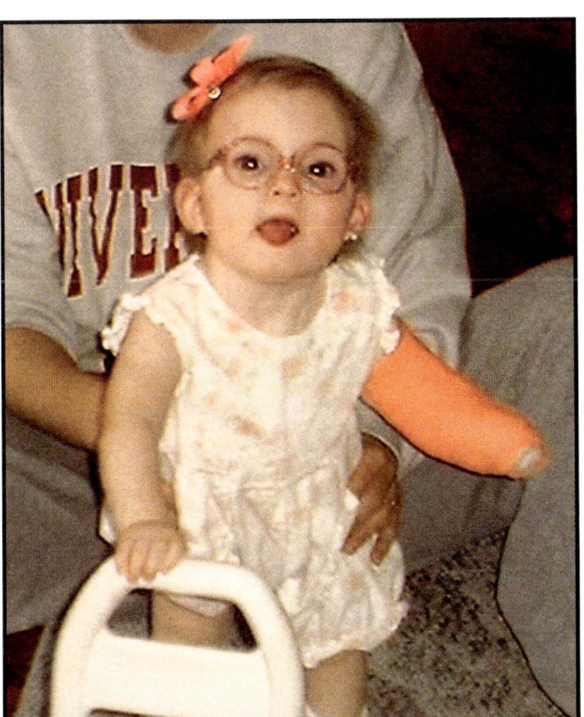

A child with cerebral palsy wears a cast on her stronger arm to help develop motor skills in the weaker one. The cast can be opened to monitor for skin problems.

TOP Trends

ADHD: NOT JUST FOR KIDS

In a reversal of the usual pattern, a childhood condition is now being recognized as an adult problem as well. Some experts estimate that about 4 percent of adults in the United States have attention deficit hyperactivity disorder (ADHD). (At least 7 percent of school-age children are believed to have ADHD, and research is finding that more than half of them never outgrow it.) The effects can be significant: A recent survey of adults with ADHD found that they experience lifelong impairments in several areas of their lives, including self-image, professional achievements, and relationships.

Because ADHD has been thought of as a children's condition, the diagnostic criteria are geared toward kids, and many doctors don't realize that symptoms may be different in adults. For example, in adults, inattention is often the dominant symptom, with hyperactivity playing a minor role or none at all. Many adults first recognize the condition in themselves when their children are diagnosed. In fact, a study from the University of Maryland found that parents of children with ADHD were 24 times more likely to have the condition themselves than parents of children without ADHD.

How it works. Edward Taub, Ph.D., and his colleagues tested CI therapy against conventional physical therapy in 18 children, ranging in age from 7 months to 8 years, who had more impairment in one arm than the other. In the CI group, each child's stronger arm was restrained using a cast—the same type used on a broken bone, except that it was split down the middle and taped together so it could be removed if necessary.

For 6 hours a day, the children "played" with a therapist, performing activities designed to improve their motor skills in the weak arm. Each time they succeeded in a task, they were encouraged to reach for the next level. For example, a child might start by removing and replacing a large puzzle piece with a knob on it. As he progressed, the puzzle pieces

A 15-month-old child with cerebral palsy uses her weaker hand to pop bubbles. Before treatment, she had almost no use of her left arm and hand.

would be replaced with smaller ones. In another activity, the child would reach for a soap bubble, with the ultimate goal of popping it with the tip of one finger.

After three weeks, children in the CI group had gained an average of nine new motor skills and functions in their affected arms, compared with just two new skills in the conventional therapy group. "In some cases, children start from zero use of the affected arm," says Dr. Taub, "and at the end of three weeks, they may be pushing up to a sitting position or crawling for the first time in their lives."

As exciting as the improvements are, Dr. Taub cautions that CI therapy does not make the children "normal." For children with cerebral palsy and their parents, though, it's a giant reach—with both arms—in the right direction. ■

Depression

Depression Causes More Than Heartache

Feelings of sadness, hopelessness, worthlessness: There's no question that depression breaks the spirit. As it turns out, for older women, it may also break the heart.

Results of a recent study provide the strongest evidence to date that depression significantly increases a woman's chances of dying from a heart attack or stroke. The sobering conclusions were based on data collected as part of the Women's Health Initiative, the largest study of postmenopausal women ever undertaken, with more than 90,000 participants age 50 and older.

What the study shows. The study looked at symptoms of depression—such as sad feelings, crying spells, restless sleep, and loss of pleasure from activities once enjoyed—as well as classic cardiovascular disease risk factors, including age,

ethnicity, high blood pressure, high cholesterol, smoking, overweight, physical inactivity, and diabetes. "After accounting for all of the other established risk factors, depression was still a risk factor for cardiovascular death," says Sylvia Wassertheil-Smoller, Ph.D., a lead investigator for the study.

Women with symptoms of depression were 12 percent more likely to have high blood pressure and 60 percent more likely to have experienced stroke or angina (heaviness or pain in the chest). Women who had depression but none of the classic risk factors for heart disease were 50 percent more likely to die of heart disease during the four years of the study than women who were not depressed.

What's the connection? It's not clear what links depression to heart disease, but theories abound. There is some evidence that depression lowers estrogen levels, and the loss of estrogen that occurs after menopause is known to increase the risk of cardiovascular disease. Another possibility is that stress hormones released during depression contribute to heart disease.

No one knows yet whether treating depression lowers the risk of heart disease. Nevertheless, experts say, the other effects of depression are significant enough that women with depressive symptoms should be monitored and treated. ■

Restless Legs and a Restless Mind

It attacks at night: an odd sensation in your legs that doesn't go away unless you move or rub them. Lie still, try to sleep... and back it comes. For people with restless legs syndrome (RSL), insomnia comes with the territory—and so, it seems, can mental distress. Researchers in Turkey found that people with RSL have higher levels of anxiety and depression than people with well-behaved legs, and the more severe the RSL, the more severe the anxiety and depression. No one knows for sure, but it's thought that the mental distress results from the RSL, not the other way around.

RESEARCH ROUNDUP

Brain Is Different in Depressed Teens

Adolescent depression is not a character flaw or the result of bad parenting, but a real medical illness, says Frank MacMaster of the National Research Council of Canada. And he should know, because he's done something that countless parents wish they could do: He's peered inside the brains of adolescents.

In his study, 34 adolescents, half of whom had major depression, underwent MRI scans. The scans showed that an area of the brain called the hippocampus was 17 percent smaller on average in the depressed teens than in those who weren't depressed. The hippocampus plays a critical role in memory, and a disruption of this function may help explain why depression has a negative impact on academic performance. One goal of the research is to aid doctors in diagnosing teen depression.

Depression Linked to Low Testosterone

According to researchers at the University of Washington in Seattle, 30 percent of men over age 55 have low testosterone, which can lead to diminished appetite and libido, fatigue, decreased muscle mass, and irritability. Now depression has been added to that list. The researchers examined the medical records of 278 men age 45 and older who had no signs of depression. Over a two-year period, nearly 22 percent of the men with low testosterone levels (less than 200 mg/dL) developed depression, compared with just 7 percent of men with normal levels. A simple blood test can reveal your testosterone level. Unfortunately, if it's low, testosterone supplementation may not be the answer, since it may raise the risk of prostate cancer and stroke.

Headache

Epilepsy Drugs Head Off Headaches

There are plenty of drugs that treat headaches, from over-the-counter pills for dull aches to powerful prescription medicines for migraines. But people who have frequent headaches are much better off if they can prevent the pain in the first place rather than trying to control it once it starts. Now, help may be coming from a seemingly unlikely source: anti-seizure drugs.

In clinical trials, two drugs approved to prevent seizures in people with epilepsy are showing that they can also keep headaches at bay. How these drugs, topiramate (Topamax) and gabapentin (Neurontin), work against headaches isn't entirely understood. Stephen D. Silberstein, M.D., professor of neurology at Thomas Jefferson University in Philadelphia, says Topamax—and probably other drugs for epilepsy—may work by calming an overactive brain. During a migraine, nerve cells that respond to pain become activated. They release a chemical that causes inflammation of the nerve endings, "the same thing that happens in the skin during hives," says Dr. Silberstein. "It's a very new way of thinking about migraine."

What the studies show. In the latest study of Topamax, nearly half of the patients taking the drug experienced at least a 50 percent reduction in migraines after six months, with about 6 percent of patients becoming completely migraine-free. In an Australian study of Neurontin, after three months, 36 percent of people with chronic headaches stopped having them entirely. "Some say that gabapentin is far better for management of pain than it is for the management of epilepsy," says Roy G. Beran, M.D., study author and neurologist at Liverpool Hospital in New South Wales.

While all medications have potential side effects, Topamax and Neurontin appear to be free of a particularly distressing one—weight gain—that's common with many other drugs used to prevent headaches, such as the antidepressant amitriptyline (Elavil), beta blockers, and valproate (Depacon), another anti-seizure drug. In fact, people taking Topamax tend to lose weight, at least initially, which could keep them from quitting the medication.

Availability. Neurontin is not currently approved for treating headaches, but many doctors prescribe it for patients who aren't getting relief with other preventive medications. The FDA approved Topamax for migraine prevention in adults in August 2004.

RESEARCH ROUNDUP

Sticking It to Headaches

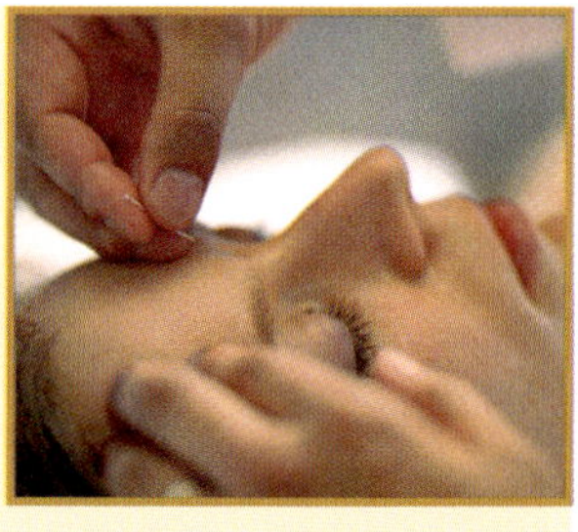

Acupuncture has been around for some 2,000 years, but convincing Western medicine of its value hasn't been easy. Critics have managed to poke holes in several small studies that showed that the ancient healing method eases headache pain. Now, a large, well-designed study should help persuade holdouts that acupuncture is a useful treatment for chronic headaches.

Most of the study's 401 participants in England and Wales had migraines, and a few had chronic tension headaches. Half received standard care, including medication, for their headaches, while the other half got standard care plus acupuncture—up to 12 treatments over three months. At the end of the year-long study, people in the acupuncture group had significantly fewer and less severe headaches than people in the standard care group. They also used less medication, had fewer doctor visits, and took fewer sick days.

Headache

Migraines May Harm the Brain

The pain and other disturbing symptoms of a migraine can be so intense that some patients suspect the headaches might actually inflict damage on their brains—and they may be right. Dutch researchers have found that migraines increase the risk of brain infarcts, or areas of dead brain tissue.

In the study, more than 400 randomly selected people underwent MRI scans. The risk of brain infarcts was 13 times higher in people who had a history of migraine with visual disturbance (an "aura," such as sparkling lights) than in those who had never had a migraine. People who had experienced migraines with or without aura had higher risks of infarcts in the cerebellum, the brain region responsible for controlling voluntary movement, posture, and balance.

Infarcts have been linked to increased risk of stroke and mental impairment, including dementia. It remains to be seen if the risk of these disorders is increased in migraine sufferers. It's also not known what causes the infarcts and whether preventing migraines, or nipping them in the bud, will lower the risk. ■

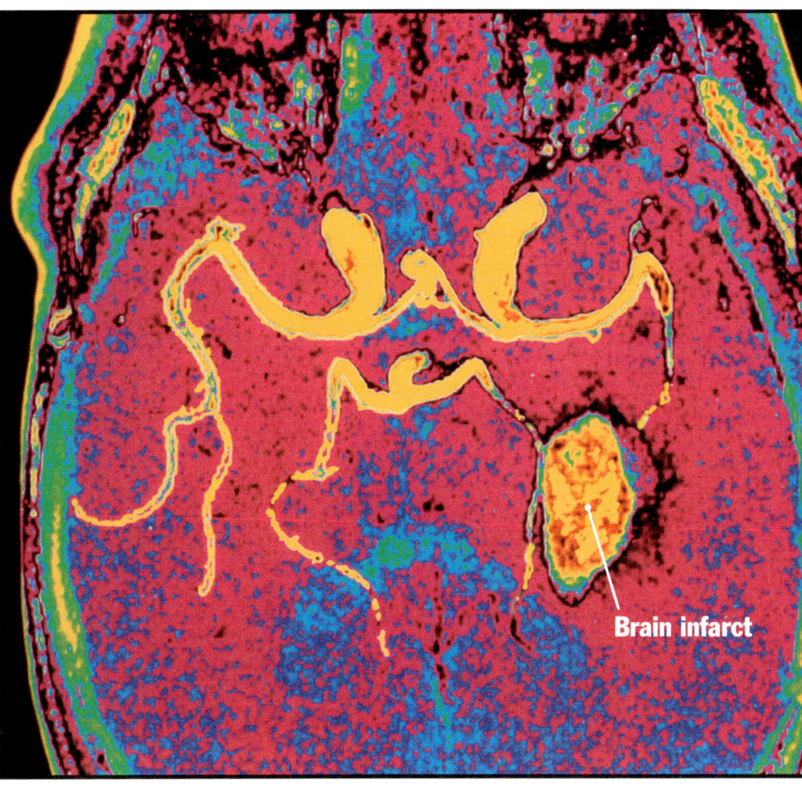

This MRI scan indicates the patient has had a brain infarct—that is, brain tissue has died. The link between such infarcts and migraines is under study, and that research may lead to new methods for managing the debilitating headaches.

RESEARCH ROUNDUP

Waking Up with Headaches? Call a Psychiatrist

Morning headaches were once believed to be the exclusive problem of people with sleep disorders, such as insomnia, snoring, and obstructive sleep apnea. While it's true that sleep disorders are associated with morning headaches, a large study of Europeans found that waking up with headaches is actually more likely to point to other culprits: anxiety and depression.

Of the nearly 19,000 people surveyed, 7.6 percent reported waking up with a headache at least sometimes. People who suffered from anxiety or depression were at least twice as likely to wake up with headaches as happier, calmer folks. The researcher notes that the relationship between headaches and depression is likely to go both ways: The headaches can be a symptom of depression, but if they're severe enough, they can also be the cause.

Humor

The Funny Bone Is All in Your Head

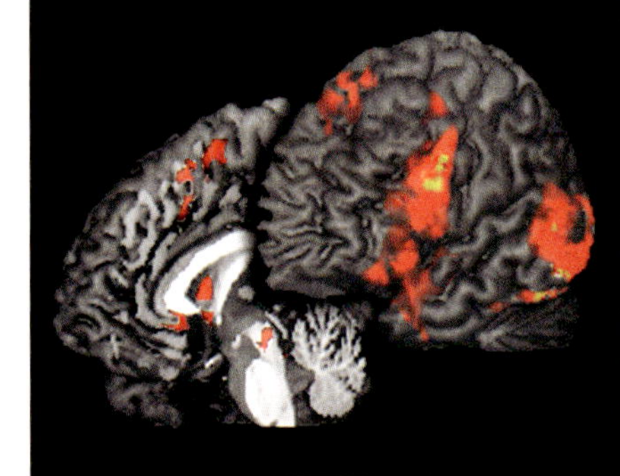

The brain's reward centers "light up" with a good chuckle, induced in this case by a funny cartoon.

Have you ever wondered why we're drawn to humor—why we'll watch *Seinfeld* reruns over and over or put up with an unreliable friend who has a rapier wit? For Allan Reiss, M.D., of Stanford University, such rumination led to a discovery. Using MRI scans, Dr. Reiss went looking for the brain's "funny bone." What he found was that humor makes us feel good because it activates the brain's reward centers—the same areas that are activated by amphetamines, cocaine, monetary rewards, and even the sight of an attractive face.

What the study shows. Dr. Reiss and his colleagues at the Stanford Psychiatry Neuroimaging Laboratory used MRIs to monitor volunteers' brain activity while they read cartoons. When participants thought a cartoon was funny, they pushed a button. But here's the joke: Some cartoons had crucial information omitted, rendering them unfunny. The scans revealed that the funnier a person found a cartoon, the more intense the activity in the brain's reward centers. The study was published in the December 2003 issue of the journal *Neuron*.

The study findings could help us understand normal variations in personality and behavior. For example, some people use humor as a coping mechanism and stress reducer, but we all know people who don't. It's possible that people who rely less on humor simply find it less rewarding. "Perhaps they are missing this reward link in their circuitry," says Dr. Reiss.

Understanding the brain mechanisms that underlie humor may one day help scientists identify people who are at risk for depression because, Dr. Reiss points out, the loss of the ability to appreciate humor is a common symptom of depression. The Stanford team's findings also support the theory that humor can be used to fight depression and other ailments. ■

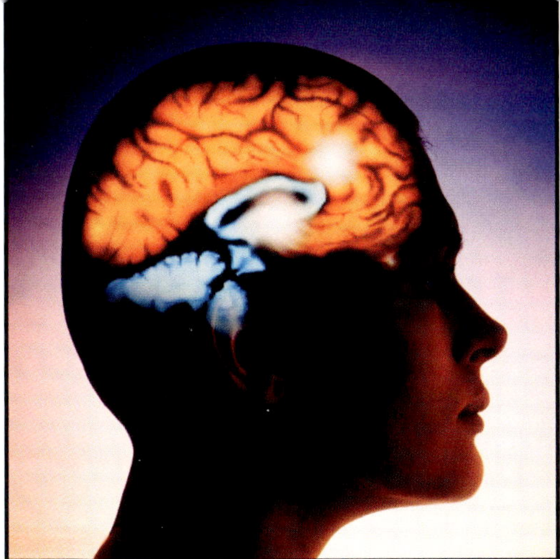

Memory

Bad Memories? Forget about Them!

Is it possible to intentionally forget unwanted memories? Yes, but it takes some effort. Researchers at the University of Oregon had volunteers memorize pairs of words, then asked them to remember some pairs and forget others. When the volunteers tried to forget some of the word matches, MRI scans revealed that certain areas of their brains—particularly the prefrontal cortex—became extremely active. This region "manages" other areas of the brain, including the hippocampus, which controls conscious memory. The amount of forgetting that occurred was directly related to how activated the prefrontal cortex was—and that forgetting could become permanent. When you try not to think about something, says Michael Anderson, Ph.D., lead study author, "you're actually reducing your ability to recall that memory later on, even when you want to."

The research could one day help researchers understand a number of conditions, including post-traumatic stress disorder (PTSD). Dr. Anderson points out that only a fraction of people who experience traumatic events develop PTSD. "Now that we know which areas of the brain are activated when things are working normally," he says, "we can take this knowledge and ask, Do people with PTSD have damage in this network?" ■

FUTURE BREAKTHROUGHS

Patches for Pain

If you've ever been in the hospital for major surgery, you know what a pain pain control can be. With your arm attached to an IV that's connected to a pump delivering morphine, it's difficult to maneuver in bed, let alone do something complicated like, say, make your way to the bathroom. In the near future, recovering patients who need pain relief could be trading IVs, pumps, and needles for skin patches the size of credit cards. Worn on the upper arm or chest, the patch has a button that the patient pushes to deliver small doses of the pain medication fentanyl (Duragesic). It's been tested at 33 North American hospitals, where postsurgical patients found that it worked just as well as standard self-administered pain control. And the patches need far less attention from nursing staff than IV lines and pumps. The new pain control method is currently under review by the FDA.

Stroke Helmet: Cooler Heads May Prevail

Stroke patients may someday arrive at the hospital with cool heads, thanks to special helmets with liquid cooling technology originally developed by NASA. Researchers say the soft, aviator-style helmets are a safe and effective way to lower brain temperature, which may reduce stroke damage and allow more time for other treatments to be administered.

In animal studies, cooling the brain after a stroke has reduced damage to brain tissue by as much as 70 percent. The tricky part is cooling the brain without cooling the entire body, which would interfere with the heart and the immune system. In a recent study, the special helmet cooled brains an average of 6 degrees Fahrenheit in the first hour without much effect on body temperature. Researchers were able to use the helmets for an average of 6 to 8 hours before body temperature dropped too low. They envision the helmets being used in ambulances to keep brain tissue alive while stroke patients are transported to the hospital.

Stroke

A Corkscrew for Blood Clots

If a blood clot lodges in a brain artery, can a corkscrew save your life? Some researchers think so.

A clot in the brain is a ticking time bomb. Because blood can't get by, the parts of the brain fed by the artery are starved of oxygen and begin to die. That's what happens in an ischemic stroke, by far the most common type. Some 8 to 12 percent of people in the United States who have this type of stroke die within 30 days. Of those who make it, 15 to 30 percent are permanently disabled by paralysis or weakness, loss of balance or coordination, problems with language use and speech, memory loss, or vision impairment.

At the tip of a catheter, a tiny clot-grabbing corkscrew.

Once an ischemic stroke occurs, there is a very narrow window in which to administer an emergency clot-dissolving drug, called tissue plasminogen activator (TPA), to minimize damage. After 3 hours, it's too late—and most people arrive at the hospital too late. TPA also takes time to work, and in the meantime, brain cells in the affected area continue to die.

Now, imagine that instead of waiting for a drug to dissolve the clot, doctors could reach in and remove it. It's possible with a new corkscrew-shaped wire designed to grab blood clots and pull them out. Called the MERCI Retrieval System, the device can be used up to 8 hours after a stroke occurs. ("MERCI" stands for mechanical embolus removal in cerebral ischemia. *Embolus* is the medical term for "clot.")

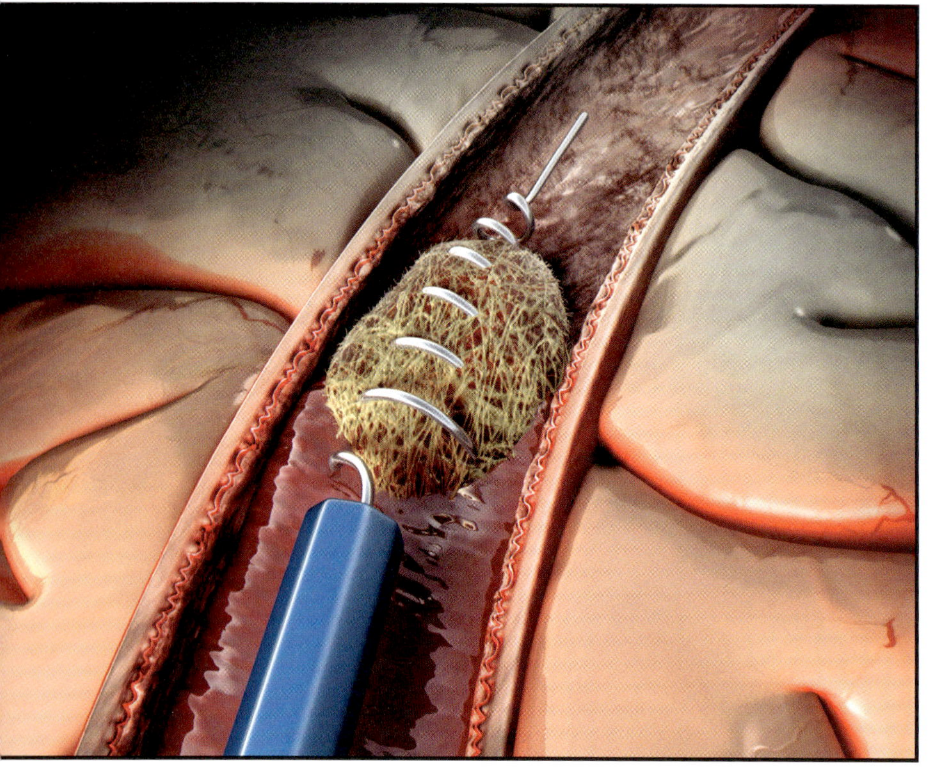

The MERCI Retrieval System pulls a blood clot out of a vessel in a stroke patient's brain. The device can be used up to 8 hours after a stroke. In contrast, the clot-dissolving drug TPA must be used within 3 hours.

How it works. The device is inserted through a catheter into an artery in the groin and then guided by angiography, a special type of x-ray that involves a dye, to the blood clot in the brain. The retriever itself is a thin metal wire with a "memory." It's straight when it's threaded through the catheter, but after it's sent into the artery, it takes on its unique corkscrew shape. Once the clot is captured in the corkscrew, a balloon inflates to stop blood flow momentarily, and both clot and corkscrew are retracted into the catheter, which is then pulled out of the body.

Success stories. The MERCI system was tested on 114 patients who had suffered severe strokes but could not receive TPA. (Not everyone can receive the drug, including those who have had recent surgery, because it can cause bleeding in the brain.) "These were the most severe stroke patients, and without the procedure, they were likely to be dead or severely disabled," says Sidney Starkman, M.D., an investigator in the study and codirector of the University of California, Los Angeles, stroke center. The blocked vessels were successfully opened—the clot was retrieved, dislodged, or broken into pieces—in 54 percent of the patients. Three-quarters of them survived, and about 40 percent had little or no lasting disability. In some cases, the procedure immediately reversed paralysis and loss of speech.

"If the blood vessel was opened and the brain had not yet suffered severe irreversible damage, then the patients had a chance for a very good to excellent recovery," says Dr. Starkman. "What was remarkable in this series of patients was that some were made nearly normal the moment that the vessel was opened with the MERCI retriever."

Availability. The MERCI Retrieval System is still in the testing stage. The manufacturer, Concentric Medical of Mountain View, California, is seeking FDA approval, but it's too early to tell when the device may be available. The procedure isn't an option for all stroke patients. In order for the MERCI system to be used, the blockage must be in a major brain artery, and the clot must show up on angiography. Furthermore, the procedure can be performed only by doctors specially trained in neurology and radiology (and even then, they require extra training). Theoretically, about 90 percent of the U.S. population could be within 8 hours' reach of an expert able to perform the procedure.

IN Brief

Injure the Brain, Damage the Mind

People who experience traumatic brain injuries have something else to worry about: psychiatric problems. A recent study found mental illness in 49 percent of people with moderate to severe brain injuries and in 34 percent of people with mild injuries. By comparison, in a group of randomly selected people with no brain injury, 18 percent had some form of mental illness (which includes depression). Thus, people who sustain brain injuries should be screened for psychiatric illness for up to three years afterward, say the researchers from the Group Health Cooperative of Puget Sound in Seattle.

Legacy of Lead: Mental Illness

In the early 1960s, lead was still a common gasoline additive in the United States. It's been banned for more than two decades now, but some people may still be living with its effects. Scientists from Columbia University in New York City found that adults whose mothers had high levels of lead exposure during pregnancy in the 1960s had double the risk of schizophrenia compared with those whose mothers had less exposure.

Stress a Factor in MS

Some experts believe that stress can contribute to the development of multiple sclerosis (MS), a neurological disorder. To test this belief, Danish researchers conducted a large study of people who had experienced the worst stressor of all—the death of a child. Sure enough, parents who had lost children had a 50 percent higher risk of developing MS than parents who had not. The risk was doubled in parents whose children died unexpectedly.

Stroke

Bat Saliva: A Stroke Remedy with Teeth

Doctors who treat stroke patients have something in common with vampire bats: They're both keenly interested in keeping blood flowing. Scientists have long struggled to devise ways of dissolving clots that block blood flow to the brain and cause strokes. Meanwhile, vampire bats have been happily feeding on their victims while a natural enzyme in their saliva keeps the blood coming. So why not take that enzyme and put it to work in humans?

Why not, indeed. An experimental drug named desmoteplase (in honor of the vampire bat, *Desmodus rotundus*) is a synthetic version of the bat saliva enzyme. It could become the second clot-busting drug ever approved to treat strokes.

The first, tissue plasminogen activator (TPA), revolutionized stroke treatment when it was introduced in 1996. Suddenly there was a drug that increased by 50 percent the number of stroke patients who could return to work and lead normal lives. But TPA has a major catch: It must be given within 3 hours of the stroke, or it can do more damage than good, degrading the body's clotting system and causing bleeding in the brain.

Because the window of opportunity is so small, only about 5 percent of people who have ischemic strokes (the most common type, which involves a clot) get the drug. Left untreated, a clot may dissolve on its own but is more likely to continue obstructing blood flow, leading to disability or death.

Researchers are optimistic that the newer drug will prove to be a kinder, gentler clot buster because it has the almost magical ability to zero in on a clot without disrupting the rest of the body's clotting mechanism. That means it can safely be given many hours after a stroke occurs.

Teaming up with MRIs. The bat-saliva drug is only part of the story. Researchers have begun pairing it with ultrasophisticated MRI machines that can identify with stunning accuracy which patients will benefit from the drug. With ECHO-Planar MRI, "you can image the whole brain every second," says George C. Newman, M.D., Ph.D., director of the stroke program at the University of Wisconsin in Madison. Neurologists use the technology to measure the portion of the brain that has already been injured and areas where there are injured but salvageable brain cells.

During an international study, the high-tech MRIs allowed researchers to give desmoteplase up to 9 hours after a stroke. "A lot of people have potentially salvageable tissue at 6, 9, 12—up to 24 hours" after a stroke, says Steven Warach, M.D., chief of the stroke diagnostics and therapeutics section at the National Institute of Neurological Disorders and Stroke. "There's individual variability," he explains. "The MRI can tell us which patients have salvageable tissue."

The impact of desmoteplase combined with the advanced MRIs could be enormous. Dr. Newman says, "We're potentially moving 50,000 people a year from disability and dependence into back-to-work range," he says.

Availability. Desmoteplase is still in early-phase clinical trials. More studies will be needed before the drug can gain FDA approval, which is still several years away. ■

RESEARCH ROUNDUP

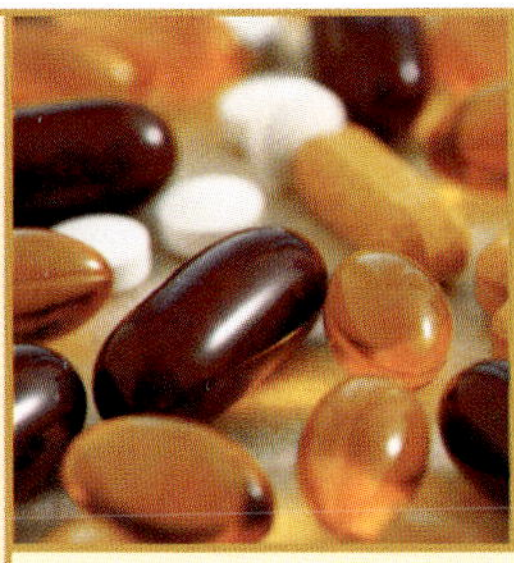

Smokers, Load Up on Vitamins

If you smoke, quitting is the best way to prevent a stroke. Short of quitting, eating foods with plenty of vitamins may reduce your risk.

A study from Rotterdam, the Netherlands, found that smokers who consumed plenty of vitamin C were about 70 percent less likely to have strokes than those who got less of the vitamin. Study participants whose diets were highest in vitamin C took in more than 133 milligrams a day, while people consuming the lowest amounts got less than 95 milligrams daily.

How can you get enough? A red pepper contains 226 milligrams of vitamin C, and a cup of fresh orange juice provides 124 milligrams. You'll get about 100 milligrams from a cup of strawberries or a cup of cooked broccoli.

Smokers also saw a benefit—although not as dramatic—from consuming vitamin E. Eating a diet rich in that vitamin resulted in a 20 percent reduction in stroke risk. Good food sources of vitamin E include vegetable oils, margarine, and nuts.

The Better Way to Treat Brain Aneurysms

Aneurysms are weakened parts of blood vessels that bulge out and can rupture, causing bleeding in the brain—what's known as a hemorrhagic stroke. Typically, aneurysms are treated with a surgical procedure called clipping, in which a piece of the skull is removed to gain access to the blood vessel, then the aneurysm is "clipped" at its base (like tying off a balloon) to prevent further blood flow. But a less invasive procedure called coiling may be a better option, according to Harvard researchers. Coiling involves threading a catheter through a blood vessel from the groin or leg to the brain. There, tiny metal coils are packed into the aneurysm, slowing blood flow and causing a clot to form at the bulge's base. The clot prevents blood from reaching the aneurysm and causing a rupture.

The researchers looked at data for nearly 4,000 patients who were treated for aneurysms. Clipping was the more popular choice, but patients who underwent the coiling procedure had fewer brain-related complications, spent fewer days in the hospital, and were more likely to be sent home rather than to a rehabilitation center.

IN *Brief*

Patching Up Parkinson's

The Parkinson's drug rotigotine, which controls involuntary movements, may soon be added to the list of drugs available in patch form. The patches, applied once a day, deliver the drug continuously, so they may smooth out symptom fluctuations that are common with pills. And there's no swallowing, a boon to some Parkinson's patients. The drug makers were expected to seek approval in the United States and Europe by the end of 2004. The patches could be available by the end of 2005.

Taking the Edge Off a Parkinson's Treatment

At high doses, levodopa (Larodopa)—the drug commonly used to treat Parkinson's disease—can cause twitching and jerking. Lowering the dose stops the side effects, but it usually makes the Parkinson's symptoms reappear. A French study of 50 patients with severe Parkinson's showed that low doses of the antipsychotic drug clozapine (Clozaril) control involuntary movements in patients taking levodopa better than placebos (dummy pills).

Stifling Saliva in Parkinson's Patients

Drooling is an embarrassing problem and potential choking hazard for many people with Parkinson's. It occurs when the disease interferes with the ability to swallow saliva. Now, help may come from an unlikely source: botulinum toxin B, a relative of Botox. When injected into the salivary glands of 16 people with Parkinson's disease, the toxin substantially decreased drooling. The treatment is still experimental.

CANCER

IN THIS SECTION

SCIENTISTS ARE BUSY TRYING TO FIGURE OUT HOW TO USE STEM CELLS TO CURE MAJOR DISEASES.

But meanwhile, a radical theory rapidly gaining acceptance holds that "bad seed" stem cells are the root of all cancers. If this theory is true, it could completely change the way cancer is treated.

For people who have cancer now, major drug developments are big news. The first cancer drug that works by starving a tumor of its blood supply has been approved for colon cancer and may soon be approved for other cancers as well. Women who survive breast cancer may stop taking tamoxifen to prevent the cancer from recurring, now that three new major studies have found that drugs called aromatase inhibitors are more effective. Researchers are also mining the sea for new cancer cures and have found at least one sea sponge that may be many times more powerful than today's cancer drugs.

Finally, experts have identified several factors that increase a person's chances of surviving cancer. Exercise is one. There's also new evidence that cancer patients need their sleep—their lives may depend on it.

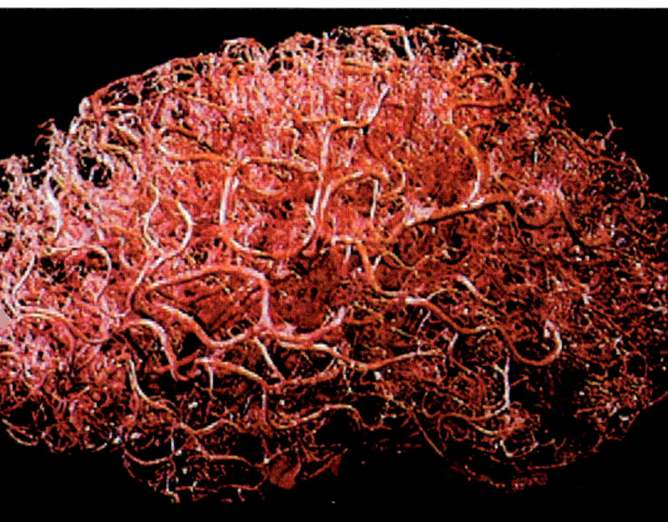

The 400 miles of capillaries in your brain have a surface area of about 100 square feet. Only tiny molecules can slip through the tightly knit cells lining these blood vessels.

Brain Cancer

Sneaking Cancer Drugs into the Brain

Despite breakthrough after breakthrough for nearly every kind of cancer in recent years, one part of the body has remained cut off from most advances: the brain. Finally, that seems to be changing, as doctors are discovering how to sneak chemotherapy drugs past the gates that bar access to the body's all-important command center.

"We spend untold millions and billions on drugs to treat disease in the nervous system, including brain tumors, but most drugs won't ever get to the tumor," says Edward A. Neuwelt, M.D., professor of neurology and neurosurgery at Oregon Health and Science University in Portland. That's because of what Dr. Neuwelt calls the Achilles heel of the brain—the blood-brain barrier, or BBB.

The barrier—really a single layer of cells that line blood vessels throughout the brain—is designed to protect the brain from toxins and keep its environment as stable as possible. That means it lets in only certain molecules, usually very small ones and only those that are fat soluble. Most chemotherapy drugs are made up of large, water-soluble molecules.

Dr. Neuwelt first succeeded in slipping standard chemotherapy treatments past the BBB nearly 20 years ago, but those drugs were often ineffective against brain cancer. In the past few years, he's been able to use a unique procedure he developed to sneak through new targeted treatments called monoclonal antibodies. These drugs, which include rituximab (Rituxan) and trastuzumab (Herceptin), attach to specific proteins on cancer cells and can be up to 100,000 times as large as the standard molecules the BBB allows in. Next on his to-do list: gene therapy, which uses deactivated viruses to deliver healing genes to the brain—and those viruses are

TOP Trends

MARROW TRANSPLANTS FOR OLDER PATIENTS, TOO

Bone marrow transplants can save the lives of some cancer patients, but older patients typically don't receive them because the treatment is so physically debilitating. That's changing as more doctors turn to kinder, gentler "mini" bone marrow transplants. In a traditional transplant, doctors remove a quantity of bone marrow, then deliver massive doses of chemotherapy to kill any cancer cells and the patient's remaining bone marrow. Finally, they replace the marrow by infusing either the patient's own marrow or a donor's to restore blood-making stem cells. Intense chemotherapy is responsible for most of the hardships inherent in the transplants. But the mini-transplant uses lower doses of chemotherapy and thus leaves some of the patient's original bone marrow intact. Patients who receive mini-transplants appear to do just as well and are much less likely to develop acute graft-versus-host disease, in which the infused cells attack the patient's organs.

LUNG CANCER IN WOMEN SURGES

It's not good news for women. A study published in an April 2004 issue of the *Journal of the American Medical Association* found that the death rate from lung cancer in American women has skyrocketed in the past 60 years, now surpassing breast cancer as the leading cause of cancer death in women. Overall, researchers found, the death rate from lung cancer in U.S. women rose 600 percent between 1930 and 1997. Even more disturbing, new lung cancer cases in women jumped 60 percent between 1990 and 2003. The most obvious reason for the increase is the higher rate of smoking among women today compared to the early 20th century. The researchers note, however, that smoking rates don't come close to explaining the jump. No one knows what's causing the epidemic.

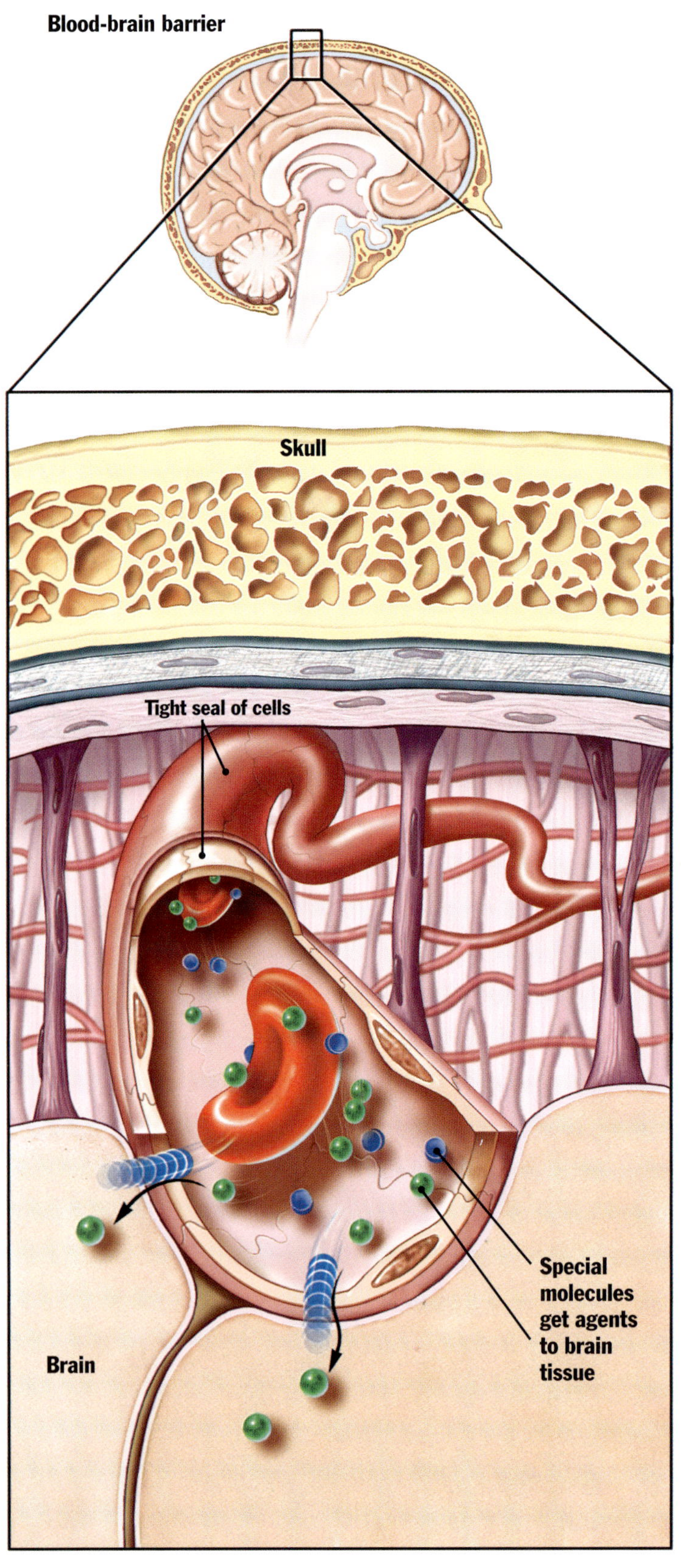

even *bigger* than the monoclonal antibodies. Finally, it appears, patients with brain tumors may have access to the same kinds of "gee whiz" therapies other cancer patients have been getting for years.

How it works. Getting the drugs to a brain tumor isn't easy. Patients have to be hospitalized for the procedure, and it requires careful cooperation among medical specialists. A catheter is snaked through a patient's groin into a main artery that supplies the brain, then a concentrated sugar solution is fed through the catheter. The solution sucks the water out of the barrier cells lining the blood vessels, creating a 30-minute window of opportunity for the cancer drug, now dripping into the patient's veins, to get through. Once the barrier closes, the patient receives a different drug that neutralizes the cancer treatment in the rest of the body, preventing it from harming healthy cells.

Although Dr. Neuwelt's work is the furthest along, it isn't the only effort to breach the BBB. Most of the other techniques are still being tested in animals, but one is in experimental use in humans. In May 2004, the British biotech company Xenova Group received FDA approval to begin late-stage clinical trials of its approach, which pumps a chemotherapy drug called TransMID directly into the tumor via two catheters implanted in the brain. Other biotech companies are investigating different drugs that open the BBB.

Availability. Seven medical centers in the United States and Canada have joined in the International Blood Brain Barrier Consortium to employ Dr. Neuwelt's procedure to get different types of chemotherapy and other treatments to brain tumors. Xenova's drug application with the FDA is on a fast track for consideration once the final clinical trials are complete, and other biotech companies are enrolling patients for additional trials of approaches to disrupting the BBB.

The blood-brain barrier keeps out not only toxins but medicines, too. One approach to sneaking medicine past the barrier: Identify molecules that are already able to pass through, then attach drugs to them.

Breast Cancer

Better Drugs May Topple Tamoxifen

For more than 25 years, women who have survived bouts with breast cancer have taken a drug called tamoxifen to prevent the cancer from coming back. Some women who are at high risk for breast cancer also take tamoxifen to avoid developing it. But now, thanks to the results of three major studies—two unveiled in late 2003 and the other in March 2004—drugs called aromatase inhibitors may be set to topple tamoxifen from its perch as the preeminent weapon against breast cancer.

Aromatase inhibitors include anastrozole (Arimidex), exemestane (Aromasin), and letrozole (Femara). Taken after menopause, they work by reducing the amount of estrogen women make. Tamoxifen, on the other hand, prevents estrogen from doing its job in cells. Either way, reducing estrogen's effects slows down or stops the growth of breast cancers that depend on the hormone.

The studies compared either Arimidex, Aromasin, or Femara to tamoxifen in breast cancer survivors. In all three trials, researchers found that the aromatase inhibitors did a better job of preventing breast cancer recurrences than tamoxifen did. In fact, in the Femara trial, the drug worked so much better than tamoxifen that the study was stopped early so the women who weren't taking Femara could receive it.

Potential for prevention. Larry Norton, M.D., deputy physician in chief and director of breast cancer programs at Memorial Sloan-Kettering Cancer Center in New York City and a lead researcher in the Femara trial, envisions a day when postmenopausal women might take an aromatase inhibitor every day to prevent breast cancer in the same way that they brush their teeth every day to prevent cavities.

That probably won't happen with the current line of aromatase inhibitors, however. Arimidex and Femara, nearly identical compounds that work by suppressing the enzyme that contributes to estrogen production, seem to increase a woman's risk of osteoporosis. No one knows for sure yet if Aromasin, which also destroys the estrogen-producing enzyme, has the same effect, but researchers think it doesn't. All three drugs also cause hot flashes.

Drug companies are working hard to find new versions that have fewer side effects. "Eventually, we could see other drugs of this type actually preserving or even promoting bone," says Dr. Norton.

Making the switch. Dr. Norton and other cancer specialists have already begun switching patients to aromatase inhibitors after they have been on tamoxifen for a couple of years. "With all three trials coming one right after another, unquestionably there's more use of aromatase inhibitors after initial cancer treatment," he says. "There are only two things left to figure out: Do the benefits last, and is it better to use an aromatase inhibitor right off the bat or after two to three years of tamoxifen?" Large clinical studies are currently under way to answer both of these questions.

How long should women take the drugs? Dr. Norton tells his patients to take it one year at a time. "In an area of science with constantly evolving information, you don't have to make long-term commitments," he says. "You can make short-term commitments and stay in tune with what's happening in the world of science."

Heading Off Cancer

When estrogen binds to receptors on certain cancer cells, the cells divide, and the tumor gets larger. Drugs called aromatase inhibitors prevent estrogen production.

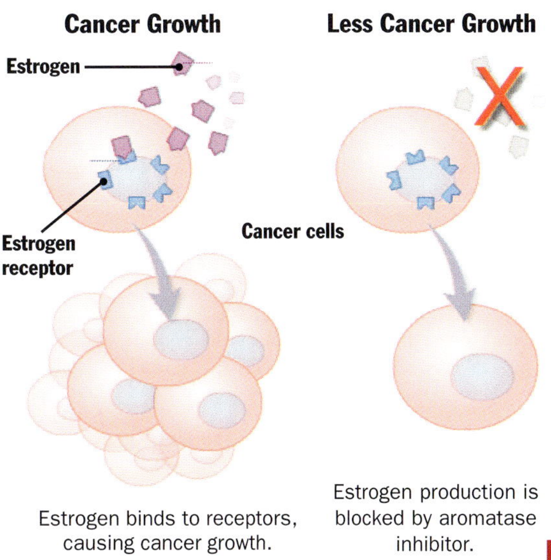

Breast Cancer

Antibiotic Use Linked to Breast Cancer

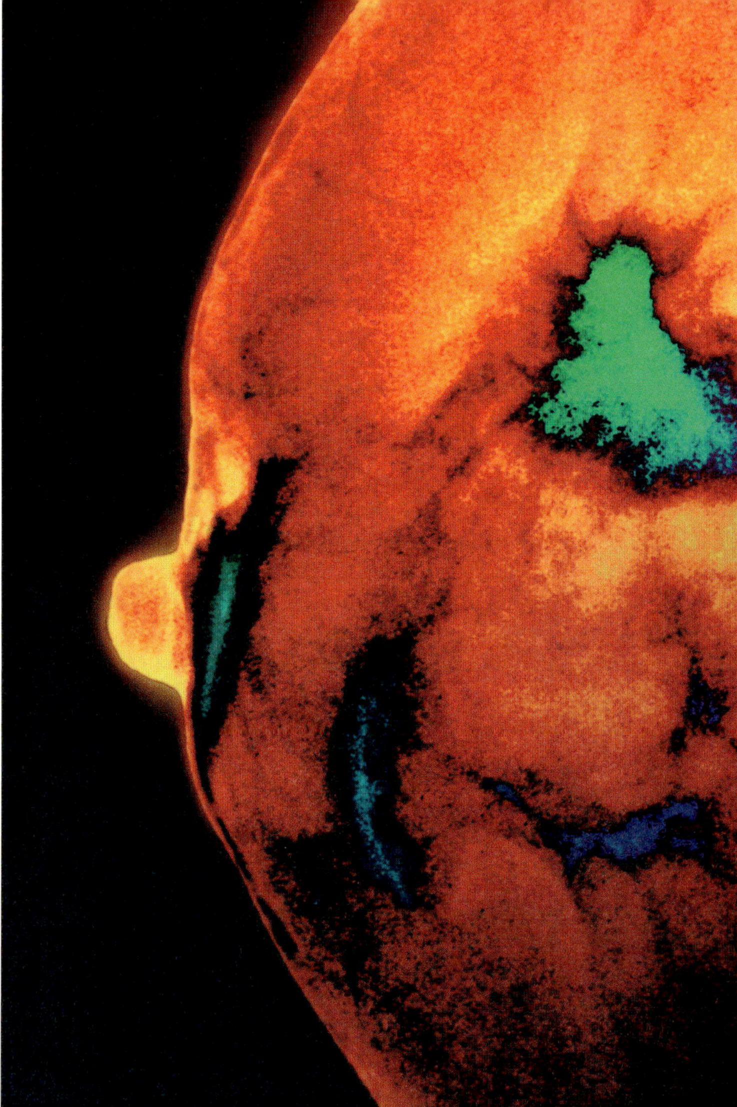

A cancerous tumor shows up green in this mammogram. Being overweight is one risk factor for breast cancer. Now it appears that heavy use of antibiotics may be another.

Long-term use of antibiotics, some of the world's most commonly used medications, may join the list of factors that cause breast cancer. That's the finding from the second study ever designed to look at a possible connection between the drugs and the cancer.

After reading a 2000 Finnish study that suggested antibiotic use might contribute to breast cancer risk, Christine Velicer, Ph.D., a research associate at the Group Health Cooperative Center for Health Studies in Seattle, decided to conduct her own study. Because Group Health has a pharmacy database dating back to 1977, is located within an area that requires that all cancers be tracked, and is part of the National Cancer Institute's Breast Cancer Surveillance Program, she and her colleagues had access to all the data they needed to explore the connection in more detail.

They compared medical information and history of antibiotic use for more than 10,000 women who have been enrolled in the health insurance organization for an average of 17 years. About 2,000 of the women had developed breast cancer.

What the study found. The researchers discovered that women who took antibiotics for more than 500 days (or more than 25 individual prescriptions) over an average period of 17 years had double the risk of breast cancer of women who took none. The more antibiotics the women took, the greater their risk of the disease was. The risk remained the same across all classes of antibiotics, a finding that surprised the researchers.

"We thought we'd see that some types increased the risk and others decreased the risk, and the whole thing would be a wash," says Dr. Velicer. "We were very surprised at the consistency of our findings."

Understanding the link. Dr. Velicer emphasizes that this study does not mean that antibiotics—drugs that have saved countless lives since their invention—cause breast cancer. There are several possible reasons for the link the research revealed.

- Antibiotics may affect various immune functions that in turn affect the production of estrogen, the hormone that plays a role in the development of breast cancer.
- Antibiotics disrupt the "good" bacteria in the gut, the kind that aid digestion. That may affect a woman's ability to absorb important chemicals that are found in plant foods and known to protect against breast cancer.
- Antibiotics affect certain chemicals that contribute to inflammation in the body, such as prostaglandins, cytokines, and COX 1 and 2 enzymes, all of which may also be involved in the development of cancer.

"As the research develops, we'll be able to see what's going on," says Dr. Velicer. For instance, it may not be the antibiotics themselves that are responsible for the increase in breast cancer risk but rather the fact that women who need to use antibiotics frequently have weaker immune systems that make them more susceptible to cancer.

Overall, she says, the possible increased risk to women who often take antibiotics is about the same as for any other common risk factor for breast cancer, including early menstruation, having children later in life or never having children, hormone therapy, and being overweight.

The bottom line, says Dr. Velicer, is that women should still take antibiotics when they need them. "Antibiotics have a huge benefit in our society, and they need to be used wisely, and that's not going to change," she says. But she emphasizes the phrase "used wisely," because antibiotics are often overused—for instance, to treat viral infections such as colds, even though the drugs have no effect on viruses. The results of Dr. Velicer's study were published in a February 2004 issue of the *Journal of the American Medical Association.*

RESEARCH ROUNDUP

Antidepressants May Interfere with Cancer Treatment

About 1 in 12 cancer patients suffers from depression. Now, a small study suggests that the medications most commonly used to treat depression—selective serotonin reuptake inhibitors (SSRIs) such as paroxetine (Paxil) and fluoxetine (Prozac)—could interfere with one of the drugs most commonly used to prevent a breast cancer recurrence: tamoxifen.

The study followed 12 women with breast cancer who were given Paxil for four weeks during their standard course of tamoxifen therapy. Blood tests revealed significantly lower amounts of a chemical related to the breakdown of tamoxifen after the women took Paxil than before they took it. This indicated that their bodies were less effective at breaking down and absorbing the tamoxifen.

The researchers emphasize that this is a very preliminary study and that more studies are required before recommending any changes in current treatments for depression.

Exercise Improves Breast Cancer Survival

Everyone knows by now that exercise is good for you. It reduces the risk of most cancers, diabetes, heart disease, diabetes, depression...the list goes on and on. And of course, it helps keep off extra pounds that themselves contribute to disease. Now, a Harvard study has found that exercise also significantly improves a woman's chance of surviving a battle with breast cancer.

Earlier studies had shown that exercise improved a woman's quality of life after a breast cancer diagnosis. This study, however, found that just 1 to 3 hours of walking a week cut a woman's risk of dying from breast cancer by 19 percent, while women who walked 3 to 5 hours a week slashed their risk by 54 percent.

What's the connection? "Exercise may lower the levels of hormones that stimulate cancer to grow," says lead researcher Michelle D. Holmes, M.D., Dr.P.H., who presented the study at a major cancer meeting in March 2004.

Breast Cancer

Virtual Reality Makes Chemotherapy a Walk in the Park

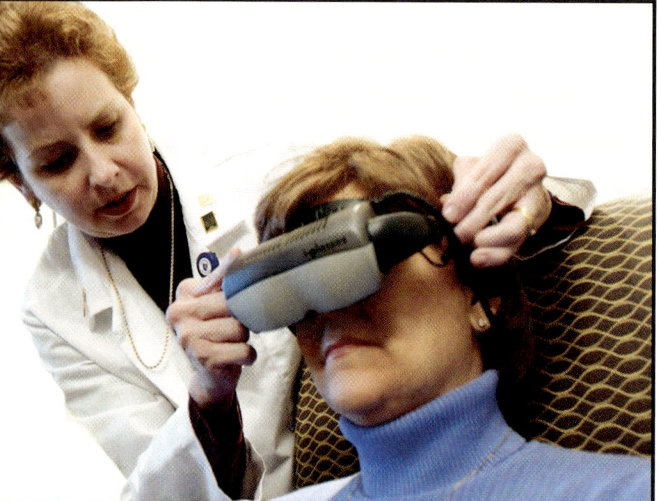

Susan M. Schneider, R.N., Ph.D., fits a chemotherapy patient with virtual reality goggles at Duke University Medical Center. The "mental vacation" reduces the ill effects of the treatment.

Which would you rather do while undergoing chemotherapy for breast cancer: sit in a room filled with other sick people who are also getting infusions of toxic chemicals, or walk on a beach? How about deep-sea diving or touring an art gallery?

Chemotherapy patients can't actually do any of these activities while in the hospital, of course, but soon they may be able to put on a pair of goggles and experience them through computer-generated virtual reality.

A small study recently found that women with breast cancer who used virtual reality during their chemo sessions experienced less fatigue, nausea, vomiting, and inability to concentrate immediately after chemotherapy than women who didn't use the technique. Such symptoms affect about 60 percent of chemotherapy patients. Additionally, the women who "escaped" via virtual reality thought the chemotherapy sessions—which averaged 67 minutes—lasted an average of only 42 minutes. The results were published in the January 2004 issue of *Oncology Nursing Forum.*

"Just the process of receiving chemotherapy can be stressful," says Susan M. Schneider, R.N., Ph.D., director of the graduate oncology nursing program at Duke University School of Nursing in Durham, North Carolina, and lead researcher in the study. "Deciding with the physician which chemotherapeutic agents are best, completing lab work, and waiting for appointments can wear someone down. By the time a woman gets to the clinic for her treatment, she is often emotionally exhausted. The virtual reality provides folks with a mental vacation."

In 2004, Dr. Schneider was completing larger studies of patients who have colon, lung, and breast cancer to better understand who might benefit most from virtual reality and how to achieve more lasting reductions in post-chemo symptoms and fatigue.

Availability. Currently, virtual reality is in use at just a couple of hospitals that are evaluating it, says Dr. Schneider. Look for that to change as more studies like this one demonstrate its benefits. ■

FUTURE BREAKTHROUGHS

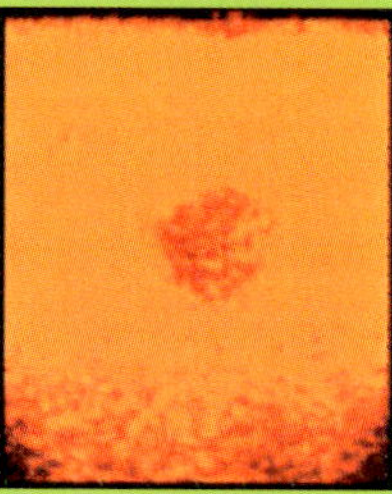

Low-frequency vibrations make tumors stand out in a special ultrasound scan.

Breast Cancer Screening without Radiation

Someday your doctor may be able to screen you for breast cancer simply by waving a handheld device over your skin—no uncomfortable mammogram required. A group of surgeons, computer specialists, and physical scientists at the University of Dundee in Scotland have invented just such a device, dubbed Sonoelastographic Breast Imaging. The device can detect the tiniest of breast lesions because the lesions are stiffer than surrounding breast tissue, so they move differently when the imaging tool hits them with sound waves. Instead of waiting days for your results, you'd get them immediately. Researchers are now gearing up for large-scale clinical studies to test the device's effectiveness.

Breast Cancer

Fight Cancer with Your Eyes Closed

"Rest when you're ill." That common wisdom is often ignored, particularly by women who try to be all things to all people. Now, a study from Stanford University researchers suggests that poor sleeping patterns, often the result of stress, can affect the course of breast cancer.

What the study found. David Spiegel, M.D., associate chair of psychiatry and behavioral sciences at Stanford, has conducted groundbreaking work showing that women with breast cancer who participate in support groups or psychotherapy live longer than women who don't. In searching for the reason behind this finding, Dr. Spiegel tested levels of the so-called stress hormone cortisol throughout the day in 17 women whose breast cancer had spread, then compared those numbers with cortisol levels in 31 healthy women.

Normally, he says, cortisol levels are highest in the morning and lowest at night. Two-thirds of the breast cancer patients tested, however, had altered cortisol levels—they rose throughout the day, a sign of a disrupted circadian rhythm (the normal cycle of sleep and waking). When questioned, the women with disrupted hormone levels admitted they had trouble falling asleep and sleeping through the night. As it turned out, they also died sooner than women with more normal cortisol cycles did. The results of that study were published in the online version of the journal *Psychoneuroendocrinology* in January 2004.

The link between cortisol, cancer, and sleep is complex, and much remains to be understood, notes Dr. Spiegel. A possible explanation for the connection is that high levels of cortisol, which belongs to a class of chemicals that suppress the immune system, might prevent the immune system from effectively fighting the cancer. Additionally, cortisol may trigger a response similar to that of estrogen or progesterone, hormones that stimulate growth in many breast cancer tumors.

What it means. One way to control cortisol levels is to get enough uninterrupted sleep, says Dr. Spiegel. Many of the women he sees don't get enough sleep because they're trying to do too much during a time when they should be taking it easier, he says. Additionally, women with breast cancer should try to manage stress as best they can. "Cancer is a message to you that your resources are not infinite," he says. ■

Breast Cancer

MRI Screenings Help Women at High Risk

Say your mother died of breast cancer. And your aunt. And an older sister had it. Also say that when you went for genetic counseling and testing, you learned that you carry a genetic mutation that dramatically increases your risk of the disease. How can you ensure that if you do get breast cancer, you catch it early?

Until recently, the answer might have been to have regular mammograms. But a major dutch study published in a July 2004 issue of the *New England Journal of Medicine* found that women at high risk are better off if they also have MRI screenings. The study, involving nearly 2,000 high-risk women, found that MRIs identified breast cancers that mammograms missed, particularly more deadly, invasive types.

Beyond mammograms. Most of the major cancer organizations already recommend that all women receive annual mammograms beginning at age 40. But women with family histories of breast cancer or those who carry genetic mutations that substantially increase their risks should begin screening earlier.

The problem is that younger women have denser breasts, and mammograms aren't very good at telling the difference between a mammary gland, which shows up white on a mammogram, and cancer, which also shows up white. "It's like trying to find a polar bear in a snowstorm," explains Marissa Weiss, M.D., a Philadelphia-based radiation oncologist who is also president of the consumer Website www.breastcancer.org.

MRI screening, on the other hand, "allows you to separate the appearance of regular gland tissue from the appearance of cancer, and that's powerful," she says.

There are downsides to MRIs, however, which is why the tests aren't used for screening on all women. First, they're much more expensive than mammograms—about $1,500 compared with about $100. Second, MRIs are more likely to produce false positives—that is, suspicious readings that result in biopsies that turn out to be negative. In fact, in the study, MRI screening led to three times as many unneeded biopsies as mammography.

Still worth doing. Nonetheless, notes Dr. Weiss, "if a woman is at high risk because she has a gene abnormality or because breast cancer is prevalent through her family, absolutely she should consider having regular MRIs." That doesn't mean she should give up on mammograms, though. The two should be used in conjunction, she says, because "they provide different pieces of information." For instance, the study found that mammography is better than an MRI at identifying ductal carcinoma in situ, the most common type of noninvasive breast cancer.

For best results, Dr. Weiss recommends having MRIs performed at centers that do lots of them. Make sure the machine is equipped with a breast coil, an instrument that improves the quality of the pictures. And take along your mammogram films so the radiologist can read the MRI along with the mammogram, she says. "You want them to have as much information as possible to best interpret the study," she says. ■

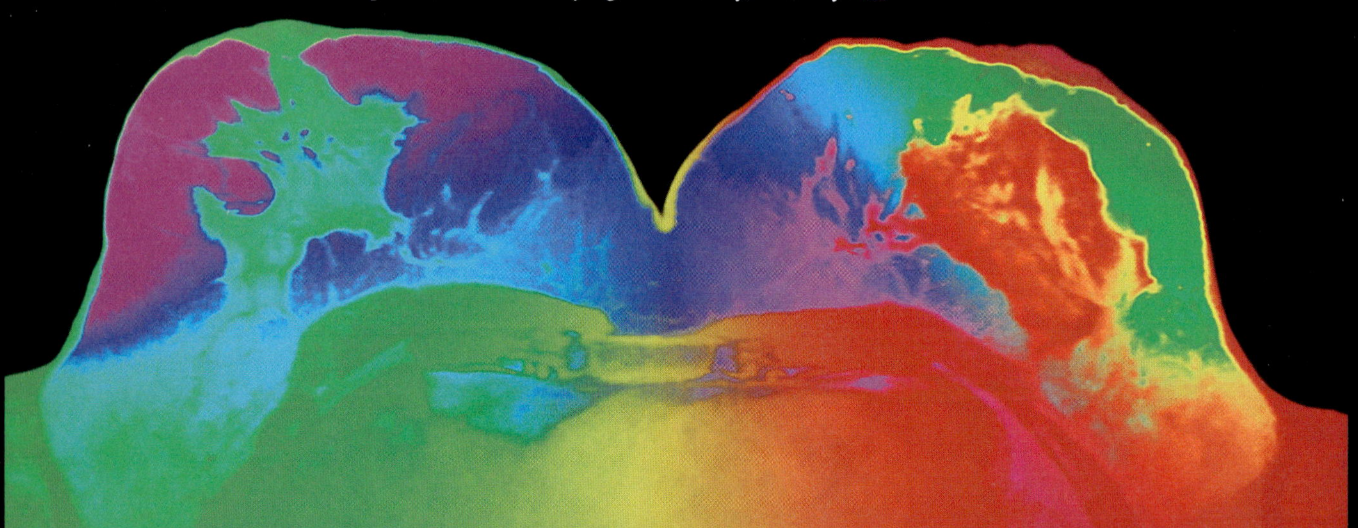

Colon Cancer

Tumor-Starving Drug Approved

Cancer survivor Grace Vanhoose credits Avastin with saving her life.

Grace Vanhoose received her death sentence in February 2002. That's when the colon cancer she thought she'd beaten three years earlier returned with a vengeance, showing up in her spine and neck. She had Stage IV cancer, the worst and final stage, and just a few months to live. But Vanhoose didn't give up. She found a doctor who enrolled her in a clinical trial to test a new idea in cancer treatment—that a tumor could be killed by choking off its blood supply. Today, Vanhoose, 57, of Everett, Washington, is back at work as an administrative assistant, feeling great and looking forward to living for many more years. In February 2004, the FDA approved the drug she credits with saving her life, bevacizumab (Avastin). When she heard the news, she says, "I felt such joy."

Avastin is the first of a new class of cancer drugs, called angiogenesis inhibitors, to be approved. The drugs were the subject of a controversial article in the *New York Times* in the late 1990s, which declared they would be the long-awaited cure for cancer. While it's doubtful the drugs will ever justify that early hype, researchers remain hopeful that Avastin and other angiogenesis inhibitors currently in the pipeline will radically change cancer treatment for the better.

How they work. The drugs work on the theory that to survive, tumors form a network of blood vessels—a process called angiogenesis—and that shutting down that network leads to a tumor's ultimate demise. Avastin works in conjunction with chemotherapy; in addition to shutting down a tumor's blood supply, it decreases the pressure between cancer cells, allowing more chemotherapy drugs into the tumor.

In clinical trials, late-stage colon cancer patients taking Avastin lived an average of five months longer. That may not seem like a lot, but to oncologists like Deborah Lindquist, M.D., of Northern Arizona Hematology and Oncology Associates in Flagstaff, who had five patients enrolled in the trial, it's tremendous. All five had cancers that had spread to the liver, a certain death sentence, yet three are still alive nearly three years after starting on the drug. That, says Dr. Lindquist, gives patients the time they need to enroll in other trials and try other treatments.

Availability. Avastin, produced by the biotech company Genentech, is currently approved only for treatment of late-stage colon cancer, although it is in clinical trials for lung and breast cancer. The drug is also awaiting approval in Europe.

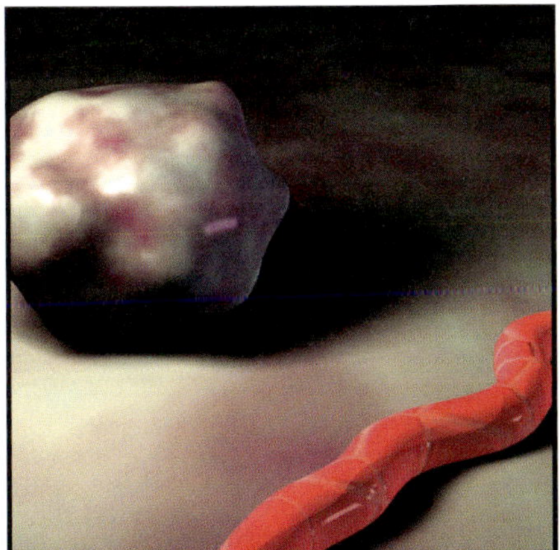

A tumor is an abnormal mass of cells that divide without control. To grow, these cells need nutrients from surrounding blood vessels.

When a tumor needs a bigger food supply, it secretes a protein that appears to stimulate blood vessels to grow toward the tumor.

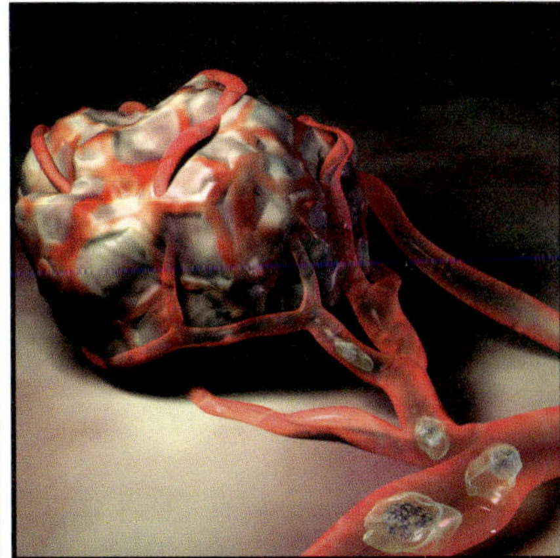

The new blood vessels reach the tumor, feeding it nutrients and allowing it to grow even more.

General Cancer

What Causes Cancer? A New Theory

When you hear "stem cells," what comes to mind? Probably those highly sought-after cells that have the power to transform themselves into any other kind of cell—heart, lung, muscle, brain—and may have the potential to repair damaged tissue and cure terrible diseases such as Alzheimer's and Parkinson's, and even paralyzing spinal injuries. These cells are so highly valued not only because they can turn into other types of cells but also because they can replicate, or divide, indefinitely, creating an infinite supply.

But what if stem cells had evil twins, "bad seeds" whose powers of limitless regeneration were used not to heal but to spread disease—specifically cancer—throughout the body?

This theory is called the cancer stem cell hypothesis, and it's getting further from hypothesis and closer to fact. If it's proven true, everything we've ever thought about what cancers are, how they grow, and how to treat them may be only about 10 percent right.

"It gives us a new framework to think of in studying cancer and targeting treatments," says Peter Dirks, M.D., a neurosurgeon, assistant professor at the University of Toronto, and a leader in cancer stem cell research.

The worst of the worst. Put simply, the cancer stem cell hypothesis theorizes that aberrant stem cells, a kind of "black sheep" of stem cells, are to blame for the rapidly dividing cells that become cancer. If it's true, instead of hitting cancer with the big guns of chemotherapy and radiation, which take their toll on patients, targeting just those stem cells could eventually make treating cancer almost as simple as treating strep throat.

The theory is an old one, dating to the 1960s. Back then, however, scientists didn't have the tools to prove it. The explosion of research into stem cells in the past decade, along with techniques to fish out stem cells from organs, has reinvigorated scientific interest.

"Essentially, the theory says that in a cancer, not every cell in the tumor has the ability to regrow the tumor," says John E. Dick, Ph.D., who directs the Program in Stem Cell Biology at the University of Toronto. This in turn goes against all we've ever thought about cancers.

Dr. Dick, Dr. Dirks, and others have found that in leukemia and brain and breast cancers at least, there are several different types of cancer cells in the same tumor. In leukemia, which is Dr. Dick's area of specialty and in which the bulk of the cancer stem cell work has been conducted, a tiny minority of rogue stem cells creates other cells called progenitor cells, which rapidly divide and produce billions of abnormal cells that overwhelm the blood.

Stem cells divide quite slowly, and sometimes they hibernate, hiding out in the body (exactly where is unknown) for months or even years before "turning on" again. Thus, the traditional approach to cancer treatment—attacking rapidly dividing cells with chemotherapy drugs or radiation—is likely to miss them, leaving them to potentially revitalize and start producing more cancer cells down the road. This helps to explain why Dr. Dirks might remove a

"Bad Seed" Cancer Theory

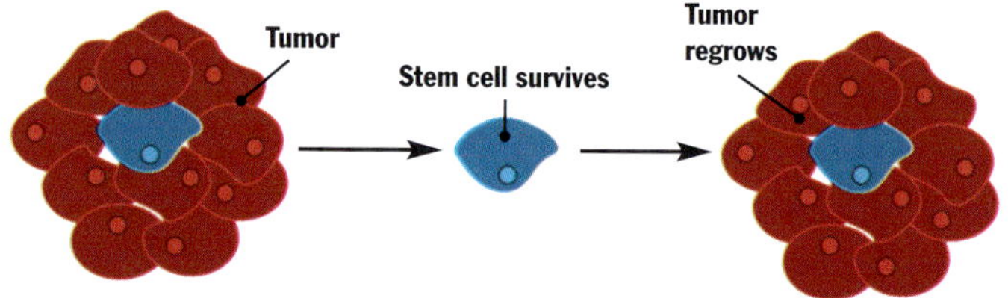

Traditional cancer therapies kill rapidly dividing tumor cells (red) but may spare the slowly dividing stem cells (blue), allowing the tumor to regrow.

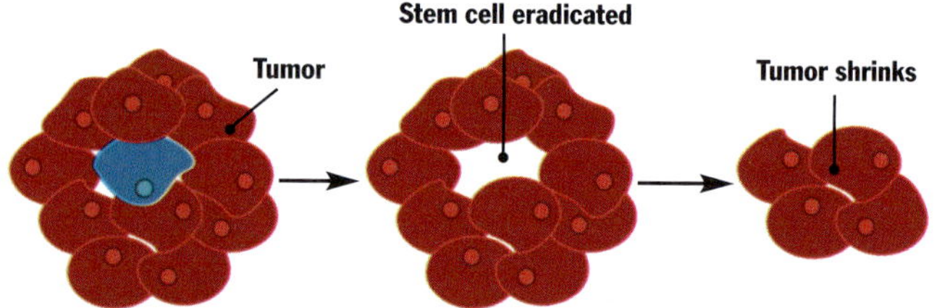

In theory, killing the cancer stem cell should halt the tumor's growth and perhaps lead to its disappearance.

Tumor cells, magnified here 7,500 times, grow and divide without restraint. If cancer stem cells indeed spawn them, destroying those cells is vital to killing the cancer.

brain tumor, think he got it all, and then have the patient relapse a few months or years after treatment. "The whole stem cell cancer hypothesis suggests that we might wipe out 99 out of 100 cells. But if we don't get the key cell, the cancer is just going to regrow," he says.

The future of cancer treatment. Although so far stem cells have been identified only in leukemia and in brain and breast cancers, researchers suspect they're at the root of all cancers. The question, of course, is how to stop them.

There are several potential approaches. Drugs could be designed to attack the mechanism within the stem cells that makes them self-renewing or to turn on a signal that makes them die. Antibodies could be developed that target proteins on the surface of the stem cells, delivering a poison directly to the cells. Or, in a kind of counterintuitive process, treatments may involve getting stem cells to mature into cancer cells; once mature, they stop regenerating and die off.

Researchers will have to tread carefully, however. Dr. Dirks and Dr. Dick suspect that cancer stem cells are actually normal stem cells gone bad. It will be vitally important that treatments targeting the black sheep cells don't inadvertently hit normal stem cells, they say.

The idea of stem cells as the root of all cancers also suggests new ways of determining how deadly a cancer might be. In the brain cancers he's studied so far, for instance, Dr. Dirks has found that the higher the ratio of stem cells to other cancer cells, the more aggressive the tumor.

The next steps. The whole field of stem cell cancer research is barely a decade old. It will take many more years of basic research before the findings bear fruit, but that doesn't keep scientists like Dr. Dick and Dr. Dirks from being very excited. Says Dr. Dirks, "Finding this culprit gives us hope that further research on these key cells will yield further breakthroughs about how cancer grows so we can more effectively treat it."

General Cancer

Fishing for Cancer Cures

The deep-sea sponge Discodermia may yield one of the most powerful anti-cancer compounds ever discovered.

Creatures that spend their lives anchored in one place on the ocean floor have evolved powerful chemical defenses to keep their enemies at bay. Now, scientists have discovered that those same unique compounds can apparently protect your body, too—against a broad range of cancers.

Researchers from Harbor Branch Oceanographic Institution in Fort Pierce, Florida, are leading the quest to find breakthrough medicines in the cells of organisms such as sponges, sea squirts, and mollusks. They're probing the depths of the Earth's oceans with state-of-the-art, deep-diving, manned submersibles equipped with sophisticated robotic equipment to collect marine organisms 3,000 feet beneath the surface.

Nature's defenses. The sea creatures garnering so much attention are "sessile," meaning that once they become adults, they remain firmly attached to one spot. This makes them ideal for research, says Amy Wright, Ph.D., director of Harbor Branch's division of biomedical marine research. "Because they're stuck in one place, they make chemical compounds to protect themselves from predators and keep other organisms from crowding their space," she explains. As it turns out, those compounds may be powerful weapons against human diseases.

Back in 1984, Harbor Branch scientists exploring the deep waters off the Bahamas found a small piece of sponge that contained a chemical with remarkable cancer-killing ability. But it took 20 more years before scientists were able to find the sponge again, says Dr. Wright, who has spent much of her career searching for it. In October 2003, she and her colleagues located it in water 1,000 feet deep in the Bahamas, in an area known as the dead zone because it has so little animal or plant life. Dr. Wright and her colleagues are now testing chemicals in the sponge for anti-cancer properties. (The chemical that first attracted their attention has also been identified by a second marine research team—in a different sponge in a different part of the world.)

Pancreatic cancer cure? Meanwhile, lab tests suggest that a compound called discodermolide, isolated by the Harbor Branch team from a Caribbean Sea sponge, may be up to 80 times more potent than Taxol, a chemotherapy drug initially derived from the bark of yew trees and often used to treat breast and ovarian cancer There's also some evidence that combining the compound with Taxol produces more powerful results than using either one alone. A synthetic version of discodermolide

Harbor Branch marine scientists catalog a sea sponge collected by a submersible for later study.

Harbor Branch's research submersible, capable of exploring 3,000 feet underwater, starts a dive. Its mission: to find marine sources of new drugs.

entered the first phase of human clinical trials for pancreatic cancer in late 2003 at the Cancer Therapy and Research Center in San Antonio, Texas. Other cancer killers from the sea currently under investigation include:

- A synthetic drug called ecteinascidin, which mimics a molecule found in saclike sea squirts that live on Caribbean coral reefs. Early studies indicate it could be hundreds to thousands of times more powerful than any cancer drug now in use. The drug is being tested in human clinical trials in Europe.
- Dolastatin-10, isolated from a sea hare found in the Comoros Islands in the western Indian Ocean. It is undergoing clinical trials in the United States for treating a variety of cancers.
- Bryostatin 1, isolated from a tiny, plantlike marine invertebrate found off the coast of California. It is being studied in more than 40 clinical trials throughout the United States and appears to prevent the growth of numerous tumors, including those of melanoma, non-Hodgkin's lymphoma, and kidney cancer.
- Halichondrin B, isolated from a sponge that's part of the Lissodendoryx species, found in New Zealand. It is currently undergoing testing in animals for its ability to combat numerous cancers.

All told, more than 5,000 new compounds have been derived from marine organisms in the last decade alone, says Dr. Wright. Her own division has discovered more than 300 bioactive compounds (compounds that have effects on other living organisms) and has filed more than 100 patents on them. Most recently, she and her colleagues have begun exploring deep-sea sites in the Gulf of Mexico, including abandoned oil rigs and an ancient shoreline—the first time such research has been conducted on the biomedical potential of the deep-sea life in that body of water. ■

General Cancer

Another Reason to Eat Your Spinach

You can bet that Popeye the Sailor Man never had cancer. That's because the gargantuan quantities of spinach he ate probably did more than just keep him strong: They also may have helped prevent prostate and bladder cancer.

That's the finding from two studies presented at a major cancer meeting in April 2004, both of which found that getting vitamin E from food can significantly reduce your risk of either of these cancers—and spinach is a great source.

Food, not supplements. If you're used to getting your vitamin E from a gel cap, that won't do the trick here. The studies, one from the National Cancer Institute (NCI) and the other from the University of Texas M. D. Anderson Cancer Center in Houston, found that only vitamin E from food made a difference.

The NCI study, which looked at blood samples of 100 Finnish men, found that those with the highest concentrations of a form of vitamin E called alpha tocopherol were 53 percent less likely to get prostate cancer. Those with the highest concentrations of the other major form of vitamin E, gamma tocopherol (the most common form in the American diet) were 39 percent less likely to get prostate cancer. The Texas study found that for those with the highest alpha tocopherol concentrations, the risk of bladder cancer was reduced by 42 percent, but no amount of gamma tocopherol had any effect.

Just 8 percent of men and 2.4 percent of women in the United States get the recommended amounts of alpha tocopherol (about 50 milligrams a day) from their diets. It's not hard to get, though: An ounce of sunflower seeds contains about 14 milligrams. Other great sources include almonds (8 milligrams per ounce), spinach (6 milligrams in one package of frozen spinach), wheat germ oil (26 milligrams in 1 tablespoon), mustard greens (1 milligram per cup of chopped raw greens), green and red peppers (1 milligram per large pepper), and canola oil (about 4 milligrams per tablespoon). ■

People with diabetes may now want to have liver enzyme tests annually as well as monitoring their blood sugar.

Liver Cancer

Diabetes Raises Liver Cancer Risk

Researchers have known for years that there is a connection between diabetes and liver cancer, because people with diabetes have more cases of liver cancer and other liver disease than those without diabetes. What they didn't know was which came first, the diabetes or the liver problems. Now, results from the largest study of its kind show that having diabetes doubles the risk of liver cancer and chronic liver disease.

The findings may have tremendous public health implications because of the growing epidemic of diabetes in the United States and other Western countries, says lead researcher Hashem El-Serag, M.D., associate professor of medicine at Baylor College of Medicine in Houston and the Houston VA Medical Center.

Behind the connection. Although they don't know for sure why liver cancer and diabetes are linked, researchers do know that people who are overweight and have diabetes are more likely to develop a condition called nonalcoholic fatty liver disease (NAFLD). It's probably related to fat accumulating in the liver because the organ can't transform enough of the fat into a form that can be eliminated. By itself, NAFLD usually isn't dangerous. However, it can develop into what Dr. El-Serag calls an uglier condition—NASH, or nonalcoholic steatohepatitis, in which inflammation of the liver damages liver cells, in some instances leading to cirrhosis and liver cancer. This may be what's happening with diabetes patients.

What it means. "If even a small percentage of those with diabetes develop NASH and liver cancer, it will translate into a very large number of patients," says Dr. El-Serag. In the meantime, he notes, it's important that people with diabetes or other insulin-related conditions, such as insulin resistance, have annual blood tests to track their liver enzyme levels, which can indicate liver disease. ■

Drug That Brought Down Martha Stewart Approved

Just a month before domestic doyenne Martha Stewart was convicted by a federal jury on charges of obstructing justice and lying to investigators about a well-timed stock sale, the FDA approved the drug at the heart of the whole mess, cetuximab (Erbitux), produced by ImClone Systems.

Erbitux is a monoclonal antibody, a laboratory-produced substance that locates and binds to cancer cells throughout the body, preventing proteins that encourage cancer cell growth from doing their job.

Prosecutors argued that Stewart sold her ImClone stock after learning that the company's founder, Sam Waksal, was trying to sell his stock based on a tip that the FDA would not review the company's application for the drug's approval without more clinical trials.

ImClone conducted those trials, and in February 2004, the FDA approved Erbitux to treat colorectal cancers that have spread to other parts of the body. The drug is administered intravenously, either along with a chemotherapy drug called irinotecan (Camptosar) or alone in patients who can't tolerate Camptosar.

Lung Cancer

An Aggressive Weapon against Aggressive Cancer

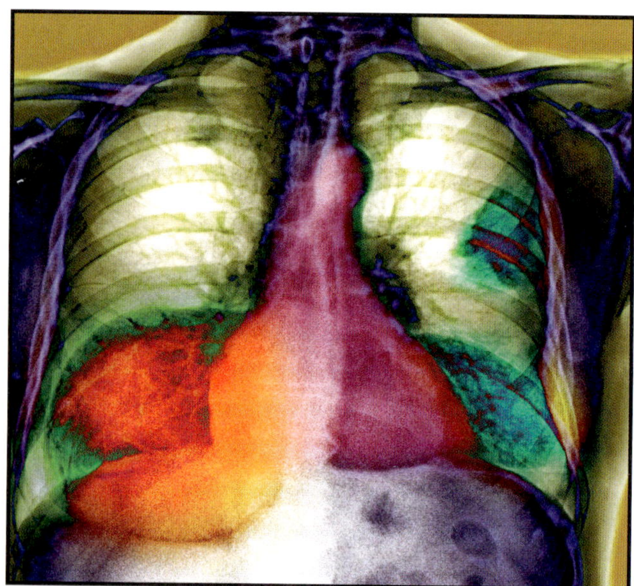

In people with certain genetic profiles, lung cancer (red and green shadings) is particularly vulnerable to the drug Iressa.

Thank goodness the director of the Massachusetts General Hospital Cancer Center reads the *Boston Globe*. If he didn't, one of the most important developments in lung cancer treatment this year might never have occurred.

Daniel Haber, M.D., Ph.D., read about a patient's amazing recovery from terminal lung cancer in 2002, after she was treated with the then-experimental drug gefitinib (Iressa). He was intrigued. He knew that Iressa worked in only about 10 percent of patients and that genetics were the likely reason, but no one knew which genes made some patients so responsive to the drug. Dr. Haber set out to find out, with the help of some colleagues. What the doctors found could mean that more patients who could be saved by the drug will get it sooner.

How it works. Iressa, approved in 2003 for patients with non-small-cell lung cancer, the most common form, works by blocking signals within the cancer cells, thus preventing a series of chemical reactions that cause the cells to grow and divide. Specifically, it works through structures known as epidermal growth factor receptors (EGFRs). Proteins called epidermal growth factors attach to these receptors, triggering reactions that enable the cells to grow and divide. Iressa blocks the receptors, halting the process.

Dr. Haber and his colleagues, as well as a group of researchers at Dana Farber Cancer Center in Boston who were working separately on the problem, found that patients in whom Iressa worked had genetic mutations in the EGFRs. The mutations made the cells grow much faster and more aggressively than "normal" cancer cells. Additionally, the mutant receptors seem to bind more tightly to Iressa, in effect creating a tighter seal against cancer growth. In other words, although the mutations make the cancer more aggressive, they also make it more susceptible to the drug.

What it means. The discovery is already changing the way some people with lung cancer are treated. "Right now, all lung cancer patients are treated the same way," Dr. Haber says, "but now we know that if you have a certain genetic mutation, you're so likely to respond to Iressa that it should be part of your first line of treatment." The drug is currently approved for use only after every other avenue of treatment fails, but it can be prescribed "off-label"—that is, at a doctor's discretion.

Although the test for the mutation can be performed at most large hospitals, it requires more tissue from lung biopsies than doctors usually get with the current, noninvasive method, so biopsy methods may have to change.

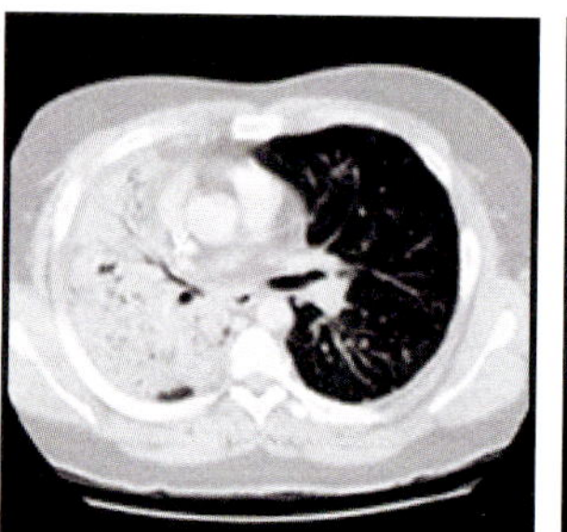

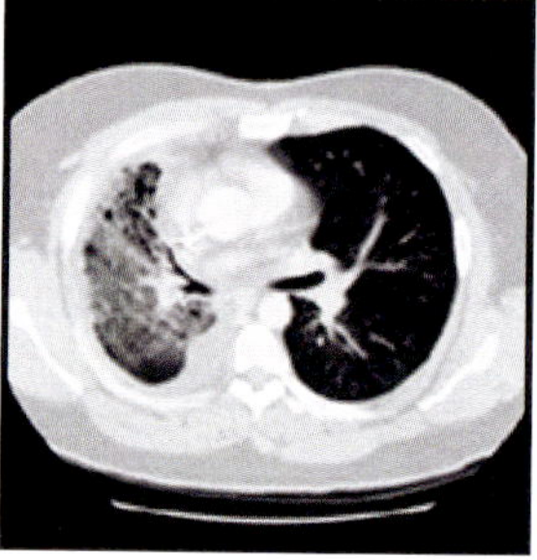

Left: CT scan shows cancer in a patient's right lung. Right: marked improvement after six weeks on Iressa.

Prostate Cancer

Radiation for Prostate Cancer: The Earlier, the Better

More than 15,000 lives could be saved each year in the United States if doctors began treating recurrent prostate cancer with radiation immediately, a practice that rarely occurs. That's the finding in a groundbreaking paper published in the *Journal of the American Medical Association* (JAMA) in March 2004.

About 30,000 men in the United States find that their cancer returns, most often showing up in the bone, after their prostates are removed. Once it recurs, only radiation will cure it, but studies show that less than half of the men who qualify for radiation get it, primarily because most doctors don't think radiation works well for fairly aggressive cancers. Their opinions are based on earlier studies that researchers now say were flawed. Instead, most doctors prescribe hormone therapy, which slows the cancer's growth but doesn't kill it.

Now, the largest evaluation ever conducted of radiation as a treatment for recurrent prostate cancer has found that the old thinking is wrong. Given early enough, radiation *can* cure the cancer, or at least significantly improve a patient's prognosis, researchers from Baylor College of Medicine in Houston found.

PSA levels not enough. Part of the confusion stemmed from a misunderstanding about what it meant when levels of PSA, a protein released by prostate cells, rose after the prostate was removed. For years, doctors assumed that rising PSA rates meant the cancer had spread to other organs and was thus incurable. The new study found that this wasn't necessarily true.

The findings highlight the need for men to stay vigilant about their care for prostate cancer after surgery, says Mitchell S. Anscher, M.D., a radiologist at Duke University Medical Center in Durham, North Carolina. Dr. Anscher wrote an editorial about the study that appeared in the same issue of JAMA. "They need to be aware of the findings at the time of surgery and whether they're really in a group that has a very high chance of being cured just with surgery or are in the group that is at risk of a recurrence."

That means tracking their PSA levels after surgery, finding out their Gleason scores—an indication of the cancer's severity—and learning if there were positive margins (cancer cells) at the edges of the tissue that was removed. The main reason a man wouldn't qualify for radiation would be that the cancer had spread to his lymph nodes.

Experts hope the findings change the way recurrent prostate cancer is treated. "I hope people will be sent for evaluation to see if they qualify for radiation much earlier," Dr. Anscher says. The lead author of the study, Kevin M. Slawin, M.D., is creating a formula to help doctors determine if they should send their patients for radiation after a cancer recurrence.

RESEARCH ROUNDUP

More Confusion about PSA Results

One of the most controversial cancer screenings is the PSA test, used to check for prostate cancer. The blood test checks for levels of prostate specific antigen (PSA), a protein released by prostate cells. When the test should be done in healthy men and how the results should be interpreted in both healthy men and those with cancer are subjects of debate. In April 2004, the waters got a bit murkier with the publication of a study finding that even low PSA levels in men who already have prostate cancer could represent serious situations.

Typically, PSA levels of 4.0 or less are thought to be relatively benign, even in men being treated for cancer. This study, from researchers at the University of Chicago, found that cancer specimens from men with levels less than 4.0 were still clinically significant, indicating that they required treatment. The findings mean that doctors should not rely on PSA readings alone to determine the status of a man's cancer and shouldn't assume that a low-PSA cancer doesn't require immediate treatment.

Skin Cancer

New Way to Predict Skin Cancer's Spread

The earlier skin cancer is detected, the better the chance that it can be cured before it spreads to other organs.

The incidence of malignant melanoma, the deadliest form of skin cancer, continues to rise around the world. Currently, about 132,000 melanoma skin cancers occur globally each year, resulting in more than 33,000 deaths. In the United States, melanoma is the most rapidly increasing cancer, growing from 17,000 cases in 1979 to 53,600 in 2002 (and causing some 7,000 deaths). That's a 68 percent increase. Now, researchers at Bristol University in England think they've found a new way to predict whether melanoma will spread (metastasize) to other organs, which dramatically increases the risk of death from the cancer.

How it works. To date, doctors have focused on the thickness of a melanoma, believing that the thicker the cancer, the more likely it is to metastasize. But only one in four thick melanomas spread, while many thin ones metastasize as well.

Most melanomas, if they spread, travel to nearby lymph nodes through lymph vessels—vessels that connect lymph nodes, carrying lymph fluid in and out. Knowing that in animals, the growth of lymph vessels is associated with the spread of cancer, the British researchers focused their efforts on those vessels. They recorded the density of lymph vessels surrounding melanoma samples from 21 patients, then followed the patients for at least eight years. As predicted, the denser the lymph vessels were, the more likely the patient was to develop additional cancers. In fact, the correlation between lymph vessel density and cancer metastasis was much greater than the correlation between melanoma thickness and cancer metastasis.

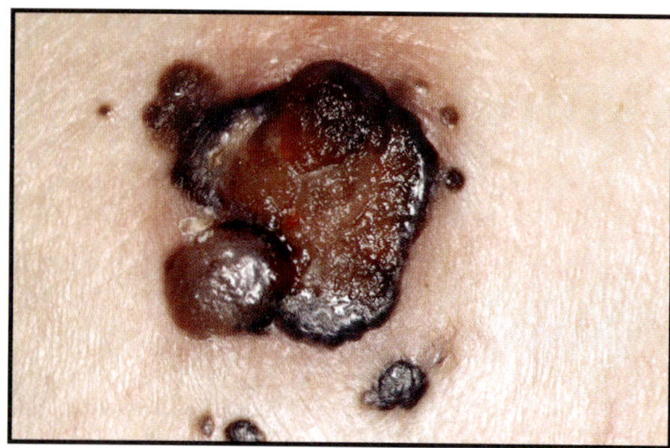

Melanomas are typically asymmetrical with an irregular border. They tend to be multicolored and 1/4 inch wide or more.

Availability. Because this was a small study, the researchers now have to see if their findings hold up in a study of hundreds of patients. If verified, the findings could provide important information to doctors about which patients should receive more extensive treatment and be more closely followed for signs of metastasis—and which are free to breathe a sigh of relief.

Skin Cancer

Melanoma Can't Hide from New Vaccine

It sounds crazy—deliberately killing healthy skin cells in order to treat skin cancer. But a group of Mayo Clinic researchers in Rochester, Minnesota, believe it may be a powerful new approach to making the body's immune system destroy melanoma tumors. In fact, they tried it on mice, and it eradicated the tumors.

Using therapeutic "vaccines" to get the immune system to kill cancer cells hasn't worked very well in the past. (Although they're called vaccines, they are intended to treat people with cancer.) The vaccines are designed to teach the immune system to recognize malignant cells so the body can destroy them, but that's a tough job because cancer cells look so much like healthy cells. The Mayo Clinic scientists tried a new approach involving healthy, pigment-producing skin cells called melanocytes, the same cells that later morph into melanoma.

How it works. The scientists placed melanoma tumors in mice, then injected the mice with a vaccine composed of the antiviral drug ganciclovir and two types of DNA—one that codes for an immunity-boosting protein called heat shock protein and another that codes for an enzyme that attracts ganciclovir, which then kills melanocytes.

As the cells died, the heat shock proteins spilled out, sending "help" signals to immune system cells called T cells. The T cells charged in and began destroying the melanocytes. Then, since melanoma cells look identical to melanocytes (at least to T cells), the T cells turned on the melanoma cells and begin destroying them, too. The researchers published their findings in the August 2004 issue of the journal *Nature Biotechnology.*

Study coauthor and Mayo oncologist Gregory A. Daniels, M.D., Ph.D., and his team hope their approach might work with other cancers. He notes, however, that not all tumors grow from nonessential cells. You wouldn't want to kill healthy lung tissue, for instance, in order to mount an immune response against lung cancer. Nevertheless, he thinks there may be a way to induce the immune response without actually having to kill the normal cells—something he and his team are working on.

Availability. The researchers hope to begin human clinical trials on their vaccine approach sometime in 2005.

IN Brief

Early Infections Fight Leukemia

If you worry because your infant seems to get sick all the time, you can take some comfort. A French study found that children who had any common infection before age 1 were 20 percent less likely to get a common form of childhood leukemia than kids who never got sick. If the child's infection was related to the stomach—for instance, gastroenteritis—the risk dropped by 90 percent. Not surprisingly, the earlier children attended daycare, the less likely they were to get leukemia, probably because kids in daycare are exposed to more infections.

A New Reason to Dust under the Bed

Numerous studies find that regular exercise can keep cancer at bay. Now, a new study from Vanderbilt University and the Shanghai Cancer Institute in China has found that routine household tasks—dusting, laundry, cooking, and cleaning—performed 4 or more hours a day cut a woman's risk of endometrial cancer by 20 percent. Can't stand to clean house? An hour a day of walking cut the risk by up to 40 percent.

New Drug for Prostate Cancer

The FDA has approved abarelix (Plenaxis), the first in a new class of drugs designed to treat prostate cancer that has spread. Given by injection, it belongs to a class of drugs called luteinizing hormone-releasing hormone antagonists. They work by shutting down the production of testosterone, which feeds prostate cancer cells. Unlike similar drugs, Plenaxis doesn't cause an initial surge of testosterone, which can result in tumor growth and bone pain. Some people may be severely allergic to it, however, so the manufacturer requires that doctors enroll in an education program before prescribing it.

DIGESTION
AND METABOLISM

IN THIS SECTION

RESEARCHERS HAVE RECENTLY MADE A NUMBER OF IMPORTANT DISCOVERIES ON THE DIABETES FRONT.

First the bad news: Today's kindergarteners face approximately a 1-in-3 chance of developing the disease in their lifetimes. And many more people now have *pre*-diabetes—a condition that often turns into full-blown diabetes—because health authorities have lowered the criteria for diagnosing the condition.

On the bright side, research points to new ways to use food to lower your risk of diabetes—namely, by eating antioxidant-rich foods, drinking coffee (especially decaf), and sprinkling cinnamon on foods. If you do develop diabetes, a breakthrough drug that's based on the saliva of Gila monsters can help control your blood sugar. Also, there's new evidence that being physically fit will help you live longer—even if you're overweight.

Here's another bit of news to digest: Researchers have discovered links between emotional health and bowel disorders. People with inflammatory bowel disease may reduce flare-ups by avoiding or treating depression, and those with irritable bowel syndrome can find years of relief with a few sessions of hypnotherapy.

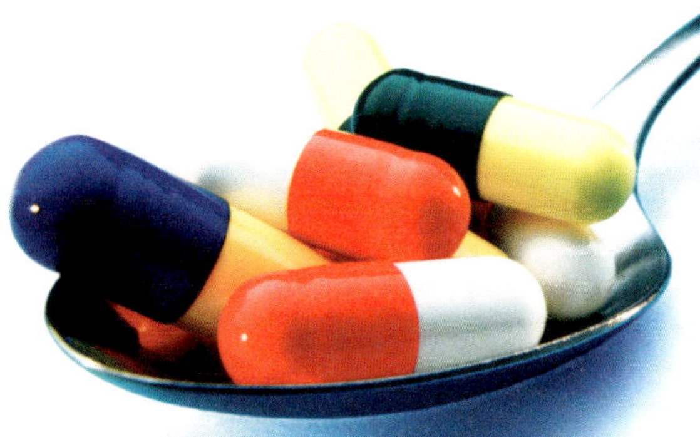

Bowel Problems

Antibiotics May Increase the Risk of Crohn's Disease

Experts know little about what causes Crohn's disease, a type of inflammatory bowel disease. It seems to run in families, so it's regarded as a genetic condition, but it's becoming more common, suggesting that something may be triggering the disease in susceptible people. Researchers have been searching for that trigger, and now British scientists have discovered clues that point to antibiotics.

Using cases from a vast, computerized medical database that contains detailed records on approximately 5 percent of the United Kingdom's population, researchers compared the histories of 587 patients who'd been diagnosed with Crohn's with those of 1,460 healthy people. They discovered that 71 percent of people with Crohn's had taken antibiotics in the two to five years before their diagnoses, compared with 58 percent of people without Crohn's. The study was published in the journal *Gut* in February 2004.

This study doesn't prove that antibiotics cause Crohn's but merely that the drugs seem to be associated with the disease. More studies are needed to confirm a link. Antibiotics may contribute to Crohn's by killing off beneficial bacteria found in the digestive system, the authors say. ■

TOP Trends

TODDLING TOWARD DIABETES

Babies who were born in the United States in 2000 face a "substantial" probability of developing diabetes at some point in their lives, according to new research published in the *Journal of the American Medical Association* in October 2003. Overall, males have almost a 33 percent chance of developing the disease, and females have more than a 38 percent chance. Some groups are at even higher risk: More than 45 percent of Hispanic males and more than 52 percent of Hispanic females will develop diabetes.

Unfortunately, these estimates may be low, according to the study authors, since they don't take into account the number of people who will develop diabetes but won't be diagnosed, which is the trend for an estimated one-third of people who now have the disease.

The study didn't differentiate between type 1 and type 2 diabetes. The latter, though, is by far the most common, representing about 95 percent of cases. Obesity and a sedentary lifestyle raise the risk of developing the disease.

FEED YOURSELF AND SOME LITTLE FRIENDS

You probably think of bacteria as something you don't want in your food—but many manufacturers would disagree. A growing number of them are adding beneficial bacteria, known as probiotics, to some of their products. These "good" bugs, which exist naturally in the gut, are thought to boost immune function and stave off intestinal woes, such as diarrhea, as well as vaginal and urinary tract infections. They work mainly by keeping "bad" bacteria in check.

In January 2004, Dannon unveiled a dairy drink called DanActive, which is enriched with three strains of beneficial bacteria. The company claims the drink contains 10 times more bacterial cultures than yogurt. It was previously available in health food stores as Actimel, and it's been popular in Europe for years under that name.

Companies also are now offering "prebiotics"—food ingredients that nourish the good bacteria in the intestine. Yogurt maker Stonyfield Farm says it adds to its yogurts a prebiotic called inulin, a natural fiber found in chicory root as well as some fruits and vegetables. Horizon Organic Dairy adds a type of soluble fiber called NutraFlora, which acts as a food for healthy bacteria, to its kids' yogurts. In the U.K., Kellogg's introduced a breakfast cereal called Rice Krispies Muddles, which also contains inulin.

Worm Your Way Out of IBD

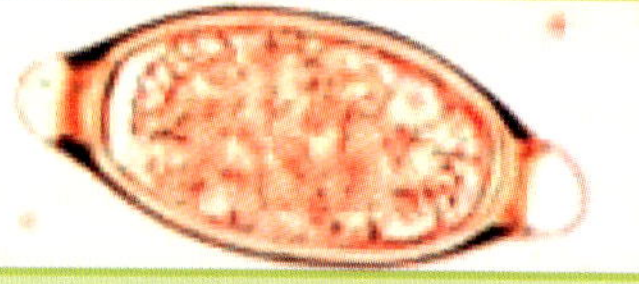

It may not be the most appealing remedy, but taking a dose of worm eggs may reduce the symptoms of inflammatory bowel disease (IBD), according to a small study at the University of Iowa.

Researchers gave a swig of Gatorade containing 2,500 eggs from the Trichuris suis worm, which normally infects pigs' intestines, to seven people who had either Crohn's disease or ulcerative colitis, then monitored them for 12 weeks. None suffered any significant negative effects, and the IBD went into remission in six of the patients, although the results were temporary.

Although the potential treatment may sound radical, it's not surprising to researchers, since populations around the world that have more intestinal worms have lower rates of IBD. The worms may help reduce symptoms by activating an immune system response that counteracts inflammation in the intestine. Although the worm eggs release larvae into the intestine, the larvae can't survive in humans as they do in pigs, and they're eliminated from the body after a few weeks.

Bowel Problems

For IBS Patients, a Good Gut Reaction to Hypnosis

Your belly is getting *verrry* sleepy…

Researchers have known for some time that in the short term, hypnotherapy can help relieve the symptoms of irritable bowel syndrome (IBS), which is characterized by abdominal pain, bloating, and alternating constipation and diarrhea. Now, a British study has shown that such therapy can offer long-term relief lasting five or more years.

The researchers, at University Hospital of South Manchester in England, gave questionnaires to 204 IBS patients before, immediately after, and up to six years following treatment with hypnotherapy. The participants were asked about their symptoms, anxiety, and quality of life.

Seventy-one percent of the patients improved "very much" or "moderately" immediately following the therapy, which consisted of up to a dozen 1-hour sessions. Of those people, 81 percent maintained that improvement years later. The patients who responded to hypnotherapy also had lower anxiety scores following the completion of treatment and reported scheduling fewer doctor visits and using less medication.

How it works. Hypnotherapy helps patients enter a relaxed, daydream-like state in which they're more open to suggestion. For treating IBS, patients are encouraged to imagine themselves calming their troubled digestive systems. This may involve placing their hands on their abdomens and envisioning a feeling of warmth, as opposed to pain. The study participants then practiced self-hypnosis at home with the help of a CD or tape.

Part of the benefit of hypnotherapy may come simply from the stress relief it provides. Lab studies suggest that hypnosis may also help a person damp down muscle activity in the gut and even the sensitivity of the gut lining—factors that aren't usually under conscious control and that contribute to IBS symptoms.

Availability. Using hypnosis to treat IBS hasn't become common yet, although some gastroenterologists are beginning to recommend it. If you're interested in trying it, ask your doctor how to go about it.

Low Moods Linked to IBD Flare-Ups

People with inflammatory bowel disease (IBD) are prone to depression, but those who remain more upbeat and less anxious may have fewer relapses, according to an Austrian study.

Researchers at University Hospital of Vienna followed 60 adults with Crohn's disease and ulcerative colitis for 18 months. At the start of the study, 28 percent of the patients were found to be depressed. These patients had their first relapses an average of 97 days later, compared with nearly a year for those who weren't depressed. The more depressed the people were, the sooner their relapses occurred. The depressed patients also had more flare-ups during the study period. Having anxiety was also associated with more frequent flare-ups.

Since these diseases can't yet be cured, the goal in treating them is to reduce flare-ups, the researchers note. Thus, people with IBD should also be screened and treated for depression as part of treatment for their bowel disease. ■

RESEARCH ROUNDUP

Montezuma Gets an Extra Measure of Revenge

If you're not careful while traveling to Mexico, you may bring home a lasting but unwanted souvenir of your trip: irritable bowel syndrome (IBS).

In a study conducted at the University of Texas-Houston Medical School, 98 American students responded to a survey six months after they visited Mexico. Sixty-two had suffered from diarrhea while traveling, and roughly 10 percent of these students reported that they later developed symptoms of IBS, such as diarrhea, constipation, and crampy abdominal pain relieved by a bowel movement. None of the students who stayed diarrhea-free while traveling had IBS symptoms six months later. Whether the delayed symptoms were a result of some infectious organism or a lingering response to the infection is unknown, says lead researcher Pablo Okhuysen, M.D., of the university's General Clinical Research Center.

To reduce your risk, follow the usual advice for eating and drinking while traveling in Mexico and other developing countries: Drink bottled water only, stick with cooked foods and fruits you can peel, and avoid buffets and beverages with ice. If you have digestive upset while traveling, and it persists after you return home, talk to your doctor, suggests Dr. Okhuysen.

Too Much Iron Has Heavy Consequences

Iron plays a crucial role in health, since it helps your blood carry oxygen around your body. Having too much iron, however, may raise your risk of diabetes.

Harvard researchers checked the records of more than 32,000 women from the long-running Nurses' Health Study and found that those who developed diabetes had significantly higher levels of ferritin, a protein that stores iron in the body. The higher your ferritin levels, the more stored iron you have. The researchers found that women with the highest ferritin levels were more than twice as likely to develop diabetes as those women with lower levels.

It's uncertain why iron may contribute to diabetes, but the researchers point out that the mineral is thought to increase the activity of free radicals, molecules that damage cells. The damage may decrease the body's sensitivity to the hormone insulin, leading to high blood sugar.

Don't run out and ask your doctor to check your ferritin levels yet, though. More research is needed to clarify the relationship between iron and diabetes.

Diabetes

Fitness Weighs In Over Weight

It's possible to be overweight yet physically fit. If you need convincing, just watch a professional football game. Those massive linebackers are certainly hefty, yet they're aerobically fit enough to hustle up and down the field. Now it turns out that among overweight men with diabetes, those who are physically fit live longer than those who aren't—and maybe just as long as those who aren't overweight. That's according to a recent study led by Tim Church, M.D., Ph.D., medical director of the Cooper Institute in Dallas.

Another reason to exercise: If you have diabetes, even if you're overweight, your chances of living a long life are good if you're in shape.

What the study showed. The study involved nearly 2,200 men who were followed for up to 26 years. Their fitness levels were rated based on their performance on treadmill tests. During the study period, normal-weight men who were the fittest were six times less likely to die than those who were least fit. Even among overweight and obese men, the fitter the men, the better their chances of a longer life. In fact, the study suggests that the obese men who were "somewhat" to "very" fit were no more likely to die prematurely than the fittest normal-weight men.

"I was really surprised that weight had a far lesser role than fitness," says Dr. Church. The study didn't look at causes of death or exactly how fitness protected the participants, but diabetes does increase a person's risk of heart disease and stroke, and staying in shape reduces those risks.

How much exercise is enough? Maintaining a fitness level that can improve your health doesn't require marathon-level training, says Dr. Church. Just a half-hour of moderate physical activity (such as brisk walking) five times a week can do the trick.

These findings don't mean that you should give up on shedding some pounds if you're overweight, but they do offer a good reason to get more exercise in addition to watching what you eat. ■

Diabetes

Lizard Spit Inspires Cutting-Edge Diabetes Drug

Gila monsters, the venomous lizards with a tenacious bite, have never been known for their healing powers, but now a hormone derived from their saliva is the basis for what could be the next breakthrough drug for type 2 diabetes.

The drug, exenatide, is a synthetic version of a compound found in the mouths of Gila monsters. It does a lot of impressive things, according to Steve Edelman, M.D., professor of medicine at the University of California, San Diego, who has been involved in clinical trials of the drug.

Exenatide can lower blood sugar without dropping it low enough to cause hypoglycemia, a condition marked by shakiness and dizziness. It also leads to weight loss—which many people with diabetes need—and it may even rejuvenate cells in the pancreas that make insulin, a boon to people with diabetes who don't make enough of the hormone naturally, Dr. Edelman says.

How it works. Exenatide functions much like the human hormone GLP-1 (short for glucagon-l ike peptide), which is produced in the intestine. GLP-1 spurs the pancreas to produce insulin after a meal so that the insulin can help keep blood sugar levels from rising too high as the food is digested. People with type 2 diabetes have trouble making or using their own insulin.

Existing drugs to reduce blood sugar can work *too* well, causing hypoglycemia, but exenatide works more like a dimmer switch. Its effects taper off as blood sugar drops toward normal. "If you were to design something to treat diabetes, that's what you might design," says John Eng, M.D., who discovered that Gila monsters carry the compound used in exenatide. The drug works with one or two daily injections.

In the most recent studies, the highest tested dose of exenatide reduced people's hemoglobin A1C—a long-term measure of glucose control—an average of 1 percent, a sizeable drop. (A 5 percent A1C level is normal. Patients in the study started at an average of 8 percent.) The most common side effect was nausea. Subjects also lost an average of 4.4 pounds over 30 weeks—which is unusual, since many medications that improve blood sugar levels cause weight gain.

Availability. The companies developing exenatide have completed Phase III trials—the studies on large groups of people that are the last tests required before a drug can win FDA approval—and planned to submit the drug for approval in mid-2004. Exenatide is in the running to be the first medication of its kind to hit the market, but other companies are working on their own versions of drugs that are similar to GLP-1. ■

Diabetes

Antioxidant-Rich Foods May Lower Diabetes Risk

Researchers from Finland have found more reasons why you should eat your vegetables and whole grains: The antioxidants they contain may steer you away from type 2 diabetes.

The researchers analyzed the eating habits of more than 4,000 men and women who were surveyed in the late 1960s and early 1970s. Based on this data, they were able to calculate the amounts of several different antioxidants the people consumed, including vitamins E and C and various carotenoids (plant chemicals that give certain fruits and vegetables their bright colors).

During a 23-year follow-up period, 383 of the men and women developed diabetes. The study authors calculated that people who consumed the most vitamin E were roughly 30 percent less likely to develop the disease than those who consumed the least. And those who ate the most b-cryptoxanthin, a type of carotenoid that's turned into vitamin A in the body, were roughly 40 percent less likely to develop diabetes. The results were published in the February 2004 issue of the journal *Diabetes Care*.

The people in the study got most of their vitamin E from whole grain foods, vegetable oils, and margarines, says Jukka Montonen, M.Sc., the lead study author and a researcher at the National Public Health Institute in Helsinki. Vitamin E is also found in leafy green vegetables and nuts. Most of the healthy Finns' carotenoids came from red and yellow vegetables, Montonen says. Good food sources of vitamin A and carotenoids include carrots, red bell peppers, and cantaloupe.

Count on carrots, as well as other colorful vegetables, to help protect you from diabetes (not to mention heart disease and cancer).

Explaining the effect. How might antioxidants protect against diabetes? By neutralizing free radicals (unstable oxygen molecules that damage cells), says Montonen. One way free radicals may contribute to diabetes is by damaging beta cells in the pancreas, which produce the insulin that helps blood sugar enter cells. Beta cells are particularly susceptible to free radical damage, and if they stop producing insulin as they should, blood sugar rises. Another way free radicals could contribute to diabetes is by causing cells in the body to take in less blood sugar.

The anti-diabetes effects of the antioxidant-rich foods may also have been due to other protective components of the foods, such as fiber, Montonen says, as well as the possibility that people whose diets contain plenty of good-for-you foods have healthier lifestyles overall.

New Diabetes Fighters, Right in Your Kitchen

Want to fight diabetes? Reach for a cup of java, a glass of Cabernet, or even a slice of apple pie. Groundbreaking new research suggests that coffee, wine, and cinnamon may all be strong weapons against the disease.

Protection in a mug. Several recent studies link coffee—the most popular beverage in the world—with lower risk of type 2 diabetes. They also offer several reasons why the drink may pack a disease-fighting punch.

One study, published in the January 2004 issue of the journal *Annals of Internal Medicine*, looked at data on roughly 42,000 men and 84,000 women who participated in large-scale studies that tracked their diets and the diseases they developed. When the researchers took into account the volunteers' age, weight, and other risk factors for diabetes, they found that men who drank at least six cups of coffee daily had less than half the diabetes risk of men who drank none. Women who drank at least six cups daily had roughly a 30 percent lower risk than women who drank none.

Another study, published in March 2004 in the *Journal of the American Medical Association*, looked at nearly 15,000 men and women in Finland, which leads the world in per capita coffee consumption, over the course of about 12 years. It also found that the more coffee people drank, the lower their risk of developing diabetes.

Why coffee reduces diabetes risk remains something of a mystery, although most experts agree that caffeine isn't the force at work—good news if you prefer decaf. The authors of the first study speculate that the potassium, niacin, magnesium, and antioxidants in coffee may improve glucose metabolism (the way the body uses blood sugar) and lower insulin resistance (which contributes to high blood sugar).

The authors of the second study put their money on a chemical called chlorogenic acid, which may disrupt an enzyme that regulates the release of glucose from the liver. It may also help keep blood sugar in check by limiting the ability of cells in the intestines to move sugar from the gut into the bloodstream.

Drinking coffee—a lot of it—appears to dramatically lower the risk of developing diabetes. Two other staples, wine and cinnamon, can actually lower blood sugar levels.

These studies don't *prove* that coffee prevents diabetes, and the authors don't recommend that you start drinking it for diabetes prevention. If you already have a coffee habit, though, the new research may make you feel better about it. You might want to switch to decaf, however, since there's evidence that caffeine impairs the ability of insulin to do its job of clearing the bloodstream of glucose.

Tasty spice, especially nice. Cinnamon does more than lend flavor to apple pie, iced rolls, and other baked treats: It may also help lower your blood sugar when you make it part of your daily diet.

Pakistani volunteers swallowed capsules containing either cinnamon or wheat flour every day for 40 days. After that time, those who took cinnamon

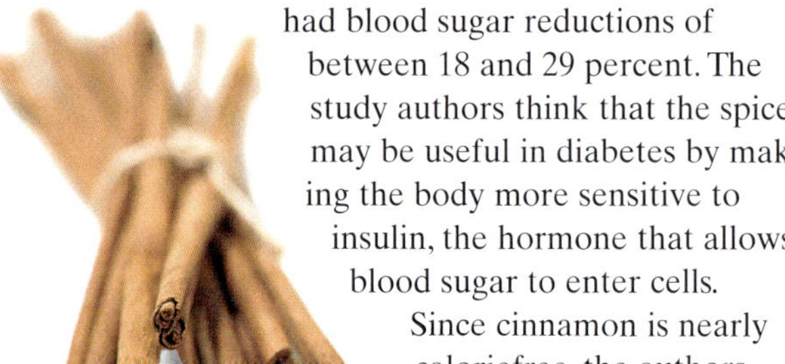

had blood sugar reductions of between 18 and 29 percent. The study authors think that the spice may be useful in diabetes by making the body more sensitive to insulin, the hormone that allows blood sugar to enter cells.

Since cinnamon is nearly caloricfree, the authors suggest that people who have diabetes, or those who wish to prevent it should regularly sprinkle the spice on their food. As little as 1/2 teaspoon a day could do the trick.

Vintage medicine. People with diabetes were once told to avoid alcohol, but according to a French study, components of red wine can actually help lower high blood sugar—at least in lab animals. For six weeks, researchers fed healthy and diabetic rats either pure alcohol extracted from wine, polyphenols (a type of antioxidant) extracted from wine, both, or neither. The diabetic rats that consumed both the polyphenols and the alcohol had about the same blood sugar levels after a meal as healthy rats—essentially becoming nondiabetic, at least in the short term. The animals that received only alcohol had better blood sugar levels than those that received only polyphenols or neither substance. Both alcohol and polyphenols may work by increasing cells' sensitivity to insulin.

Some of the animals were consuming the human equivalent of three glasses of wine daily—too much for people. The American Diabetes Association advises men with diabetes to drink only up to two 5-ounce glasses of wine daily, and women only one—and only if the alcohol doesn't interfere with medications. And of course, no food or beverage is a substitute for taking your diabetes medication or getting more exercise and eating right. ■

Pre-Diabetes

More of Us Need to Worry about Pre-Diabetes

In November 2003, the number of Americans with the condition known as pre-diabetes skyrocketed. These people didn't become sick overnight. Rather, the American Diabetes Association (ADA) lowered the bar for defining pre-diabetes, increasing the number of people who could be classified as having it by 20 percent.

The previous criteria were letting some people who were at risk for diabetes slip through without being diagnosed, says Gene Barrett, M.D., president of the ADA. The lower cutoff point means that more people can be alerted that they need to take steps to avoid diabetes, such as exercising more and eating better.

According to the Centers for Disease Control and Prevention, roughly 16 million U.S. adults ages 40 to 74 have pre-diabetes, also called impaired glucose tolerance. It's marked by blood glucose levels that are higher than normal, but not high enough to warrant a diagnosis of diabetes. According to the ADA, most people with pre-diabetes develop type 2 diabetes within 10 years. Previously, a glucose reading of 110 milligrams of glucose per deciliter of blood (mg/dL) meant a diagnosis of pre-diabetes; the new level is 100 mg/dL. Glucose levels are measured with a simple blood test after an overnight fast.

Grave implications. The threat of high blood sugar goes far beyond an increased risk of developing diabetes. Glucose intolerance is a symptom of a larger problem, often referred to as insulin resistance syndrome. It's generally found in people who are

OLD Criteria Fasting Glucose Level (mg/dl)

NORMAL	PRE-DIABETES	DIABETES
	110	126

NEW Criteria

NORMAL	PRE-DIABETES	DIABETES
	100	126

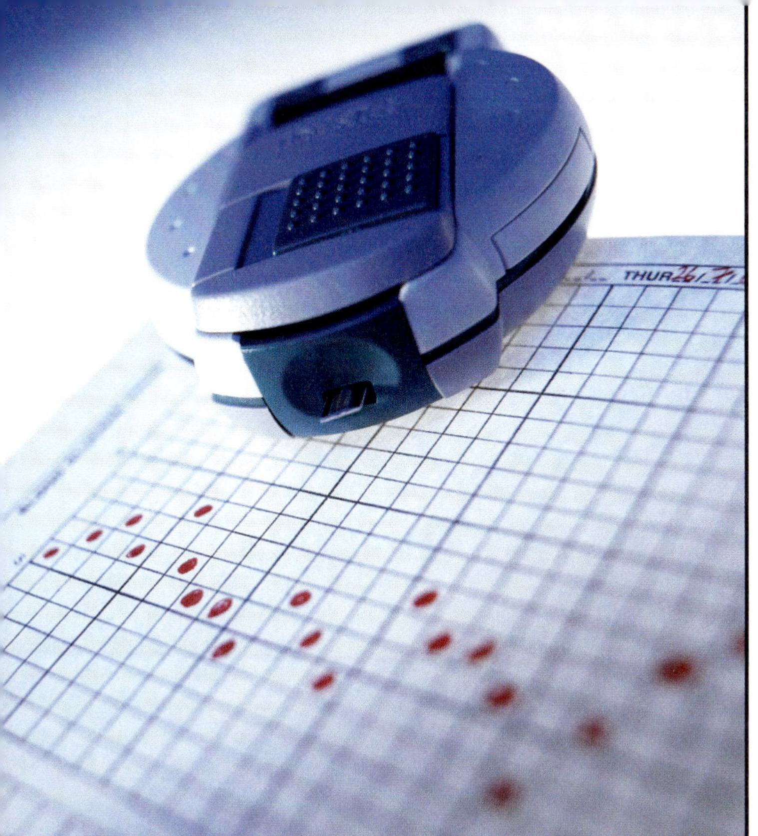

Is there a bloodsugar testing device in your future? People with pre-diabetes—marked by higher-than-average bloodsugar levels—are at increased risk of developing full-blown diabetes.

sedentary and overweight, with fat accumulation particularly around the waist. Insulin resistance occurs when the body's cells don't respond as they should to the hormone insulin, which helps the sugar from foods enter the cells. When the sugar can't enter cells, it builds up in the bloodstream. Excess body fat contributes to insulin resistance.

Insulin resistance is linked to an increased risk of unhealthy cholesterol levels, buildup of plaque in the arteries, and a resulting higher risk of heart disease and stroke. According to the American Heart Association, adults with diabetes are up to four times more likely to have heart disease or strokes than those without diabetes.

Another condition linked to insulin resistance is polycystic ovary syndrome (PCOS), a cause of infertility in women. Up to 70 percent of women with PCOS, which is marked by lack of ovulation, may have insulin resistance.

Who should be tested. The ADA recommends that everyone who is 45 or older and overweight should be tested for pre-diabetes. Even if your weight is normal, if you're 45 or older, talk to your doctor about the test at your next visit. Also consider having the test if you're under 45, overweight, and have other risk factors for pre-diabetes, such as high blood pressure, low HDL cholesterol, high triglycerides, a family history of diabetes, or Hispanic or Native American ethnicity. ■

IN *Brief*

Digestive Disorder, Mental Illness May Travel Together

A Danish study has found that having celiac disease—or a family history of it—may be a risk factor for schizophrenia. In celiac disease, eating grains containing a protein known as gluten causes damage to the small intestine.

Researchers compared nearly 8,000 people with schizophrenia who were admitted to a psychiatric facility with 200,000 people who did not have schizophrenia. They concluded that for people with celiac disease, the chance of having schizophrenia is more than 200 percent greater than for those who don't have celiac disease.

Video Capsule Pinpoints Hidden Bleeding

If you have gastrointestinal bleeding, swallowing a camera in a pill could help you and your doctor figure out what's causing it. An Italian study found that tiny capsules containing cameras and lights found the source of bleeding in 92 percent of people who had visible digestive bleeding. This technology—called capsule endoscopy (CE)—allows doctors to see portions of the small intestine that can't be viewed by putting a scope down the esophagus or up through the rectum.

The authors say that CE is best for people whose bleeding is ongoing, whether it's visible to the eye—as with bloody bowel movements—or hidden in the stool and discovered through stool tests.

EYES

AND EARS

IN THIS SECTION

JUST AS BABY BOOMERS ARE REACHING FOR READING GLASSES, THERE COMES A NEW, MINIMALLY INVASIVE PROCEDURE TO RESTORE VISION.

Called conductive keratoplasty, it's the first surgery approved to enhance close-up vision, which begins to evade just about everyone after age 50.

Older eyes affected by age-related macular degeneration may benefit from a host of new therapies, including common and experimental medications, radical surgery that involves moving the retina, and a miniature telescope that's implanted right inside the eye.

There are new positive effects from aspirin, cholesterol-lowering statins, and certain blood pressure drugs: All of them seem to benefit the eyes in one way or another.

While you may have been unknowingly helping your eyes, you may also have been damaging your hearing without realizing it. Recently, hormone replacement therapy and heavy drinking have been implicated in hearing damage. Even being short may put people at risk for hearing loss.

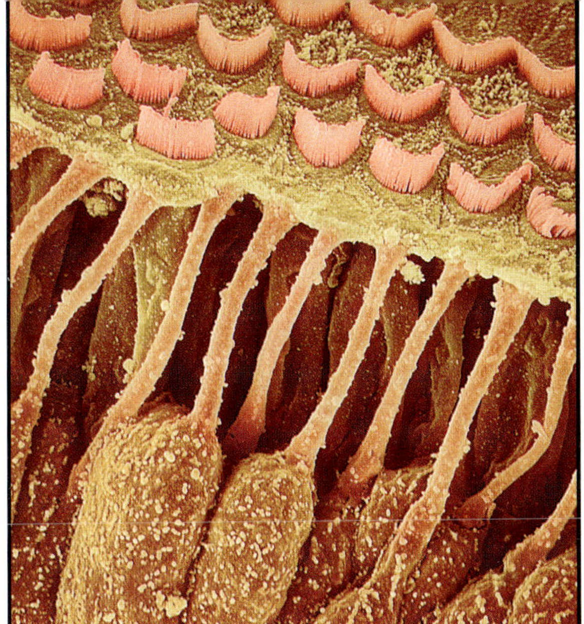

When microscopic hairs in the inner ear are bent by sound waves, they release chemicals that generate nerve impulses which then travel to the brain and are interpreted as sound.

Hearing Impairment

Growing Hair to Repair Hearing

Some human hairs are not even visible, yet their loss causes far more distress than a balding patch on a middle-aged head. They are tiny hair cells in the inner ear, and they're responsible for your hearing. When sound waves move the fluid in the inner ear, the hairs vibrate, causing nerve cells below the hairs to generate electrical impulses that are sent to the brain and interpreted there as sounds.

When too many of the 15,000 or so sensory hair cells in each ear are damaged—most often due to aging, heredity, or the use of certain antibiotics—hearing is permanently lost. Reptiles and birds can regenerate sensory hair cells, but humans can't. Now, though, perhaps modern medicine can.

A future cure for hearing loss? European scientists working with a research project called the Bionic Ear have taken the first steps down a path that could very well lead to replacement sensory hair cells for the human ear. They isolated inner ear hair cells from adult mice and, by exposing them to proteins that promote cell growth, got them to multiply—something they never do under normal circumstances. The scientists were also able to manipulate them into becoming different types of cells necessary for the transmission of sound, including auditory nerve cells and glial cells, which nourish the nerve cells.

This means that the cells the scientists found in the mice were stem cells—the "master" cells that can turn into other types of cells and multiply indefinitely. (Unlike embryonic stem cells, which have been the subject of heated political debate for the past several years, these stem cells exist in adults, so there is no moral quandary regarding their use.) The researchers expect to find similar stem cells in the ears of humans and hope to nudge them in the laboratory into becoming sensory hair cells—and perhaps a cure for hearing loss.

What's next? Finding out whether such new hair cells could actually replace damaged ones in the human ear—and figuring out how to get them to do it—will take years of research, but this discovery could pave the way to therapy that could restore hearing using a patient's own hair cells. And that would be music to the ears of many.

TOP Trends

A HEART FOR AN EYE?

Remember the advent of eyebrow piercing and tongue studs? Just when you thought humans were running out of body parts to adorn with jewelry, surgeons in the Netherlands have begun implanting "jewels" into the eyes.

Those who feel the need to adorn their eyeballs can choose from shapes such as hearts and half moons. The tiny ornaments, called JewelEye, were designed specifically for implantation in the conjunctiva, the mucous membrane that lines the front of the eyeball. The brief surgical procedure is performed by a registered ophthalmologist using local anesthesia and an operating microscope.

The American Academy of Ophthalmology is not pleased about the trend and issued a press release warning about the possibility of scar tissue and infection. But the Rotterdam-based Netherlands Institute for Innovative Ocular Surgery, which patented the procedure, claims there have been no side effects or complications to date.

According to the FDA, the implants would most likely be considered medical devices in the United States, meaning that they would have to undergo an approval process before becoming available.

RESEARCH ROUNDUP

Heavy Drinking Hurts Hearing

By now you've probably heard that moderate drinking is good for your heart. Heavy drinking, on the other hand, has been shown to cause all sorts of problems, including increased risk of heart disease and liver damage. If you need yet another reason to keep your drinking in check, consider this: German scientists have new evidence that heavy drinking causes hearing loss.

Researchers recruited two groups of men for the study: one made up of heavy drinkers and one of moderate social drinkers. All the participants answered questions about their alcohol use and had blood tests and hearing exams. Then, with each participant, the scientists recorded and evaluated certain electrical currents in the brain that are responses to sound. They found that in the heavy drinkers, it took longer for the brain stem to process sound.

Short on Hearing

As if tall people didn't have enough advantages in life, Swedish researchers at Göteborg University say that short people may be more prone to hearing loss. Researchers tested the hearing of 479 men ages 20 to 64 who were exposed to noise in their jobs. Among them, short men were three times more likely to have worse hearing for their age than taller workers. The researchers also tested 500 randomly selected men who were born in 1974. In that group, men with hearing loss were twice as likely to be short as men with normal hearing. The researchers suspect that adult hearing loss may go all the way back to the womb: A low level of a kind of growth hormone during fetal development may lead to a reduced number of cells at birth, resulting in short stature and early onset of hearing loss.

Hearing Impairment

Another Blow for HRT

In recent years, hormone replacement therapy (HRT) has been reported to increase women's risk of heart disease, stroke, breast cancer, and dementia. Alas, the bad news seems to have no end: Now it appears that HRT is associated with hearing loss.

In a small study at the University of Rochester and the Rochester Institute of Technology in New York, three different hearing tests were given to women who had taken HRT and women who had not. Women in the HRT group performed worse on all three tests, but the most dramatic difference was discovered on a test of how well the brain processes sounds detected by the ear. Women in the HRT group did 30 percent worse than women in the non-HRT group. A deficit in the brain's ability to filter and prioritize sounds is most noticeable in situations where there is a lot of background noise.

The results were surprising to the researchers. Because the ear contains receptors for the hormone estrogen, they thought HRT might help women's hearing, not make it worse. The team has begun researching a number of questions raised by their finding, including why HRT may be linked to hearing loss, how much and what type of HRT may be to blame, and whether hearing improves when HRT is stopped. ■

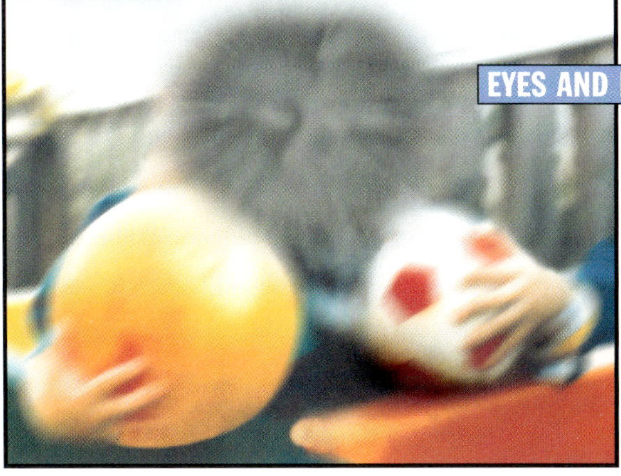

Two views of the same scene: With normal vision (left) and as it would appear to a person affected by macular degeneration.

Macular Degeneration

A One-Two Punch for Advanced Eye Disease

Many people approaching retirement envision a future of gazing at their grandchildren and reading all those books they never got around to while they were still working. For the unfortunate ones struck by age-related macular degeneration (AMD), though, the vision they need to enable that future to unfold is all but lost.

AMD spares peripheral vision but steals the sharp central vision necessary for recognizing faces, reading, and other activities. At its worst, central vision is replaced by a black blotch. Nobody knows what causes it, and there is no cure. Conventional treatment for advanced AMD, called photodynamic therapy, uses medication and a laser to slow or stop the disease, but it rarely improves vision. Many who receive it continue to lose sight despite multiple treatments, and once their central vision is gone, it's gone for good.

Now, a radical, two-part surgical procedure, developed and refined at Duke University Eye Center in Durham, North Carolina, is helping some people with advanced AMD. It's certainly not restoring 20/20 vision, but patients who had little hope of seeing again have regained enough central vision to continue their normal activities.

Cynthia A. Toth, M.D., associate professor of ophthalmology and biomedical engineering at Duke, says the average outcome of surgery is an improvement of one line on an eye chart and improved reading speed of about 25 words per minute. That may not seem like much, but it's significant for many people faced with a visionless future. "The majority of patients get back to reading using reading glasses—they're actually able to sit down and read a book again," says Dr. Toth, who has performed hundreds of the procedures. "Patients are telling us it has an impact on their quality of life at home."

How it works. AMD affects the macula, the central part of the retina, where light-sensitive cells are concentrated. In advanced AMD, scarring and leaky blood vessels form underneath the retina and begin to damage the macula. The two-phase procedure, technically known as macular translocation surgery with 360-degree peripheral retinectomy, moves the retina away from the diseased area of the eye wall to a spot with healthy tissue before more damage can occur. (You could compare it to moving a steak away from the hot spot on a grill before it burns.)

In the first surgery, fluid is injected underneath the retina, which is cut away from the eye wall. The optic nerve is left intact and acts as a pivot point as the retina is rotated away to a healthy area, and leaky blood vessels are removed. After the first procedure, the patient's vision is tilted because of the rotation. Two months later, after the eye has healed, a second surgery fixes the tilt by detaching and repositioning four of the six muscles that hold the eye in place.

Limits and risks. The surgery is available only to patients with advanced AMD who are already blind in one eye and have lost vision in the other within the previous six months. It's the less-damaged eye that gets the procedure. Complications do occur. The risk of retinal detachment, which can cause permanent vision loss, is about 10 percent at the Duke Eye Center. Some patients have double vision or some residual tilting after the surgery, which can be treated with special glasses or additional surgery. ■

Macular Degeneration

A Shot in the Eye for Age-Related Blindness

Their delivery method is not for the squeamish, but people with severe age-related macular degeneration (AMD) may soon get help from two new medications, pegaptanib (Macugen) and ranibizumab (Lucentis), if they can literally take a shot in the eye.

The drugs treat the "wet" form of AMD, which affects more than one million people in the United States alone and can steal vision in a matter of months. Both drugs are in clinical trials, which means hundreds of people with wet AMD have endured multiple injections into their eyeballs (and lived to tell about it).

In the latest clinical trial of Macugen, the drug was 27 percent more effective than a placebo (dummy injection) at limiting vision loss in patients with wet AMD. Patients treated with Lucentis for about three months had small gains in vision, while those receiving standard care (observation or a laser treatment called photodynamic therapy) lost the ability to see an average of five letters on an eye chart.

How they work. In wet AMD, abnormal vessels grow behind the retina and leak blood and fluids, ultimately destroying the center of the retina (the macula), where light-sensitive cells are concentrated. Crucial to the development of Lucentis and Macugen was the recent discovery of vascular endothelial growth factor (VEGF), a protein that helps stimulate the formation of new blood vessels. Both drugs block VEGF, preventing it from activating vessel-forming cells.

Availability. The drugs are still in clinical trials. If they continue to prove safe and effective, Macugen could be available by the end of 2005, with Lucentis following in 2006.

Macular Degeneration

A Telescope for "Black Holes" in Vision

Forget the Hubble. There's a new telescope that sees right around black holes, and it's so tiny it fits inside a human eye.

The telescope is the Implantable Miniature Telescope (IMT), and the black holes it sees around are caused by age-related macular degeneration, a condition in which the macula—the central portion of the retina—deteriorates. In its advanced stage, the disease causes a permanent blurred or blind spot in the center of the visual field. Peripheral vision isn't affected, but anything requiring "straight-ahead" vision, such as reading, becomes nearly impossible.

About 300 people have had the IMT implanted during clinical trials. The average improvement in vision has been two or three lines on an eye chart (three lines represent double the vision—say, from 20/100 to 20/50), allowing patients to get back to some of their normal activities.

"This is an amazing technology. Even I have to admit that this is particularly cool," says Baruch Kuppermann, M.D., Ph.D., an investigator in the clinical trials of the IMT who has been involved in eye research for 15 years.

A tiny telescope six weeks after implantation in an eye.

How it works. The IMT is implanted in the eye's lens during a 1-hour outpatient procedure. The device magnifies images two to three times their normal size and projects them over a wide field of the retina, beyond the damaged parts. The eye with poorer vision gets the IMT, while the other eye is left untreated to handle peripheral vision (although it's reduced compared with having side vision in both eyes).

Dr. Kuppermann, who is chief of the retina service at the University of California, Irvine, says his patients report that the eye with the implant doesn't feel any different. "But you see a little glint in their eye," he adds. "The implant comes just beyond the pupil."

People can use natural eye movements to see with the IMT, but using it requires training. Once the device is implanted, the eyes don't work together anymore because the brain can't merge the larger image from the telescope with the normal-size image from the other eye. Patients typically work with a low-vision therapist for about six weeks after the procedure, learning to suppress the smaller image and focus their attention on the larger one—similar to what people do when they look through a regular telescope.

Availability. The IMT is being evaluated for safety and effectiveness in a two-year clinical trial at 28 ophthalmic centers across the United States. The manufacturer, VisionCare Ophthalmic Technologies, expected to seek FDA approval of the device after the study's first year, near the end of 2004. If it's approved, the IMT would be available in late 2005 at the earliest. ■

RESEARCH ROUNDUP

Inflammation May Be Linked to Eye Condition

You may have heard that inflammation in the body, measured by a "marker" protein called CRP, signals an increased risk of heart disease and stroke. Now, a new study has found that high CRP levels are linked with age-related macular degeneration (AMD). Researchers already knew that smoking, obesity, and high blood pressure raise the risk of both cardiovascular disease and AMD. There is no cure for inflammation, but quitting smoking, exercising, losing weight, and eating more fatty fish seem to help.

Eye Damage Affects Sleep

Getting some shuteye is not so easy for people with damage to the optic nerve, according to researchers at Washington University in St. Louis. They looked at sleep/wake cycles in 25 visually impaired young people ages 12 to 20, as well as 12 young people with normal sight. The people with optic nerve disease were 20 times more likely to have daytime sleepiness than those with normal sight and 9 times more likely to have daytime sleepiness than those with vision impairment not involving the optic nerve. Those with optic nerve damage also had highly variable wakeup times and had trouble falling asleep.

Recent research has found that the retina contains nonvisual, light-sensitive cells that determine light levels and communicate with the part of the brain that's involved in sleep/wake cycles. These special cells are concentrated at the head of the optic nerve. People with optic nerve disease may have difficulty using daylight to synchronize their internal rhythms to the outside world, say researchers, whose results were published in February 2004.

Vision Impairment

Over 40? Can You Read This without Glasses?

"What a drag it is getting old," sang the Rolling Stones, and many baby boomers are likely to nod their heads in agreement. An estimated 90 million of them need reading glasses or will need them within the next 10 years. The reason? A condition called presbyopia, which is caused by stiffening of the eye's lens and which makes it difficult to see clearly up close. Many people first notice the problem in their forties, and by age 50, nearly everyone has it.

For the first time, there's a way to dodge those reading glasses. In March 2004, a procedure called conductive keratoplasty (CK) received FDA approval for the treatment of presbyopia. It was approved for treating farsightedness in 2002.

"It's not a laser, and no tissue is removed. The procedure is minimally invasive and very safe," says Penny Asbell, M.D., director of the Cornea Service and Refractive Surgery Center at Mount Sinai Medical Center in New York City.

How it works. In CK, a probe thinner than a human hair is used to apply radiofrequency energy to the cornea. Like an electrical current, the radio waves seek to complete a circuit and return to their source. When they meet resistance—in this case, the cornea—they produce heat, which is used to shrink the corneal tissue in a circular pattern, akin to tightening a belt. The cornea becomes more dome shaped, and near vision is brought back into focus.

The procedure is typically performed in just one eye, at a cost of $1,500 to $2,000, to restore close vision without compromising distance vision. Some people who need bifocals to correct both their distance and near vision can have CK done on both eyes, with a little correction for the "distance vision" eye and more correction for the "near vision" eye.

In clinical trials, 87 percent of people who had CK came out of the procedure with 20/20 vision and could read phone-book-size print. A minority of patients didn't get full correction, says Dr. Asbell, who was a researcher in the trials and performs the surgery herself. But, she says, "We're talking about getting good vision for most activities. We're not going for extremes. Most days, we're not reading the smallest letter on the chart—that's not normal, everyday vision." In fact, most people would be happy to be able to read the morning newspaper without having to hold it at arm's length.

Does it last? CK isn't likely to fix your vision forever, either. The procedure is permanent, but the eyes continue to age. Some people need touch-up procedures every few years, "maybe as often as they would upgrade their glasses," says Dr. Asbell.

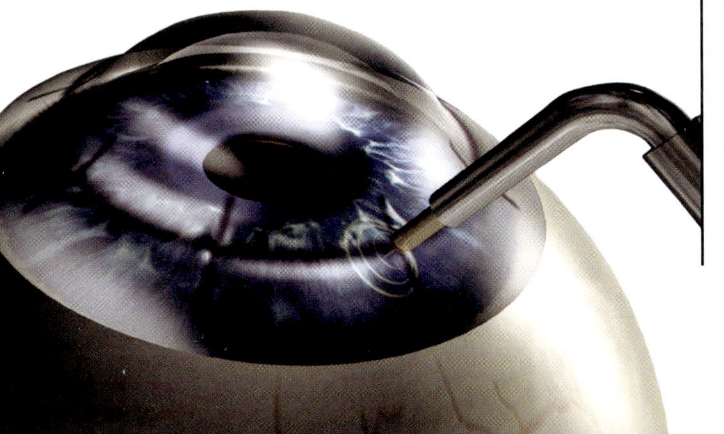

Adjusting the focus: A probe thinner than a hair corrects vision by shrinking corneal tissue with radio waves.

IN *Brief*

A Little Pressure Prevents Ear Infections

Your child has yet another ear infection. You've been through several rounds of antibiotics, and now your pediatrician is suggesting surgery to insert ear tubes. You're reluctant, but what else can you do?

There may be benefit in an alternative therapy called osteopathic manipulative treatment (OMT), which involves gentle stretching and pressure to move the muscles and joints. During a six-month study of 57 children with frequent ear infections, the ones who received OMT in addition to routine care had fewer ear infections and surgical procedures. Researchers at Oklahoma State University in Tulsa, who published their results in September 2003, say OMT helps partly by relieving compression of the bones surrounding the ear's Eustachian tube, allowing it to drain more freely.

Blood Pressure Drugs for Dry Eyes

Blood pressure drugs called angiotensin-converting enzyme (ACE) inhibitors seem to reduce the risk of dry eye syndrome, common in the elderly. When researchers followed nearly 2,500 people without dry eye syndrome for five years, only 9 percent of those taking ACE inhibitors to lower their blood pressure developed dry eyes, versus 14 percent who were not taking them. The protective effect of the drugs may involve their anti-inflammatory properties. It remains to be seen whether taking an ACE inhibitor helps once dry eye syndrome has developed.

Early Treatment Best for Eye Disease in Preemies

A leading cause of vision loss in premature babies is retinopathy of prematurity (ROP), the growth of abnormal blood vessels in the back of the eye. A study of 317 infants at high risk for ROP showed that early and aggressive treatment, using a laser or freezing the retina to reduce the number of blood vessels, is best. Infants who would have been treated later, based on current recommendations, retained better vision with early intervention.

HEART

AND CIRCULATORY SYSTEM

IN THIS SECTION

RESEARCHERS CONTINUE TO INVESTIGATE NEWER AND BETTER WAYS OF GETTING HEART DISEASE UNDER CONTROL.

Gene therapy is improving angina symptoms by growing brand new blood vessels to feed the heart. Statin drugs and implanted defibrillators are saving the lives of more people with heart failure. And researchers have discovered a simple trick to prevent cognitive problems in people who undergo bypass surgery.

That surgery, much less popular now than angioplasty (the newer, less invasive approach to dealing with clogged arteries), may actually be the better option, at least when performed by the best surgeons, because it delivers longer-lasting results. This conclusion surprised even researchers who conducted a study of the procedure.

On the low-tech side, there are new reasons why alcohol and the Mediterranean diet are both good for the heart: They control inflammation of the arteries, now thought to be intimately connected with heart disease. Recent studies found that people who drink moderately, and those who follow the traditional Mediterranean diet, have lower levels of CRP, a protein that indicates levels of inflammation.

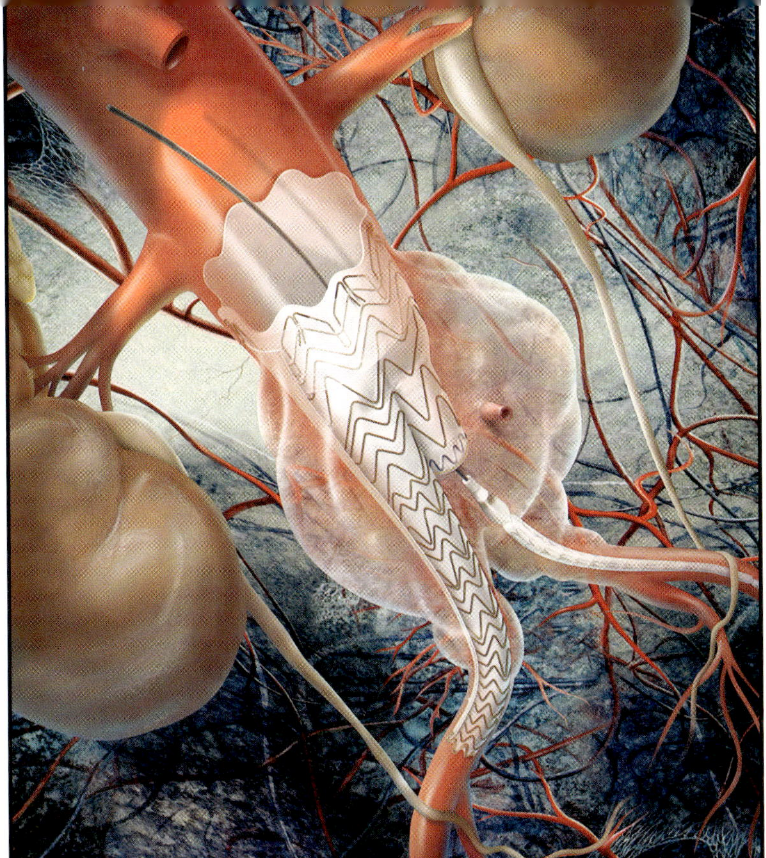

A tiny support structure called a stent is inserted via a catheter into a bulging abdominal aortic aneurysm. The stent's two branches extend into the arteries that lead toward each leg.

Aneurysms

Stent Beats Traditional Aneurysm Surgery

An abdominal aortic aneurysm (also known as an AAA) is a dangerous bulge in the part of the body's largest blood vessel located in the belly. Although aneurysms often aren't detected until it's too late, there are actually two ways of repairing these deadly bubbles—traditional "open" surgery and a less invasive approach that involves a catheter threaded through a small incision. For years, the experts have passionately debated which approach is better, but now the argument may be over. A study shows that compared with the open surgical technique that many doctors have come to rely on, the newer, less invasive technique gets high marks for improving chances of survival and promoting quicker recovery.

The traditional procedure, which involves making a long incision in the abdomen and stitching up the aneurysm, was the only option until 1999, when the FDA approved a device

TOP Trends

HEART SURGERY GETS A NEW "THEME SONG"

Many surgeons like to play music while they operate, and now some heart patients at renowned hospitals—including Columbia University Medical Center in New York City, the Cleveland Clinic in Ohio, and Cedars-Sinai Medical Center in Los Angeles—are getting their own audiotapes to listen to, via headphones, while they're under the knife. These aren't just any old tapes, though; they are designed to help patients through their surgeries and possibly speed recovery.

Unlike generic relaxation tapes, these tapes deliver positive messages geared to specific surgical procedures. The voice on the recording might reassure patients about tubes or medical devices or have them imagine that their arteries are becoming wider and more flexible. The patients listen to the tapes before, during, and after their operations. (Research suggests that people do process information while under anesthesia.)

To find out just how well the tapes work, doctors at Columbia have launched a study involving coronary bypass patients. The patients will be given either standard care, standard care plus relaxing music, or standard care plus music and targeted messages. They will be assessed after their operations to see whether the messages helped to alleviate postsurgical depression—a common problem with bypass surgery—and the need for pain medication, among other outcomes.

WEST NILE REACHES THE BLOOD SUPPLY

A bite from an infected mosquito is no longer the only way to contract the dreaded West Nile virus, now that it has reached the blood supply. Despite screenings for the virus, in 2003 there were six confirmed cases and three more possible cases of Americans who became infected through blood transfusions. Improved screening tests introduced since then have greatly improved the safety of donated blood. Even more sensitive tests are being developed to better detect the low levels of virus that could lead to infection in someone who is sick enough to require a transfusion.

TOP Trends

SAY "ADIOS" TO ANGIOGRAMS?

Scientists are developing more and more sophisticated ways to peer into your body to find out whether you have heart disease—meaning better information for your doctor and less discomfort for you. The latest generation of high-tech imaging machines includes "16-slice" computed tomography (CT) scanners that capture details of the body in tiny, half-millimeter slices. These scanners are being used to look inside blood vessel walls with little risk or discomfort for patients. Many major hospitals and cardiac centers already consider the stunning images produced by these super-fast (and super-expensive) CT machines to be the gold standard for diagnosing heart ailments. They could make the more common angiogram (which requires threading a catheter into the coronary arteries in order to inject a dye) a thing of the past.

called a stent graft. The device is a collapsible reinforcement for the aorta that's shaped like a tiny pair of trousers; it's designed to be positioned inside the aneurysm and extend slightly down into the artery that leads to each leg. The graft is inserted via a long, thin catheter inserted through an incision in the groin. For doctors who took to the new minimally invasive technique, the idea of open surgery started to look outmoded and extreme, but surgeons who swore by the older method considered the new technique too iffy to become the new standard.

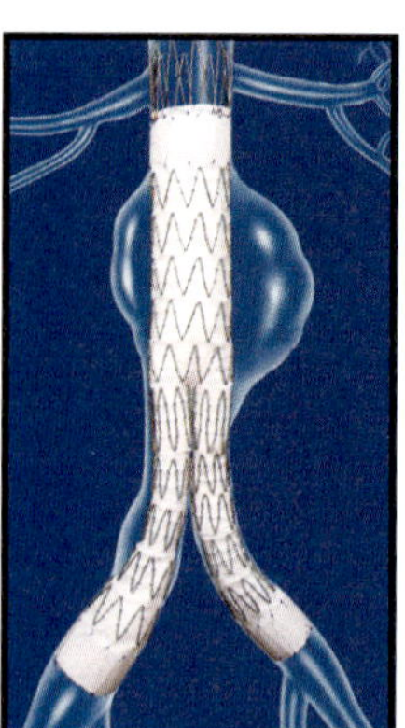

AAA stent repair improves recovery times and survival rate.

The first study to compare the two, published in January 2004, analyzed information from thousands of AAA repairs performed in hundreds of hospitals in New York State over a two-year period. The bottom line: Use of the stent graft boosts a person's chances of surviving the procedure. Fewer than 1 percent of stent recipients died, compared with 4.2 percent of those treated with surgery. The study also showed that people who had the stent-graft repair were able to return home in less than 4 days and needed to recover for only about two weeks. People who underwent open surgery stayed in the hospital an average of 10 days and needed up to two months of recovery time to get back to their normal activities.

Angina

Homegrown Blood Vessels Relieve Angina

For people with angina, any exertion—walking, talking, and even simply standing—can bring on debilitating chest pain caused by reduced blood flow to the heart. Think of what happens when traffic flow on a major highway narrows because one lane is closed: fewer cars can get through. Likewise, when coronary arteries grow narrower due to the buildup of plaque (made largely of cholesterol), less blood can get to the heart. Now, there may be a way to help the body add more "lanes"—by injecting a gene that encourages extra blood vessel branches to sprout from the coronary arteries.

How it works. The gene, called Ad5FGF-4, is delivered by way of a harmless virus (a modified, deactivated version of the common cold virus), which is injected directly into the heart with a syringe. The gene can stimulate growth of both heart muscle cells and cells lining the arteries. The therapy had previously been studied in animals, and in 2003, researchers took the big step of testing the procedure—successfully—in people.

Cindy Grines, M.D., of William Beaumont Hospital in Royal Oak, Michigan, led the study, which was published in an October 2003 issue of the *Journal of the American College of Cardiology*. All the patients had angina that was not responding to treatment with medicines, and none of them could have surgery. Thirty-five patients received gene therapy, and 17 received placebo (dummy) injections. Eight weeks after the one-time gene injection, the areas of the heart that showed low blood circulation were reduced by an average of 4.2 percent in the people who had the gene therapy. Those who received the placebo treatment experienced no such improvement. The researchers hoped that blood circulation would continue to improve within the hearts of the gene therapy patients.

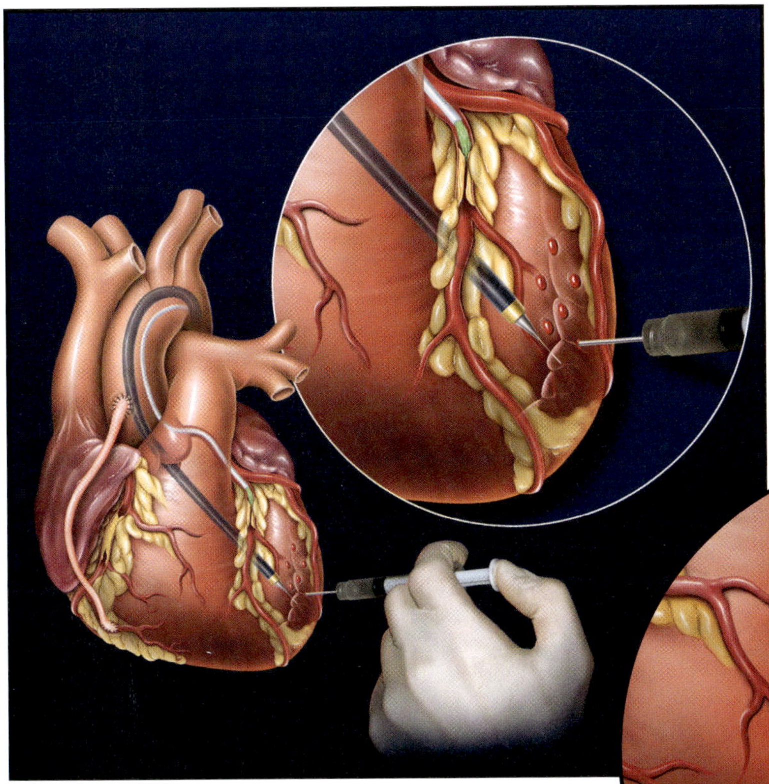

Genes that encourage the growth of new blood vessels are injected directly into the left ventricle of the heart (left). The new blood vessels provide improved circulation to the heart muscle (below), relieving angina.

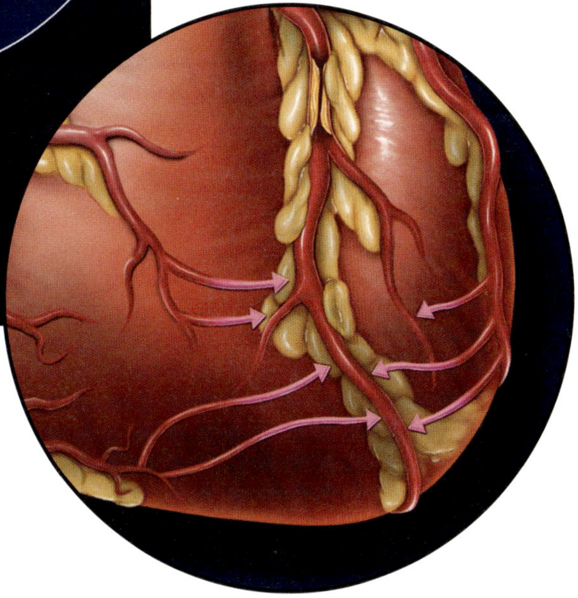

Availability. Two larger clinical trials, involving 450 patients each, are starting up to gather more information on long-term, symptom-relieving effects of the gene therapy. If all goes well, the treatment could be an FDA-approved option for treating angina within the next five years. Until then, it will remain experimental.

RESEARCH ROUNDUP

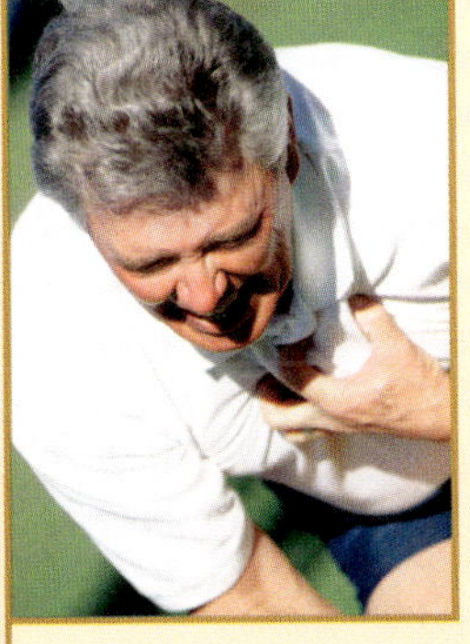

A New Pill for Chest Pain

Chest pain that isn't life-threatening can still threaten a person's quality of life. Millions of people experience chronic chest pain caused by reduced blood flow to the heart, a condition called angina. This difficult-to-treat problem, usually the result of heart disease, can reduce a person's ability to exercise, work, and enjoy regular daily activities. For more than a quarter of people with angina, the most commonly prescribed medications, such as nitrates and beta blockers, just don't help.

Now there's an experimental drug, called ranolazine, that could benefit people who don't respond to other medicines. It's thought to work by helping the heart get more mileage out of less oxygen by increasing its ability to use glucose to make energy. In studies, ranolazine let people exercise longer without experiencing angina and reduced the overall number of angina attacks.

Ranolazine was expected to gain approval in Europe by the end of 2004. In the United States, the FDA has asked for one more clinical trial before it will approve the drug. If it's approved (probably around 2006), it will become the first new type of medication for angina approved for U.S. use in more than 20 years.

Atrial Fibrillation

Putting Dangerous Arrhythmia on Ice

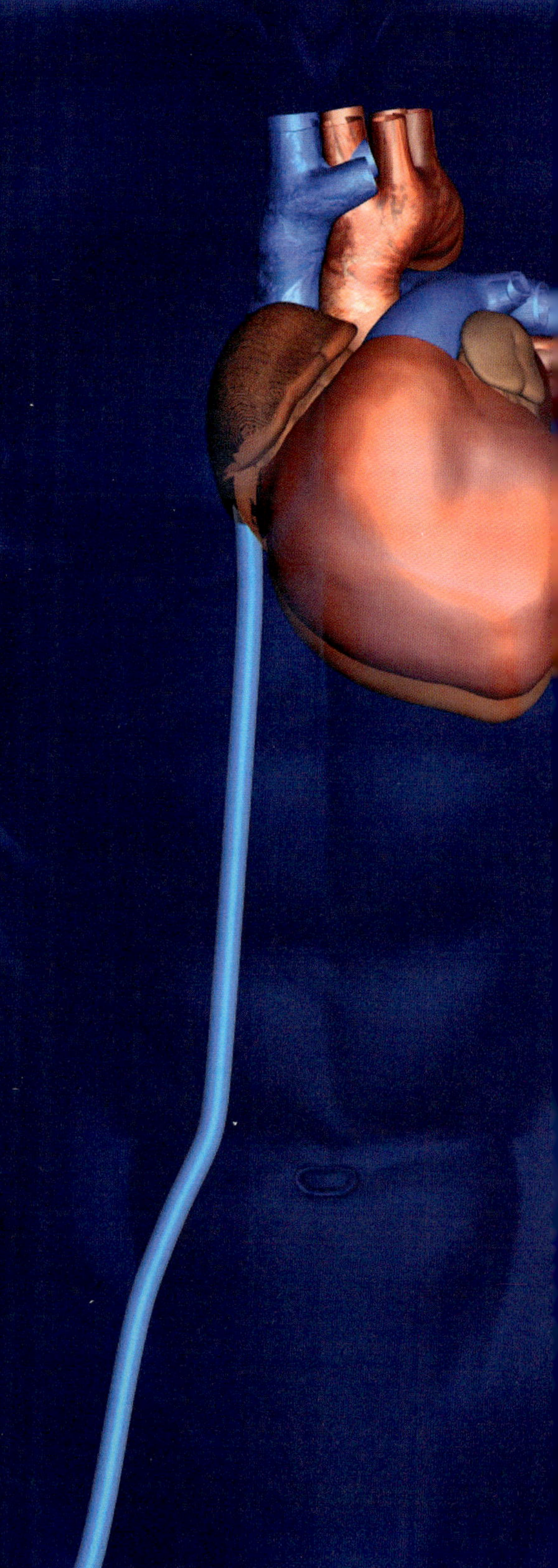

A new "cool" treatment for atrial fibrillation (the most common form of heart rhythm abnormality) may be safer than the standard approach.

Atrial fibrillation can cause heart palpitations, shortness of breath, dizziness, and, perhaps most worrisome, an increased risk of stroke due to blood clots. (Blood clots can form when an uneven heart rhythm allows blood to stagnate between beats instead of being evenly pumped and mixed.) The American Heart Association recommends aggressive treatment for atrial fibrillation in order to prevent stroke and improve quality of life.

The standard surgical fix uses radio waves to generate heat that selectively scars the heart, creating "inactive" spots that interrupt the electrical signals that cause the arrhythmia. But this approach (called radiofrequency ablation) can actually lead to the blood clots that the procedure aims to prevent, because intense heat has a coagulating effect on blood cells. In addition, the inactive sites must be relatively large in order to effectively stop atrial fibrillation, and the risk of clotting grows along with the size of the treated areas.

Luckily, applying heat is not the only way to stop an electrical signal gone wrong. Early studies of a new treatment device called CryoCor show that freezing tiny areas of heart tissue appears to be as effective as using heat—and the cold method does not seem to lead to clot formation.

Like radiofrequency ablation, the cold treatment uses a minimally invasive technique to thread a catheter through an artery and into the heart. Once in position, the tip of the catheter delivers a medical refrigerant gas that can reach temperatures as low as –176°F, low enough to freeze small bits of heart tissue.

Availability. CryoCor is already available in Europe, and more than 300 patients have been treated worldwide so far. The manufacturers expect the device to be approved by the FDA and available to U.S. patients before the end of 2005. ■

A catheter with a tip that can freeze tissue is threaded through the groin and along an artery into the heart, where it's positioned against a vein in the left atrium.

A "mapping catheter" with a ring-shaped tip confirms electrical activity in the vein before tissue is frozen to interrupt the electrical signals that can lead to atrial fibrillation.

Sudden Death Warning

An Illinois woman named Shalon Gardner was only 17 years old when she suddenly developed a very rapid heartbeat. Preben Bjerregaard, M.D., a cardiologist at St. Louis University Hospital, recalls that when he looked at her EKG, a test that measures the electrical signals during each heartbeat, "I saw this incredible, short QT interval, which I had never seen before." The QT interval is the length of time separating electrical impulses in the heart. People with long QT intervals are known to be at higher risk for sudden death, but based on Gardner's symptoms of heart palpitations and her short QT measurements, Dr. Bjerregaard feared she might face the same tragic fate.

Dr. Bjerregaard was surprised to discover that Shalon's mother and brother also showed short QT intervals, indicating a family propensity for serious heart trouble. To head off sudden death, each Gardner family member had a defibrillator surgically implanted. If erratic heart rhythms occur, the devices will kick in and save the day.

The short QT interval has also been identified in some families in Europe and is most likely related to a rare genetic defect. Dr. Bjerregaard advises anyone with a family history of sudden death, especially among younger family members, to have their QT intervals measured with an EKG.

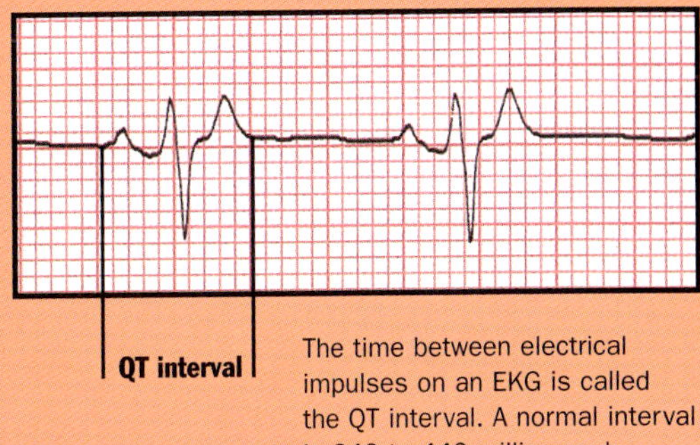

The time between electrical impulses on an EKG is called the QT interval. A normal interval is 340 to 440 milliseconds.

Cardiovascular Disease

Greek Diet Douses Inflammation

Scientists may have just uncovered the mystery of the Mediterranean diet. Since the 1970s, doctors, nutritionists, and gourmands alike have praised the traditional Greek diet as being particularly heart healthy, but exactly how a cuisine rich in olive oil, fruits, fish, and vegetables (and short on red meat) might help the heart was not totally clear. Some experts believe the diet's effect on blood pressure is responsible; others point to cholesterol reduction. They may all be right—but according to new research, the Mediterranean diet does something else, too: It fights inflammation, a major contributor to heart disease.

A study involving more than 2,000 healthy Greeks used a specially developed food questionnaire to track food preferences, and the participants were divided into groups based on how closely they followed a Greek-style diet. When given blood tests, the top Greek-style eaters showed 20 percent less C-reactive protein (CRP) in their blood than people who ate a diet that was less rich in vegetables, olive oil, and other foods associated with the classic Greek diet. CRP is a chemical that indicates chronic, low-level inflammation, including inflammation within artery walls. Elevated levels of CRP are now known to signal increased risk of heart disease, because the inflammation ultimately leads to dangerously fragile blockages in the blood vessels, which could lead to a heart attack. Those who ate the Greek cuisine also had fewer other signs of inflammation.

Another recent Greek study offered more proof of the heart-protecting power of the Mediterranean diet. Researchers at the University of Athens Medical School followed more than 22,000 volunteers for 44 months. Those who most closely followed the traditional Greek diet had a much lower risk of death from heart disease. ■

RESEARCH ROUNDUP

Tummy Tuck Tissue to Heal Hearts?

Body tissue extracted during tummy tuck procedures may one day be put to good use in healing damaged hearts. Tissue generally referred to as "body fat" also contains large numbers of non-fatty (stromal) cells that can be separated from tissue removed through procedures such as liposuction. According to test-tube research being performed by scientists in France and the United States, these stromal cells can be coaxed to develop into other types of tissue, including blood vessel and heart tissue.

Researchers believe that these cells could then be injected (using a catheter) into areas needing repair and improved blood flow, such as a damaged region of the heart or a blocked artery. One major benefit of this approach is that unlike a transplanted heart, for instance, the stromal cells won't be rejected by the immune system because the body recognizes them as its own.

Cardiovascular Disease

Controversial Calcium Scans Have Their Day

Many heart attacks occur without any warning. How can you know if you're at risk? One way is to have a scan that detects calcium deposits within the coronary arteries. At up to $400 a pop, the scans, known as electron-beam computed tomography (EBCT), have been considered by many doctors to be an expensive waste of time. Now, however, new research shows that for some people—those seemingly at moderate risk for heart disease—they may indeed be worth the money.

In EBCT, a beam of electrons (invisible particles of energy) is aimed at targeted parts of your heart as you lie flat on a table that glides into position within the scanning machine. Powerful magnets detect the electrons as they pass through your body. The images that result can show minute details, including calcium deposits on the lining of the arteries. Some doctors think that those layers of calcium—which have nothing to do with your dietary calcium intake—form around plaques in order to keep them from bursting and causing a heart attack. No matter why they form, though, the bottom line is clear: The more calcium deposits you have in your arteries, the more plaque you have.

Who can benefit? EBCT scans are worthless for people who already know they are at high risk for heart attacks. What would be the point of further proof? Their doctors already know they need aggressive treatment. The scans are probably also a waste of time and money for people who already know their risk is very low (for instance, those who are under 45, have never smoked, and have low cholesterol levels, low blood pressure, and no family history of heart problems). It's the "in-betweeners" who, according to findings from three U.S. medical schools, could benefit from the additional information an EBCT scan provides.

How do you know if you're in between? A person's risk of cardiovascular disease is usually measured by a grading system called the Framingham scale, which takes into account risk factors including cholesterol levels, smoking, blood pressure, family history, and diabetes. People with high Framingham scores are considered at high risk; those with low scores are considered at low risk. About 40 percent of adults score somewhere in between, and their risk may not be considered high enough to warrant treatment with drugs—unless the EBCT shows trouble.

The new study, published in the *Journal of the American Medical Association* in January 2004, followed more than 1,400 people who were at risk for heart disease. All of them were scored on the Framingham scale and received EBCT scans. They were then contacted yearly for eight years. In the end, among people with midrange Framingham scores, those with the highest arterial calcium levels also had the greatest risk of heart attack or death from heart disease.

What it means. If you think you're at moderate risk for a heart attack, consider asking your doctor about having an EBCT scan, but be aware that currently, most health insurance companies don't cover the test. Also know that if your scan shows no calcium deposits, it doesn't mean you can feel free to eat all the steak and cheeseburgers you want; in the study, 7 of 195 "moderate-risk" people with calcium scores of zero had heart attacks.

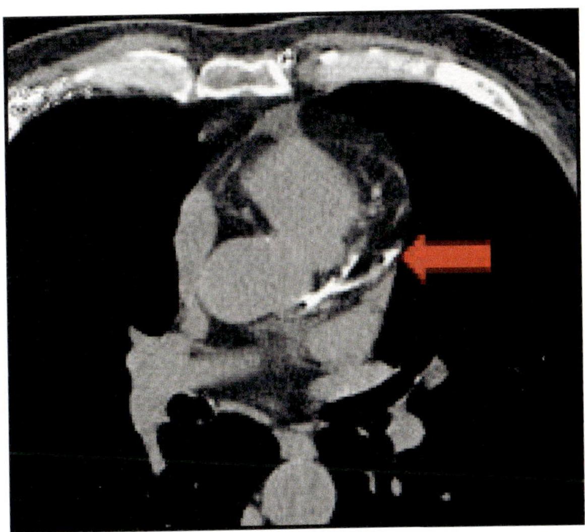

White areas of this scan indicate calcium deposits—meaning there's plaque in the arteries, increasing heart attack risk.

Deadly Heart Attack Gene Discovered

If you could take a simple blood test that would let you know if you were at greatly increased risk for heart attack and stroke, would you do it? Scientists have found a gene mutation that nearly doubles the risk of both. The discovery was made by a team led by deCODE Genetics, a developer of drugs and diagnostic tests, during a study of 296 families in Iceland.

The mutation is a change in the genetic code of a gene called ALOX5AP, which is involved in inflammation—now considered a leading cause of heart disease. The oddball gene is believed to increase the production of a chemical identified in the blood of people who have a history of heart attack. The researchers speculate that the chemical, leukotriene B4, is an indicator of inflammation in artery walls, which contributes to plaque formation.

A test to detect the chemical isn't currently available, since developing such tests often takes two to three years. Meanwhile, the deCODE group has also begun clinical trials of a drug designed to inhibit the gene's activity and dampen its damaging effects.

Other genes that increase the risk of cardiovascular disease have also been identified. If you learn through genetic testing that you have an increased risk of heart attack, it's all the more important to be vigilant about maintaining a heart-healthy lifestyle by exercising, eating right, and managing stress.

Cardiovascular Disease

New Reasons to Imbibe a Bit

Doctors know that moderate drinking—a daily glass of wine, beer, or spirits—lowers heart attack risk. No one's exactly sure why, but alcohol does seem to raise levels of HDL (the "good" cholesterol that sweeps up LDL, or "bad" cholesterol) and help "thin" the blood to prevent dangerous blood clots. But according to new research, it may also counter a process now thought to be intimately linked with heart disease: inflammation.

Inflammation is the body's response to injury, whether from a cut, invasion by bacteria, or some other insult—such as the attack on artery walls by LDL cholesterol. Researchers have recently linked heart attacks to arterial inflammation, a process that encourages plaque to accumulate inside artery walls and causes clumps of plaque to burst. In the body, inflammation can be measured indirectly by determining levels of chemicals called C-reactive protein (CRP) and interleukin-6 (IL-6).

Researchers in Italy measured these chemicals in 2,574 men and women ages 70 to 79. The volunteers also filled out questionnaires detailing their drinking habits. Sure enough, levels of CRP and IL-6 were lowest in people who drank one to seven alcoholic beverages each week.

Don't take the news as permission to drink with abandon, however. The researchers note that people who had eight drinks or more a week were more likely to have higher levels of CRP and IL-6, possibly because regularly drinking more than about one cocktail a day may lead to early-stage liver disease, which can be indicated by increased levels of the two inflammation markers measured. ■

RESEARCH ROUNDUP

Mentally, Men Fare Better after Bypass

Men and women can both benefit from bypass surgery, but for women, the benefits may be smaller. A study at Duke University Medical Center in North Carolina looked at a group of men and women who were about to undergo the surgery. Before surgery and a year later, each patient took a series of tests that measured life-quality factors, including depression, anxiety, and perception of health. At the one-year mark, the women had more depression and anxiety and felt that their ability to carry out their daily activities had decreased since the surgery.

Why the difference? One reason may be that the surgery just doesn't help women as much as it helps men. Women have smaller arteries, and the blood vessels used in bypass surgery tend not to last as long. After surgery, women typically show less improvement in angina symptoms and spend more days in bed.

Cardiovascular Disease

Bypass Surgery? Tell Your Doctor to Cool It

If you're about to undergo coronary artery bypass, consider this: People who have the surgery may have memory and concentration problems afterward. In fact, up to one-third of bypass patients report some mental impairment following surgery. Now, researchers at Duke University in Durham, North Carolina, think they have figured out the problem—and the solution.

Bypass surgery typically involves using a heart-lung machine to temporarily take over for the heart by mechanically pumping blood throughout the body. This allows the surgeon the advantage of working on a motionless heart. (Technology now allows some bypass surgeries to be performed on beating hearts, but most still rely on heart-lung machines.) When blood is circulated through the machine, it is cooled to a relatively low temperature (approximately 86°F, or 30°C) to help protect the brain and other organs from damage during surgery. When the surgery is over, the blood must be rewarmed to normal body temperature; the heart-lung machine does this by gradually increasing the temperature of the blood as it passes through the pumping equipment.

Heating the circulating blood too quickly can cause the core of the brain to become overheated before the heat can be transferred to the brain's outer surface. This overheating, called hyperthermia—think of it as a high fever within the brain—is known to cause cognitive problems. According to the Duke researchers, who analyzed more than 6,000 cases of bypass surgery, nearly all patients who underwent bypass before 1993 became hyperthermic. The analysis exposed the common problem of overheated blood, and Duke doctors now take the necessary steps to rewarm patients' blood more slowly.

The researchers hope to spread the message of the danger of rapid blood rewarming to other medical centers. They recommend that doctors spend an extra 10 to 15 minutes to avoid overheating delicate brain tissue. If you are facing bypass, you may want to talk to your doctor about his approach to rewarming after surgery. "The small amount of extra time it takes to rewarm slowly is definitely worth the benefits to our patients," says Hilary Grocott, M.D., cardiothoracic anesthesiologist at Duke.

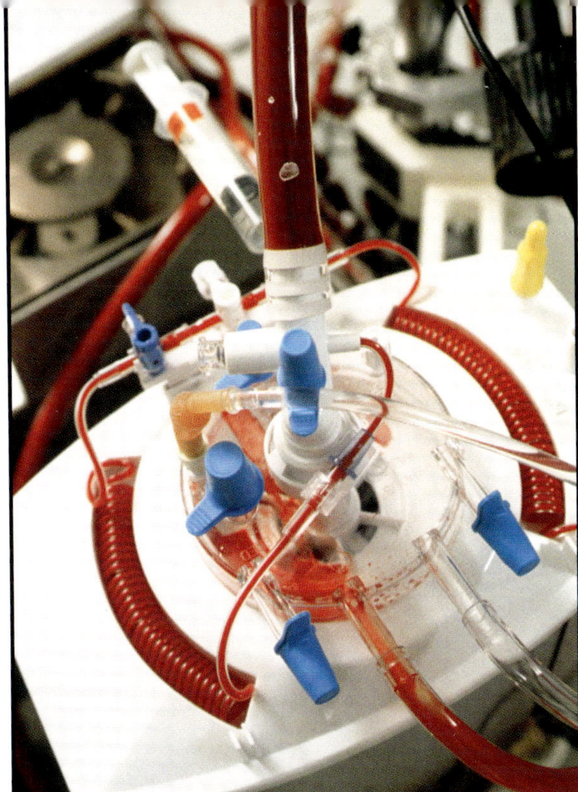

A heart-lung machine adds oxygen to a patient's blood, removes carbon dioxide, and returns the blood to the body.

RESEARCH ROUNDUP

Buddy Up to Protect Your Heart

Engaging in "guy" activities—think watching basketball and tinkering with the car—can be good for the heart, at least when men do them together. According to a Swedish study, men who have a support group of friends are much less likely to develop heart disease than those who tend to go it alone. The researchers followed 741 50-year-old men for 15 years. The men who regularly spent time with good friends were almost half as likely to be diagnosed with heart disease as those with the least social interaction. Researchers also noted greatly reduced heart disease risk in the men who were most emotionally attached to their buddies. So guys, don't be afraid to open up when you need to—you'll be doing your heart a favor.

Cardiovascular Disease

Bypass May (Still) Be Better for You

Sometimes a new, "easy" way to get something done just isn't as reliable as a time-honored technique. Although angioplasty is the more modern, less invasive treatment for coronary artery disease, a surprising study showed that bypass surgery saves more lives.

Bypass uses open-heart surgery to literally bypass the damaged artery by stitching in a healthy section of blood vessel. Angioplasty, on the other hand, is much less invasive and requires a fraction of the recovery time, a benefit to weaker and sicker patients who wouldn't be able to undergo the extensive surgery that bypass requires. In angioplasty, instead of cutting open the patient's chest, the doctor reaches the blocked artery by inserting a catheter via a narrow slit (usually in the groin, sometimes in the armpit), then uses tiny tools to clear out the blocked arteries and prop them open with miniature wire tubes called stents. Angioplasties now outnumber bypass surgeries in the United States by more than three to one.

Why bypass may be better. Heart doctors who regularly perform angioplasty, including Sorin J. Brener, M.D., a cardiologist at the Cleveland Clinic in Ohio, were extremely skeptical of the idea that open-heart surgery might be preferable for the highest-risk patients. The study Dr. Brener led comparing the two procedures, however, showed that traditional bypass delivered longer-lasting results than angioplasty, which opens up relatively small sections of artery. The results were published in the May 2004 issue of the journal *Circulation.*

"My own findings surprised me," says Dr. Brener. He found that for nearly 900 patients who he termed "at the worst end of the illness spectrum" (people with heart disease plus diabetes or high blood pressure), the potential surgical complications and tougher recovery were worth it. Five years after surgery, patients who had their diseased or blocked arteries completely bypassed had close to half the risk of dying from heart disease compared with similar patients who had undergone angioplasty.

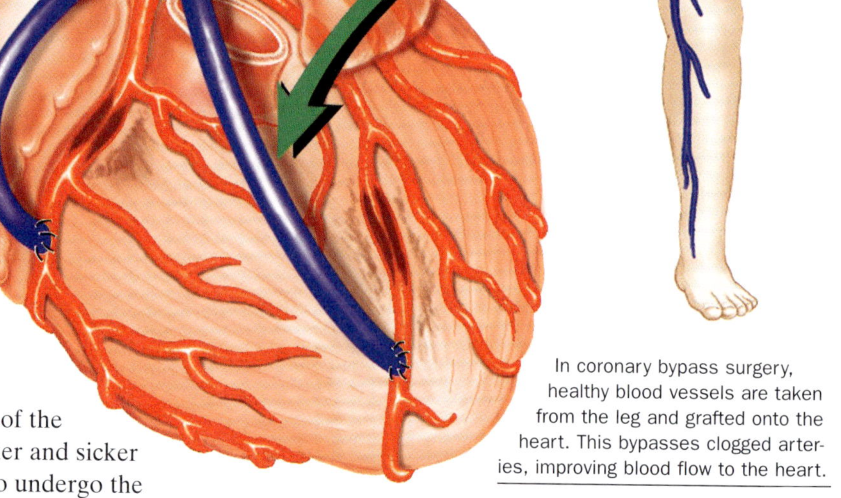

In coronary bypass surgery, healthy blood vessels are taken from the leg and grafted onto the heart. This bypasses clogged arteries, improving blood flow to the heart.

Choose the right hospital. Where a patient has the surgery matters. Dr. Brener says that the results of his study were greatly influenced by the Cleveland Clinic's above-average rate of surgical success—the clinic boasts bypass-related mortality rates that are approximately one-third of the national average. Bypass performed at another hospital with a less experienced staff may not be the better option as compared with angioplasty at that same location, he says. If you're choosing between bypass surgery and angioplasty, Dr. Brener advises, requesting as much information as possible regarding the facility's rates of complication and death. This information is already readily available from many hospitals and clinics, and it will be widely available from medical facilities in every U.S. state within the next two years, he says.

Heart Failure

Statins for Heart Failure

You probably think of statins as cholesterol-lowering drugs, but a study published in February 2004 showed that these drugs may also dramatically reduce the risk of death from heart failure when added to standard treatment.

Millions of people have heart failure, in which the heart loses the ability to pump enough blood through the body. Despite the availability and frequent use of drugs (such as ACE inhibitors, beta blockers, and aldosterone antagonists), more than five million Americans with heart failure remain at great risk for hospitalization and death from the condition, says Gregg Fonarow, M.D., professor of medicine in the division of cardiology at the University of California, Los Angeles, and coauthor of the study. "New heart failure medications are urgently needed," he says, "and our research shows that statins offer the potential to provide additional benefits to those patients who are already on standard medical treatment for heart failure."

Statins, which include atorvastatin (Lipitor) and pravastatin (Pravachol), are often prescribed to treat both high cholesterol and coronary artery disease, but medical experts have been unsure whether the drugs would help or hurt heart failure patients. First of all, people with heart failure frequently have low cholesterol, so using a cholesterol-lowering drug didn't seem to make much sense. In addition, some researchers worried that statins might have negative effects when used for heart failure, because the drugs lower levels of coenzyme Q_{10}, a heart-protective substance produced by the body.

Other experts, though, had a hunch that statins could save the lives of some patients. Dr. Fonarow and his colleagues followed 551 people with heart failure. In addition to taking standard medication, nearly half of the group was also taking statins to treat other heart-related problems. Over the course of one year, those taking statins had a reduced need for heart transplants and a substantial 55 percent reduction in the risk of dying from heart failure.

How it works. Statins may help heart failure patients in a number of ways, says Dr. Fonarow. They may either reduce inflammation in the heart and blood vessels, rejuvenate damaged heart tissue by improving blood flow to the area, or somehow improve the way the nervous system controls heart function. All of these positive effects could ultimately lead to reduced incidence of heart attack and death. The researchers concluded that adding statins to existing treatment is safe—and smart—for people with heart failure.

RESEARCH ROUNDUP

Implanted Defibrillators: More People Could Benefit

For people who have had heart attacks due to heart failure, surgically implanted defibrillators—those "guardian angels" that monitor heart rhythm and automatically administer an electric jolt if it should go awry—are godsends. But according to a recent study, even more people could benefit from them, including those with moderately severe heart failure who have never had heart attacks.

The study, sponsored by the National Heart, Lung, and Blood Institute, looked at more than 2,500 patients at nearly 150 hospitals in the United States, Canada, and New Zealand. The participants each had been diagnosed with heart failure; 52 percent had had heart attacks, and 48 percent had heart failure stemming from viral heart infections. The study showed that defibrillators reduced sudden death by 23 percent. After five years, only 28.9 percent of people who had implanted defibrillators had died, compared with more than 36 percent of those who didn't have the devices.

The study also compared the benefit of defibrillators to that of a drug that can prevent irregular heartbeat. People who got only the anti-arrhythmia drug had a 28 percent chance of dying from the problem, substantially more than the 17 percent chance for those who had defibrillators.

There's a catch, of course. Although you can't put a price on saving a life, defibrillators cost $20,000 (not including the cost of surgery). As things stand now, Medicare and private insurance companies have not proven particularly eager to provide reimbursement to everyone who might benefit.

RESEARCH ROUNDUP

Say Goodnight to High Blood Pressure

If you have high blood pressure, you may want to check your clock—your body clock, that is. A small study at the Netherlands Institute for Brain Research showed that men with high blood pressure lowered their nighttime numbers with regular use of melatonin, a hormone often used in supplement form for insomnia and jet lag. Researchers stress, however, that anyone who needs medication for high blood pressure should continue their treatment until larger studies clarify who might benefit from melatonin.

Hands Up for Better Blood Pressure

Want lower blood pressure? Just raise your hand. A study featured in a January 2004 issue of the journal *Annals of Internal Medicine* tested the blood pressure of 100 men and women when they had their arms raised to chest level and then dangling at their sides while they were standing, seated, and lying down.

The researchers found that regardless of their overall body position, the test subjects' blood pressure was lower when their arms were raised than when their arms were resting at their sides. While the subjects were seated with their arms down, for example, the average systolic blood pressure (the top number) was 8.8 mm/Hg (millimeters of mercury) higher, and the average diastolic pressure was 10.1 mm/Hg higher. Overall, this change in position increased the number of subjects who could be classified as hypertensive from 22 percent to 41 percent.

The researchers didn't suggest how patients should hold their arms during a blood pressure reading. However, the American Heart Association recommends that you be seated during a blood pressure check, with your upper arm held at roughly a 45-degree angle to your body.

High Blood Pressure

The Pressure Is Off: Moderate Drinking's Okay

If you have high blood pressure, your doctor has probably warned you that drinking alcohol could put you at risk for even higher blood pressure or other health problems. According to new research, though, the heart-protective benefits of moderate drinking may outweigh any negative effects on blood pressure.

Researchers from the University of Massachusetts Medical School analyzed data from the Physicians' Health Study, a huge initiative involving more than 80,000 male doctors who contribute to medical research by submitting annual health questionnaires. Specifically, they looked at some 14,000 men who had past or current high blood pressure but no history of heart attack or stroke at the outset of the study. The men who drank alcohol regularly—lightly or moderately—had a lower risk of death from heart disease than those who didn't.

"Alcohol does not lower blood pressure per se," says Howard Sesso, M.P.H., Sc.D., assistant professor of medicine at Brigham and Women's Hospital in Boston and coauthor of the study. "However, we found that among men with hypertension, drinking no more than one drink a day reduced their risk of dying from cardiovascular disease." Dr. Sesso says it is most likely the ethanol (the type of alcohol in all alcoholic beverages) that does the trick. Scientists believe that ethanol may protect the heart by raising good cholesterol and preventing dangerous blood clots. ■

High Cholesterol

Super-Low Cholesterol a Super Idea

Think your cholesterol is low enough? Think again, because "low enough" may be getting lower. A recent experiment showed that cutting cholesterol to well below the current recommended level could significantly reduce the risk of death from cardiovascular disease.

The eye-opening study, led by researchers at Harvard and Brigham and Women's Hospital in Boston, showed that for people with unstable angina or those recovering from heart attacks, a drug that aggressively lowers "bad" LDL cholesterol—far below the level currently recommended—kept arteries clearer and prevented more heart disease–related deaths than the standard cholesterol-lowering drug. The findings may mean that all of us could benefit from cholesterol levels that are even lower than those previously considered safe.

The power of high-dose statins. The study was the first to pit the older statin drug pravastatin (Pravachol) against the newer and more potent atorvastatin (Lipitor). Pravachol was designed to reduce LDL cholesterol to 100 mg/dL (milligrams per deciliter of blood), the accepted target for people at high risk. High-dose Lipitor was designed to drop LDL levels to the much lower goal of 70 mg/dL.

More than 4,000 people who had heart attacks or chest pain at 350 hospitals in eight different countries took part. People who got Lipitor typically saw their LDL cholesterol drop to the sub-basement level of 62 mg/dL—and it paid off. After two years, only 22.4 percent of those people had repeat heart-related problems, while more than 26.3 percent of people who took Pravachol had either died, had heart attacks or strokes, required bypass surgery, or been hospitalized for severe angina.

Not surprisingly, the super-powered statin drug is more expensive (Lipitor costs about $1,400 a year, while Pravachol is $900) and carries a slightly higher risk of side effects. The benefits of the stronger drug regimen, however, may outweigh any of those concerns, according to Christopher Cannon, M.D., Harvard cardiologist and lead researcher for the study. "Starting today, patients going home after a heart attack should be given a high-dose statin regimen," he says.

Benefits for everyone? Dr. Cannon and his colleagues later completed an analysis of people taking Lipitor six months after their heart attacks—by which time their conditions had stabilized. The results showed that Lipitor delivered the same powerful cholesterol-lowering, heart-protecting benefit, which hints that the drug could be useful as a preventive measure in people with no history of heart trouble. And despite some speculation that super-low cholesterol could backfire and turn out to be a *bad* thing (studies have associated very low cholesterol levels with severe depression, anxiety, and a risk of suicide), no side effects were noted.

The findings carry a powerful message for people without existing heart problems, says Dr. Cannon. Although it's not possible to lower LDL to such extreme levels without taking medication, lower is clearly better for ensuring heart health.

Lowering Cholesterol, Improving Survival

Lowering heart attack patients' cholesterol below current standards improves their survival, according to a new study. It suggests that the newer, more potent statin drug, Lipitor, works better with high-risk patients than the older statin drug Pravachol.

Percent of patients taking 40 milligrams of **Pravachol** daily who died or experienced a cardiac event, such as a new heart attack.

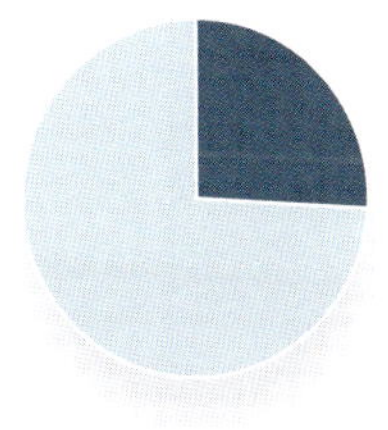

26 Percent

Percent of patients taking 80 milligrams of **Lipitor** daily who died or experienced a cardiac event, such as a new heart attack.

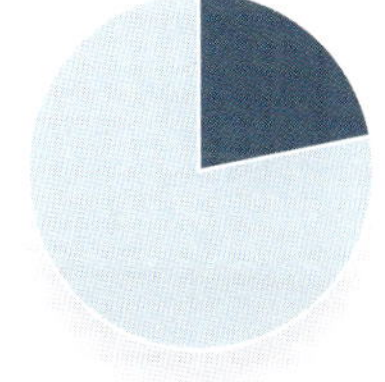

22 Percent

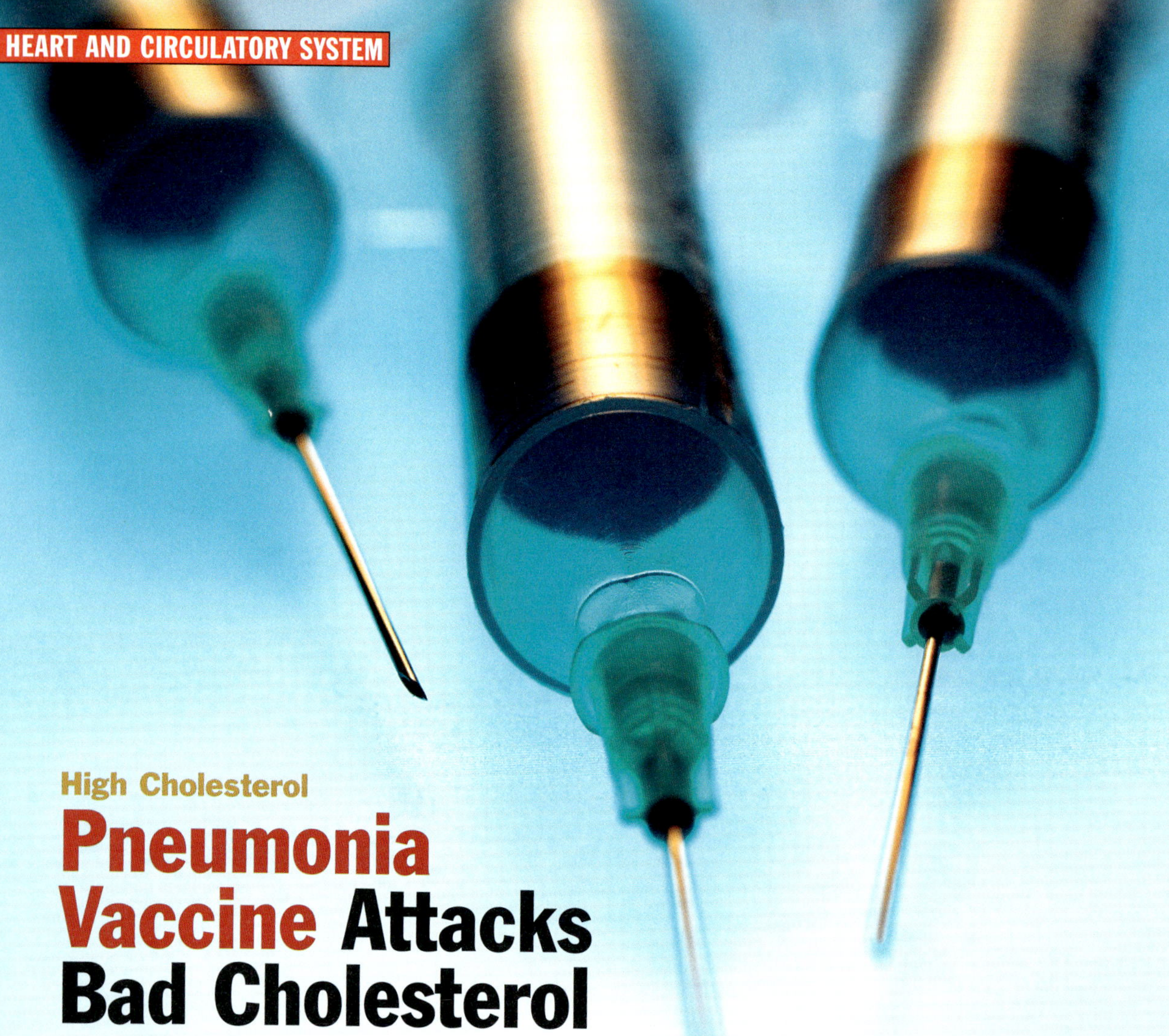

High Cholesterol

Pneumonia Vaccine Attacks Bad Cholesterol

High cholesterol may someday be treated—or even prevented—with a familiar, low-tech vaccine that will protect your arteries from sticky plaque.

Immunologists and cholesterol experts working together at the University of California, San Diego, have found that in mice, a simple pneumonia vaccine can help protect against heart disease by increasing the body's immune response to "bad" LDL cholesterol. Mice that were vaccinated against pneumonia showed a 21 percent reduction in plaque buildup compared with unvaccinated mice.

How it works. The vaccine works by activating a naturally present antibody—the antibody for the pneumonia bacterium. Antibodies "flag" dangerous substances by attaching to them so the body can attack and destroy them. The pneumonia vaccine also works against LDL cholesterol because, as it turns out, the surfaces of both the pneumonia bacterium and LDL have an identical chemical marker. When the immune system is "primed" by the pneumonia vaccine to recognize the pneumonia bugs, it also spots the bad cholesterol and binds with it. The connection disables the cholesterol and makes it less likely to stick to artery walls.

This isn't the first study to link vaccines with better heart health. A study of 286,000 seniors hospitalized for heart disease or stroke found that they were able to leave the hospital sooner if they'd had flu shots.

What it means. Should you run out and roll up your sleeve for a pneumonia vaccine to defend yourself against heart disease? Study coauthor Gregg Silverman, M.D., says it's possible that current pneumonia vaccines deliver such a benefit, but no one is certain. "The vaccines we studied were not specifically designed to boost this response. Based on what we now know, a more focused vaccine could be made for treating or even preventing cardiovascular disease in patients." Research in primates is now under way.

Sickle Cell Disease

Treat High Lung Pressure—Stay Alive

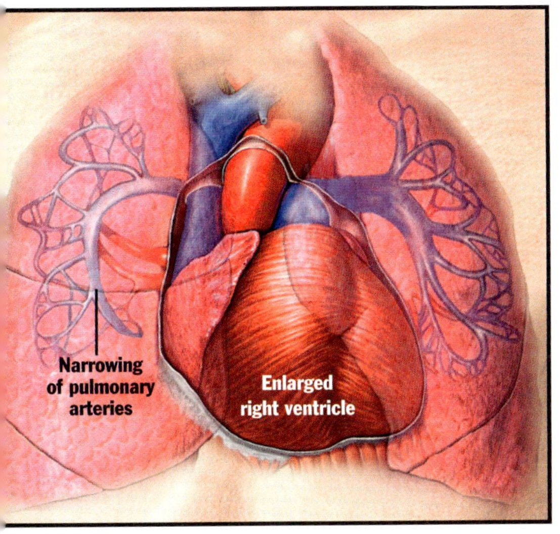

Pulmonary hypertension: Lung arteries narrow, and the overworked heart enlarges.

Anyone with sickle cell disease should be regularly screened for high blood pressure in the arteries that deliver oxygen to the lungs. Not only is this problem very common in people with sickle cell disease—a genetic blood disorder that distorts the shape of red blood cells—but it can also be extraordinarily deadly.

High blood pressure in the lungs, called pulmonary hypertension, affects 20 to 40 percent of people with sickle cell disease. Researchers believe that it's caused by sickle cell–related changes that break down red blood cells and leave excess hemoglobin (the blood component that carries oxygen) floating in the bloodstream. The extra hemoglobin binds to nitric oxide, a chemical that is important for keeping blood vessels open. Without enough usable nitric oxide, blood flow in the lungs can become restricted, leading to sudden death.

A study by researchers from the National Institutes of Health (NIH) recently confirmed the lifesaving value of treating pulmonary hypertension. They followed 190 men and women with sickle cell for 18 months. At that end of that period, 12 of the 62 people with pulmonary hypertension had died (20 percent of that group), compared with only 2 of the 128 sickle cell patients without the lung condition (less than 2 percent). The increased risk of death was very high even in people with only mild or moderate pulmonary hypertension, leading one researcher to call the lung condition the "number one predictor of sudden death syndrome" for people with sickle cell disease.

What it means to you. If you or someone you know has sickle cell disease, be sure to ask about testing and treatment for pulmonary hypertension. The NIH researchers used noninvasive Doppler echocardiology, a form of ultrasound, to spot the condition. They recommend aggressive treatment, including medications that increase nitric oxide in the blood, inhaled nitric oxide gas, and blood transfusions. Drugs called calcium channel blockers (which relax blood vessels and allow more blood to get through) may also help. ■

FUTURE BREAKTHROUGHS

A 6-in-1 Heart Pill

Imagine popping a single pill every day that contains six powerful protective medicines to stave off heart attack and stroke. Cutting the incidence of cardiovascular disease by as much as 80 percent is the grand idea behind the proposed Polypill, which would contain a cholesterol-lowering statin drug, three blood pressure medicines, the heart-friendly vitamin folic acid, and a small dose of clot-melting aspirin. The pill would be recommended for people age 55 and up regardless of heart disease risk factors, since everyone stands to benefit. Clinical trials have not yet begun, however, so it could be 10 or more years before the super pill becomes available.

Red Wine in a Pill

If you prefer the natural approach to heart health but want or need to forgo red wine, you may soon be able to get the same benefits in a pill. Researchers at the Pavese Biochemical Institute in Pavia, Italy, are freeze-drying wine and condensing it into alcohol-free pills that, they say, could provide all of the known benefits of a glass of wine, including protection against heart disease. The ingredients include wine's antioxidants, which neutralize cell-damaging free radicals, contributors to heart disease. Not only would swallowing a pill be faster than drinking a glass of wine, you'd still be able to pass muster as a designated driver.

MUSCLES
BONES, AND JOINTS

IN THIS SECTION

THE POPULATION IS AGING, AND THAT MEANS MORE CASES OF OSTEOPOROSIS.

So it's good news that taking a common vitamin—either singly or in a multivitamin—can help keep your bones strong and fracture-free. According to other research, supplements containing red clover or components derived from tofu can also help, thanks to their high content of estrogen-like plant chemicals.

For aching joints, science is bringing out the big guns. By pairing two rheumatoid arthritis drugs never before used together, researchers have come closer to stopping the crippling disease. Thinking bigger, other researchers have taken a giant step toward using stem cells to repair joints damaged by arthritis. And one team has a startling theory about what causes most cases of osteoarthritis—one that could lead to previously unimagined treatments and preventive measures.

In the war on pain, two old favorites for joint pain relief, glucosamine and ibuprofen, turn out to be like Astaire and Rogers, working better together than either one alone. And speaking of old favorites, there's now another reason to love Botox, the popular toxin: New research shows it works wonders for eliminating certain types of back pain.

Arthritis

Stem Cells Shown to Reverse Arthritis

Goats have joined the growing list of animals involved in stem cell research. Unlike the cats, sheep, and mice that have been cloned using stem cells, however, these goats aren't being replicated. Instead, scientists are using stem cells to cure the animals' arthritis.

The stem cells involved are not the controversial embryonic stem cells culled from the earliest stages of human (or, in this case, goat) life. Rather, they are adult stem cells that survive throughout life in bone marrow, muscle tissue, and the bloodstream.

How it works. Like embryonic stem cells, adult stem cells seem to have the ability to become just about any type of tissue in the body, and they are capable of replicating almost indefinitely. Thus, they serve as remarkable little "repair engines." Researchers had already shown that adult stem cells can be used to repair some human organ tissues, such as the heart. Up until now, though, it was uncertain whether they could successfully mend the notoriously hard-to-repair cartilage and bone found in joints. The goats have helped to answer that question.

Researchers from Osiris Therapeutics in Baltimore extracted stem cells from the goats' bone marrow and allowed

TOP Trends

ARTHRITIS? YOU'RE NOT ALONE

According to new figures from the Centers for Disease Control and Prevention, about a quarter of all adult Americans have been diagnosed with some form of arthritis (including osteoarthritis, rheumatoid arthritis, gout, lupus, and fibromyalgia), and another 17 percent probably have arthritis but haven't been diagnosed. That's a lot of aching joints. Those numbers are higher than they've ever been—and will probably climb much higher. The youngest baby boomers are reaching their forties, and the oldest are nearing 60, when osteoarthritis is almost the rule. The upside to the trend is that it's stimulating vigorous research into new arthritis treatments and preventive measures.

Meanwhile, experts say you can lower your risk by keeping your weight down, exercising regularly, getting plenty of joint-saving antioxidants by eating fruits and vegetables and supplementing with vitamin C, and getting your joints into a doctor's office as soon as you suspect anything is wrong.

TWO DECADES LATER, THE LIVIN' IS EASIER

Experts are seeing a positive rheumatoid arthritis trend: Over the past two decades, the quality of life for people with the serious joint disease has improved significantly. By examining California hospital records, researchers from the National Institutes of Health found that admissions as a direct result of rheumatoid arthritis were much lower between 1998 and 2001 than they were between 1983 and 1987. The number of arthritis-caused problems such as inflamed blood vessels and knee replacements was also down.

Even though powerful drugs for rheumatoid arthritis existed 20 years ago, questions about their safety made doctors reluctant to prescribe them. As time passed, however, the drugs' safety records proved to be good, so doctors began to use them more aggressively. They also started using them earlier in the disease's progression, which is key to preventing potentially crippling complications.

Butt out, arthritis. Stem cells repaired worn tissue in goats' knees.

The Future of Arthritis Relief?

A close-up of a goat's knee tissue shows early-stage arthritis damage (top) and repair after stem cell treatment (bottom)

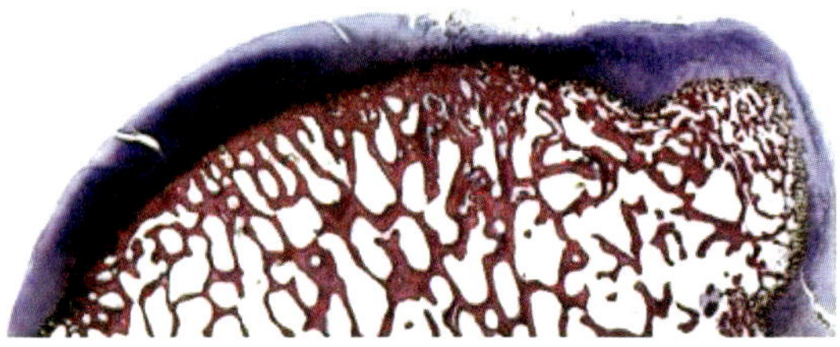

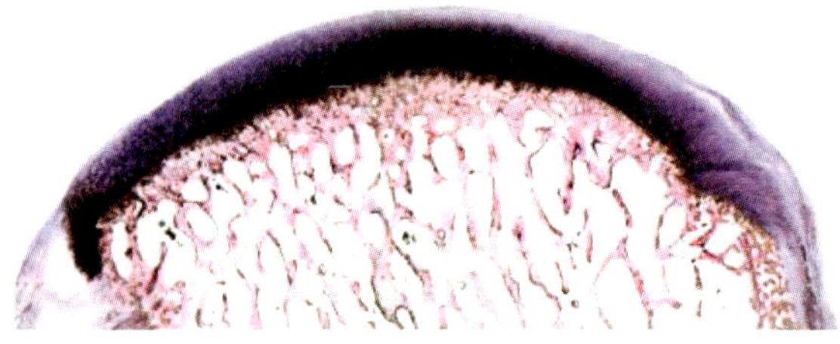

them to multiply in a petri dish. Then they injected some 10 million of the cells into the goats' arthritic knees. The result? Joint tissue that had been worn away by arthritis began to grow back. The progression of cartilage damage was significantly slowed, and bone erosion was reduced.

The study also showed that stem cell therapy may be useful for preventing knee arthritis as well as treating it, since timely joint repair discourages cartilage damage from progressing to full-blown arthritis. The results were published in the December 2003 issue of the medical journal *Arthritis and Rheumatism.*

Availability. Since goats aren't people, a lot of work needs to be done before stem cell transplantation becomes a proven and safe treatment for human arthritis.

Arthritis

One-Two Punch May Knock Out Rheumatoid Arthritis

In rheumatoid arthritis, the joints are attacked by the body's immune system and systematically destroyed. There is no single drug that can halt the crippling disease, although medicines known as DMARDs (disease-modifying anti-rheumatic drugs) and TNF (tumor necrosis factor) inhibitors can ease symptoms and slow the damage. Now it appears that an unusual approach—using both types of drugs at the same time—is much more effective than using either type alone. It works so well, in fact, that it seems to stop the disease in its tracks.

That's what Swedish researchers found when they studied 686 rheumatoid arthritis patients from across Europe and Australia. The patients were divided into three groups. One group received both the DMARD methotrexate (Rheumatrex, Trexall) and the TNF inhibiter etanercept (Enbrel); the others received either one drug or the other.

After one year, joint damage was slowed significantly more in the volunteers who were treated with both drugs. More than 33 percent of those patients virtually stopped having arthritis symptoms while on the drugs, compared with 13 percent on methotrexate alone and 16 percent on etanercept alone. The study results were published in the British medical journal *Lancet* in February 2004.

How it works. The two drugs tackle rheumatoid arthritis differently. Methotrexate suppresses the overactive immune system that triggers the disease. Etanercept works by interfering with the activity of TNF, a protein that's a major culprit in the swelling and joint damage caused by this type of arthritis. Having different methods of action

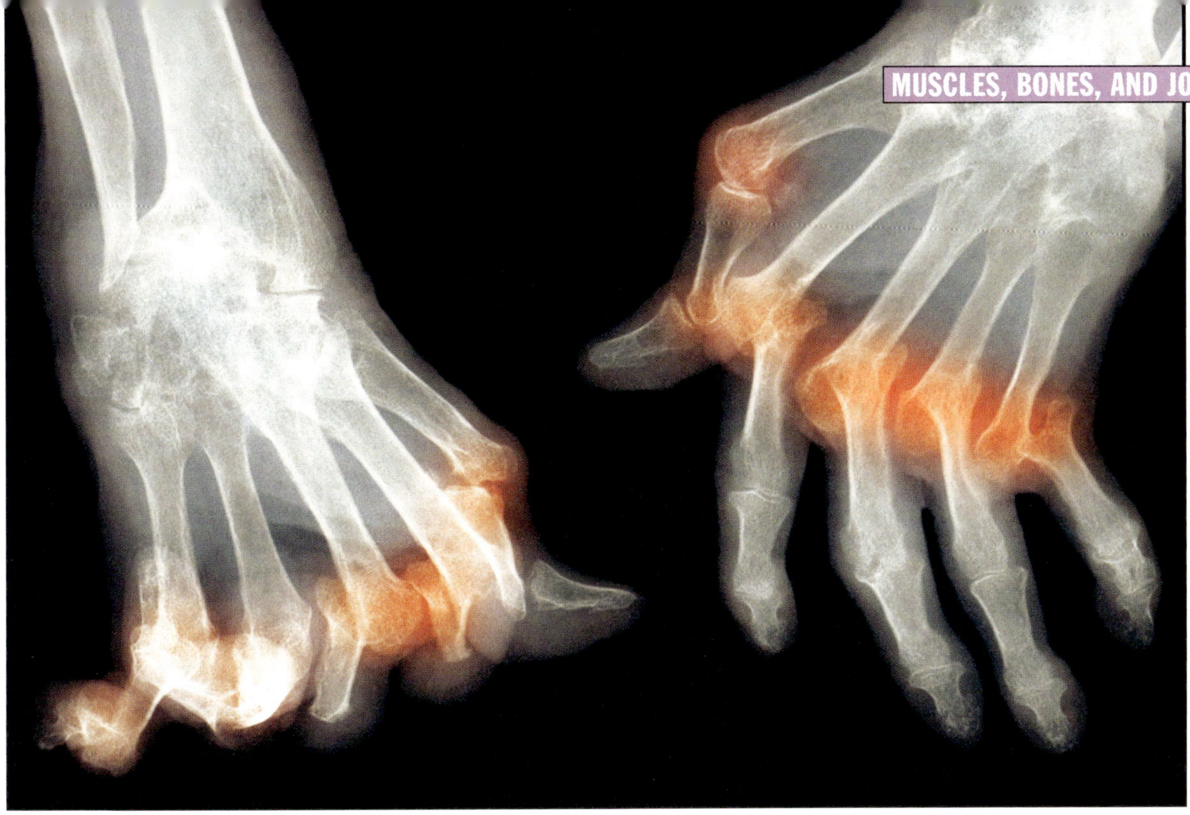

The red on this x-ray indicates fingers bent abnormally by rheumatoid arthritis. Joints damaged by the disease can become inflamed and painful, limiting movement.

doesn't necessarily guarantee that medications can work together effectively, but this study showed that these two drugs do. "If we initiate treatment with etanercept in combination with methotrexate, we can stop the inflammatory process," says study author Lars Klareskog, M.D., Ph.D., of the Karolinska Institute in Stockholm. "The body recovers and can begin to heal."

Availability. You can ask your doctor now about combination therapy, but the study authors expect progress toward routine use of the treatment to be gradual. Further studies are needed to determine long-term safety and identify which patients are most likely to benefit. Studies are planned to test the drug combination's effectiveness in recently diagnosed rheumatoid arthritis patients. (The Swedish study looked at patients who had had the disease for an average of 6 1/2 years.) The hope is that treating the disease with the two drugs very early in its progression will be effective enough to actually heal joint damage. ■

Arthritis Medications' Heart-Saving Bonus

The drugs you're taking for rheumatoid arthritis may be reducing your risk for heart disease, including heart failure. One of those drugs, the immune system suppressant methotrexate (Rheumatrex, Trexall), is already known to do so. Now, new research, published in the March 2004 issue of the *American Journal of Medicine*, shows that drugs called TNF inhibitors, such as infliximab (Remicade) and etanercept (Enbrel), also help guard against heart disease. This is an especially welcome finding, since these drugs were previously suspected of worsening certain heart conditions. The study also found that having rheumatoid arthritis raises the risk of heart failure, in which the heart can't pump enough blood to the organs. Earlier research connected rheumatoid arthritis to other kinds of heart disease, including fatal heart attacks.

Arthritis

A New Power Hitter in the Anti-Arthritis Lineup

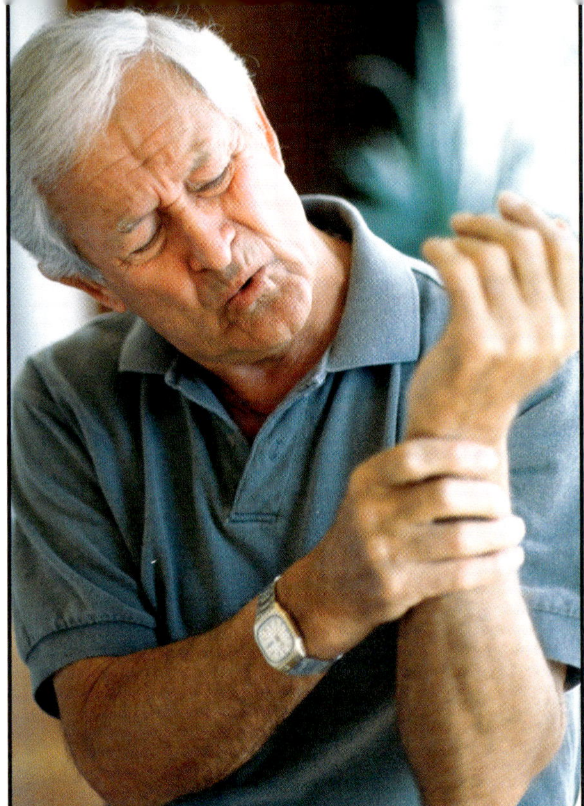

Not satisfied with your current rheumatoid arthritis medicine? A powerful new alternative is on the way.

A rheumatoid arthritis drug that works wonders for one person may be useless to another. That's why doctors depend on having a variety of options to choose from. The next option on deck is a powerful drug that suppresses the immune system. It's so powerful, in fact, that it's currently used to prevent organ rejection in transplant recipients. Since rheumatoid arthritis is caused by an overactive immune system, immunosuppressants make up a key treatment category.

The drug, tacrolimus (Prograf), is already being prescribed for arthritis "off-label"—that is, outside the use for which it was approved—in a number of countries. Most doctors in the United States are waiting for the FDA to approve it specifically for rheumatoid arthritis before prescribing it for that purpose. A recent study, reported in the British medical journal *Rheumatology* in March 2004, brought that approval a step closer.

What the study showed. The study involved almost 900 rheumatoid arthritis patients, all of whom had been treated unsuccessfully with disease-modifying anti-rheumatic drugs (DMARDs), the most common class of rheumatoid arthritis medications. All of them were given Prograf daily. After 14 months, the researchers found that the drug benefited a significant portion of these users: About 26 percent showed at least a 70 percent improvement in swollen and painful joints. However, many volunteers reported side effects, such as headache and diarrhea.

Availability. If you're not getting relief with your current medication, you can ask your doctor about Prograf, but it can have serious side effects, including pneumonia and even diabetes.

The drug was expected to be approved for rheumatoid arthritis treatment in Japan by the end of 2004. In the United States and Europe, where more studies were still under way in 2004, approval will take a year or two longer. ■

RESEARCH ROUNDUP

Want Arthritis Relief? Treat Your Depression

If you feel better, so will your joints, suggests a study of more than 1,800 depressed seniors in five U.S. states, which found that aggressive treatment of depression has a welcome side effect: less arthritis pain. A lot of people stand to benefit from this discovery, since four out of five adults over age 70 have arthritis, and about one in six has depression.

Researchers have known for a while that some antidepressant drugs can reduce pain under certain circumstances, but their success as pain relievers has been inconsistent. This latest study showed that people who took antidepressants and underwent psychotherapy experienced less arthritis pain (not to mention fewer depressive symptoms) after 12 months than people who simply took medication. No one fully understands why.

Arthritis

Double-Barreled Relief for Joint Pain

Millions of people take glucosamine to prevent damage to bones and cartilage. The supplement (a synthetic version of a substance found in the body) has also been shown to help repair joint damage. Now, researchers from Temple University in Philadelphia have discovered that glucosamine has a third trick up its sleeve: providing relief from joint pain. The only catch is that you need to combine it with ibuprofen.

Glucosamine appears to have no pain-blocking effect of its own (although, of course, reducing joint damage lessens pain, which is why people taking the supplement often feel better). When the researchers tested glucosamine along with ibuprofen on mice, it noticeably boosted the power of the pain reliever. This "drug synergy" didn't happen when glucosamine was teamed with other painkillers, such as aspirin and acetaminophen.

The next step is to find out whether the combo has the same effect in humans. Studies are already under way. The result may be a single pill containing the optimal doses of both ibuprofen and glucosamine to deliver immediate pain relief along with ongoing joint benefits. Meanwhile, both are available at any drugstore. Talk to your doctor before taking ibuprofen on an ongoing basis.

RESEARCH ROUNDUP

Now They Know Squat about Arthritis

Amateur gardeners in the Western world and typical residents of China's capital city have at least one thing in common: They squat a lot. As a result, they're statistically more likely to have arthritis of the knee later in life. According to a study of more than 1,800 Chinese men and women over age 60, the more you squat in early adulthood, the higher your risk of eventually developing knee arthritis (or more accurately, a specific type of arthritis called tibiofemoral osteoarthritis).

Besides sounding a warning to softball catchers, weight lifters, and avid gardeners, the results, published in April 2004, clear up a lingering question among rheumatologists: Why are knee arthritis rates higher in China than in the West, even though obesity (a major arthritis risk factor) is less of a problem there? The answer seems to be that squatting is a traditional resting and working position in China. In the study, many residents of Beijing reported having squatted for more than 3 hours a day in their twenties. Those people were as much as twice as likely to develop knee arthritis in their sixties as people who reported squatting less often.

Is It Rheumatoid Arthritis?

An Earlier Test Can Tell You

Is the joint pain that's been bothering you caused by osteoarthritis or the more serious disease rheumatoid arthritis? It often takes years before your doctor can determine which it is. And since rheumatoid arthritis (a malfunction of the immune system) is treated differently than osteoarthritis (an age-related disease), a delayed diagnosis also means a delayed prescription for the drugs that can help—and that's highly unfortunate, since the sooner rheumatoid arthritis is treated, the less damage the joints sustain.

That's about to change. Dutch researchers have announced that with a new diagnostic test, which measures blood levels of an antibody called anti-CCP, it's now possible to predict accurately whether early-stage arthritis will develop into rheumatoid arthritis.

In results of a 936-patient study, 93 percent of people who tested positive for anti-CCP at the early stage of joint pain went on to develop rheumatoid arthritis within three years, compared with only 25 percent of those who tested negative for the antibody. The next step: Studies under way in 2004 will confirm whether treatment at the prediagnosis stage of rheumatoid arthritis is beneficial.

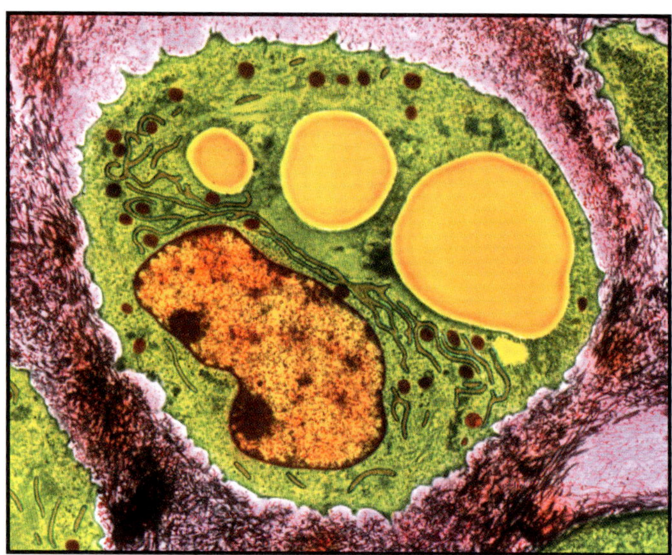

A new theory holds that aging cartilage cells lose their ability to replicate, possibly causing arthritis. Antioxidants could extend the life of these cells.

Arthritis

What Really Causes Arthritis?

If you have osteoarthritis, the most common form of arthritis, you've probably been told that simple wear and tear is to blame—that the cartilage that keeps the bones in the joints from rubbing against one another has been worn away by a lifetime of mechanical stress. In other words, your joints hurt because you've used them so darn much. That's the usual explanation—but it could be all wrong.

Groundbreaking research presented to the American Academy of Orthopaedic Surgeons in March 2004 revealed an entirely different explanation for osteoarthritis that may assign the wear-and-tear theory to the dustbin of medical history. According to a team of orthopedists led by Joseph Buckwalter, M.D., professor of orthopedics at the University of Iowa in Iowa City, the cartilage damage of osteoarthritis has little to do with wear and tear and lots to do with aging cartilage cells and that ubiquitous health bugaboo known as oxidation.

That view, if proven correct, could open up a whole new universe of preventive strategies, treatment options, and perhaps even a cure. "Within a few years, we hope to have some important new ways of decreasing the risk of osteoarthritis,"

Dr. Buckwalter says. One preventive step might be as simple taking supplemental antioxidants such as vitamin C.

The real problem. After analyzing cartilage tissue in patients ranging in age from 1 to 87, Dr. Buckwalter and his colleagues concluded that a major reason cartilage breaks down is that cartilage cells, known as chondrocytes, lose their ability to generate new tissue with age. The solution? Discover a way to postpone the chondrocytes' retirement. Dr. Buckwalter and others are working on it. "We're already getting some interesting preliminary results in our efforts to prolong the functional life of chondrocytes," he says.

Dr. Buckwalter's analysis also pointed to another arthritis culprit: free radicals. Experts have long known that these unstable oxygen molecules, released as by-products of natural chemical reactions in the body, harm cells. The damage they cause to chondrocytes, Dr. Buckwalter concluded, hastens the aging of those cells and increases the risk of osteoarthritis. Joint injuries, because they bring excess oxygen to the cartilage tissue as blood rushes in to heal the damage, also speed the death of chondrocytes.

A potential solution. If free radicals contribute to the problem, antioxidants, which neutralize them, could be part of the solution. Antioxidants, such as vitamin C, vitamin E, and beta-carotene, are abundant in many fruits and vegetables and other foods, as well as in green tea and dietary supplements. While there's not yet any evidence that antioxidant supplementation helps prevent arthritis, many orthopedists consider it a good idea. "Antioxidants, especially vitamin C, are useful for protecting your entire musculoskeletal system," says Nick DiNubile, M.D., clinical assistant professor of orthopedic surgery at the Hospital of the University of Pennsylvania in Philadelphia.

A joint effort: Eating fruits and vegetables that are rich in vitamin C, vitamin E, and beta-carotene may help to fend off osteoarthritis.

RESEARCH ROUNDUP

Osteoporosis Drugs May Do Double Duty

Could osteoporosis drugs such as alendronate (Fosamax) and risedronate (Actonel) also help protect against arthritis and help ease joint pain? According to one study, the answer is a resounding "Yes."

Researchers at the University of Tennessee in Memphis studied more than 800 women, most of whom reported knee pain from osteoarthritis, the most common type of arthritis. All were 69 or older, and most took some kind of zbasis—either raloxifene (Evista), the hormone estrogen, or a bisphosphonate drug such as Fosamax or Actonel.

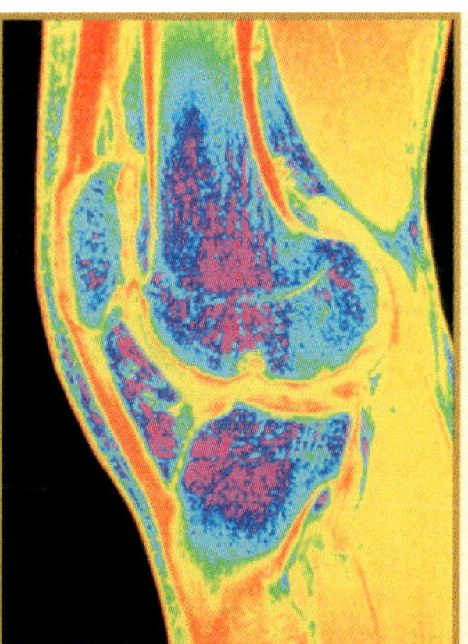
MRI scans showed that women who took osteoporosis drugs called bisphosphonates had less severe arthritis.

MRI scans showed that women who had been taking bisphosphonates in the months or years preceding the study had, on average, less severe knee arthritis than those who'd either been taking another type of osteoporosis drug or weren't taking any medication for osteoporosis. The bisphosphonate users also tended to have less knee pain and suffered less from arthritis-related problems, such as bone marrow swelling, bone spurs, and the wearing away of the bone itself. The apparent slowing of arthritis progression may come from drugs' ability to reduce damage from inflammation.

Back and Neck Pain

Simple Shots Ease Back Pain

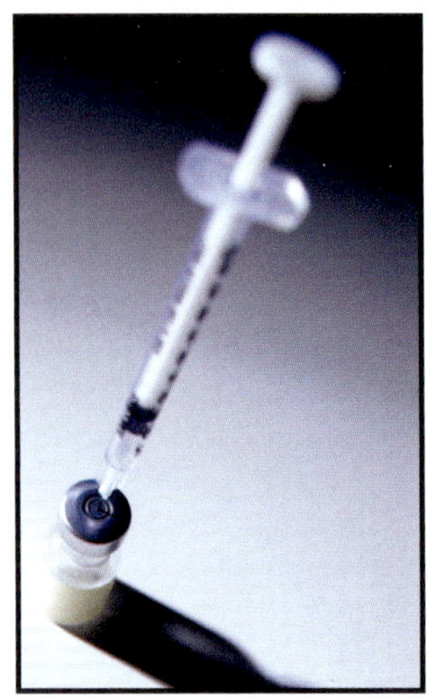

Shots to soothe your aching back may have just gotten cheaper and easier. Australian researchers say the most effective ingredient in common ligament injections to treat back pain may very well be the needle itself. That surprising possibility arose in January 2004, when published study results revealed that patients who were given "prolotherapy" injections every other week for three months reported no more improvement than those who were injected with a simple salt solution.

Prolotherapy involves injecting a substance such as phenol, glycerin, or glucose, usually blended with a local anesthetic, directly into the ligaments in the area of pain. The prolotherapy agents are thought to speed recovery by strengthening the ligaments. But researchers from the University of Queensland found that in a group of volunteers with chronic back pain, those who received inert saline injections got the same amount of pain relief at the same rate as those who received prolotherapy.

If prolotherapy is no more helpful than saltwater, why does either treatment provide any benefit at all? "The effect may lie in the needle rather than the specific injection solution," say the study authors. In other words, it's possible that the needle produces a counterirritant effect. In this phenomenon, the body's response to a new, less severe pain effectively blocks the nervous system's response to preexisting pain.

In fact, saline shots are sometimes used currently to relieve certain kinds of lower-back pain. Whether they work because of the counterirritant effect or some other action, these injections can disrupt what orthopedists call the pain/spasm cycle. (First, a muscle spasm causes pain, then the body's reaction to that pain causes a spasm.) Temporarily blocking that cycle helps your body focus on healing the underlying cause of the pain, such as a pinched nerve, a disk problem, or arthritis. The Australian study suggests that it may be worth asking your doctor about using such an approach for your back pain. ■

Back and Neck Pain

Artificial Disk Is No Pain in the Neck

Just a few months after having an experimental disk surgically inserted between two of her neck vertebrae, a female study volunteer rammed her minivan head-on into a tree. She survived, thanks to the vehicle's airbag. The artificial disk weathered the impact so well that the emergency room physicians called the study leaders to ask, "What is that thing?"

"That thing" was a synthetic version of the shock-absorbing disks that keep the vertebrae in the neck from rubbing against each other and from pinching nearby nerves. Soon it could save tens of thousands of Americans—and even more people worldwide—from having to choose between excruciating pain caused by damaged vertebral disks and a surgical procedure that drastically limits freedom of movement.

The indication of the artificial disk's durability provided by the woman's accident is what medical researchers call anecdotal evidence—an interesting story to be sure, but not exactly scientific proof that the disk works. In March 2004, however, researchers at Loyola University in Chicago unveiled the results of a laboratory study in which the disk withstood impact forces far beyond anything a person's spine will ever experience in the real world. That *does* count as scientific evidence.

How it works. When our ancestors began to walk upright, they bucked the trend among mammals. Thanks to gravity, modern sedentary ways, and ever-increasing life spans, that move pretty much guaranteed that by the 21st century, virtually all adults over 40 would suffer from degeneration of the spongy disk tissue that serves as

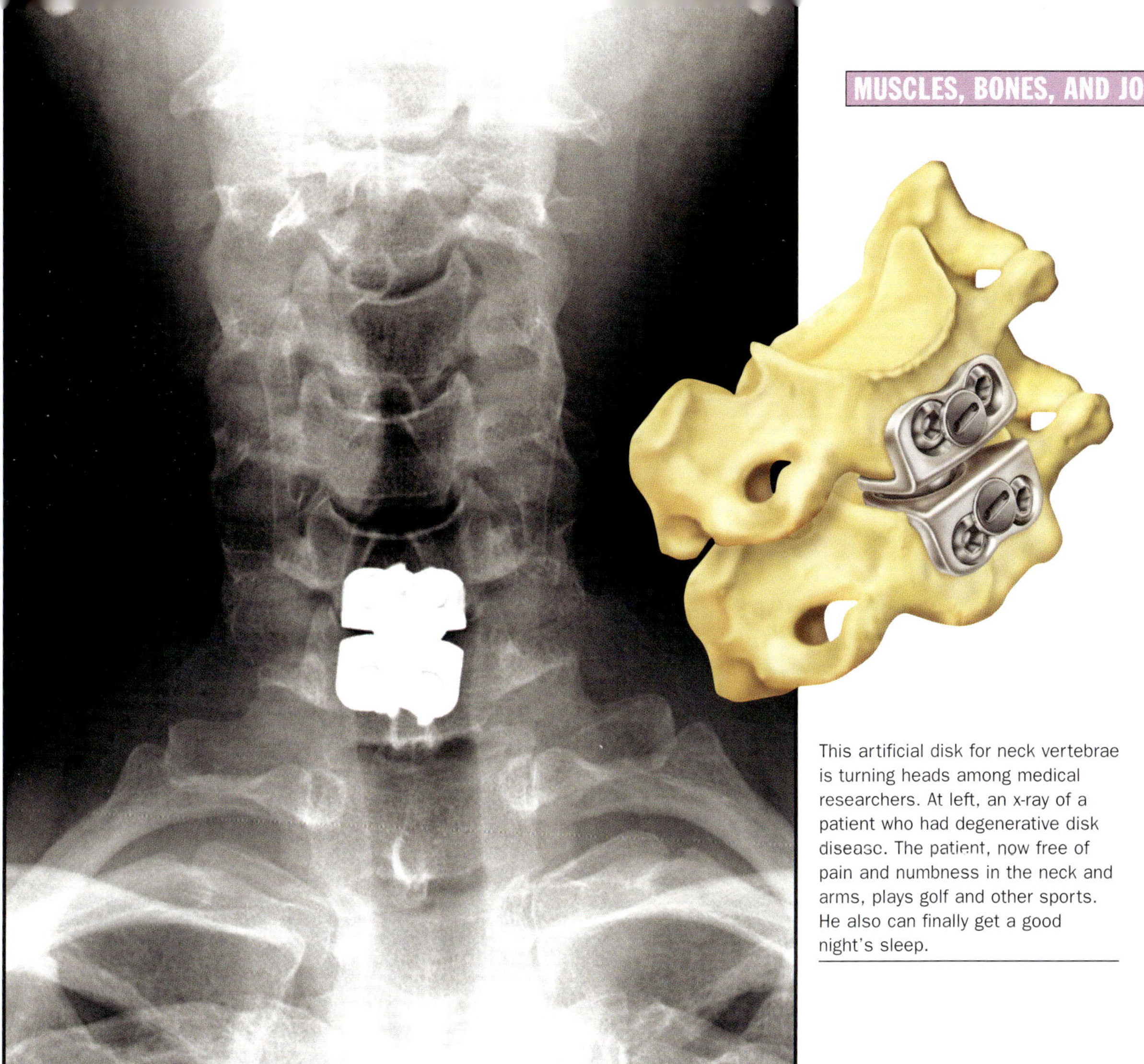

This artificial disk for neck vertebrae is turning heads among medical researchers. At left, an x-ray of a patient who had degenerative disk disease. The patient, now free of pain and numbness in the neck and arms, plays golf and other sports. He also can finally get a good night's sleep.

a buffer between vertebrae in the spine. When the problem occurs in the seven upper vertebrae that run from the base of the skull to the top of the back, it's called cervical disk disease. And it can hurt a lot.

The current surgical solution gives up on saving the disk, instead removing it and fusing the two neighboring vertebrae together with the help of bone grafted from the hip. Since the surgery leaves the patient with limited ability to make up-and-down or side-to-side neck movements, it's usually reserved for people whose pain has become unbearable or who are in danger of serious nerve damage.

The artificial disk changes all that. Although made of metal, it serves the same protective function as a real disk. Thus, unlike fusion surgery patients, artificial disk recipients are literally as good as new, enjoying full freedom of movement. The cervical disk's design differs from that of an artificial disk meant for the lower back, which is already in use in some parts of the world. The new disk includes tiny screws to help firm up its placement in the neck area, where there's much more spinal movement to accommodate and less natural pressure to help hold it in place.

Availability. The researchers are so pleased with the preliminary results of the ongoing study that they predict FDA approval as soon as a year after the final results are evaluated in 2006. Russ Nockels, M.D., one of the study leaders, thinks the availability of an artificial disk will bring about a new approach to dealing with the pain of cervical disk disease. "The balance between the positive and negative aspects of surgery will change," he says. "More people will say, 'Why wait?'"

Back and Neck Pain

The Latest Wrinkle in Back Pain Relief—Botox

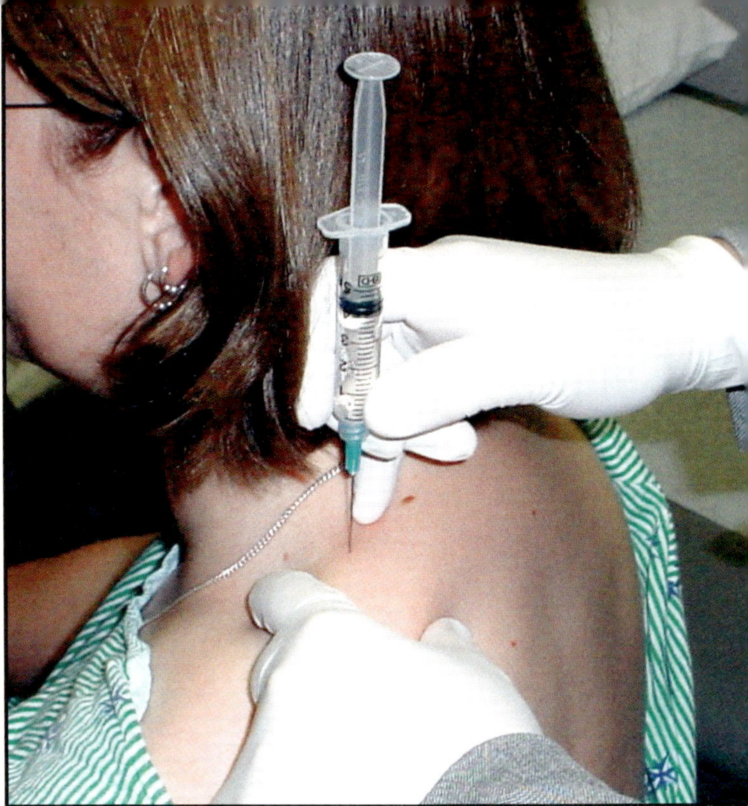

Botox injections into neck and upper back muscles give some patients relief from persistent pain for six months to a year.

Botox shots have been successfully used to treat everything from facial wrinkles and migraine headaches to bladder problems and even body odor. So why not back and neck pain as well?

Eight weeks after 25 volunteers in Georgia received injections of botulinum toxin directly into the muscles causing their persistent neck and upper-back pain, the average reported pain level dropped by nearly 40 percent.

Botox makes perfect sense as a back pain treatment. It was, after all, originally developed to relax muscle spasms, which are often responsible for back pain. And study author Amy Lang, M.D., a Lawrenceville, Georgia, rehabilitation medicine specialist who published her research in the January 2004 issue of the *Journal of Pain Management*, thinks the effect of Botox on upper-back muscles can go beyond pain relief. In many cases, she says, it helps correct postural imbalances that may be causing the spasms.

How it works. Botox's original fame as a wrinkle smoother has left the impression that it "freezes" or "paralyzes" muscles. Instead, injecting it into painfully contracted upper-back or neck muscles actually relaxes the muscles as it inhibits the release of contraction-triggering chemicals. Further pain relief may come from Botox's interference with proteins that carry pain messages to the central nervous system.

As Botox relaxes upper-back and neck muscles, it lengthens them from their contracted state, making it easier for them to be strengthened with physical therapy and exercise. By selecting the appropriate muscles for Botox injections and strength training, doctors can help the body realign itself, putting an end to posture-induced pain.

The number of shots needed for pain relief varies from person to person. According to Dr. Lang, some people get relief for six months to a year with just one injection session. Others need regular follow-ups. The patient's attitude about the treatment counts. "The ones who do the best are the ones who make a commitment to their own recovery," she says. "It's not just a matter of getting a few shots. You need to follow your physical therapy program and make whatever ergonomic or other lifestyle adjustments are needed."

Availability. Because Botox is an approved medication, doctors can administer it as they see fit, including for upper-back and neck pain. Some have been using it for lower-back pain, encouraged by other recent studies that show it relieves spasm-induced pain for as long as three to four months. The new study, although small, suggests that similar treatments make sense for the upper back and neck.

The use of Botox for any type of back pain is still considered experimental and will continue to be until larger and longer studies confirm its beneficial effects. That means that Medicare and private insurance companies won't cover such treatment except in very rare cases. It also means, of course, that not all doctors and clinics will offer it, but since Dr. Lang and other pioneers have been training their colleagues in the technique for several years, the number of orthopedists who will perform the treatment is growing. ■

Carpal Tunnel Syndrome

A Pain-Free Way to Sound Out Carpal Tunnel

Ultrasound, the same technology that provides expectant parents with wavy moving pictures of their developing fetuses, may soon be the diagnostic tool of choice for spotting the condition known as carpal tunnel syndrome, which can cause tingling or numbness in the hand and pain in the wrist and forearm. That's good news for anyone with carpal tunnel symptoms, because ultrasound is quicker, easier, and much more comfortable than the usual diagnostic technique, electromyography, which involves the insertion of wire electrodes into muscle tissue and mild electric shocks to the fingers and wrist.

Egyptian researchers assembled 78 people who had carpal tunnel syndrome and 78 people who did not, then used both diagnostic procedures on all of them. The test showed that ultrasound, which uses sound waves to create images of the nerve that runs through the carpal tunnel in the wrist, was as good as electromyography at revealing nerve damage. But ultrasound was the clear winner in pinpointing the exact cause of the damage.

For example, ultrasound could "see" better whether the pain was the result of an inflamed tendon sheath pressing on the nerve, damage within the nerve itself, or some other cause. The study also showed that ultrasound is more effective in evaluating how well carpal tunnel patients respond to treatment. ■

Typing and other repetitive hand movements are common causes of carpal tunnel syndrome. At left, a patient undergoes an ultrasound scan to test for compression of the median nerve, which runs through the carpal tunnel in the wrist.

Osteoporosis

Time to Bone Up on Vitamin B_{12}

Here's yet another reason to make sure you take a multivitamin every day: The B vitamins it contains could very well help you avoid debilitating fractures. One of the 11 members of the B-vitamin family—vitamin B_{12}—has recently been shown to play a bigger role than previously thought in keeping bones strong as you grow older, thus fending off osteoporosis and the serious fractures that often go with it.

New research from the University of California, San Francisco, looked at how much vitamin B_{12} was circulating in the bloodstreams of 83 volunteers age 64 and up. Measurements taken over a six-year period yielded a clear finding: Those who had the highest blood levels of B_{12} showed the least loss of bone density in their hips over that period, while those with the lowest levels of B_{12} showed the most bone loss.

How it works. No one knows for sure why lack of B_{12} would speed bone loss. Like folate, another B vitamin, B_{12} helps reduce levels of the protein homocysteine, which has recently been connected with osteoporosis risk (as well as heart attack risk). But additional factors, as yet unkown, could be at work.

What it means to you. The finding is especially important because B_{12} deficiency, rare in younger adults, is much more common in women over 60, the people who are most at risk for osteoporosis and hip fractures. If you think you may not be getting enough B_{12}, ask your doctor if it's a good idea to have a blood or urine test to determine how much of the vitamin is circulating in your system. If the levels are low, you need to find out why.

Vitamin B_{12} deficiency is sometimes due to pernicious anemia, a serious condition that requires medical treatment. It's also possible that you're simply not getting enough shellfish, milk, cheese, eggs, organ meats, and other sources of vitamin B_{12} from your diet. More likely, your digestive system just isn't absorbing the vitamin B_{12} from those foods the way it used to—which means you'll need a B_{12} supplement.

The recommended daily intake of vitamin B_{12} for people 50 and over is 2.4 micrograms. Most multivitamins offer more than that, prompting the study authors to note, "Our data indicate that long-term use of multivitamins may be an effective means of reducing B_{12} deficiency in older women."

RESEARCH ROUNDUP

A Rising Star among Bone Boosters

On the periodic table of elements, you'll find strontium occupying the same vertical row as calcium and magnesium. Just like its close cousins, strontium plays a role in bone formation. Now, after decades of trying, medical researchers have discovered a way to use strontium's bone-building capacity in an osteoporosis treatment.

In January 2004, French researchers published results of a study showing that a patented strontium compound called strontium ranelate not only increases bone density in women who have osteoporosis but also reduces their risk of vertebral fractures. The researchers followed 1,442 women with osteoporosis who took strontium ranelate for three years. Their risk of new vertebral fractures was cut almost in half, and the bone mineral density in their lower spines increased by 14.4 percent.

Strontium ranelate has proven so effective in recent studies that it's expected to become available in Europe sometime in 2005 in the form of a daily pill called Protelos. In the United States, its approval is awaiting completion of a study examining the compound's ability to reduce the incidence of nonvertebral fractures in women who have osteoporosis.

Osteoporosis

Early Warning for Osteoporosis

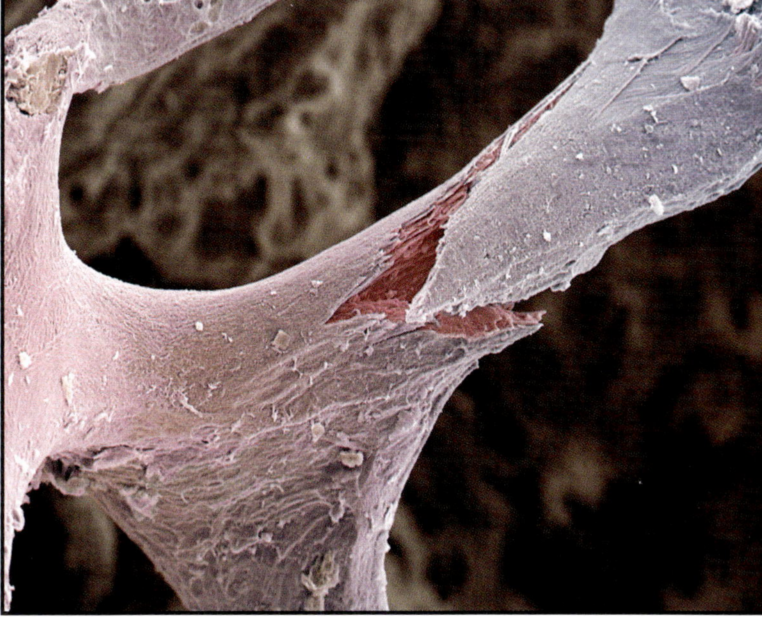

This is a magnified image of fractured bone tissue from a patient with osteoporosis. Genetic tests may soon reveal who's at high risk.

Scans and x-rays can reveal whether your bones are brittle, but by then the damage is pretty much done. The fact is, it's far easier to prevent osteoporosis than to try to cure it—but few people take the threat seriously enough to do anything to protect their bones while they still can. That could change in the coming years, now that researchers have discovered a gene variation that triples the osteoporosis risk of anyone who has it.

All of us carry the gene, dubbed BMP2 by biotech scientists at the Icelandic company deCODE Genetics, but it exists in several different variations. Three of those variants signal high osteoporosis risk. If you discover you have a high-risk variation, you'll have all the motivation you need to start taking preventive measures. Those include high calcium intake (up to 2,500 milligrams a day), adequate vitamin D (400 to 600 IU a day), regular exercise, and bone-protecting prescription medication such as alendronate (Fosamax), risendronate (Actonel), or raloxifene (Evista).

Two factors were key in connecting the BMP2 gene with high osteoporosis risk: the recent completion of the human genome map and the easily traceable genealogy of Iceland's population. By scanning the genomes of 207 Icelandic families, the deCODE team was able to isolate genes common to the osteoporosis patients (living and long dead) who were analyzed. The finding does not mean that BMP2 is "the" osteoporosis gene, since researchers suspect that several other genes have variants that also contribute to osteoporosis risk. Nor does it doom its owners to brittle bones and certain fractures. It does, however, issue a loud wakeup call to people with any of the three high-risk variations of the gene, the most significant genetic risk factor for osteoporosis yet discovered.

Availability. A genetic test for BMP2 won't be ready until 2006 at the earliest. First, scientists must confirm the gene's role as a risk marker in broader and more varied populations than Iceland's. Meanwhile, a much more limited test of fracture risk, based on a previously verified genetic marker called collagen 1A1, will be introduced in 2005.

RESEARCH ROUNDUP

Safer Estrogen for Your Bones

The popularity of estrogen replacement plummeted among postmenopausal women when it was shown to increase the incidence of breast cancer and heart disease. But many women over 50 have wondered if there may be some way to take advantage of estrogen's bone-saving properties without the risks. Soon, the answer may be yes.

In August 2003, a University of Connecticut study revealed that ultra-low doses of a type of synthetic estrogen called micronized 17 beta-estradiol clearly increased bone mineral density in older women without the negative effects associated with estrogen. For example, none of the 167 women involved in the study developed breast cancer over the three-year study period. The rate of other unwanted side effects, such as breast tenderness and abnormal mammograms, was similar in women who took estradiol and those who took placebos (dummy pills).

As promising as this form of estrogen seems, though, it won't be considered an osteoporosis treatment option until larger studies assess its safety over a longer period of time as well as its effectiveness in preventing fractures rather than just bone loss.

For Bone Strength
Tofu in a Capsule

Tofu, the jiggly form of soy that's held an exalted place in Asian diets for centuries, has a new role: osteoporosis prevention. The best part is that you don't need to change your diet to benefit from tofu's bone-saving powers. A study by Israeli researchers has shown that a tofu-derived supplement boosts bone mineral density in postmenopausal women, reducing their risk of osteoporosis and the fractures that often go with it.

Researchers gave 98 volunteers either a 344-milligram or a 644-milligram daily dose of the supplement, dubbed DT56a for now, for a year. While the low-dose group showed no improvement, those who received the higher dose had a significant 3.6 percent increase in bone density in their lower spines.

Tofu's health value is attributed to its rich concentration of phytoestrogens, plant chemicals that provide many of the same benefits as the human hormone estrogen—including bone density improvement—but without the risks that estrogen supplementation carries. DT56a works so well because it preserves all of the key phytoestrogens in their natural form. As a dietary supplement, DT56a needs no FDA approval and is already available in capsule form in Europe and North America, sold as Tofupill or Femarelle.

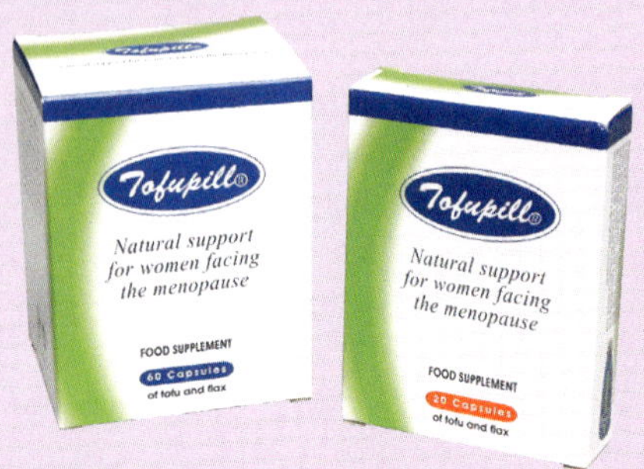

Osteoporosis
Diuretics Are Hip New Treatment for Bones

Diuretics are making a major-league comeback. Recently, a panel of experts designated these age-old urination-promoting medications as the first-choice treatment for high blood pressure. Now, a new study has shown that taking diuretics is also an excellent way to protect against hip fractures.

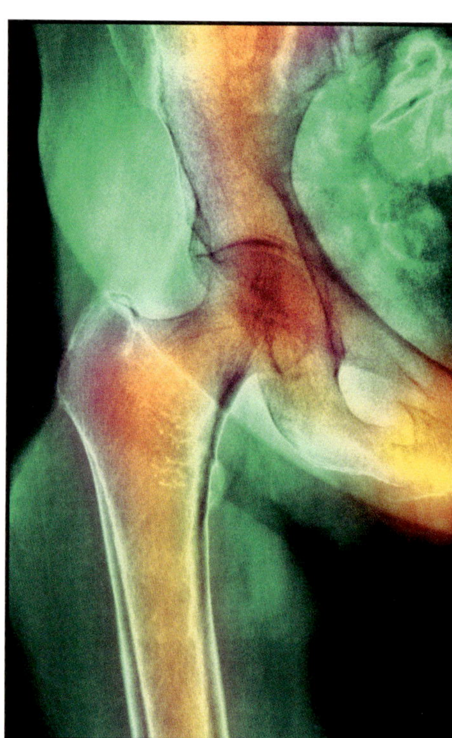
Diuretics, typically prescribed for high blood pressure, may have a welcome side effect: fewer hip fractures.

Dutch researchers studied the medical records of nearly 8,000 men and women over age 55. The scientists concluded that those who had been taking diuretics for at least a year had, on average, a 50 percent lower risk of hip fractures than those who hadn't been taking the drugs.

The finding makes sense because diuretics are known to slow age-related bone loss by cutting down on the amount of calcium excreted in urine. However, this study, published in the September 2003 issue of *Annals of Internal Medicine*, was the first to connect diuretic use with protection against hip fractures, which are often the consequence of the bone-wasting disease osteoporosis. The study also found that the fracture-prevention benefits of diuretics disappear soon after you stop taking the drugs. Although the study authors consider long-term diuretic use to be safe under a doctor's supervision, they say further study is needed before diuretics can be recommended as an osteoporosis treatment for people who don't have high blood pressure. ■

Osteoporosis

Bone Strength Is Rolling in Clover

Worried about thinning bones? Take a tip from hungry cows. They like to graze on red clover, and it turns out that this common pasture herb packs a bone-boosting wallop. Available in supplement form, red clover is teeming with isoflavones, plant compounds that deliver the bone-protecting benefits of estrogen without the risks associated with hormone replacement therapy. In a recent British study of 200 women ages 49 to 65, those who took red clover supplements daily lost much less bone density in the lower backbone after a year than those who didn't take them.

How it works. Low estrogen levels after menopause take much of the blame for the increased risk of osteoporosis after age 50. Since replenishing estrogen through hormone replacement therapy increases the risk of heart disease and breast cancer, researchers have been looking at so-called plant estrogens such as isoflavones as alternatives. Scientists have yet to prove the safety of these compounds, but researchers are encouraged by the relatively low rates of breast cancer and heart disease among Asian women, who eat large amounts of isoflavone-rich soy.

The British researchers didn't use soybeans as their isoflavone source, as most previous studies had. Rather, they used a supplement derived from red clover, which could explain why this was the first well-designed study of significant size to clearly show the bone-saving benefits of isoflavones. Red clover is not only richer in isoflavones than soy, it also contains different kinds of isoflavones.

Availability. The researchers, who published their study results in the February 2004 issue of the *American Journal of Clinical Nutrition,* are looking for a few more answers before they'll recommend red clover to help prevent or treat osteoporosis. They want to see proof that the isoflavones will reduce fractures in addition to helping to maintain bone density. They also want to confirm that red clover's isoflavones work as well on hipbones as they do on the backbone. Since bone mass is greater in the hip, a longer study period is needed to come to any conclusions.

Red clover is available over the counter at pharmacies and health food stores in various forms, including teas, tinctures, capsules, and tablets. The red clover product used in the study was Promensil, which is typically used to relieve menopausal discomforts. ■

RESEARCH ROUNDUP

Love Cola? Your Bones Don't!

The pause that refreshes may also be the pause that weakens your bones. It doesn't matter if your favorite cola is Pepsi or Coke, diet or caffeine-free; a survey of the drinking habits of more than 2,500 volunteers showed that those who consumed more than three 12-ounce servings a day of any kind of cola had up to 5.1 percent lower bone mineral density in their hips than those who didn't drink that much. It does matter whether you're a man or a woman, though; only women showed low bone mineral density as a result of drinking cola.

Carbonated sodas have long been suspected of weakening bones, but these study results, reported in September 2003, are the first to single out colas. The study, by researchers at Tufts University in Boston, also challenges earlier assumptions by pinning the blame on cola drinking itself rather than on a concurrent decrease in calcium-rich foods, such as vegetables and milk and other dairy foods. The problem, the study leaders suspect, is that colas are loaded with phosphoric acid, which can interfere with bone formation.

IN Brief

A Blood Test Predicts Fracture Risk

Bone density tests can help reveal how vulnerable your bones are, but the calcium content they measure is not the only indicator of fracture risk. Another kind of test may soon be available to help your doctor decide early on if you need medication to combat osteoporosis. The new test measures blood levels of a protein known as RANKL; low levels of the protein indicate that there's less than a 1 percent chance of a fracture in the next five years.

REPRODUCTION
AND SEXUALITY

IN THIS SECTION

MANY OF THIS YEAR'S BIGGEST BREAKTHROUGHS HAVE A COMMON THEME: MORE POWER TO WOMEN.

While men have Viagra, women may soon have their own options for enhancing libido. Three of them were in late-stage clinical trials in 2004 and could hit pharmacies sometime in 2005.

In the area of infertility treatment, frozen eggs have resulted in a handful of successful pregnancies; egg freezing could allow women to delay childbearing or to conceive after undergoing cancer treatment. Even more remarkable, doctors have used frozen pieces of ovarian tissue to produce viable eggs, which may mean more options for women who face early menopause because of cancer treatment.

For women with heavy periods, there's a technique that uses microwave energy to permanently remove the uterine lining, significantly reducing bleeding or even stopping it entirely. There's also a new birth control pill that cuts periods from 13 a year to 4.

Also, an over-the-counter fertility supplement has been proven to work, and a common allergy drug helps relieve hot flashes.

Contraception

Bye-Bye, Periods

Nothing ruins a romantic weekend more than getting your period. Or how about finding out you're due to have it the same day you were planning to throw a party? Women taking a new brand of birth control will have fewer of these conflicts. In September 2003, the FDA approved Seasonale, an oral contraceptive designed to cut the number of periods a woman experiences each year from about 13 to about 4.

How it works. Seasonale is exactly the same as any other birth control pill containing the hormones estrogen and progestin. Essentially, it tricks the body into thinking it is pregnant so the ovaries don't release any eggs, rendering a real pregnancy impossible. The uterine lining builds up more or less as it would during preparation for pregnancy (although not as much), and then it's shed when the woman takes inactive pills that don't contain any hormones.

The only difference between Seasonale and traditional oral contraceptives is how the pills are taken. With traditional birth control pills, the woman takes the hormone pills for 21 days, then takes the inactive pills for a week, during which she has her period. With Seasonale, women take the active pills for 12 weeks (84 days) in a row, followed by 1 week of inactive pills. In the absence of menstrual periods, the uterine lining eventually is absorbed by the body.

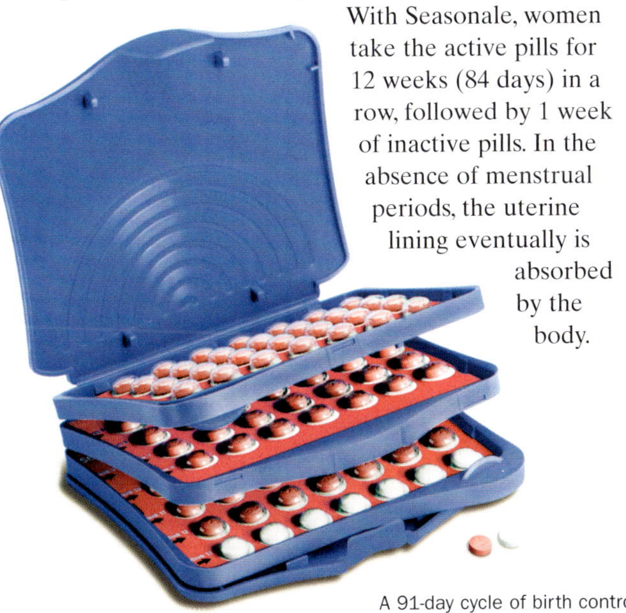

A 91-day cycle of birth control pills reduces periods to four per year.

TOP Trends

NEW ROLE FOR VIAGRA

When sildenafil (Viagra) first hit pharmacies, aging senator Bob Dole promoted it as a treatment for erectile dysfunction, also known as impotence. Since then, the ads for Viagra and its newer competitors, tadalafil (Cialis) and vardenafil (Levitra), have changed dramatically, as have the drugs' users. According to a December 2003 article in the *New York Times*, both straight and gay men in their twenties, thirties, and forties are turning to the drugs to improve their sexual performance. In fact, about 10 percent of the 16 million prescriptions written for Viagra in the United States since its introduction in 1998 have been for men under age 39—most of whom do not have problems with impotence.

The drug companies' ads now feature 30- and 40-something hunks. In racy ads for Levitra that began running in April 2004, an attractive brunette implied that the drug improves erection quality in her partner. The message seems to be getting out. Actress Demi Moore's under-30 actor boyfriend Ashton Kutcher even told the *Times of India* in January 2004 that he'd been taking the little blue Viagra pills to keep up with his woman.

MORNING-AFTER PILL: ACCESS DENIED

In early May, the FDA quashed hopes for over-the-counter sales of the morning-after pill—against the advice of its own advisory panel—citing a lack of evidence that young teens could use such emergency contraception safely. (Emergency contraception is currently available over the counter in numerous other countries, including Canada and England.)

Meanwhile, in Seattle, where emergency contraception has been available without a prescription since 1998, eight pharmacies began a government-funded, year-long study in February 2004 to see whether conventional birth control pills should be made available over the counter nationally.

The researchers, funded by the National Institutes of Health, expected to enroll 300 women ages 18 to 45. The volunteers complete a 23-item questionnaire and have their weights and blood pressures checked. Then they purchase a three-month supply of birth control pills, contraceptive patches, or vaginal rings from specially trained pharmacists without a prescription. The women pay $25 per pharmacist visit, plus the cost of the contraception.

While taking Seasonale as recommended, women will only have four periods a year once their menstrual cycles become regular. Initially, however, they may have some breakthrough bleeding until their bodies adjust.

Pill is controversial. The idea of a drug that enables women to have fewer periods has been somewhat controversial. Some women's groups are concerned about the long-range health effects of fewer periods. They also criticize statements by Seasonale's manufacturer, drug company Barr Pharmaceuticals, that menstruation has a negative effect on women's lives.

On the other hand, Michael P. Goodman, M.D., an obstetrician/gynecologist in Davis, California, who has been practicing for more than 34 years, says Seasonale is not a big shift. For years, he and other doctors have been prescribing regular, 28-day oral contraceptives to be taken in succession—that is, without the week of inactive pills—for women who have very heavy periods or who want to skip their periods for some reason. "It's amazing the drug companies have waited so long to bring something like this to market," says Dr. Goodman, author of *The Midlife Bible: A Woman's Survival Guide*. "I've been telling patients to take birth control pills this way for years."

Taking hormones continuously is safe, he says. In fact, some researchers believe that it's unnatural for women to have as many periods as they do these days. Until fairly recently, the experts say, women spent most of their reproductive lives either pregnant or breastfeeding and therefore had far fewer periods than women have today—and, perhaps related to that, fewer incidences of hormone-related ovarian cancer and breast cancer.

RESEARCH ROUNDUP

Don't Blame the Pill for Extra Pounds

For more than 40 years, some women taking oral contraceptives have blamed the pills for weight gain. In fact, about one out of five women either quits taking birth control pills or avoids them altogether because of concerns about weight gain. One study even found that women who stopped taking oral contraceptives were more likely to report that they'd gained weight while on the Pill, even when they hadn't.

Now women will have to find another scapegoat for their widening waistlines. Researchers from Family Health International in Research Triangle Park, North Carolina, and the University of Leiden in the Netherlands reviewed 42 different studies of women on birth control patches or pills. The Pill, the researchers reported in the February 2004 issue of the journal *Obstetrics and Gynecology*, doesn't appear to cause much, if any, weight gain.

Male Birth Control Gets Boost

The search for a male contraceptive has gotten a shot in the arm—or rather an implant in the arm. A December 2003 study showed that implanting tubes containing a synthetic hormone that resembles testosterone into a man's arm may be an effective form of male birth control. The implants work by fooling the brain into thinking the body is already making enough testosterone. This causes it to shut down production of natural testosterone, which is required for sperm production.

Called MENT, the implant has a significant advantage over taking natural testosterone because it doesn't enlarge the prostate. The synthetic hormone is also more potent than natural testosterone when it comes to reducing sperm count, but it doesn't affect sexual desire or performance. In the study, the implant was left in place for 9 to 12 months, during which it remained effective. This study was the second of three research phases required before the drug can be submitted for FDA approval. Researchers hope to complete all studies and submit their application by 2008.

Fertility

Frozen Ovarian Tissue Yields Eggs Years Later

It sounds like something out of Aldous Huxley's *Brave New World*: A 30-year-old woman has to undergo cancer treatment that will leave her infertile, so beforehand she has a minor surgical procedure to remove a tiny piece of her ovary, which is frozen. Six years later, when her medical treatment is long over and she's ready to have a child, the tissue is thawed and implanted just under the skin of her abdomen, where, after a few months, it starts doing what all healthy ovarian tissue does: producing hormones and manufacturing eggs. Doctors remove some of the eggs, mix them with sperm in a petri dish, and *voilà!*—an embryo.

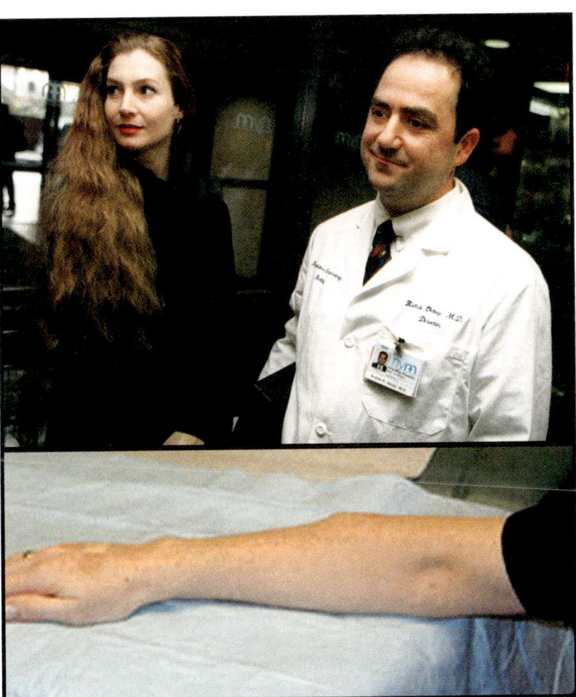

Kutluk H. Oktay, M.D., above right, aims to restore women's fertility by freezing their ovarian tissue and reimplanting it later. The bulge in a patient's forearm (bottom) is the site where implanted ovarian tissue has resumed functioning like a normal ovary.

Only it's not science fiction. It's fact, published in the journal *Lancet* in March 2004. And it suggests that a woman's fertility can be restored years after cancer treatment has destroyed it or even after natural menopause has ended it.

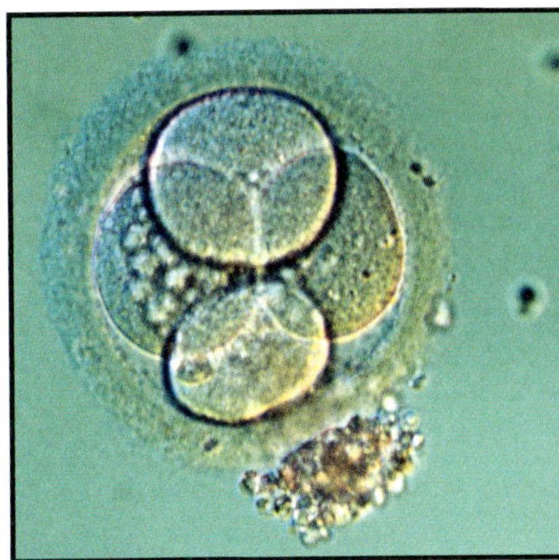

Eggs produced by transplanted ovarian tissue can be harvested and fertilized in a petri dish, creating an embryo, above.

Fertility after cancer treatment. Growing ovarian tissue in other parts of the body isn't completely new—the same researchers did it a couple of years ago when they implanted ovarian tissue into a woman's arm. However, using the eggs produced by the tissue to produce a viable embryo was a major leap forward, says lead researcher Kutluk H. Oktay, M.D., associate professor of reproductive medicine and obstetrics and gynecology at the Center for Reproductive Medicine and Infertility at Cornell University in Ithaca, New York. The embryo didn't result in a pregnancy when it was implanted in the woman's uterus, but Dr. Oktay says that fact doesn't worry him, given that there is just a 10 to 20 percent chance of pregnancy with any in vitro fertilization (IVF) procedure.

In July 2004, researchers from Brussels announced that a 32-year-old woman had become pregnant naturally—without using in vitro fertilization—after her frozen ovarian tissue was transplanted back.

Freezing and later reimplanting ovarian tissue could prove a boon to women undergoing treatment for cancer, which often renders them infertile. The method offers an advantage over egg freezing (See "Egg Freezing Becomes Reality" on page 204), which requires more than a month to stimulate and extract the eggs, because ovarian tissue can be collected with just a day's notice.

The next step. Dr. Oktay believes this procedure will become a regular path to pregnancy in the near future as tissue preservation techniques are perfected and pregnancies result. Because it is a procedure, not a drug, no government approval is necessary.

Fertility

Freezing Eggs Becomes a Reality

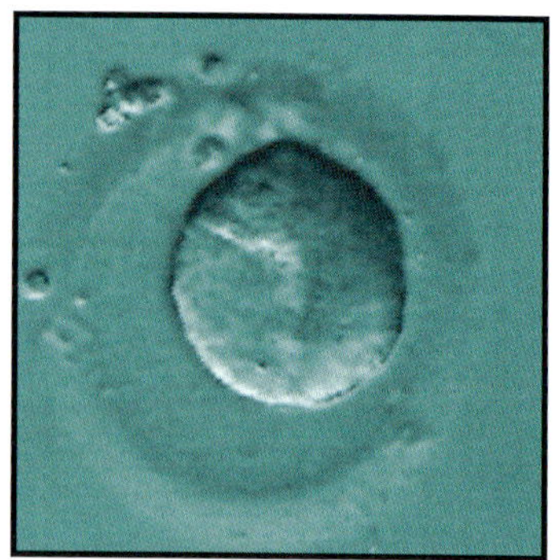

This egg has been placed in a solution that removes water from it, protecting it from damage during freezing and thawing. It has shrunk to 50 percent of its original size.

Just like the eggs in a grocery store, a woman's reproductive eggs begin to spoil as they age, shrinking her chances of pregnancy. That's not good news for the millions of women who want to delay motherhood. But it now appears that decades-old research into freezing eggs is finally paying off, with doctors around the world reporting the first significant numbers of successful conceptions and births using frozen eggs.

Egg freezing holds great promise not only for women who want to delay starting families but also for couples undergoing in vitro fertilization (IVF). Today, those couples often wind up with several extra embryos (eggs united with sperm) that remain frozen for years and sometimes decades. Deciding what to do with those embryos (there are now more than 400,000 in the United States alone) poses great ethical and moral questions.

If women could have their eggs frozen, however, they could repeat the IVF procedure relatively simply whenever they decided they were ready for children, or they could dispose of the unfertilized eggs without having to deal with the issues surrounding disposal of embryos. Egg freezing would also benefit women undergoing chemotherapy or radiation, which affects ovulation. They could have their eggs frozen beforehand for use at a later date.

Although several groups around the world have been working on the problems of egg freezing, one of the most successful is Assisted Fertility Services in Indianapolis, where eight women have delivered healthy babies who were conceived using frozen eggs, and a ninth was expected to deliver in fall 2004.

How it works. The challenge with freezing eggs, says Jeffrey Boldt, Ph.D., program and scientific director, is that unlike easily frozen sperm, an egg is a very big cell filled with water. When frozen, the water forms ice crystals big enough to "blow the egg apart," he says. "The trick is to get the water out of the cell before it freezes."

To do that, researchers devised a special solution that pushes the water out of the egg and fills the space it once occupied. They also kept the eggs in the solution longer than other researchers in this area had done to ensure that they had wrung as much water as possible out of them.

The babies born so far came from eggs that had been frozen, on average, for six to nine months, Dr. Boldt says. The eggs were thawed and fertilized in a procedure called ICSI, or intracytoplasmic sperm injection, in which a single sperm is injected into each egg. Researchers used ICSI, he says, because they think that freezing the egg damages its outer layer, making it more difficult for sperm to penetrate. So far, he says, the fertilization rate for frozen eggs using ICSI is running just 5 percent behind that for fresh eggs using the same procedure.

Availability. Egg freezing is available only as an experimental procedure at a handful of IVF clinics around the world. Most clinics still require that participants pay for the fertility drugs required to produce numerous eggs and for the egg retrieval.

RESEARCH ROUNDUP

Saliva Test for Ovulation

The days of peeing onto a stick and lying in bed with a thermometer in your mouth to see if you're ovulating may be over. In February 2004, the FDA approved the first home saliva test to reveal when a woman is ovulating. The test, called Ovulite, applies the same technology medical laboratories use to measure hormones that pinpoint times of fertility and infertility. A woman places a drop of her saliva on the miniature microscope first thing in the morning, then peers through the lens. If a fern-like pattern appears, she's ovulating. The test, available in drugstores nationwide, costs about $40.

Fertility

Over-the-Counter Fertility Supplement Gets Results

When the study results were unveiled, they surprised even the researchers conducting the clinical trial. That's because no one expected an over-the-counter, $30 supplement to really make a difference when it came to helping infertile women get pregnant. But in a small pilot study of the nutritional supplement FertilityBlend on 30 women, ages 24 to 46, that's exactly what happened.

The women, who had been trying unsuccessfully to conceive for six months to three years, were randomly assigned to receive either daily doses of the supplement or placebos (dummy pills) for three months. After that time, 4 of the 15 women who received the supplements were pregnant, compared with none who received placebos. Another woman became pregnant after taking the supplement for an additional two months. Although 5 out of 15 may not sound like a lot, it is statistically significant, says Lynn Westphal, M.D., assistant professor in the department of obstetrics and gynecology at Stanford School of Medicine and one of the researchers on the study. "I was surprised [by the results]," Dr. Westphal admits. "I think I was skeptical that a supplement could have that much of an impact."

How it works. The results may stem from the supplement's effects on a woman's ovulatory cycle, says Dr. Westphal.

An herb in FertilityBlend affects ovulation and may increase a woman's chances of pregnancy.

FertilityBlend, which contains the herb chasteberry, green tea extract, the amino acid L-carnitine, and a handful of vitamins and minerals, increased women's progesterone levels and extended the second half of their menstrual cycles, both of which play a role in fertilization.

Dr. Westphal suspects that while the chasteberry affected ovulation, the other ingredients improved the women's nutritional status, thus increasing their chances of conception. She and her study coauthors were so impressed with the results that they began a larger clinical trial with 100 women in early 2004.

FertilityBlend isn't a cure-all. "It's a nice thing women can take when they're trying to get pregnant," says Dr. Westphal, but if women over 35 haven't conceived within six months (with or without the supplement), they should see their doctors for testing. Also, women with blocked fallopian tubes or other physical abnormalities probably won't benefit from the supplement, she says.

Availability. FertilityBlend is available in most drugstores around the United States and worldwide from the company's Website at www.fertilityblend.com. The company also makes a supplement for men, which Dr. Westphal and her colleagues are currently testing. Results from that trial were expected in late 2004. ■

Fertility

Stem Cells Offer Hope for Infertility

Stem cells, depicted here in lab solution, are the master cells that can turn into virtually any kind of cell in the body.

In an experiment that could have significant implications for male infertility, Japanese researchers have transplanted frozen sperm stem cells into infertile male mice, which then went on to father live baby mice. Stem cells, you recall, are the "genesis" cells from which all other cells grow. Although researchers have known since 1996 that infertile mice that received sperm stem cell transplants could make their own sperm containing their own DNA, the male mice were never able to get female mice pregnant. By implanting the cells into very young mice, before they reached their "adolescence," researchers at Kyoto University enabled four out of eight infertile mice to father normal babies after normal sex. Those figures dropped to one out of nine when adult mice were used.

One out of 12 adult mice that received cancer drugs to destroy their sperm cells also fathered live babies after transplants. In this case, however, the sperm was injected directly into the egg in a mouse version of in vitro fertilization.

What does it mean? If the results can be duplicated in humans, the implications are particularly important for children. Because young boys don't produce sperm, they don't have any sperm to freeze prior to undergoing cancer treatment that could destroy their fertility. With this procedure, their stem cells could be frozen, then transplanted after the cancer treatments are finished. Worldwide, an estimated 1 in 650 children develop cancer during childhood, and by 2010, 1 in 250 young adults (ages 20 to 29) will be long-term survivors of childhood cancer. Approximately 16 to 85 percent of them become infertile.

Sperm on demand? In another Japanese-led study, researchers created sperm cells from embryonic mouse stem cells. Their efforts marked the first time anyone has ever created sperm cells in the laboratory. The work may be applied to developing specialized sperm—for instance, sperm without certain genetic defects—or to adding certain traits to the sperm. Given that scientists have already turned embryonic stem cells into eggs, it opens the possibility of creating life—at least mouse life—with no parental involvement whatsoever. ■

Estrogen Therapy Increases Stroke Risk

Back in 2002, a major study on the hormone replacement therapy (HRT) drug Prempro was halted because the drug was found to increase the risk of heart disease, breast cancer, and stroke. As a result, millions of women went off HRT. But some experts were convinced that it was Prempro itself—a combination of estrogen and progestin—that was the problem and that taking estrogen alone was still safe and effective. It turns out they were wrong.

In March 2004, researchers ended an estrogen-only study early, concluding that the hormone provided few health benefits to postmenopausal women. The seven-year study was designed to answer one key question: Does estrogen therapy prevent heart disease? It doesn't, says JoAnn Manson, M.D., Dr.P.H., professor of women's health at Harvard Medical School and a researcher for the Women's Heath Initiative study. In fact, the trial found that supplemental estrogen slightly increased a woman's risk of stroke.

Although there's no longer any good reason to take estrogen to prevent heart problems, that doesn't necessarily mean you have to toss those estrogen pills. "The estrogen trial didn't address the role of estrogen in the short-term treatment of hot flashes and other menopausal symptoms, for which estrogen has clear benefits," Dr. Manson says. "I think the message here is that hormone therapy is still appropriate for recently menopausal women with significant symptoms."

Menopause

Allergy Medicine for Hot Flashes

Relief from hot flashes may come from an unexpected source: allergy medication. When doctors at Baylor College of Medicine in Houston began hearing that patients had fewer hot flashes when they took the prescription allergy drug cetirizine (Zyrtec), they decided to investigate. They had 100 postmenopausal women take either Zyrtec or a placebo (dummy pill) for four weeks. The women also completed a daily hot flash questionnaire for one week before they started the study, resulting in a "hot flash score" based on the severity and frequency of their flashes. That score plummeted by 40 percent in the women who took Zyrtec.

No one is certain why an antihistamine might help relieve hot flashes. The cause of hot flashes—the most common menopause symptom—isn't known. Ironically, Zyrtec's package insert warns that the drug may cause hot flashes. ■

RESEARCH ROUNDUP

Estrogen in Gel Form Approved

Menopausal women turned off by the bad news about oral hormone replacement therapies such as Prempro and Premarin got a new option in February 2004, when the FDA approved the first hormone therapy gel.

Available in European countries for more than 25 years, EstroGel is a clear, odorless gel that's applied once a day on one arm, from the shoulder to the wrist, and dries in a few minutes. Because it isn't taken by mouth, it isn't processed by the liver, so it may have fewer negative health effects than Prempro and Premarin, say doctors. Also, the gel contains a form of synthetic estrogen called estradiol, which is identical to a woman's natural estradiol. Prempro and Premarin, on the other hand, contain estrogen taken from the urine of pregnant mares.

Hot flashes? You'd probably be a fan of the allergy medicine Zyrtec, research suggests.

Menstruation

Zapping Away Heavy Bleeding

For much of her life, 40-year-old Andrea Graley suffered from excessive menstrual bleeding, sometimes using 10 to 15 pads a day during the first days of her periods, ruining clothes, missing work, and becoming so anemic from blood loss that she required prescription iron pills. Like an estimated one in five other women, Graley, a single mother of two in Parma Heights, Ohio, had a condition called menorrhagia, or heavy menstrual bleeding. Traditional treatments such as birth control pills didn't work, and because Graley had fibroids (benign uterine cysts) and an enlarged uterus, she couldn't undergo surgical treatments such as balloon endometrial ablation, which destroys the lining of the uterus. Her only option, her doctor told her, was to have a hysterectomy.

Then Graley heard a radio spot about a clinical trial for a new procedure for menorrhagia called microwave endometrial ablation, or MEA. It uses microwave energy to permanently remove the uterine lining, the tissue that produces menstrual bleeding. Three years after the procedure, Graley has no periods at all. "Life now is wonderful," she says. "I still go through the monthly cycle but without the bleeding and cramping, and I no longer have to plan my life around one week."

How it works. The 3-minute procedure is performed in the doctor's office under a local anesthetic that numbs the patient from the waist down, explains Susan Wheatley, M.D., of Crabapple OB & GYN in Atlanta. Dr. Wheatley, who participated in the MEA clinical trials, first dilates the woman's cervix to about 8 millimeters (the cervix dilates to 10 centimeters during childbirth), then inserts the microwave probe and turns on the machine. She sweeps the probe back and forth around the uterus, receiving information via a monitor that tells her when the tissue has been destroyed.

Studies have found that MEA causes amenorrhea (total cessation of bleeding) in more than 60 percent of women and significantly reduces monthly bleeding in 96 percent of cases. Other forms of ablation, including the balloon procedure, in which a hot-water-filled balloon destroys the uterine lining, and cryosurgery, in which the lining is frozen off, have amenorrhea rates ranging from 13 to 54 percent.

Microwave ablation can be performed on all women, regardless of the size or position of their uteruses (some women's uteruses are very large or are "tipped," precluding the use of other ablation techniques). There is also some evidence that it may be successful in treating endometrial cancer.

Availability. MEA has been used since 1996 to successfully treat women in the United Kingdom, Canada, and Australia. The FDA cleared it for use in the United States in September 2003, and the company that markets it, Microsulis Ltd., is currently training physicians around the country in its use.

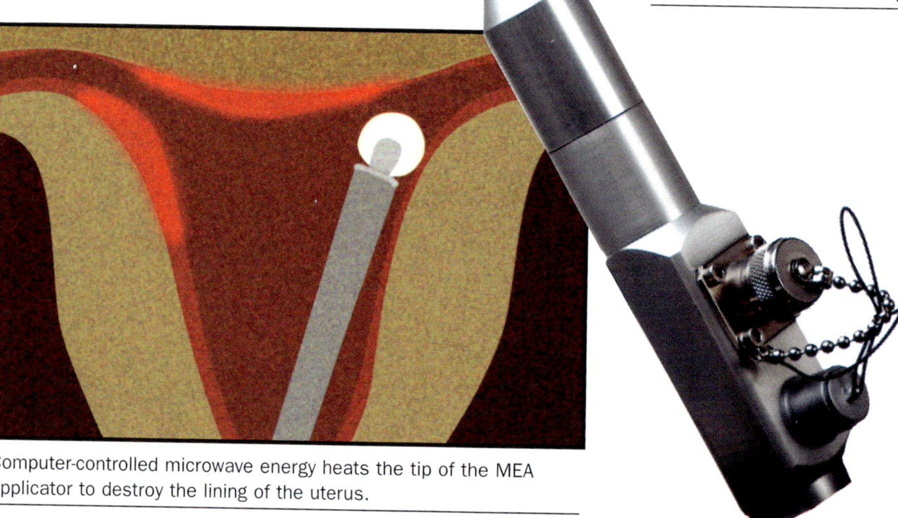

In a brief and painless procedure, microwave endometrial ablation (MEA) reduces or eliminates excessive menstrual bleeding.

Computer-controlled microwave energy heats the tip of the MEA applicator to destroy the lining of the uterus.

Pregnancy

First Guidelines Released for Morning Sickness

Women have been vomiting and feeling nauseated during pregnancy since the first egg met the first sperm. Until recently, though, they had little expert advice on what to do about the problem, which affects an estimated 75 to 80 percent of pregnant women. Now, the world's leading gynecological organization has released its first-ever guidelines for treating pregnancy-related nausea, also known as morning sickness.

Morning sickness has always been "off the beaten path" of research because women don't die from it, says T. Murphy Goodwin, M.D., assistant professor in the department of obstetrics and gynecology at the University of Southern California Women's Hospital in Los Angeles. He chaired the committee that drafted the American College of Obstetrics and Gynecology (ACOG) guidelines. "There has been a growing appreciation in the college that this was a problem worthy of specific attention," he says. That's because the costs—both physical and economic—are tremendous. Some women have abortions because they're so sick, and about 2 percent of women become so dehydrated and ill that they have to be hospitalized.

As with many health conditions, the sooner morning sickness is treated, the better the outcome. However, Dr. Goodwin says, "unless it's life threatening, most women won't take anything, and 99 percent of doctors just tell women they'll get over it." Of those who do seek treatment, 90 percent are offered therapies that aren't likely to be effective, according to one study.

The ACOG guidelines recommend a variety of therapies. Among them:

- **A multivitamin around the time of conception.** No one knows why, but studies on the benefits of multivitamins on fetal defects found that women who took the vitamins while trying to conceive also had less morning sickness.
- **Antihistamines, such as Zyrtec.** When taken as directed, these medications are very safe for pregnant women, says Dr. Goodwin, and can help with morning sickness.
- **Vitamin B_6 or B_6 plus doxylamine.** Studies find that taking 75 milligrams of vitamin B_6 can significantly reduce morning sickness, although no one knows why. The vitamin is available over the counter as well as in a prescription prenatal vitamin called PremesisRX, marketed especially for nausea during pregnancy. It delivers 75 milligrams of vitamin B_6 in a single, time-released dose.

  A prescription medication called Bendectin combines vitamin B_6 with the antihistamine doxylamine. It was used for years to treat morning sickness, but concerns about its potential role in birth defects led to its removal from the U.S. market in the early 1980s, although it is still available in Canada under the brand name Diclectin. Studies since then have shown the drug is safe for use during pregnancy, and the manufacturer has asked the FDA for permission to make it available again in the United States.
- **Ginger.** This herb has been used for centuries to quell nausea (think about the ginger ale your mother gave you when you were sick). The ACOG doesn't recommend a specific dose, but research suggests that one 250-milligram capsule of ginger a day may do the trick. ■

RESEARCH ROUNDUP

Go Ahead, Indulge—Chocolate's Good for Baby

A new study shows that eating chocolate during pregnancy can result in a happier baby. Finnish researchers asked pregnant women to rate their stress levels and chocolate consumption during pregnancy, then compared the data with infant behavior six months after birth. Babies of women who ate chocolate every day during their pregnancies were more active and were "sweeter," smiling and laughing more than babies of women who didn't eat much chocolate. Also, infants of stressed women who ate chocolate during their pregnancies showed less fear during new situations than babies whose mothers were stressed but didn't indulge. The chemicals in chocolate that put women in a good mood seem to do the same for their babies.

Pregnancy

Study Argues More Women Should Be Offered Prenatal Testing

Typically, only women age 35 or older are offered amniocentesis or chorionic villus sampling (CVS), invasive prenatal tests that check for Down's syndrome and certain other chromosomal birth defects. (Younger women may be offered the tests if screening finds that their fetuses are at high risk). The original age threshold was chosen largely because, when testing guidelines were first developed in the United States back in the 1970s, 35 was the approximate age at which amniocentesis was cost-beneficial. But a new study published in the British medical journal *Lancet* calls that thinking into question, suggesting that the age thresholds should be tossed out so that women can decide for themselves whether to be tested.

The risk of having a child with Down's or another chromosomal disorder rises significantly with age—a main reason that only older women are routinely offered the invasive tests, which carry a risk of miscarriage. According to the study authors, "This threshold was chosen because at that age, the procedure-related miscarriage risk was approximately equal to the chance that a child would be born with Down's syndrome, and the cost of offering amniocentesis would be offset by the savings associated with preventing a birth of an infant affected by Down's syndrome."

Lead study author Miriam Kuppermann, Ph.D., explains, however, that the early researchers who helped develop the guidelines assumed that women put equal weight on two of the potential outcomes after invasive testing—having a miscarriage or having a child with Down's. "We have shown in our previous work that this assumption is not true."

The study, conducted at the University of California, San Francisco, based on data from 534 pregnant women, factored in the women's preferred outcomes (many preferred a miscarriage over giving birth to a child with a chromosomal disorder). Performing their own cost-utility analysis, the researchers compared the cost of the tests with the benefit gained in "quality-adjusted life years." The bottom line: The tests can be cost-effective at any age depending on a woman's "preferences for reassurance about the chromosomal status of her fetus and, to a lesser extent, for miscarriage."

What it means. Many insurance companies make coverage decisions based on clinical guidelines that limit tests such as amniocentesis to pregnant women 35 and older. According to Dr. Kuppermann, her findings suggest the decision should be up to the woman. "You need to get information on all the tests and think about your own situation—whether that risk of miscarriage is worth getting the kind of definitive results only an invasive test can give you."

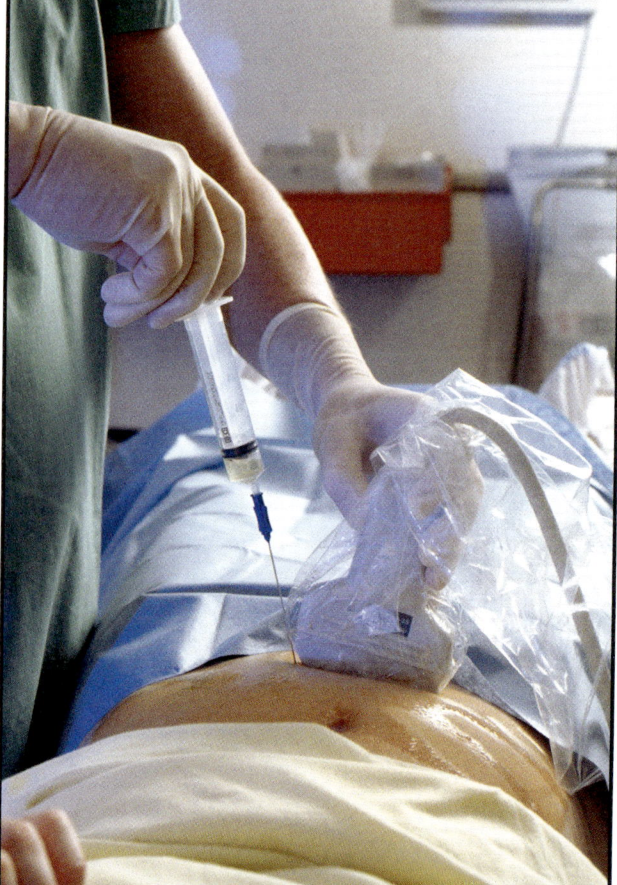

In amniocentesis, a needle guided by ultrasound is used to take a small sample of fluid from the sac surrounding the fetus.

Pregnancy

An Earlier Option for Prenatal Screening

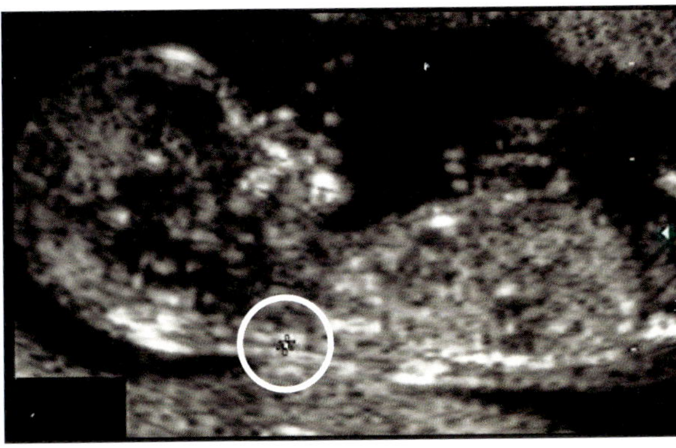

The circle on this ultrasound image indicates the baby's fetal nuchal translucency, or neck thickness.

The agony of waiting until nearly midway through your pregnancy to learn if your baby may have Down's syndrome may be a thing of the past. A large government-funded study found that a combination of blood testing and ultrasound, done in the first trimester, was just as effective at detecting Down's syndrome as the current second-trimester screenings.

What it is. The blood test measures chemicals in the mother's blood called pregnancy-associated plasma protein-A and free-beta human chorionic gonadotropin. (The traditional second-trimester "quad" blood test measures four other Down's markers.) The ultrasound examination, done 10 to 14 weeks into the pregnancy, measures fetal nuchal translucency, or the thickness of an area at the back of the fetus's neck, another way of detecting the condition.

Although the first- and second-trimester screenings performed similarly well, says lead researcher Mary E. D'Alton, M.D., the advantage of the first-trimester screening is that parents can get the results earlier. If the results are negative, parents can stop worrying sooner about genetic defects because the risk is low. If the results are positive, they may choose to have further diagnostic tests, such as chorionic villus sampling or amniocentesis, to rule out a false positive result.

The study, which involved more than 38,000 pregnant women at 15 medical centers, also found that combining the first-trimester test with the traditional second-trimester screening provided significantly more accurate results than using either one alone, reducing the number of women who needed further tests to clarify the results.

Availability. The first-trimester screenings are available at about 50 medical centers nationwide, including the 15 centers that participated in the trial. More medical centers are likely to offer the screening as they train ultrasound staff and doctors in its use. ■

FUTURE BREAKTHROUGHS

Press "O" for...

No more faking it, ladies. Soon you may be able to have a device implanted near your spine that triggers an orgasm. About the size of a pack of cigarettes but thinner, the Orgasmatron is permanently implanted under the skin of the lower back and is operated by remote control.

Anesthesiologist Stuart Meloy, M.D., who heads a pain management clinic in Winston-Salem, North Carolina, stumbled upon the idea while using a spinal cord stimulator to treat a woman's back pain. The device stimulates nerves that control sexual response in women, including orgasm. In a small, FDA-approved clinical trial in the summer of 2004, 9 of the 10 women in the study reportedly experienced enhanced sexual feelings while using the Orgasmatron. Dr. Meloy is talking to two medical device companies about manufacturing his invention and had plans to begin licensing it to other doctors by the end of 2004.

Pregnancy

Skip the Epidural; Head for the Tub

Forget epidurals and back rubs. A study published in the *British Medical Journal* in February 2004 found that first-time mothers who spent the first part of their labors lying in birthing pools were less likely to need pain medication than women who didn't labor in water and had more traditional assistance.

The study, conducted by British midwives, followed 96 first-time mothers whose labors were progressing slowly. Half were randomly assigned to labor in the warm water, and half received standard care. (Although some women actually give birth in labor pools, many simply labor there and get out when they are ready to push.)

Fewer than half of the women (47 percent) who labored in the pool needed epidural anesthetic, which causes numbness from the waist down, for delivery, compared with two out of three (66 percent) who labored conventionally. Plus, nearly all the women who didn't use the pool either had to have their water broken, needed oxytocin to cause the uterus to contract, or required both in order to move labor along. Just 71 percent of the women who used the water pool required such interventions.

Laboring in water helps women with the pain of labor both physically and psychologically, says lead researcher Elizabeth R. Cluett, a lecturer in midwifery at the University of Southampton. The warm water helps women relax, which reduces stress and pain. It also encourages the body to produce natural painkillers called endorphins. Additionally, she says, the buoyancy provided by water means that women can change positions easily, also helping them cope with labor pain. Overall, there was an average of 6 hours between the time the women left the pool (whenever they felt comfortable doing so) and the time they gave birth.

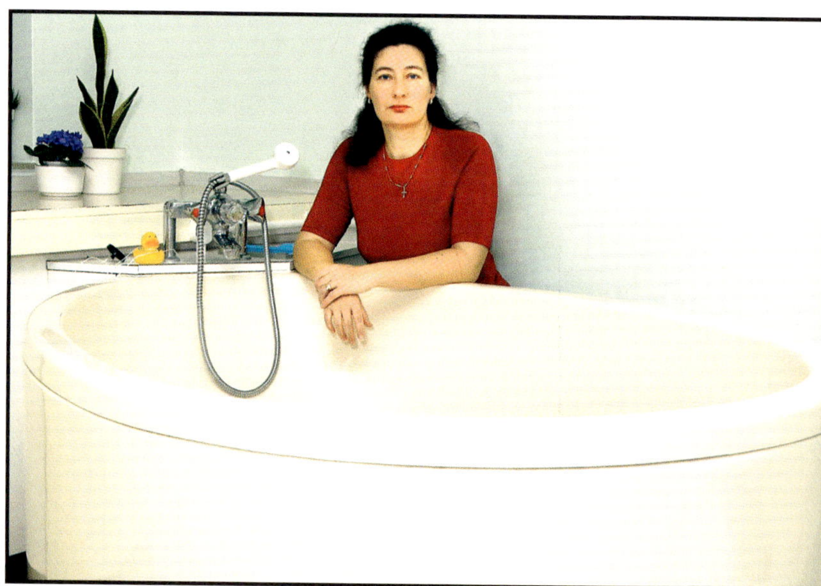

The water's fine: Researcher Elizabeth R. Cluett, above, says birthing pools ease women through labor—both physically and psychologically.

RESEARCH ROUNDUP

Cesarean Delivery Linked to Stillbirth

A British study found that women with one previous cesarean delivery are twice as likely to deliver a stillborn baby during subsequent pregnancies.

Researchers linked a database of information from pregnant Scottish women with a database that tracks stillbirths and infant deaths in Scotland. They found that after the 39th week of pregnancy, the rate of unexplained stillbirth was 1.1 (per 1,000 women) for those with previous cesarean deliveries and 0.5 for those with previous vaginal deliveries.

The findings, published in late 2003, should cause any woman who's considering an elective or "on demand" cesarean to think twice about her decision, note the authors. In the United States, which has one of the highest cesarean rates in the world, the number of such births is growing, according to the American College of Obstetricians and Gynecologists. Overall, cesarean rates in the United States hit their highest level ever in 2002, the latest year for which data is available, with more than one-fourth of all children (26.1 percent) delivered by cesarean. In the United Kingdom, cesarean rates have increased from an estimated 10 percent of all births in 1987 to 22 percent in 2002.

Premature Birth

Help for Tiny Babies: Artificial Amniotic Fluid

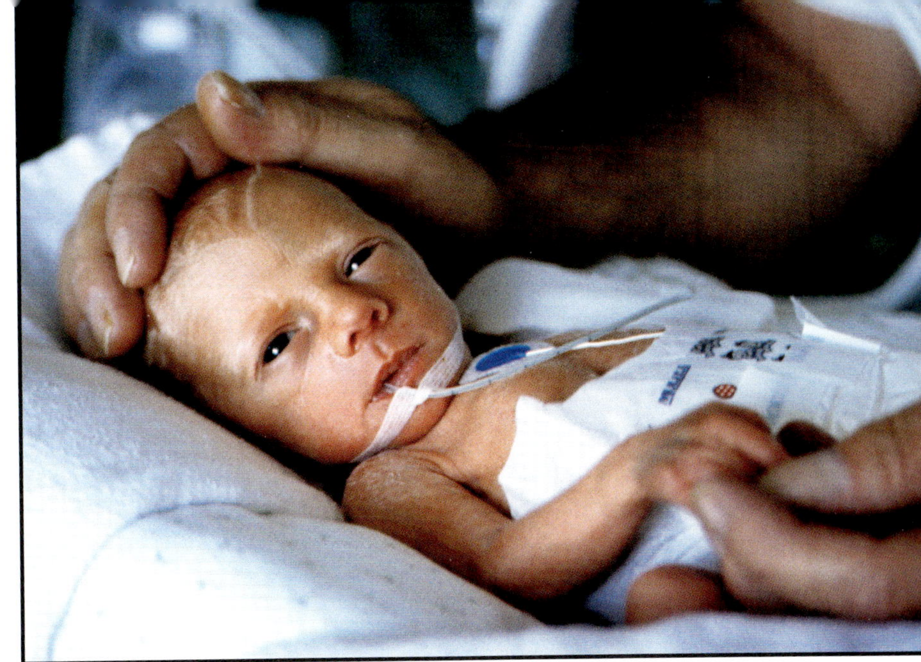

As any woman who has ever felt her unborn baby hiccup knows, fetuses continually gulp the salty brew in which they float. In fact, they take in about 30 ounces a day until the time they're born. Until fairly recently, doctors weren't quite sure why. Now they believe the fluid helps a fetus's immature digestive system develop properly. The finding helps explain why babies born prematurely (and therefore deprived of the fluid) often develop life-threatening gastrointestinal problems. It also presents a potential solution in the form of artificial amniotic fluid.

An accidental discovery. Two neonatology specialists at the University of South Florida College of Medicine in St. Petersburg were analyzing a freezer full of amniotic fluid specimens, hoping to find hormonal clues to certain illnesses, such as infections. Instead, they found extremely high concentrations of proteins called growth factors, which enhance the production of red and white blood cells in bone marrow.

"We figured that finding these growth factors in such high concentrations couldn't be an accident. There must be some purpose," says Robert D. Christensen, M.D. Sure enough, when he and his colleague Darlene A. Calhoun, D.O., examined human fetal tissue, they found special sites on certain intestinal cells designed for the growth factors to "lock" onto. These cells make up the villi, tiny fingerlike projections that line the interior of the intestine and absorb nutrients.

In premature babies, who often don't receive any nutrition by mouth for up to a week or more after they're born, the villi tend to atrophy. Thus, when the babies start receiving formula or breast milk, they often develop a condition called feeding intolerance, which involves vomiting, diarrhea, bloating, bloody stools, and, worst of all, a life-threatening infection called necrotizing enterocolitis (NEC).

Dr. Christensen and Dr. Calhoun theorized that if they could continue getting the growth factors into the babies' digestive tracts, they might be able to avert feeding intolerance. To do that, they created artificial amniotic fluid—a colorless, odorless, and flavorless solution of various minerals plus the growth factors. These growth factors are already available as the biomedically engineered drugs filgrastim (Neupogen) and epoetin alfa (Epogen).

What the study showed. Researchers tested the solution in premature babies by giving them varying amounts beginning on the first day of life. Eventually, the doctors increased the dose of growth factors to mimic the amount the infants would have received in utero.

In the group's most recent study, published in the March 2004 issue of the *Journal of Perinatology*, doctors in Mexico used the solution on 10 premature infants who had already been treated for NEC. All the babies tolerated the solution well, and none developed any recurrence of NEC. More important, none developed feeding intolerance, a common occurrence after an episode of NEC.

Availability. Dr. Christensen and Dr. Calhoun received approval from the FDA in the summer of 2003 to conduct more clinical trials on the solution, and they're looking for a pharmaceutical partner to help fund the studies. ■

Sexual Health

Female Viagra Gains Ground

From the moment the male impotence drug sildenafil (Viagra) hit pharmacy shelves six years ago, researchers have been scrambling to find a similar medication for women. It won't be Viagra, though; Pfizer, the manufacturer, halted all trials on the drug for women in March 2004 because of disappointing results. Other drug makers are having better luck. Three possibilities, including a gel, a patch, and a spray, showed strong results in studies in 2004.

The challenge of finding a drug to enhance women's libido is that women's sexual desire is governed by emotional as well as physical factors, says sexual health researcher Marc Gittleman, M.D., of the South Florida Medical Research Center in Miami. Simply enhancing blood flow to the genitals, as Viagra does, won't increase a woman's desire if she has relationship problems, is coping with dropping hormone levels, or is just plain tired.

Nevertheless, you have to start somewhere. Among the leading contenders for the title "first female Viagra," is topical alprostadil (Alista). When the gel is rubbed onto the clitoral area, it stimulates blood flow to the vagina and clitoris, enhancing lubrication. Results of late-stage clinical trials showed that Alista significantly increased women's arousal (measured as the women watched what scientists call "visual sexual stimulation").

Another option is a testosterone patch called Intrinsa, which is applied to the abdomen and changed twice a week. In a study of 562 women who had had their ovaries removed—and were therefore in surgically induced menopause—those who used Intrinsa reported significant improvements in sexual desire and satisfaction. (Menopause causes a sharp decline in testosterone, which is produced by the ovaries and adrenal glands and plays a role in female sexual desire and function.) A spray called Testosterone MDTS is also being tested.

If approved, all three treatments may be available in the United States sometime in 2005. ■

Bacterial Infections

More Common Than You Think

That vaginal itching and odor you're experiencing? Hold off on buying a yeast infection treatment. You could have a case of bacterial vaginosis (BV), the most common cause of vaginal discharge among women in the United States. Left untreated, it may lead to significant health complications in pregnant women or women undergoing gynecological surgery, including premature delivery, postpartum infections, endometriosis, infertility, and increased vulnerability to HIV infection.

The condition has been considered by some to be a sexually transmitted disease, but a study in the journal *Obstetrics and Gynecology* found BV to be very prevalent in virgins as well as much more common overall than previous estimates suggested.

The study, which involved young women entering the military, found that 27 percent of the 2,000 women evaluated had BV. Among those who were sexually active, 28 percent had BV, as did 18 percent of those who were virgins. Additionally, the researchers found lower rates of BV in women who were using hormonal contraception, such as birth control pills, suggesting that hormonal treatments may provide some protection against the infection.

BV is treated with antibiotics but often recurs. Symptoms include a change in the color and consistency of vaginal fluid, itching and burning, and an unpleasant odor, but up to half of women have no symptoms.

Sexually Transmitted Diseases

Promising Vaccine May Wipe Out Herpes

Herpes is the sexually transmitted disease that never leaves. Once you have it, you're prone to painful flare-ups throughout your life. There is no cure, but a new vaccine that was midway through its final stages of clinical testing in 2004 may eventually vanquish the virus for good by preventing new infections in uninfected women.

The problem. "Clearly, genital herpes is a huge problem in this country," says Rhoda Sperling, M.D., vice chair of the department of obstetrics, gynecology, and reproductive science at Mount Sinai School of Medicine in New York City, which is participating in the herpes vaccine trials. The National Institutes of Health estimates that genital herpes affects an estimated 67 million Americans, and, Dr. Sperling notes, rates are rising. Rates are similarly high in other countries around the world, with an estimated one in four patients at sexually transmitted disease clinics in the United Kingdom and 5 to 40 percent of various other European populations infected. Plus, she says, "people express more worry and concern about herpes than any other sexually transmitted disease"—even more than HIV.

Herpes is caused by one of two forms of the herpesvirus, HSV-1 and HSV-2, which cause either oral herpes—marked by sores and blisters on the lips, gums, and in the mouth—or genital herpes—marked by painful sores in the genital area. HSV-1 typically causes oral herpes, but either form of the virus can cause either type of herpes.

The virus can be transmitted via sexual or other skin-to-skin contact and can be spread even when the infected person shows no symptoms. It is particularly dangerous if a pregnant woman passes the virus to her infant, potentially causing a devastating and possibly deadly illness. Herpes infection also increases the risk of HIV infection by providing easier entry for HIV through open sores.

How the vaccine works. Called Herpevac, the vaccine contains small amounts of the outer coatings of herpes viruses, along with other substances designed to boost the immune system. Once injected, the vaccine stimulates the immune system to create antibodies to the viruses. Thus, if an immunized person ever encounters the real virus, the immune system is already primed to launch an all-out attack, staving off an infection.

Earlier studies on uninfected women and men who had infected partners found that Herpevac prevented herpes in more than 70 percent of women but had no effect on men. "It may be that herpes is a different disease in women than in men," explains Dr. Sperling. For instance, in men, herpes may be more a disease of the skin, while in women, it may be more a genital disease because women have more warm, damp areas in their genitals that make perfect viral breeding grounds.

Thus, the vaccine, if approved, would be targeted at women. By vaccinating all uninfected women, researchers hope to eventually break the cycle of viral transmission and send HSV the way of the polio virus. The vaccine will not help people who are already infected.

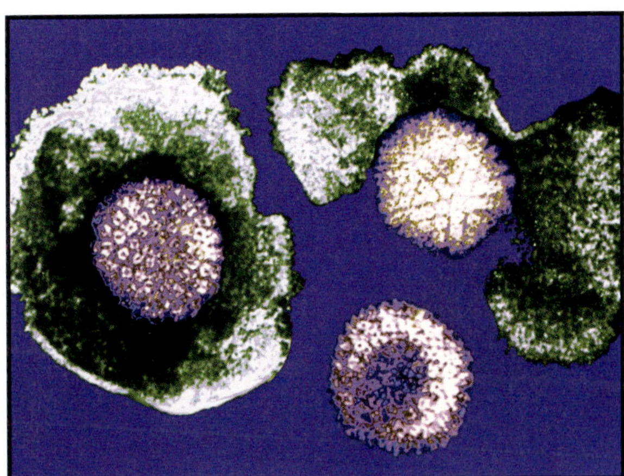

The three purple circles are herpes simplex viruses. A new vaccine could provide protection for women who aren't yet infected.

Availability. The study, funded by the National Institute of Allergy and Infectious Diseases and the vaccine's manufacturer, GlaxoSmithKline Biologicals, plans to enroll 7,550 women at 23 sites throughout the United States, including Mount Sinai. Results are expected in 2006 or 2007. To see if you're eligible to enroll in the trial, visit the Website at www.niaid.nih.gov/dmid/stds/herpevac/. ■

RESPIRATORY
SYSTEM

IN THIS SECTION

HERE'S A REASON NOT TO PRESSURE YOUR DOCTOR FOR ANTIBIOTICS YOU DON'T NEED: THEY MAY CONTRIBUTE TO ALLERGIES AND ASTHMA.

That's the news according to recent research. There's also a new, simple blood test that will tell doctors immediately whether antibiotics are the right choice for symptoms that may or may not be caused by a bacterial infection.

You and the person sleeping next to you would love to end your snoring, especially if it's a symptom of the rest-robbing breathing disorder known as sleep apnea. Now you may be able to quiet the racket with a simple orthodontic device; research shows it works as well for some people as more cumbersome breathing apparatuses.

There's also good news for cystic fibrosis patients: Researchers have confirmed that healthy genes can be safely sprayed into the lungs of people with the life-shortening disease. The new genes take over from the congenitally damaged ones, improving lung performance for about a month. The breakthrough is a major step toward the day when gene therapy will permanently restore healthy lung function.

Asthma and Allergies

Three Common Nutrients Reduce Kids' Asthma Risk

Are your children taking their vitamin C? Do they get enough grains and fish? Do they eat orange and yellow vegetables? If not, they may be running an unnecessarily high risk of asthma, the most common serious chronic condition among children under 18. Two new studies have shown a clear link between asthma risk and three nutrients: vitamin C, beta-carotene (the nutrient that gives carrots, squash, and other vegetables their yellow or orange color), and selenium (a trace mineral found in grains and fish). One of the studies found that children with low levels of vitamin C and beta-carotene in their bloodstreams were more likely to develop the airway disease. The other concluded that increased intake of vitamin C, beta-carotene, and selenium lower a child's risk of asthma.

Also, if anyone in your house smokes, you may want to be doubly sure that your children are getting at least the recommended daily allowance of vitamin C (25 milligrams for kids 4 to 8 and 45 milligrams for kids 9 to 13). The new research shows that kids who are regularly exposed to secondhand tobacco smoke have as much as a 40 percent lower asthma risk when they get enough vitamin C. The same is true for selenium and beta-carotene.

Why the three nutrients might protect children from asthma is still undetermined, but all three are antioxidants, meaning they neutralize free radicals, unstable oxygen molecules that damage cells and contribute to disease. The two latest studies, published in February 2004 in the *American Journal of Respiratory and Critical Care Medicine* and the *American Journal of Epidemiology,* follow several others in recent years that suggested that antioxidants can help combat asthma. One study even found improved lung function in children with asthma who were given antioxidant supplements, meaning that antioxidants may help treat asthma as well as prevent it.

TOP Trends

LAST GASP FOR CIGARETTES?

Smoking bans in public places are cropping up across the globe, from Norway to Australia and from Canada to the Netherlands. What's more, they're surprisingly popular. One poll found that 62 percent of New Yorkers support the recently imposed smoking limitations in their city. In Ireland, where a new policy outlaws smoking even in barrooms, a survey revealed that Irish drinkers prefer smoke-free pubs by a solid 2-to-1 margin.

So is an outright ban on smoking—anywhere, anytime—the next step? In the United Kingdom, it would be if the editors of the *Lancet* got their way. In a stunning editorial published in December 2003, the prestigious British medical journal called for making possession of cigarettes a crime. Citing an estimated 1,000 yearly deaths from secondhand smoke in the U.K. alone, the editors wrote, "If tobacco were an illegal substance, possession of cigarettes would become a crime, and the number of smokers would drastically fall....We call on Tony Blair's government to ban tobacco." In an informal poll by the online medical information service Medscape, 67 percent of the respondents (and 72 percent of those who identified themselves as doctors) said they'd support criminalizing tobacco use in their own countries.

The researchers want to await the results of larger studies on the asthma-antioxidant link, which are currently under way, before recommending that children supplement with vitamin C, beta-carotene, or selenium. One reason is that the current studies don't indicate how much of each antioxidant is best for asthma prevention. Even without that information, it's worth it to see that your kids get plenty of the fruits, vegetables, and grains that provide antioxidants, says Patricia Cassano, Ph.D., one of the study authors. "With such a healthful diet, they'll develop habits that will help reduce their risk of chronic disease throughout life," she says.

TOP Trends

WHOOPING COUGH WORRIES RETURN

Memo to all parents who thought whooping cough had been eradicated: It's back. So are the frightening, high-pitched coughing fits that gave the respiratory infection its name. In truth, whooping cough never really disappeared, but a spike in reported cases—more in 2002 and 2003 than in 1964—has forced parents to think anew about protecting their children from this serious and sometimes deadly bacterial infection.

One reason for whooping cough's comeback is underuse of the vaccine that provides protection throughout childhood. Another is that adolescents and young adults, for whom the vaccine has worn off, carry the infection in surprisingly large numbers. They have milder symptoms and usually don't experience the dreaded, fighting-for-air coughing attacks, so they often unwittingly spread the bacteria to children.

What's a parent to do? First, health officials say, vaccinate your child. In the United States, the vaccine is part of the DTaP combination (that stands for diphtheria, tetanus, and pertussis, the medical term for whooping cough), which calls for five shots between the ages of 2 months and 4 to 6 years. Also, since the vaccine is not 100 percent effective, consider the possibility of whooping cough when your child comes down with cold- or flu-like respiratory symptoms. (In the early stages of the infection, there's usually no "whoop" in the cough, or even a fever.) Remind your pediatrician that the Centers for Disease Control and Prevention recommends testing for pertussis to rule it out in young patients who have persistent coughs.

With a fingertip pulse sensor connected to his computer, a patient gets in touch with his breathing and heart rate to help him control his asthma.

Asthma and Allergies

Biofeedback Is Strong Asthma Medicine

Inhaled steroid drugs are an asthma patient's best bet for easier breathing and fewer serious attacks, yet 50 percent of people who are prescribed these drugs for asthma don't use them as often as they should. They hate the routine, fear side effects, or resent the cost.

If you're among that group, take heart. An alternative to steroids may come from a surprising source: biofeedback training. Once considered a "fringe" therapy but now increasingly accepted, biofeedback may keep asthma symptoms under control so well that for some people, it can drastically reduce the need for steroids.

In the largest study ever conducted on biofeedback as an asthma treatment, 45 adult volunteers who practiced the technique daily reported significant reductions in symptoms over the four-month study period. Doctors regularly examined the people who used biofeedback, as well as 48 asthma patients who didn't use it. Without knowing which patients fell into which category, the doctors consistently prescribed less steroid medication for those in the biofeedback group.

How it works. In biofeedback, electronic monitoring devices help a person alter body functions, such as heart rate, that aren't normally under conscious control. The kind of biofeedback training given to the asthma patients in the study helped them improve their heart rate variability (HRV), the periodic variations in the time between heartbeats. Having such variations may not sound desirable, but in fact, high HRV is associated with good health. Asthma tends to lower HRV, and raising it seems to reduce asthma symptoms, although researchers aren't sure why.

The type of biofeedback used in the study teaches people to breathe in a way that maximizes their HRV. Sensors, much like the heart-rate monitors on exercise bikes, are connected to pulse points such as the chest or fingertips. A small readout screen indicates HRV, usually in the form of a vertical bar that lengthens as HRV rises. By focusing on their breathing as they watch the screen, people eventually learn which subtle variations in breathing will lengthen the bar. With enough training, they can carry that knowledge with them throughout the day, regularly breathing in a way that helps controls asthma.

Availability. HRV biofeedback is thought to help with other conditions, such as stress and depression, so it's usually easy to sign up for guided sessions at one of the biofeedback centers that are common in urban areas. You can also order home HRV biofeedback kits from Internet sources. However, Paul Lehrer, Ph.D., professor of psychiatry at Robert Wood Johnson Medical School in Piscataway, New Jersey, who published the biofeedback-for-asthma study in the August 2004 issue of the medical journal *Chest*, recommends that beginners get some professional assistance before practicing biofeedback on their own.

Dr. Lehrer also cautions against premature substitution of biofeedback for prescribed steroid medications. "It looks like biofeedback will be a good adjunct asthma therapy and may allow some people to go off steroids," he says, "but first we need larger studies that look at biofeedback's benefits for longer than four months." In 2004, Dr. Lehrer applied to the National Institutes of Health for funding for just such a study. ■

RESEARCH ROUNDUP

Basketball Gets Losing Score

Ice hockey, rugby, and football may have the reputation as the roughest sports, but basketball appears to be the deadliest one for people with asthma. A research team from Drexel University in Philadelphia investigated all the sports-related asthma deaths over a seven-year period and found that more of them (21 percent) occurred while playing basketball than any other sport. Track was second, and standard school gym class activities were third. Almost all of the deaths involved people with a known history of asthma, and most victims were under 20. Hardly any were using long-term control medications.

The study made no attempt to explain why basketball was associated with the most deaths, nor are the mechanics of exercise-induced asthma attacks completely understood. It's thought that big increases in air intake (which the constant movement and numerous quick spurts in basketball certainly create) dry the lungs, which can constrict airways by tightening the surrounding muscles and thickening mucus.

Should people with asthma sit on the sidelines and watch others score all the baskets? No, say the researchers in the February 2004 issue of the *Journal of Allergy and Clinical Immunology*. The benefits of regular exercise far outweigh the risks. After all, only 61 sports-related asthma deaths occurred in the United States from 1993 to 2000. Nevertheless, coaches, parents, doctors, and athletes should be aware of the potential risks and be prepared to deal with emergencies.

Asthma and Allergies

Do Antibiotics Promote Asthma and Allergies?

The widespread use of antibiotics in the second half of the 20th century corresponded with soaring rates of asthma and allergies in the West that continue today. Coincidence? Mairi Noverr, M.D., and Gary Huffnagle, M.D., don't think so. The two Michigan University researchers released a report in April 2004 revealing strong evidence from a mouse study that antibiotic use promotes respiratory allergies.

If these findings are borne out by further research on humans, doctors and their patients will have at least three good reasons for using antibiotics only when they're absolutely necessary: to slow down the development of drug-resistant strains of bacteria, to spare patients unnecessary side effects from the drugs, and now, to avoid increased risk of asthma and allergies.

How it works. Simultaneous increases in allergy cases and antibiotic use don't prove that one causes the other, but the Michigan team was able to establish a link between antibiotic use and allergies. When antibiotics kill harmful bacteria to clear up an infection, they also kill "friendly" bacteria that exist naturally in the gut. Researchers think the resulting imbalance in intestinal bacteria diminishes the immune system's ability to differentiate between harmless molecules in the body and true invaders. And that's precisely what an allergic reaction is: a misguided immune system attack on benign visitors, such as mold spores.

The researchers administered antibiotics to a group of mice for five days and then exposed them to mold spores. The treated mice experienced much greater allergic immune responses to the spores than the untreated mice.

The message. With these results, the study authors see additional incentive to use antibiotics responsibly. If they're needed, take them—but if they're not necessary, use an alternative treatment. When your antibiotic regimen is complete, ask your doctor about "probiotic" tablets that can help restore proper bacterial balance in the intestines. You can also help restore that balance by eating plenty of yogurt, raw fruits, and vegetables. ■

For Many, Aspirin and Asthma Don't Mix

Up to now, about 5 to 10 percent of adults with asthma were thought to be aspirin sensitive. For them, popping an aspirin for a headache can trigger an asthma attack that in extreme cases could be life-threatening. Now it turns out the problem is worse than experts thought. After analyzing data from 21 studies, British and Australian researchers have concluded that 21 percent of adults with asthma are prone to aspirin-induced attacks. That's one in every five.

It's not just aspirin that carries a risk. According to the study results, published in February 2004 in the *British Medical Journal*, most people with asthma who are sensitive to aspirin will also react to other over-the-counter pain relievers, including ibuprofen (Motrin, Advil), naproxen (Naprosyn), and diclofenac (Voltaren, Cataflam). The findings, say the study authors, suggest that all adults with asthma should discuss the possibility of aspirin sensitivity with their doctors and, if necessary, decide on a pain-relief strategy that lowers the risk of reactions. The caution is aimed primarily at adults because children with asthma are rarely aspirin sensitive.

Asthma and Allergies

A Chinese Formula for Solving Peanut Allergies

An ancient 11-herb Chinese formula for soothing stomach ailments may soon become the basis for a modern 3-herb treatment for the growing problem of peanut allergies.

A research team at Mount Sinai School of Medicine in New York City became interested in the Chinese formula several years ago. A key breakthrough occurred in 2004, when the researchers announced that after they'd eliminated two superfluous herbs from the formula, peanut-sensitive mice treated with the nine-herb combination had virtually no reaction when fed the offending goobers.

The next step will be to whittle down the formula to the three most essential herbs. Such a streamlined formula has already shown promise in protecting mice from peanut allergy reactions, but the researchers won't divulge yet which three herbs they're working with. Whichever they are, the pared-down version could pave the way for testing the herbs—or a new drug based on their properties—on humans who have peanut allergies.

Availability. Four of the herbs from the original formula are well known in the West and are available at health food stores and Chinese markets. They are reishi mushrooms (called ling zhi), panax ginseng (ren shen), ginger root (gan jiang), and Chinese angelica (dang gui). The other herbs in the nine-herb formula are wu mei, chuan jiao, huang lian, huang bai, and gui zhi. Of course, buying the herbs individually and blending them yourself is neither recommended nor likely to work. If you can't wait for the final version to be tested and approved, the original 11-herb formula is available in the East and West through practitioners of Traditional Chinese Medicine. At this point, however, it's still used only for stomach conditions. ■

Cystic Fibrosis

Breathing In a Long-Awaited Cure

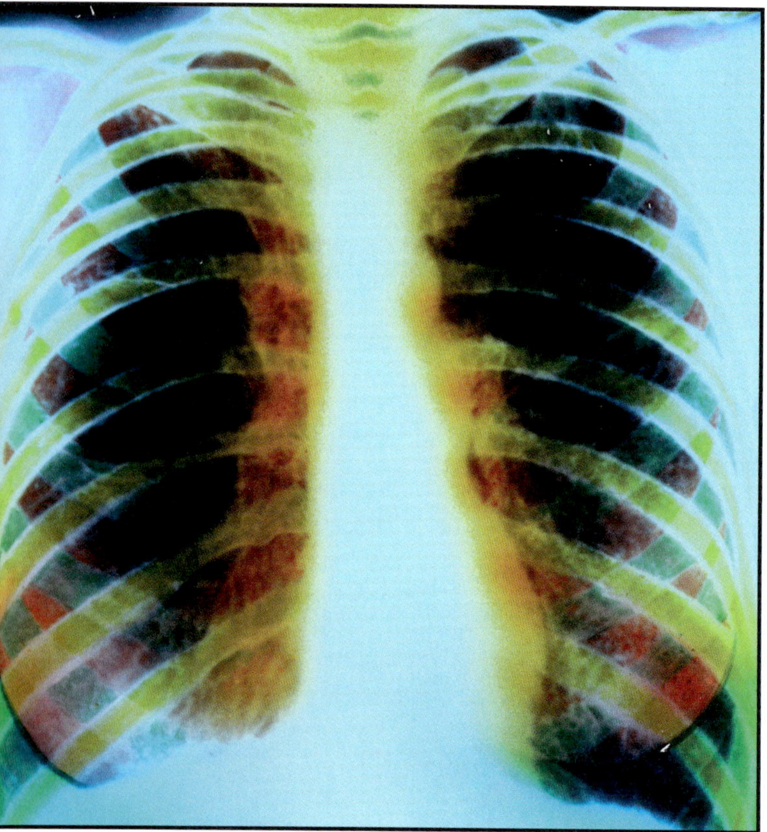

Repeated infection has thickened the air passages (orange, beside the spine) in this cystic fibrosis patient's lungs. A cure for the disease could be on the near horizon.

The most likely cure for cystic fibrosis—installing normal genes in a patient's lung cells to replace the defective genes that cause the life-shortening disease—is no longer a distant dream. In fact, such a cure may be just a year or two away, now that Stanford University researchers have successfully tested a treatment that lets cystic fibrosis patients literally inhale healthy genes into their lungs.

Medical researchers have long known that a flaw in a gene called CFTR (cystic fibrosis transmembrane-conductance regulator) is responsible for this congenital condition—the most common inherited condition among white people of North American or European descent. Previous attempts to deliver healthy CFTR genes by injection and other methods have had some limited success, but the results of the latest test, involving 37 cystic fibrosis patients, represent a major step forward for two reasons.

"Inhalation is the only method that gets the genes to the lungs, where we want them," says Richard Moss, M.D., the lead study author. "And there are much fewer side effects."

The inhalation gene delivery method significantly improved lung function for about a month after each treatment. That's key, because lung damage from abnormal mucus production is what kills most cystic fibrosis patients, usually by age 30.

How it works. In the Stanford study, published in the January 2004 issue of the medical journal *Chest*, the inhaled genes were carried into the lungs inside harmless viruses called AAV. Once there, the viruses inserted themselves into the cells lining the airways, giving those cells flawless copies of the CFTR gene. It's thought that the "good" genes took over command of the lungs, sending out correct instructions for functions such as salt and water secretion and overriding the old instructions that caused mucus to become abnormally thick and sticky.

Availability. A follow-up study of inhalant gene therapy involving 100 cystic fibrosis patients was under way in 2004, and results from an even bigger test (with 500 to 600 participants) could be available in 2005. If both studies confirm the treatment's safety and effectiveness, Dr. Moss says some cystic fibrosis patients may receive monthly gene therapy as soon as 2006.

Two hurdles will remain, however. One is the fact that the therapy has been tested only on patients age 12 and older, so more study will be needed before younger children can take advantage of it. Also, since cell turnover in the lung tissue means that cells with the congenital bad gene reclaim control of lung function a month after each treatment, ongoing monthly treatments will be required to

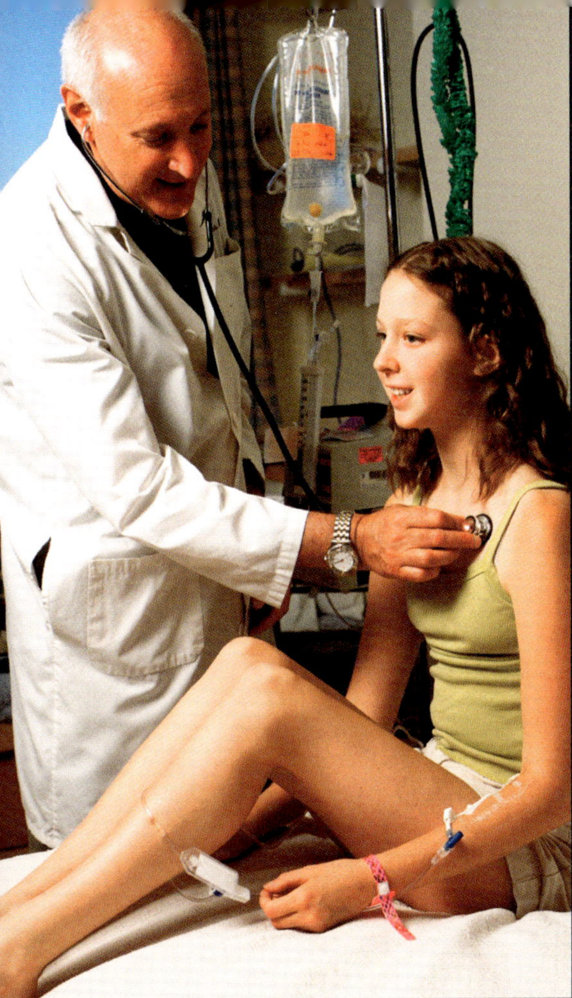

Researcher Richard Moss, M.D., examines a young cystic fibrosis patient. Inhaling healthy genes, he discovered, gives patients a month of improved lung function.

improve and prolong patients' lives. (It's unlikely that the patients—who are used to frequent, often daily, therapy to remove secretions from the lungs—will complain, though.)

A true one-treatment cure for cystic fibrosis will come only when stem cells—currently at the red-hot center of a burning political debate—replace viruses as self-renewing gene delivery vehicles. Those special cells, thought by many to be the best hope for curing a host of diseases from Parkinson's to Alzheimer's, would be able to multiply indefinitely in the lung tissue once they're delivered, assuring a lifelong supply of healthy CFTR genes for the patient. Such a permanent cure is thought to be at least a decade away. ■

Is There a Cure in Curry?

Wouldn't it be nice if a treatment for cystic fibrosis were as close as the kitchen spice rack? That could be the case, say Yale University researchers, who fed curcumin, the main compound in the common curry spice turmeric, to mice with cystic fibrosis.

According to the research team's report, published in an April 2004 issue of the journal *Science*, curcumin helps a gene called CFTR do its job correctly. In most cystic fibrosis patients, CFTR is rendered defective by the mutation responsible for the life-shortening genetic disorder. This causes the perpetual infection and inflammation that eventually lead to lung failure.

The mouse experiments were so successful that plans were under way in 2004 to begin testing curcumin in humans who have cystic fibrosis. The first phase will explore the safety of concentrated doses of the compound, and later studies will examine how well it works. Although curcumin supplements are available at health food stores, the Cystic Fibrosis Foundation recommends that patients hold off on experimenting with them on their own until the safety studies are completed, probably by the end of 2005.

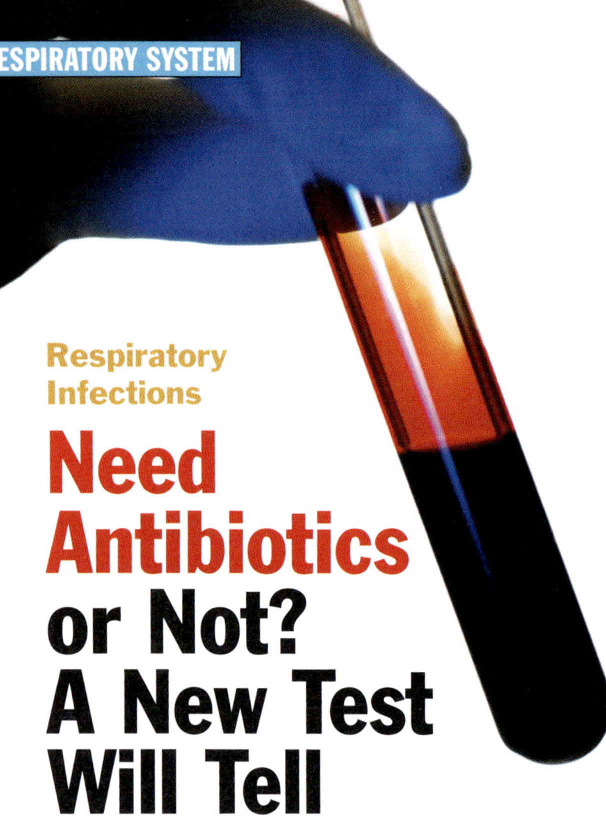

Respiratory Infections

Need Antibiotics or Not? A New Test Will Tell

You've been coughing for a week, your throat is sore, and you're running a fever. Suspecting some kind of respiratory tract infection, you visit your doctor and beg to be put on antibiotics. Your doctor complies. A week later, you're fine. Was it the antibiotics, or did your illness simply run its course?

The fact is that most respiratory tract infections are caused by viruses, and antibiotics—which work only on bacteria—are utterly useless against them. Nevertheless, doctors tend to err on the side of caution and prescribe antibiotics because they have no easy way to be sure whether they're dealing with a bacterial or a viral infection.

That may be changing. Swiss researchers announced in a February 2004 issue of the British medical journal *Lancet* that they've developed a safe and reliable blood test that reveals in less than an hour whether a respiratory infection is bacterial and therefore treatable with antibiotics. The test works so well that it could cut the frequency of antibiotic treatments in half worldwide. That would do much to undercut the growing problem of bacterial resistance to antibiotics. (The more antibiotics are prescribed, the greater the chance that bacteria resistant to those drugs will develop.) It would also spare millions of people from unnecessary antibiotic treatment and its potential side effects (such as diarrhea and yeast infections).

In the study, researchers asked doctors to decide whether to prescribe antibiotics to 243 people who had symptoms of a lower respiratory tract infection. After the patients were given the new blood test and the results were revealed to the doctors, prescription recommendations for antibiotics dropped by half. Patients who did not receive antibiotics because their infections were nonbacterial recovered just as well as those who got antibiotics for their bacterial infections.

How it works. The test measures the amount of a protein called procalcitonin—a marker for bacterial infections—in the blood. Although the protein doesn't play a major role in either the infection or the immune system's response, blood levels rise if the infection is bacterial.

Availability. According to Beat Muller, M.D., a member of the Swiss research team, any medical professional who invests in the equipment needed to measure procalcitonin can use the test right away. However, health care providers may decide not to acquire the equipment until the test is accepted by health insurance companies, which may require further testing. ■

RESEARCH ROUNDUP

Goody Kit Reduces Antibiotic Use

A Minnesota study found that patients who take home kits containing feel-good supplies such as tea bags, chicken soup, lozenges, and over-the-counter cold and flu medications are less likely to desire antibiotics for their illnesses.

That's a promising discovery, since prescribing antibiotics for viral illnesses is a common but ineffective practice. Overuse of antibiotics leads to the development of resistant strains of bacteria, making the drugs less effective against the germs they're designed to fight.

The study followed more than 10,000 patients during a cold and flu season. The researchers gave more than 4,000 adults who had upper respiratory illnesses or acute bronchitis both kits and prescriptions for antibiotics at their doctors' offices. Those patients were 34 percent less likely to fill prescriptions for antibiotics within three days of their visits than people who didn't get kits. The study was presented at the International Conference on Emerging Infectious Diseases in February 2004.

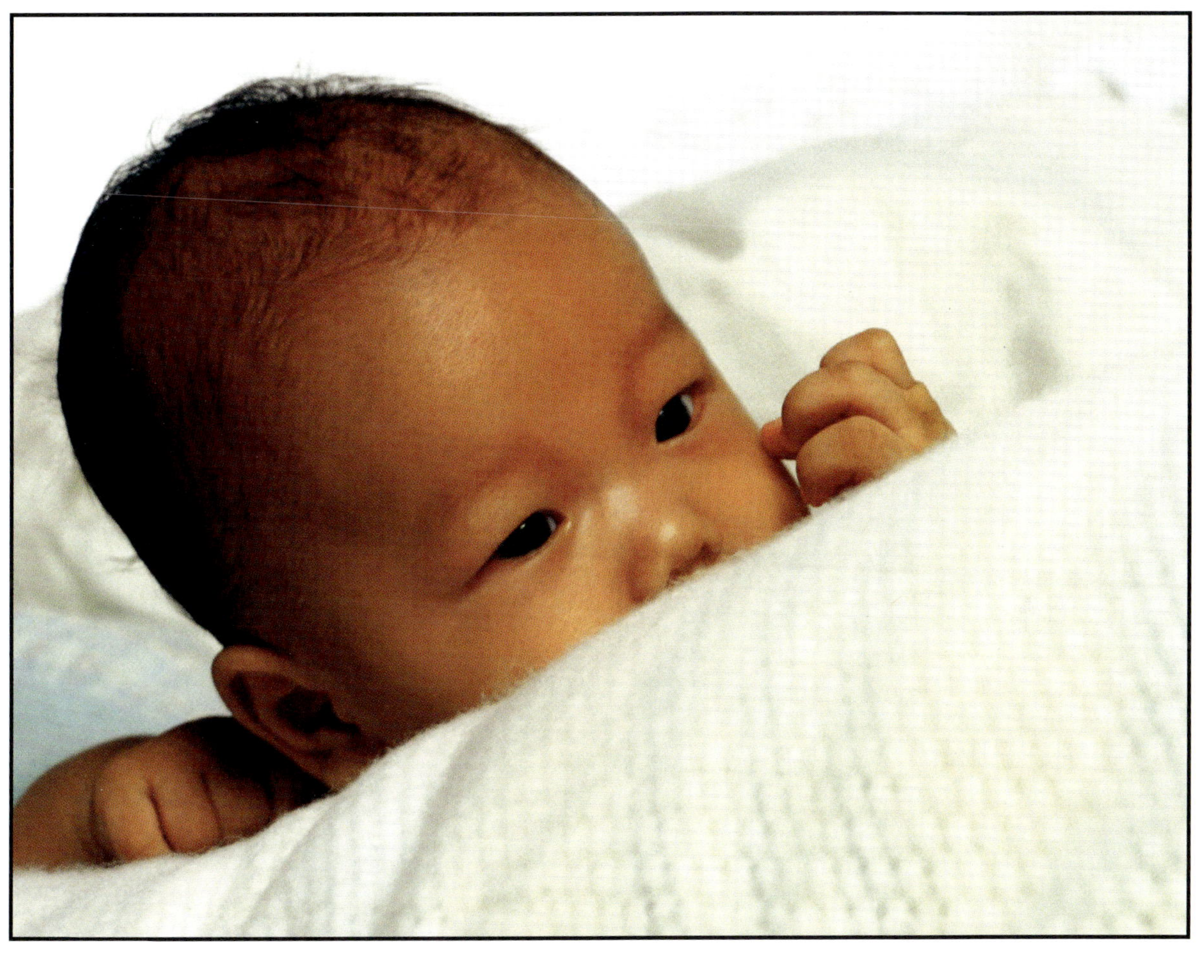

Respiratory Infections

Bronchitis? Pneumonia? Think Zinc

If your young child comes down with a lower respiratory tract infection such as bronchitis, you may want to ask his doctor about zinc supplements. While zinc, critical to a healthy immune system, had already been shown to help the body resist such infections, two recent studies found that the trace mineral also helps kids under age 2 recover faster from them.

One study, led by an Indian researcher and published in the March 2004 issue of the *American Journal of Clinical Nutrition*, found that boys between 2 and 24 months old who were given 10 milligrams of zinc daily in a syrup recovered from their illness 2.6 times faster than those who didn't receive zinc. (For unknown reasons, the zinc didn't speed recovery for girls.)

Another study, conducted in Bangladesh and published in the May 2004 issue of the British medical journal *Lancet*, found that treatment with 20 milligrams of zinc a day in addition to the usual antibiotics helped boys and girls under age 2 recover faster from the most serious lower respiratory tract infection, pneumonia.

The doses administered in the studies were far higher than those found in over-the-counter zinc lozenges used to ward off colds. In fact, 10 milligrams a day is more than double what's normally considered the safe upper limit for zinc in kids under 2, so this is definitely not a home treatment. If you're interested in zinc as a therapy for your child, talk to your doctor. ■

Spray Away Sleep Problems

A simple nasal spray may be the solution to the serious sleep problems of millions of adults worldwide. Sleep apnea—short but frequent breathing interruptions during sleep—often requires the use of mechanical devices to assist breathing, or even surgery to clear airway blockage. Now, Irish researchers have found that for certain people, spraying a steroid called fluticasone (Flonase) into the nose twice a day can cut down on apnea episodes.

The medication is already frequently prescribed for rhinitis, an inflammation of the mucous membranes in the nasal passages that causes a stuffy, itchy, or runny nose. About 26 percent of people with sleep apnea also have rhinitis. The new study confirms that fluticasone's anti-inflammatory, nose-clearing action seems to help those people get better shuteye.

Researchers at St. Vincent's University Hospital in Dublin treated 13 such patients twice a day for a month with a nasal spray containing fluticasone. According to results published in the January 2004 issue of the medical journal *Thorax*, the frequency of sleep interruptions (apneas) decreased by 40 percent in those patients compared with a group of 10 apnea-and-rhinitis patients who received no fluticasone. The people who were given the medication also reported less nasal congestion and more daytime alertness.

Sleep Apnea

Get Set for Snore-Free, Sound Sleep

What's worse: Night after night of poor sleep, or having to don a cumbersome face mask before bed and spend the night hooked up to a breathing machine? That's the choice for many people with sleep apnea, a disorder that causes frequent breathing interruptions during the night. Now, there's a third option that, according to new research from Sweden, can improve sleep without much fuss.

How it works. The device is called a mandibular advancement device because it puts the lower jaw (mandible) into a more forward position, which opens the airway from the nose on down the throat. That's key, since both snoring and sleep apnea are a result of flesh partially obstructing the flow of air from the mouth and nose to the lungs. While snoring may bother your sleeping partner more than it does you, sleep apnea can trouble your sleep so severely that you can't perform well during the day.

Many people with severe apnea get help from a continuous positive airway pressure (CPAP) machine, which keeps air passages open by supplying a steady flow of air through a nose and/or mouth mask connected by a tube to an electric pump. That's a setup, however, that many people are unwilling or unable to tolerate, says Marie Marklund, D.D.S., Ph.D., of Umea University in Sweden. So she and her research team tested an alternative—the mandibular

Wear this device, and you could kiss sleep apnea goodbye.

advancement device—on 619 volunteers who snored and had sleep apnea. The device is smaller and easier to use than the CPAP machine. Once fitted into the mouth, it can't be seen when the lips are closed, and you can speak, drink water, and give a goodnight kiss with it in place.

Air Interrupted

In a person with sleep apnea, tongue and throat tissues relax, blocking the airway.

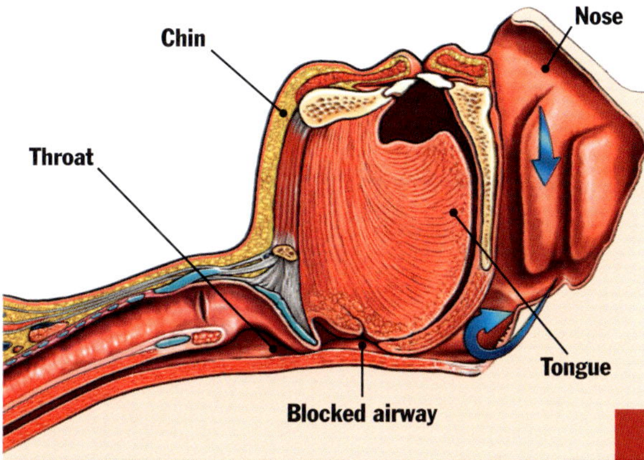

More important, the device improved sleep for a significant number of the study volunteers who used it throughout the one-year test period. According to the study results, women are most likely to get relief from the device because a more forward jaw position opens their airways more than men's, but the men in the study whose apnea occurred when they slept face-up also benefited significantly.

Not everyone liked the device, though, and nearly a quarter of the study volunteers stopped using it before the study ended. Some cited its orthodontic appearance, and others objected to side effects that included excessive salivation and discomfort associated with having the set of their jaws determined by a foreign object. But Dr. Marklund says, "Once you get used to it, you'll improve your well-being, at night and during the day."

Availability. Mandibular advancement devices are widely available; many are offered on the Internet. Don't buy one on your own, though, warns Dr. Marklund. The doctor who's treating your apnea or snoring first needs to determine if you're likely to benefit from it, and then the device should be prescribed and fitted to your mouth.

IN Brief

Antibacterial Cleaners Let Many Illnesses Thrive

Even if you wash your hands with antibacterial soap, you're just as likely to come down with a variety of common illnesses as people who use regular cleaning agents.

That's the conclusion of researchers who provided either regular soap and cleaners or antibacterial versions to 238 New York City households, then tracked their rates of illness for nearly a year. Both groups reported similar rates of coughing, runny noses, sore throats, and conjunctivitis.

Why was there no difference? These common symptoms are typically caused by viruses, which aren't affected by antibacterial cleaners.

Office Bug Zappers Reduce Illness

Blasting germs with ultraviolet light deep in the ventilation ducts of office buildings may lead to a healthier workforce, according to new Canadian research.

Researchers equipped the ventilation systems in three Montreal office buildings with germ-killing UV lights. The lights shone on air-conditioning coils and drip pans—hotbeds of mold and bacterial growth.

The scientists alternated use of the lights—on for 4 weeks, then off for 12 weeks—for 48 weeks. On repeated questionnaires, nearly 800 workers reported whether they had symptoms such as congestion, headache, fatigue, and difficulty breathing. When the UV lights were on, workers reported 20 percent fewer symptoms that started after they arrived at work. In addition, concentrations of microbes in the ventilation systems fell by 99 percent.

SKIN

HAIR AND NAILS

IN THIS SECTION

CAN YOU CHANGE THE SKIN YOU'RE IN? MAYBE NOT, BUT NEW DRUGS AND DISCOVERIES CAN IMPROVE IT.

If it's acne prone, finding ways to tame the stress monster could lead to fewer breakouts. If itchy, inflamed skin caused by a topic dermatitis is your problem, a nonprescription vitamin B_{12} cream could help. For the face-reddening condition rosacea, a new gel called Finacea is your best choice. And there's a revolutionary new "biological bandage" that can actually help burn victims grow new skin, speeding healing and possibly reducing scarring.

When it comes to the hair on your head—or an unfortunate lack thereof—stay tuned for stem cell transplants that grow brand-new hair-producing follicles.

Finally, two cosmetics companies have agreed to remove from their nail polish a substance that some consumer advocates believe could be dangerous to your health. The ingredient is still found in some other companies' nail polish.

Acne

It's True: Stress Worsens Acne

Plenty of common health beliefs turn out to be wrong, but some turn out to be true. A study from Stanford University found that stress seems to play a role in acne outbreaks—something that generations of teens and young adults have long suspected upon discovering blemishes just before a big test, the prom, or some other momentous occasion.

The study looked at 22 college students with acne. The students, average age 22, first visited a researcher during a non-exam period of the academic quarter, and the researcher evaluated the severity of their acne using a standard measurement scale. The volunteers then returned during exam time to have their skin evaluated again.

On each visit, the students completed questionnaires that are commonly used to measure people's stress levels, and they answered questions about their sleep and diet patterns.

The results showed that the students whose stress levels went up the most during exams had the greatest increase in acne severity—even taking into account changes in diet and sleep, which may also play a role in acne.

Alexa Kimball, M.D., associate professor of dermatology at Stanford and a researcher involved with the study, said the team was surprised by the results, since they launched the study "actually attempting to debunk the relationship as a myth." The results of the research were published in the journal *Archives of Dermatology* in 2003.

How it works. Although experts don't know for sure how stress might worsen acne, the authors quote previous research showing that during emotional stress, the body releases hormones that can aggravate the skin condition. Stress may also cause the release of substances in the skin that increase inflammation. It also has been shown to slow wound healing, which could make acne linger longer.

Dr. Kimball recommends that people with acne be especially vigilant about using their skin medications and other treatments to keep the condition under control during stressful times. "Most acne treatments work best preventively, and people tend to neglect them when they are stressed, making the situation worse," she says.

TOP Trends

DO-IT-YOURSELF DERMABRASION KITS RUB YOU THE RIGHT WAY

Want younger-looking skin? You could go to a dermatologist or plastic surgeon for microdermabrasion, the skin-renewing technique that uses a device not unlike a fine sandblaster to smooth out skin. Or you could buy one of the new do-it-yourself kits, available over the Internet and at upscale beauty supply shops, which promise to soften wrinkles, reverse sun damage, fade acne scars, and lighten age spots. Some of the kits include a "resurfacing" tool with various attachments that polish skin and apply an exfoliating cream to eat away dead skin cells. Others rely on textured sponges or cloths to deliver the creams. Pair one of these products with the hugely popular tooth-bleaching kits, and you have yourself a not-so-extreme at-home makeover. When you've finished your skin treatment, though, don't forget the sunscreen, since any kind of facial exfoliation makes skin much more sensitive to the sun.

Dermatitis

Vitamin Cream Heals Common Skin Rash

Atopic dermatitis, also known as eczema, is a distressing and incurable skin condition that causes itching and inflammation. The cause is unknown, but a combination of inherited, environmental, and immunity-related factors seems to be at work. Topical steroids and oral cortisone are two of the most common treatments, but both of them carry a risk of side effects, particularly when used long term. Another, safer answer may be vitamin B_{12} cream.

How it works. Compared with normal skin, the skin of people with atopic dermatitis contains elevated levels of a chemical called nitric oxide. When vitamin B_{12} is rubbed into the skin, it prevents further buildup of the chemical, according to Markus Stücker, M.D., a dermatologist at Ruhr-University Bochum in Germany and lead author of the study. Previous research has shown that other substances that inhibit nitric oxide can reduce the itching and swelling of atopic dermatitis. Vitamin B_{12} is also thought to prevent immune system cells from releasing cytokines, chemicals that are associated with inflammation.

Researchers in past studies have tried giving vitamin B_{12} by mouth for the skin condition psoriasis, with no success (the vitamin leaves the body too quickly in the urine to yield any benefit). However, vitamin B_{12} is known to be absorbed through the skin, notes Dr. Stücker, and since it's water soluble—which means it doesn't build up in the body's tissues—it is generally regarded as safe.

In the new study, researchers found that the B_{12} cream relieved symptoms much better than a placebo (dummy) cream and had no serious side effects. One small drawback was the natural red color of the vitamin, which isn't a problem if the cream is rubbed into the skin thoroughly. The study results were published in the May 2004 issue of the *British Journal of Dermatology*.

Availability. Vitamin B_{12} is available without a prescription, and government approval of its use is not necessary in Europe or the United States. Vitamin B_{12} cream isn't widely available yet, but some creams can be found on the Internet. Talk to your dermatologist for advice if you are interested in trying this treatment. ■

TOP Trends

NO MORE TOXIC TIPS AND TOES

Two major cosmetics companies have agreed to phase out the use of a common—and, according to some consumer advocates, potentially dangerous—nail polish ingredient. Chemicals called phthalates (pronounced THA-layts) are regularly used in the manufacturing industry to make plastics more flexible. One type of phthalate, DBP, an ingredient that prevents nail polish from chipping, has been linked to birth defects in the male offspring of female lab mice that had been exposed to high levels of the chemical.

The cosmetics industry as a whole insists that the chemicals used in their products pose no danger to people, despite the fact that the European Union voted to ban phthalates as of September 2004. The companies that have decided to discontinue use of DBP are Procter and Gamble, makers of Max Factor and Cover Girl, and Estée Lauder, parent company of Clinique and MAC.

Hair Loss

Stem Cells Used to Grow New Hair

Stem cells, those "master" cells that can become just about any other type of cell, have been found in the hair follicles of mice and may hold the key to effective treatments for baldness. When scientists removed these cells, grew them in the lab, and transplanted them back in the mice, the mice grew hair where none had been before the treatment.

The discovery of the stem cells in mouse hair follicles provides researchers with important clues that should help them identify and manipulate similar cells in human hair—perhaps leading to that ever-elusive Holy Grail, a cure for baldness.

"Very simplistically, one could envision a process in humans whereby we isolate stem cells from the scalp [grow them in the lab], and transplant them back to areas that need hair," says George Cotsarelis, M.D., a researcher from the University of Pennsylvania Medical School in Philadelphia, who took part in the study. The implanted stem cells would develop into new, functioning hair follicles, which could produce new hair.

The researchers also hope that their stem cell discovery will teach them more about the skin aging process in general. They suspect that increasing the amount or life span of stem cells in the skin would have visible rejuvenating effects. "In aging, we believe that there is a decrease in the number of stem cells in the skin," says Dr. Cotsarelis, "so if we know more about stem cells, we will be able to modify their number and behavior." ■

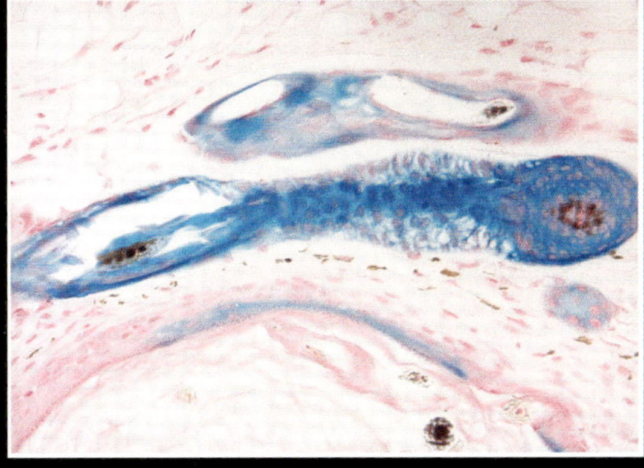

In blue, a new hair follicle, grown from donor stem cells isolated from the skin of a mouse.

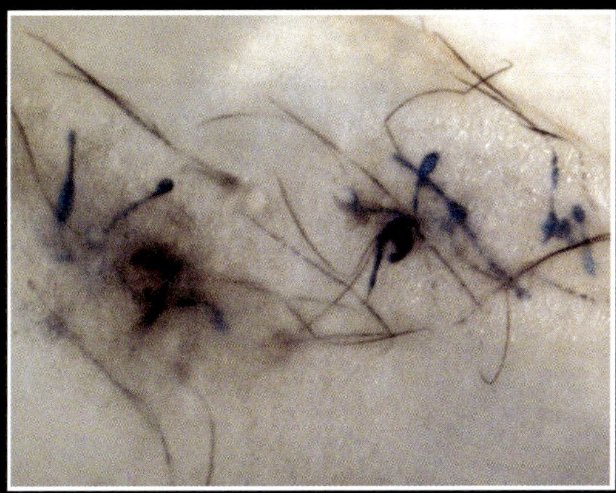

Thanks to the new hair follicles, this mouse is growing hair where it had none before.

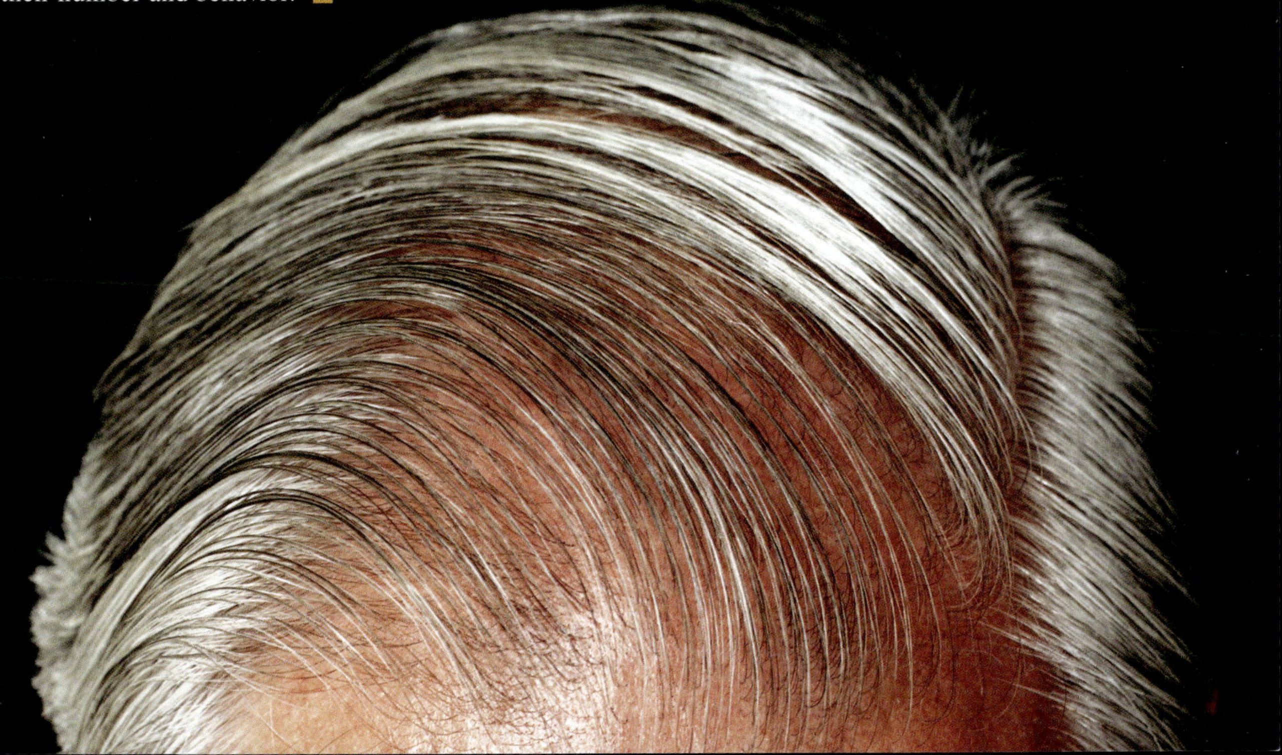

Rosacea

New Drug Wins Face-Off in Rosacea Study

There's a new topical drug for treating rosacea, and a recent study showed it does a better job of alleviating the face-reddening condition than an older medication, metronidazole (MetroGel).

Rosacea generally strikes people after the age of 30, beginning as flushing redness on the face that repeatedly flares up, then goes away. The condition can progress to cause longer episodes of flushing and noticeable blood vessels in the skin. Rosacea can also cause itching and burning on the face as well as raised bumps that are solid or contain pus. It's sometimes called acne rosacea, and its symptoms may be confused with those of plain old acne.

The new gel, azelaic acid (Finacea), was approved by the FDA for rosacea in 2003. Research published in the *Archives of Dermatology* found that it did a better job of reducing the number of lesions on study volunteers' faces than MetroGel did. It also reduced more patients' facial redness, and researchers and patients gave it better overall ratings for improving the condition. Neither Finacea nor MetroGel, however, had an appreciable effect on the appearance of visible blood vessels on the face.

How it works. Azelaic acid, also used in cream form to treat acne, may relieve rosacea by reducing skin inflammation, the authors suggest. Metronidazole is a germ-killing medication. Why it would help to treat rosacea is unknown, but other antibiotic preparations have also been used to alleviate the condition. According to the maker of the MetroGel, it may also have an anti-inflammatory effect. ■

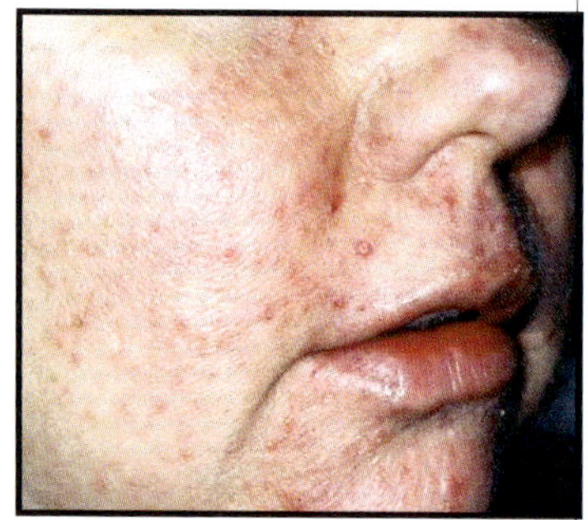

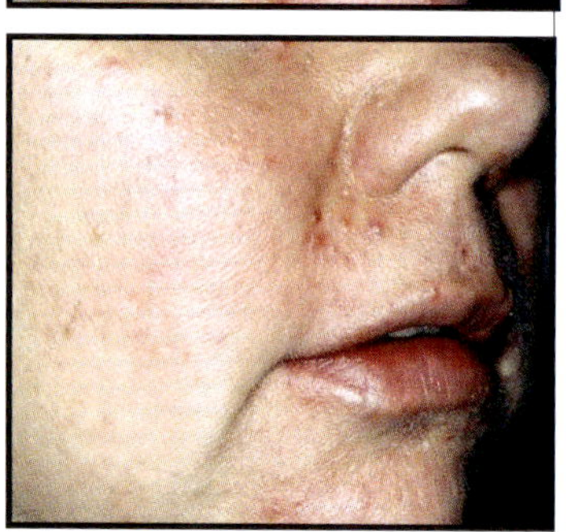

A 54-year-old woman with mild to moderate rosacea before treatment (top) and after eight weeks on Finacea.

Wounds

Biological Bandages Speed Burn Healing

More than 45,000 Americans are hospitalized each year for serious burns, which can lead to scarring and disfigurement. Speedier, more complete healing is now possible with special high-tech bandages that deliver new skin cells right to the site of the injury.

In a process that takes about one week, a small skin sample is removed from the patient (usually from the thigh or buttock) and treated in the lab so it develops into a supply of new skin cells. The fledgling cells are secured onto a specially prepared, disk-shaped bandage, which is placed on the wound. The cells move from the bandage to the injury, where they begin prompting new layers of skin to grow. They also encourage undamaged skin cells at the edges of the burn to migrate to the injured site and begin to grow. Burn patients are often too badly hurt for their bodies to jump-start this kind of healing on their own. Standard treatments

IN Brief

Smokers Left Out in the Cold

We know smoking is bad for your lungs, your heart, your skin, and most other organs in the body. Now, a study has shown that smoking puts your fingers and toes at risk, too. Research presented at the American Physiological Society meeting in April 2004 showed that people who smoke are much more susceptible to frostbite. The puffers' vessels were slower and less efficient at expanding when exposed to cold, which is the body's normal reaction to extreme drops in temperature.

A Myskin bandage is lifted out of the petri dish where new skin cells were grown. The bandage promotes faster healing of wounds and appears to leave less scarring than traditional treatments.

for serious burns, including skin grafts, take longer and are much more complicated to administer. Grafting also carries the risk of rejection in some cases.

The bandage, called Myskin, is also useful for difficult-to-heal, longstanding wounds, such as stubborn foot ulcers caused by diabetes that can lead to toe and foot amputations. Myskin also apparently leaves behind much less scarring than traditional treatments, researchers say, although additional testing is required to confirm that.

Availability. Myskin is now available to doctors and patients in the United Kingdom. CellTran, the manufacturer, is seeking an American company to get the novel bandage into clinical trials and eventually introduce it to the U.S. market.

A Dab of Pain Relief

Dread the stab of a needle? A new device developed at the Massachusetts Institute of Technology could make that pain a thing of the past. Called SonoPrep, it uses ultrasound to open tiny, temporary channels in the skin to allow an anesthetic cream to pass through. Together, the device and cream numb skin in just 5 minutes, compared with an hour for the cream alone. SonoPrep was approved by the FDA in August 2004, and may become standard equipment in doctors' offices and hospitals.

A Pill to Heal All Wounds

One day soon, if you have a bad sore or wound that's slow to heal, you may be able to pop a pill to heal the injury from inside your body. The pill, now being tested, would be a boon especially for the elderly, people who are hospitalized, and those with diabetes.

The drug contains a newly discovered amino acid (a type of protein) that occurs naturally in almost all human cells. That amino acid—thymosin beta 4, or TB4 for short—is a potent anti-inflammatory substance that plays a role in wound healing by helping new skin cells develop and migrate to injured areas. It also encourages the production of other substances that are crucial for skin strength, including laminin-5, a protein important in helping cells adhere to one another. Laminin-5 is known to be missing in people with certain skin disorders associated with an inability to heal.

The drug is currently being tested with human subjects. Small, early trials ended in the fall of 2003, and tests to determine safe and effective doses in larger numbers of patients were scheduled to begin in mid-2004. TB4 is the only known potential treatment option for an inherited skin disease called epidermolysis bullosa. If testing goes well, the FDA may give special approval (known as orphan status) for the use of TB4 to treat this disease as early as 2005.

URINARY

TRACT

IN THIS SECTION

DOCTORS ARE USING MICROWAVES TO ZAP ENLARGED PROSTATES AND PROVIDE OLDER MEN **NEW RELIEF.**

If you're taking medication for this condition, talk to your doctor; new research shows that taking two different drugs works better than taking one. And a small preliminary study has found that Botox, the infamous wrinkle treatment, may also help (although you may not like the injections).

For women who find they "leak" a bit every time they laugh or cough, a new drug holds significant promise for treating stress incontinence. Finally, a new study should put the final nail in the coffin of the pervasive "calcium causes kidney stones" myth. The truth is that consuming calcium actually lowers the risk of kidney stones—so drink your milk!

Kidney Stones

Drink Your Milk to Prevent Kidney Stones

For decades, researchers and doctors believed that too much calcium was to blame for kidney stones, the often painful mineral deposits that form in the kidney from substances concentrated in the urine. Now, though, a new study published in the journal *Archives of Internal Medicine* has found that the more calcium women get from their diets, the lower their risk of developing kidney stones. The study builds on other, similar research in older men and postmenopausal women.

Despite earlier studies showing that dietary calcium prevents kidney stones, many women who developed stones during the current study were still told by their doctors to reduce their calcium intake, says the study's lead author, nephrologist Gary C. Curhan, M.D., associate professor of medicine at Brigham and Women's Hospital in Boston. "Many things take a long time to change," he says. He hopes this study will finally end any recommendations that dietary calcium be restricted.

Calcium/kidney stone theory wrong. The idea that calcium contributed to kidney stones made sense in a simple way, says Dr. Curhan, because most kidney stones are partly composed of a salt called calcium oxalate. For years, doctors thought that reducing calcium consumption would reduce production of this salt, but the scientific picture is more complicated. It turns out that people on low-calcium diets actually have *higher* levels of oxalate because calcium binds with oxalate in the intestine, preventing it from being absorbed into the body. Thus, the more calcium you eat, the less oxalate you absorb from food. The less oxalate you absorb, the less likely you are to develop kidney stones.

Also, notes Dr. Curhan, "There may be something in calcium products that is beneficial in other ways, some unidentified factor that reduces the likelihood of stones forming."

Stay away from sugar. The study, which evaluated the dietary habits of 96,000 women ages 27 to 44, also found that eating whole grains and vegetables

RESEARCH ROUNDUP

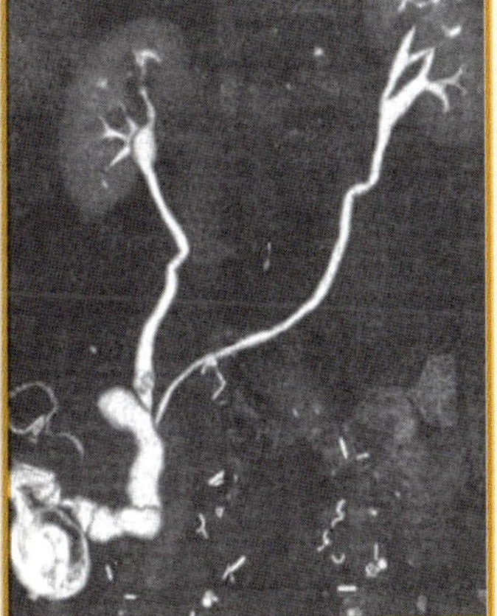

Better than an x-ray: The MDCTU scan is a special type of CT scan that reveals kidney stones and other urinary tract problems.

Detecting Kidney Stones and Bladder Cancer

Between bladder and kidney cancer, kidney stones, and other urinary tract problems, it can sometimes seem as if that part of your body is just a minefield of health problems. But detecting the mines may be easier now that researchers at the University of Michigan Health System in Ann Arbor have developed a simple, 15-minute CT (computed tomography) scan that they say can find tiny cancers, stones, and other urinary tract problems.

The researchers used a special CT technique called multi-detector CT urography, or MDCTU, to find problems in the tiny tubes of the body's urine collection system as well as to detect bladder cancer, bladder stones, kidney stones, kidney cysts, and kidney cancer. The technique, a kind of three-dimensional x-ray available at most large hospitals, was tested with more than 1,000 patients and proved much more accurate than the typical x-ray conducted on patients who are at high risk for such problems.

seemed to reduce the risk of kidney stones. Dr. Curhan thinks that's due to phytate, a naturally occurring substance found in these foods. Additionally, the more fluids—regardless of type—that the women drank, the lower their risk of developing stones.

The study did turn up one dietary substance that increased the women's risk: sugar. Although the reason isn't clear yet, researchers do know that the more sugar in your diet, the more calcium you excrete in your urine, which could increase the amount of oxalate you absorb. ■

RESEARCH ROUNDUP

Lose the Weight, Lose the Stones

As if increased risks for cancer, heart disease, and diabetes weren't enough, now comes news that being overweight also increases your risk of a certain kind of kidney stones, called uric acid stones. A study published in April 2004 found, for the first time, that the more you weigh, the more likely you are to develop this type of kidney stones, found in about 5 percent of people with kidney stones and in about 30 percent of people with diabetes who have kidney stones.

One reason, the researchers speculate, is that overweight people tend to have more acidic urine—which is not related to diet. Instead, says lead researcher Khashayar Sakhaee, M.D., professor of internal medicine at the University of Texas Southwestern Medical Center in Dallas, it's probably related to insulin resistance, a condition common in overweight people in which cells become resistant to insulin, leading to high blood sugar. "When you have this defect, the kidneys cannot produce and excrete sufficient amounts of a buffer chemical to neutralize the acid," he says. The cure? Lose weight and exercise more to reduce insulin resistance.

Prostate Enlargement

Zapping Prostates with Microwaves

Men who get up numerous times during the night for trips to the bathroom and feel as if they're never quite able to empty their bladders may be pleased to learn about a new treatment that can solve the problem. In February 2004, the FDA approved Prolieve, a microwave-based procedure to treat benign prostatic hyperplasia (BPH), or enlarged prostate.

The procedure adds to the current treatment options, which all have drawbacks as well as benefits. Medications leave four out of six men dissatisfied with the results because they don't always work and can have fairly annoying side effects, such as hot flashes, dizziness, and impo-

The Prolieve Thermodilation System

In this newly approved procedure, microwaves destroy excess prostate tissue that blocks urine flow.

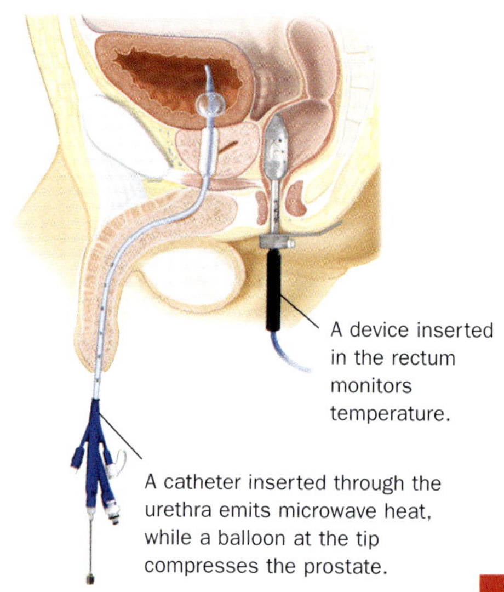

The Prolieve procedure can be performed in a doctor's office. The device on top heats the prostate to about 45°C (113°F). The device on bottom monitors temperature.

tence. Surgical removal of part of the prostate may leave men incontinent, impotent, or subject to retrograde ejaculation, in which semen flows backward into the bladder during ejaculation.

Using microwaves to shrink enlarged prostates isn't new, notes Jonathan Henderson, M.D., a urologist in Shreveport, Louisiana, but older microwave procedures are very painful, requiring extremely high levels of anesthesia. Additionally, patients need to have urinary catheters in place for a few weeks after the procedure, and it can take up to six weeks before the patients feel any relief. By contrast, men who undergo Prolieve rarely need catheters and usually feel significant relief from symptoms within a week or two.

How it works. The Prolieve procedure combines microwaves that destroy excess prostate tissue with a balloon device that circulates warm water through the urethra to prevent any damage to its lining. The warm water and balloon are keys to the treatment's success, says Dr. Henderson, and they are the primary difference between Prolieve and other microwave techniques, some of which use cool water to protect the urethra.

Cool water, says Dr. Henderson, can decrease the effectiveness of the microwave-induced heat. Additionally, he notes, the balloon keeps the urethra open while it's warm, then stays inflated during the "cooldown" period of the procedure, so it stays open. "It's like heating up plastic, bending it, and then when it cools down, it maintains its new shape," he explains. This often eliminates the need for a postoperative catheter; in one study, just 16 percent of the men who had the procedure required catheters afterward, most of them for no more than three days. Prolieve also prevents permanent damage to the urethra, which may occur with other microwave devices.

Clinical trials on Prolieve found that 75 percent of men who received the treatment experienced fewer BPH-related symptoms two weeks after the procedure than those who took finasteride (Proscar), the most commonly prescribed medication for BPH. Side effects included soreness and some blood in the urine, both of which disappeared within a few days. Significantly, the procedure requires no anesthesia. It takes about 45 minutes, and patients remain awake and able to inform the doctor if they feel any pain or heat.

Availability. Now that the FDA has approved Prolieve, its manufacturer, Celsion, is training urologists around the country in its use. Currently, the procedure is available only in the United States. ■

RESEARCH ROUNDUP

Two Drugs Are Better Than One

According to a five-year study of more than 3,000 men at 20 major medical centers, pairing two drugs commonly used to treat symptoms of enlarged prostate (benign prostatic hyperplasia, or BPH) not only relieves symptoms better than either one alone but also significantly reduces the risk that the condition will worsen and require surgery.

The drugs are doxazosin (Cardura) and finasteride (Proscar). Cardura relaxes the muscle cells in the prostate that tend to choke off urine flow and is usually the first drug given for BPH, while Proscar slowly reduces the size of the prostate by about 15 to 20 percent within 6 to 18 months. Taken individually, they reduce the risk that symptoms will worsen by about one-third; taken together, they slash it by two-thirds. (Surprisingly, Cardura alone did not keep symptoms from getting worse or reduce the risk of needing surgery.) Also, men taking both drugs reported fewer side effects, such as impotence and dizziness, than those taking either drug alone.

Prostate Enlargement

Older Men May Have Use for Botox

Along with migraine headaches, facial wrinkles, urinary incontinence, and cerebral palsy, benign prostatic hyperplasia (BPH), or enlarged prostate, is now on the list of health conditions that can be treated with botulinum toxin A, more commonly known as Botox.

"It's worked on everything else, why not BPH?" says University of Pittsburgh researcher Michael Chancellor, M.D. Actually, Dr. Chancellor, professor of urology and gynecology at the university's school of medicine, had been researching the use of Botox to treat incontinence for years. Since Botox works on smooth muscles, and the prostate gland contains smooth muscle cells, he figured it was time to try it for this condition that's so common in older men.

A 10-minute procedure. Dr. Chancellor, along with colleagues in Pittsburgh and at Chang Gung Memorial Hospital in Taiwan, tried the paralyzing poison on 11 men ages 50 to 82. The men, all of whom had BPH symptoms that didn't improve with medication, each received one injection directly into the prostate via a needle inserted through the rectum. The procedure took about 10 minutes.

The men's symptoms improved within a few days, says Dr. Chancellor. The participants found it easier to urinate, had improved urinary flow, and got up less often during the night to urinate. At the same time, they didn't have any of the side effects that sometimes occur with medication or surgery, such as impotence; urinary incontinence; and retrograde ejaculation, in which semen leaks into the bladder. Dr. Chancellor presented the results of his study at the annual meeting of the American Urological Association in April 2004.

"We have good treatments available with pills and surgery, but if the pills don't work, many men don't want to have the surgery because it's irreversible," says Dr. Chancellor. "Botox provides an option. It seems just as effective as surgery." He said the results should last at least six months.

Availability. Technically, any doctor could begin using Botox for BPH as an "off-label" use—that is, a use other than the one for which it was originally intended and approved. However, it's doubtful that insurance companies would reimburse for the treatment, which costs up to $1,000 for the medicine alone. Dr. Chancellor hopes the drug's manufacturer will eventually begin larger clinical trials on its use for BPH.

Botox can relax muscle cells in the prostate, making urination easier.

Enlarged Prostate

Enlargement of the prostate gland is common in men over 50. If symptoms are bothersome, it's usually treated with drugs or surgery.

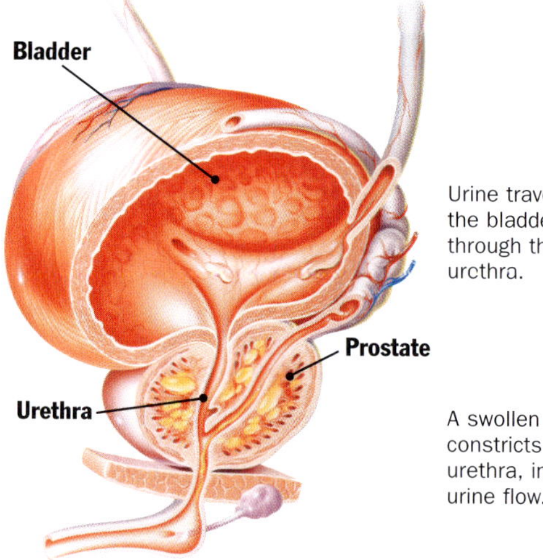

Urine travels from the bladder down through the urethra.

A swollen prostate constricts the urethra, inhibiting urine flow.

Urinary Incontinence

Drug Stops Embarrassing Leaks

Imagine how annoying and humiliating it would be if every time you sneezed, coughed, jumped up and down, or laughed hard, you also wet your pants. Yet that's a fact of life for an estimated one out of five women who must cope with stress incontinence.

Current treatments for the condition include pelvic exercises called Kegels, which strengthen the muscles that hold in urine; biofeedback; and medications that calm an overactive bladder. Now, there's a new drug in late-stage clinical trials that may provide significant relief.

How it works. The drug, called duloxetine, takes advantage of a relatively new understanding about the role of serotonin in the urinary tract. Yes, serotonin—the same chemical that plays such a large role in depression and the workings of antidepressant drugs called selective serotonin reuptake inhibitors (SSRIs), such as fluoxetine (Prozac).

Serotonin and another chemical, norepinephrine, released by nerves, signal muscles in the bladder area to contract, helping to control the urge to urinate, explains Roger Dmochowski, M.D., professor of urology at Vanderbilt University in Nashville. Duloxetine prevents the spinal cord from reabsorbing these chemicals from the bladder neck, allowing them to continue doing their job of stimulating the sphincter (valve) muscles to contract. This is similar to the way SSRIs work in the brain.

In a major study on duloxetine, the researchers found that in half of the women taking the drug, their condition was 50 to 100 percent improved, compared with just one-third of women taking placebos (dummy pills). The women who took the drug were also able to go longer before needing to urinate. In the world of stress incontinence, notes Dr. Dmochowski, these are significant improvements, and the women confirmed this in patient surveys that assessed the treatment's effect on their quality of life.

Availability. The drug's maker, Eli Lilly, expected to submit duloxetine for approval to U.S. and European authorities by the end of 2004.

Hold it! If daily physical stresses bring on bladder leaks, the new drug duloxetine may give you a lift.

FUTURE BREAKTHROUGHS

A Pacemaker for Incontinence

Imagine being able to control your bladder with the push of a button. Crazy? Not necessarily. Australian researchers are working on a device called a urinary pacemaker that would let you do just that. An implanted electrical stimulator, operated by remote control, would activate a ring of muscle created from a patient's own body and transplanted to the bladder. On command, the stimulator would send a signal telling the muscles to relax, thus allowing the release of urine when the person is ready. The research team from the University of Melbourne is currently raising money to begin clinical trials in 2005.

RESOURCE DIRECTORY

For a wealth of information on a particular ailment or other medical topic, turn to the organizations listed here. Call, write, or log on to their web sites to find out what type of news, information, and services they provide. Many offer patient guides, event listings, study enrollment, advocacy programs, support groups, newsletters, free publications, and physician referrals.

GENERAL RESOURCES

American Medical Association
515 North State Street
Chicago, IL 60610
800-621-8335
312-464-5000
www.ama-assn.org

American Medical Women's Association
801 North Fairfax Street, Suite 400
Alexandria, VA 22314
703-838-0500
www.amwa-doc.org

Center for Science in the Public Interest
1875 Connecticut Avenue NW, Suite 300
Washington, DC 20009
202-332-9110
www.cspinet.org

Centers for Disease Control and Prevention
1600 Clifton Road
Atlanta, GA 30333
800-311-3435
404-639-3534
www.cdc.gov
Clinicaltrials.gov
www.clinicaltrials.gov

MEDLINEPlus
U.S. National Library of Medicine
8600 Rockville Pike
Bethesda, MD 20894
www.medlineplus.gov

National Institutes of Health
Bethesda, MD 20892
301-496-4000
www.nih.gov

National Women's Health Information Center
8550 Arlington Boulevard, Suite 300
Fairfax, VA 22031
800-994-9662
www.4woman.gov

United Network for Organ Sharing
PO Box 2484
Richmond, VA 23218
888-894-6361
www.unos.org

U.S. Food and Drug Administration
5600 Fishers Lane
Rockville, MD 20857
888-463-6332
www.fda.gov

World Health Organization
Avenue Appia 20
1211 Geneva 27
Switzerland
011-41-22-791-2111
www.who.int

AGING

AARP
601 E Street NW
Washington, DC 20049
888-687-2277
www.aarp.org

Alzheimer's Association
225 North Michigan Avenue, 17th Floor
Chicago, IL 60601
800-272 3900
312-335-8700
www.alz.org

Alzheimer's Disease Education and Referral Center
PO Box 8250
Silver Spring, MD 20907
800-438-4380
www.alzheimers.org

American Menopause Foundation
350 Fifth Avenue, Suite 2822
New York, NY 10118
212-714-2398
www.americanmenopause.org

National Institute on Aging
Building 31, Room 5C27
31 Center Drive, MSC 2292
Bethesda, MD 20892
301-496-1752
www.nia.nih.gov

North American Menopause Society
PO Box 94527
Cleveland, OH 44101
440-442-7550
www.menopause.org

BRAIN AND NERVOUS SYSTEM

American Pain Foundation
201 North Charles Street, Suite 710
Baltimore, MD 21201
888-615-7246
www.painfoundation.org

American Pain Society
4700 West Lake Avenue
Glenview, IL 60025
847-375-4715
www.ampainsoc.org

American Parkinson Disease Association
1250 Hylan Boulevard, Suite 4B
Staten Island, NY 10305
800-223-2732
www.apdaparkinson.com

American Psychiatric Association
1000 Wilson Boulevard, Suite 1825
Arlington, VA 22209
703-907-7300
www.psych.org

American Psychological Association
750 First Street NE
Washington, DC 20002
800-374-2721
202-336-5500
www.apa.org

Brain Injury Association
8201 Greensboro Drive, Suite 611
McLean, VA 22102
800-444-6443
703-761-0750
www.biausa.org

Epilepsy Foundation
4351 Garden City Drive
Landover, MD 20785
800-332-1000
www.efa.org

National Institute of Mental Health
6001 Executive Boulevard, MSC 9663, Room 8184
Bethesda, MD 20892
866-615-6464
301-443-4513
www.nimh.nih.gov

National Institute of Neurological Disorders and Stroke
PO Box 5801
Bethesda, MD 20824
800-352-9424
www.ninds.nih.gov

National Multiple Sclerosis Society
733 Third Avenue
New York, NY 10017
800-344-4867
www.nationalmssociety.org

National Parkinson Foundation
Bob Hope Parkinson Research Center
1501 NW Ninth Avenue
Bob Hope Road
Miami, FL 33136
800-327-4545
www.parkinson.org

National Spinal Cord Injury Association
6701 Democracy Boulevard, Suite 300-9
Bethesda, MD 20817
800-962-9629
301-214-4006
www.spinalcordorg

National Stroke Association
9707 East Easter Lane
Englewood, CO 80112
800-787-6537
www.stroke.org

Parkinson's Disease Foundation
710 West 168th Street
New York, NY 10032
800-457-6676
212-923-4700
www.pdf.org

Stroke Network
PO Box 492
Abingdon, MD 21009
www.strokenetwork.org

CANCER

American Cancer Society
1599 Clifton Road NE
Atlanta, GA 30329
800-227-2345
404-320-3333
www.cancer.org

Division of Cancer Prevention and Control
Centers for Disease Control and Prevention
4770 Buford Highway NE, MS K64
Atlanta, GA 30341
888-842-6355
www.cdc.gov/cancer/index.htm

National Cancer Institute
6116 Executive Boulevard, MSC 8322, Room 3036A
Bethesda, MD 20892
800-422-6237
301-435-3848
www.nci.nih.gov

Women's Cancer Network
230 West Monroe, Suite 2528
Chicago, IL 60606
800-444-4441
312-578-1439
www.wcn.org

Y-ME National Breast Cancer Organization
212 West Van Buren Street, Suite 1000
Chicago, IL 60607
800-221-2141
312-986-8338
www.y-me.org

CHILDREN'S HEALTH

American Academy of Pediatrics
141 Northwest Point Boulevard
Elk Grove Village, IL 60007
847-434-4000
www.aap.org

Children and Adults with Attention-Deficit/Hyperactivity Disorder
8181 Professional Place, Suite 150
Landover, MD 20785
800-233-4050
www.chadd.org

DIGESTION AND METABOLISM

American Diabetes Association
1701 North Beauregard Street
Alexandria, VA 22311
800-342-2383
703-549-1500
www.diabetes.org

American Society of Colon and Rectal Surgeons
85 West Algonquin Road, Suite 550
Arlington Heights, IL 60005
847-290-9184
www.fascrs.org

Crohn's and Colitis Foundation of America
386 Park Avenue South, 17th Floor
New York, NY 10016
800-932-2423
www.ccfa.org

Hepatitis Foundation International
504 Blick Drive
Silver Spring, MD 20904
800-891-0707
301-622-4200
www.hepfi.org

International Foundation for Functional Gastrointestinal Disorders
PO Box 170864
Milwaukee, WI 53217
888-964-2001
414-964-1799
www.iffgd.org

National Institute of Diabetes and Digestive and Kidney Diseases
31 Center Drive, MSC 2560
Bethesda, MD 20892
301-496-3583
www.niddk.nih.gov

EYES AND EARS

Better Hearing Institute
515 King Street, Suite 420
Alexandria, VA 22314
800-327-9355
703-684-3391
www.betterhearing.org

Glaucoma Foundation
116 John Street, Suite 1605
New York, NY 10038
800-452-8266
212-285-0080
www.glaucomafoundation.org

National Eye Institute
2020 Vision Place
Bethesda, MD 20892
301-496-5248
www.nei.nih.gov

National Institute on Deafness and Other Communication Disorders
31 Center Drive, MSC 2320
Bethesda, MD 20892
301-496-7243
www.nidcd.nih.gov

Prevent Blindness America
500 East Remington Road
Schaumburg, IL 60173
800-331-2020
www.preventblindness.org

HEART AND CIRCULATORY SYSTEM

American College of Cardiology
9111 Old Georgetown Road
Bethesda, MD 20814
800-253-4636
301-897-5400
www.acc.org

American Heart Association
7272 Greenville Avenue
Dallas, TX 75231
800-242-8721
www.americanheart.org

Mended Hearts Inc.
7272 Greenville Avenue
Dallas, TX 75231
888-432-7899
214-706-1442
www.mendedhearts.org

National Heart, Lung, and Blood Institute
PO Box 30105
Bethesda, MD 20824
301-592-8573
www.nhlbi.nih.gov

National Stroke Association
9707 East Easter Lane
Englewood, CO 80112
800-787-6537
www.stroke.org

Sickle Cell Disease Association of America
200 Corporate Pointe, Suite 495
Culver City, CA 90230
800-421-8453
www.sicklecelldisease.org

World Hypertension League
3120 Glendale Avenue
Toledo, OH 43614
800-575-9355
419-383-6016
www.mco.edu/org/whl/

MUSCLES, BONES, AND JOINTS

American Podiatric Medical Association
9312 Old Georgetown Road
Bethesda, MD 20814
800-275-2762
301-571-9200
www.apma.org

Arthritis Foundation
PO Box 7669
Atlanta, GA 30357
800-283-7800
www.arthritis.org

Lupus Foundation of America
2000 L Street NW, Suite 710
Washington, DC 20036
800-558-0121
202-349-1155
www.lupus.org

Lyme Disease Network
43 Winton Road
East Brunswick, NJ 08816
www.lymenet.org

National Chronic Fatigue Syndrome and Fibromyalgia Association
PO Box 18426
Kansas City, MO 64133
816-313-2000
www.ncfsfa.org

National Institute of Arthritis and Musculoskeletal and Skin Diseases
1 AMS Circle
Bethesda, MD 20892
877-226-4267
301-495-4484
www.niams.nih.gov

National Osteoporosis Foundation
1232 22nd Street NW
Washington, DC 20037
800-624-2663
202-223-2226
www.nof.org

REPRODUCTION AND SEXUAL HEALTH

AIDS.org
7985 Santa Monica Boulevard, #99
West Hollywood, CA 90046
323-656-6036
www.aids.org

American College of Obstetricians and Gynecologists
409 12th Street SW
PO Box 96920
Washington, DC 20090
202-638-5577
www.acog.org

National Institute of Allergy and Infectious Diseases
6610 Rockledge Drive, MSC 6612
Bethesda, MD 20892
301-496-5717
www.niaid.nih.gov

Planned Parenthood Federation of America
434 West 33rd Street
New York, NY 10001
800-230-7526
212-541-7800
www.plannedparenthood.org

RESOLVE: The National Fertility Association
1310 Broadway
Somerville, MA 02144
888-623-0744
www.resolve.org

RESPIRATORY SYSTEM

Action on Smoking and Health
2013 H Street NW
Washington, DC 20006
202-659-4310
www.ash.org

American Academy of Allergy, Asthma & Immunology
555 East Wells Street, Suite 1100
Milwaukee, WI 53202
414-272-6071
www.aaaai.org

American Lung Association
61 Broadway, 6th Floor
New York, NY 10006
212-315-8700
www.lungusa.org

Asthma and Allergy Foundation of America
1233 20th Street NW, Suite 402
Washington, DC 20036
800-727-8462
202-466-7643
www.aafa.org

Cystic Fibrosis Foundation
6931 Arlington Road
Bethesda, MD 20814
800-344-4823
www.cff.org

National Heart, Lung, and Blood Institute
PO Box 30105
Bethesda, MD 20824
301-592-8573
www.nhlbi.nih.gov

National Institute of Allergy and Infectious Diseases
6610 Rockledge Drive, MSC 6612
Bethesda, MD 20892
301-496-5717
www.niaid.nih.gov

Nicotine Anonymous World Services
419 Main Street, PMB #370
Huntington Beach, CA 92648
415-750-0328
www.nicotine-anonymous.org

SKIN, HAIR, AND NAILS

American Academy of Dermatology
PO Box 4014
Schaumburg, IL 60168
847-330-0230
www.aad.org

American Society of Plastic Surgeons
44 East Algonquin Road
Arlington Heights, IL 60005
888-475-2784

American Vitiligo Research Foundation
PO Box 7540
Clearwater, FL 33758
727-461-3899
www.avrf.org

National Institute of Arthritis and Musculoskeletal and Skin Diseases
1 AMS Circle
Bethesda, MD 20892
877-226-4267
301-495-4484
www.niams.nih.gov

National Psoriasis Foundation
6600 SW 92nd Avenue, Suite 300
Portland, OR 97223
800-723-9166
503-244-7404
www.psoriasis.org

Skin Cancer Foundation
245 Fifth Avenue, Suite 1403
New York, NY 10016
800-754-6490
www.skincancer.org

URINARY TRACT

American Association of Kidney Patients
3505 East Frontage Road, Suite 315
Tampa, FL 33607
800-749-2257
www.aakp.org

American Foundation for Urologic Disease
1000 Corporate Boulevard, Suite 410
Linthicum, MD 21090
800-828-7866
410-689-3990
www.afud.org

American Kidney Fund
6110 Executive Boulevard, Suite 1010
Rockville, MD 20852
800-638-8299
www.akfinc.org

National Kidney Foundation
30 East 33rd Street, Suite 1100
New York, NY 10016
800-622-9010
212-889-2210
www.kidney.org

WELLNESS

Alcoholics Anonymous
Grand Central Station
PO Box 459
New York, NY 10163
212-870-3400
www.alcoholics-anonymous.org
www.aa.org

American Council on Exercise
4851 Paramount Drive
San Diego, CA 92123
800-825-3636
858-279-8227
www.acefitness.org

American Dental Association
211 East Chicago Avenue
Chicago, IL 60611
312-440-2500
www.ada.org

American Yoga Association
PO Box 19986
Sarasota, FL 34276
941-927-4977
www.americanyogaassociation.org

National Center on Sleep Disorders Research
6705 Rockledge Drive, Suite 6022
Bethesda, MD 20892
301-435-0199
www.nhlbi.nih.gov/about/ncsdr/index.htm

National Institute on Alcohol Abuse and Alcoholism
5635 Fishers Lane, MSC 9304
Bethesda, MD 20892
301-443-3860
www.niaaa.nih.gov

National Institute of Dental and Craniofacial Research
45 Center Drive, MSC 6400
Bethesda, MD 20892
301-496-4261
www.nidcr.nih.gov

National Sleep Foundation
1522 K Street NW, Suite 500
Washington, DC 20005
202-347-3471
www.sleepfoundation.org

Weight Control Information Network
1 WIN Way
Bethesda, MD 20892
877-946-4627
202-828-1028
www.niddk.nih.gov/health/nutrit/win.htm

INDEX

A

CREDITS

Cover: *background* Paula Bronstein/Getty Images; *inset top* Yorgos Nikas/Wellcome Trust; *inset bottom* DuCane Medical Imaging, Ltd./SPL/Photo Researchers. **Back cover:** Photodisc. **14 & 15** Paula Bronstein/Getty Images. **16** Romeo Ranoco/ Reuters/Corbis. **17** Daniel Pepper/Getty Images. **13 & 18** *top* Reuters/Corbis. **18** *bottom* STR/AFP/Getty Images. **19** Liu Jin/ AFP/Getty Images. **20** AFP/Getty Images. **21** Courtesy CDC/ James Gathany. **22** AP/Wide World. **23** *top left* AP/Wide World; *right New Scientist*. Reprinted with permission. **13 & 25** *All* 3D Clinic/Getty Images. **26** AP/Wide World. **27** 2003 *U.S. News & World Report*. Reprinted with permission. **29** *top* AP/Wide World; *bottom* EPA/Woo Suk Hwang/Seoul National University in Korea/*Science* Magazine. **30** Kim Kyung-Hoon/ Reuters/ Corbis. **13 & 31** *top* Yorgos Nikas/Wellcome Trust; *bottom* 2002 *U.S. News & World Report,* L.P. Reprinted with permission. **32** *top* Lucy Nicholson/Reuters/Corbis; *bottom* AP/Wide World. **34** TRBfoto/Photodisc/Getty Images. **13 & 35** ER Productions/ Corbis. **36** *top & bottom right* Courtesy Q-Med AB; *bottom left* ISM/Phototake. **37** Courtesy Dr. Jeffrey Ascherman/Columbia University Medical Center. **38** *top* Lauren Shear/Photo Researchers; *bottom* American Society of Plastic Surgeons. **40** Courtesy Dr. Wassermann. **41** James Salzano/ Imaging by Trilobyte. **42** Jane Hurd Studios. **13 & 43** Michael Amendolia/Network Photographers. **44** Jason Grow. **45** Illustration by Bryan Christie. Text: *Scientific American*. **13 & 47** Anastasia Vasilakis. **48** Reprinted from September 1, 2003 issue of *BusinessWeek* with permission; Copyright 2003 by the McGraw-Hill Companies, Inc. **49** James Salzano. **51** *top left* James Salzano; *inset* Courtesy Helicon Therapeutics, Inc. Photo by Matthew Bletsch & Rusiko Bourtchouladze. **13, 52 & 53** Victor Habbick Visions/Photo Researchers. **54** *top* 1999 Time Inc. Reprinted with permission; *bottom* Lidke et al/Nature Biotechnology; Reprinted with permission. **55** *bottom left* Carol & Mike Werner/Phototake; *top* AP/Wide World. **56** DK Images. **2 & 57** Coneyl Jay/Photo Researchers. **13 & 58** Brand X Pictures. **59** Brand X Pictures/Getty Images. **60** *top* Erik Butler; *bottom* Copyright 1997 Nature Publishing Group. Reprinted with permission. **61** Courtesy Dr. Nir Barzilai. **62** AP/Wide World. **6 & 63** Alfred Pasieka/Photo Researchers. **65** Claro Cortes IV/Reuters/Corbis. **66** Business Wire via Getty Images. **67** Justin Sullivan/Getty Images. **68** Photodisc/Getty Images. **13 & 70** Photodisc/Fotosearch. **71** *top* Brand X Pictures/Fotosearch; *inset* Courtesy Eli Lilly and Company. **72** Courtesy HemCon, Inc. **73** The Reader's Digest Association, Inc./Christine Bronico. **77** Courtesy University of Pittsburgh. **78** *top* Comstock; *bottom* Dr. Kari Lounatmaa/Photo Researchers. **79** Photodisc. **80** Ryan McVay/Photodisc/Getty Images. **81** *top* Reprinted with permission from Elsevier (The *Lancet,* vol 362-Oct. 4, 2003); *bottom* Courtesy Boston University/Kalman Zabarsky. **82** *top* The Reader's Digest Association, Inc./GID/Lisa Koening; **75 & 82** *bottom* Digital Vision/Fotosearch. **83** Image Ideas/Fotosearch. **84** Voisin/Photo Researchers. **85** *top* Courtesy Martha E. Pollack; *bottom* Courtesy Yariv Ben Yosef. **87** Courtesy Cogmed Cognitive Medical Systems. **88** *top* Courtesy Dr. Torkel Klingberg; *bottom* Reprinted with permission from Elsevier (The *Lancet,* vol. 362, 2003 Issue 9397). **89** Image State/Fotosearch. **75 & 90** Brand X Pictures/Fotosearch. **91** *left* Ross Whitaker/Image Bank/Getty Images; *bottom right* Photodisc/Getty Images. **92** *left* Courtesy Terry Drenner; *right* EyeWire/Photodisc.

93 Brand X Pictures/Fotosearch. **94** Corbis. **95** *top* Image State/Fotosearch; *bottom* Courtesy Altracel Pharmaceuticals *photo* The Reader's Digest Association, Inc./Christine Bronico. **96** *top* Comstock; *bottom* Stockbyte/Fotosearch. **97** *top left* Courtesy Roche Laboratories, Inc.; *top right* Gusto/SPL/Photo Researchers. **98** Pete Cade/Image Bank/Getty Images. **99** Image Source/Fotosearch. **100** Jim Arbogast/Photodisc/Getty Images. **101** Comstock/Fotosearch. **103** Courtesy Serin-America, Inc. **104** Courtesy Dr. Michael Phillips. **105** Courtesy Dr. David Carpenter. **106** Photodisc. **107** Nibsc/Photo Researchers. **6 & 108** Corbis. **109** *background* Comstock/Getty Images; **75 & 109** *inset* Ghislain & Marie David de Lossy/Image Bank/Getty Images. **110** Rita Maas/Envision. **111** *left* Index Stock/Fotosearch; *right* Courtesy Georgia Tech/Gary Meek. **112** The Reader's Digest Association, Inc./GID/Alan Richardson. **113** Steven Mark Needham/Envision. **114** Image Source/Fotosearch. **115** AP/Wide World. **119 & 120** *top left* Courtesy Edward Taub, Ph.D. **120** *bottom right* Corbis/Fotosearch. **121** Image State/Fotosearch. **122** *top left* Brand X Pictures/Fotosearch; *right* Image Source/Fotosearch. **123** Simon Fraser/SPL/CMSP. **124** *top* Courtesy Dr. Allan L. Reiss. **116 & 124** *bottom* Photodisc/Getty Images. **125** *top* Photodisc; *bottom* Courtesy Dr. David Wang. **126** *top right* Courtesy Concentric Medical; *bottom left* Illustration by Joe Zeff. **128** Dr. Merlin Tuttle/BCI/Photo Researchers. **129** Photodisc. **131** Courtesy Dr. Edward A. Neuwelt. **132** Illustration by Lydia Kibiuk. **133** Courtesy National Cancer Institute/NIH. **134** Zephyr/SPL/Photo Researchers. **135** Digital Vision. **136** *left* Courtesy Duke University Medical Center; *right* Courtesy University of Dundee. **137** Photodisc. **138** Simon Fraser/Photo Researchers. **139** *top* Courtesy Grace Vanhoose; *bottom* Illustrations by Gary Carlson. **140** Reprinted with permission from *Science News*. Copyright 2004 by Science Service. **117 & 141** Luis M. de la Maza, Ph.D., M.D./Phototake. **142 & 143** Harbor Branch Oceanographic Institute. **144** The Reader's Digest Association, Inc./GID/Alan Richardson. **145** Photodisc. **146** *top* DuCane Medical Imaging, Ltd./SPL/Photo Researchers; *bottom* Copyright 2004 Massachusetts Medical Society. All rights reserved. Translated with permission. **148** *bottom left* ISM/Phototake; *top right* Garo/Photo Researchers. **7 & 151** Colin Hawkins/Stone/Getty Images. **152** *left* Courtesy Dr. Bruce Lawhorn/*Merck Veterinary Manual; right* Bruce T. Brown/Stone/Getty Images. **153** Roger Harris/SPL/Photo Researchers. **154** Jose Luis Pelaez/Corbis. **155** Tim Flach/Stone/Getty Images. **156** *left (all)* The Reader's Digest Association, Inc./GID/Alan Richardson. **11, 117 & 156** *top right* Andrea Monikos/Stone/Getty Images. **157** Nino Mascardi/Image Bank/Getty Images. **158** *top* The Reader's Digest Association, Inc./GID/Alan Richardson; *bottom* Photodisc. **159** Steve Horrell/SPL/Photo Researchers. **161** Susumu Nishinaga/Photo Researchers. **162** BSIP Agency/Index Stock Imagery. **163** *both* Courtesy National Eye Institute/NIH. **164** Photodisc/Getty Images. **165** *top* Courtesy VisionCare; *bottom* Courtesy James P. Gilman, CRA. **166** *bottom left* C. Squared Studios/Photodisc/Getty Images. **117 & 166** *top right* Digital Vision/Getty Images. **167** Courtesy Refractec, Inc. **117 & 169** Courtesy W. L. Gore & Associates, Inc. **170** Courtesy Cook, Inc. **171** *top* Courtesy Arizona Heart Institute/VAS Communications; *bottom* Corbis. **172 & 173** *left* Courtesy CryoCor, Inc. **173** *bottom right* Courtesy Dr. Bjerregaard. **174** Photodisc. **175** Courtesy South Carolina Heart Center. **177** Michael Donne/SPL/Photo Researchers. **179** Gillian Lee/Wellcome Trust. **180** Image Source/Fotosearch. **181** Source: *New England Journal of Medicine,* AP/Wide World. **182** Adam Gault/Photo Researchers. **183** A.D.A.M. Medical Illustration Team. **185** Photodisc. **186** Courtesy Osiris Therapeutics, Inc. **187** CNRI/Photo Researchers. **117 & 188** Joe Polillo/Stone/Getty Images. **189** *top right* Image Source/Fotosearch; *bottom left* The Reader's Digest Association, Inc./Christine Bronico. **190** VVG/Photo Researchers. **191** *top* The Reader's Digest Association, Inc./GID; *bottom* Simon Fraser/Royal Victoria Infirmary/Photo Researchers. **192** Photodisc. **193** *both* Courtesy Dr. Russ Nockels. **194** Courtesy Dr. Amy Lang. **195** *top right* Michael Keller/Index Stock Imagery; *inset* Courtesy University of Michigan Dept. of Radiology and Dr. John Lin, Valley Radiologists, Ltd. **196** The Reader's Digest Association, Inc./GID. **197** VVG/ Photo Researchers. **198** *bottom left* Courtesy PitRok, Ltd.; *right* Princess Margaret Rose Orthopaedic Hospital/Photo Researchers. **199** Gusto/Photo Researchers. **201** Courtesy Duramed Pharmaceuticals, Inc. **202** Photodisc. **203** *bottom left (upper)* AP/Wide World; *bottom left (lower)* AP/Wide World/American Medical Association, HO; *top right* Claude Cortier/Photo Researchers. **204** Courtesy Dr. Jeffrey Boldt. **117 & 205** Stockbyte/PictureQuest. **205** *inset* Courtesy The Daily Wellness Company. **206** Laguna Design/Photo Researchers. **207** *top* Courtesy Solvay Pharmaceuticals, Inc.; *bottom* Yoav Levy/Phototake. **208** *left* The Reader's Digest Association, Inc./Michele Laseau; *right* Courtesy Microsulis Medical, Ltd. **209** Courtesy Hershey Food Corporation. **210** Index Stock Imagery. **211** Courtesy Dr. Mary E. D'Alton. **212** Courtesy University of Southampton/School of Nursing and Midwifery. **213** John Cole /Photo Researchers. **214** Digital Vision/Fotosearch. **215** Dr. Linda Stannard, UCT/Photo Researchers. **217** Banana Stock/Fotosearch. **218** Courtesy HeartMath LLC. **219** Photodisc/Getty Images. **220 & 221** Digital Vision. **117 & 222** Simon Fraser/Photo Researchers. **223** *left* Courtesy Dr. Richard Moss; *right* Corbis. **224** Mauro Fermariello/SPL/Photo Researchers. **225** Brand X Pictures/PictureQuest. **226** *top* Courtesy Marie Marklund; *bottom* Index Stock Imagery. **227** Copyright 2004 Nucleus Medical Art, All rights reserved, www.nucleusinc.com. **117 & 229** Digital Vision/Getty Images. **230** Peter Nicholson/Stone/Getty Images. **231** *background* Lauren Shear/Photo Researchers; *insets (both)* Courtesy Dr. George Cotsarelis. **232** Courtesy Berlex Laboratories. **233** Courtesy CellTran. **235** *middle* The Reader's Digest Association, Inc./GID/Lisa Koening; *bottom left* Courtesy University of Michigan Health System. **236** *left* The Reader's Digest Association, Inc./GID/Ginger Neumann. **236** *right* & **237** Courtesy Celsion Corporation/Boston Scientific Corporation. **238** *bottom left* Lauren Shear/PhotoResearchers; *top right* John Bavosi/Photo Researchers. **117 & 239** Stuart Pearce/Agefoto Stock.

Photo Research by Jeanne Leslie